PIONEERING NEW SERIALS FRONTIERS:
FROM PETROGLYPHS TO CYBERSERIALS

Proceedings of the
NORTH AMERICAN SERIALS
INTEREST GROUP, Inc.

11th Annual Conference
June 20-23, 1996
University of New Mexico, Albuquerque

PIONEERING NEW SERIALS FRONTIERS: FROM PETROGLYPHS TO CYBERSERIALS

Proceedings of the
NORTH AMERICAN SERIALS
INTEREST GROUP, Inc.

11th Annual Conference
June 20-23, 1996
University of New Mexico, Albuquerque

Christine Christiansen
Cecilia Leathem
Editors

The Haworth Press, Inc.
New York • London

Pioneering New Serials Frontiers: From Petroglyphs to Cyberserials has also been published as *The Serials Librarian*, Volume 30, Numbers 3/4 and Volume 31, Numbers 1/2 1997.

The development, preparation, and publication of this work has been undertaken with great care. However, the publisher, employees, editors, and agents of The Haworth Press and all imprints of The Haworth Press, Inc., including The Haworth Medical Press and Pharmaceutical Products Press, are not responsible for any errors contained herein or for consequences that may ensue from use of materials or information contained in this work. Opinions expressed by the author(s) are not necessarily those of The Haworth Press, Inc.

The Haworth Press, Inc., 10 Alice Street, Binghamton, NY 13904-1580 USA

Library of Congress Cataloging-in-Publication Data

North American Serials Interest Group. Conference (11th : 1996 : University of New Mexico)
    Pioneering new serials frontiers : from petroglyphs to cyberserials : proceedings of the North American Serials Interest Group, Inc., 11th Annual Conference, June 20-23, 1996, University of New Mexico, Albuquerque / Christine Christiansen, Cecilia Leathem, editors.
      p. cm.
    Published also as v. 30, no. 3/4 and v. 31, no. 1/2, 1997 of The serials librarian.
    Includes bibliographical references and index.
    ISBN 0-7890-0324-4 (alk. paper)
    1. Serials control systems–United States–Congresses. 2. Serials control systems–Canada–Congresses. 3. Serial publications–United States–Congresses. 4. Serial publications–Canada–Congresses. I. Christiansen, Christine. II. Leathem, Cecilia. III. Serials librarian. IV. Title.
Z692.S5N67 1997
025.3′432–dc21
                                              97-11234
                                                CIP

Dedication

NASIG dedicates these proceedings to Leigh Chatterton, vital contributor as member of the Program and Proceedings Committee, co-editor of the Proceedings and Executive Board Member in NASIG's early years.

Leigh exemplified the spirit of volunteerism that has characterized NASIG since its inception; she spent hours editing, communicating with authors and program participants and serving on the board. She took her responsibilities seriously, strove for quality at each stage of the process and had a quiet sense of humor that made it a pleasure to work with her. We shared a sense of dedication to our work along with gratitude for the support we received from others in and outside NASIG. We had many opportunities to acknowledge that appreciation on behalf of the organization. These gestures were important to Leigh and once the editing and other correspondence were completed, we spent part of every summer writing to the presenters and members who made each conference a valuable experience.

NASIG now remembers and thanks our loyal charter member, Leigh Chatterton. This is a most fitting way to acknowledge Leigh's role in NASIG's formative years and her deep commitment to the profession.

Mary Beth Clack
Cambridge, MA
1 March 1997

INDEXING & ABSTRACTING

Contributions to this publication are selectively indexed or abstracted in print, electronic, online, or CD-ROM version(s) of the reference tools and information services listed below. This list is current as of the copyright date of this publication. See the end of this section for additional notes.

- *Academic Abstracts/CD-ROM,* EBSCO Publishing Editorial Department, P.O. Box 590, Ipswich, MA 01938-0590

- *Academic Search: database of 2,000 selected academic serials, updated monthly,* EBSCO Publishing, 83 Pine Street, Peabody, MA 01960

- *Cambridge Scientific Abstracts,* Environmental Routenet (accessed via INTERNET), 7200 Wisconsin Avenue, #601, Bethesda, MD 20814

- *Chemical Abstracts,* Chemical Abstracts Service Library, 2540 Olgentangy Road, P.O. Box 3012, Columbus, OH 43210

- *CINAHL (Cumulative Index to Nursing & Allied Health Literature), in print, also on CD-ROM from CD PLUS, EBSCO, and Silver-Platter, and online from CDP Online (fomerly BRS), Data-Star, and PaperChase. (Support materials include Subject Heading List, Database Search Guide, and instructional video.)* CINAHL Information Systems, P.O. Box 871/1509 Wilson Terrace, Glendale, CA 91209-0871

- *CNPIEC Reference Guide: Chinese National Directory of Foreign Periodicals*, P.O. Box 88, Beijing, People's Republic of China

- *Current Awareness Abstracts,* Association for Information Management, Information House, 20-24 Old Street, London, EC1V 9AP, England

(continued)

- *Current Contents: Clinical Medicine/Life Sciences (CC: CM/LS) Weekly Table of Contents Service), and* **Social Science Citation Index.** *Articles also searchable through* **Social SciSearch,** *ISI's online database and in ISI's* **Research Alert** *current awareness service,* Institute for Scientific Information, 3501 Market Street, Philadelphia, PA 19104-3302

- *Hein's Legal Periodical Checklist: Index to Periodical Articles Pertaining to Law,* William S. Hein & Co., Inc., 1285 Main Street, Buffalo, NY 14209

- *IBZ International Bibliography of Periodical Literature,* Zeller Verlag GmbH & Co., P.O.B. 1949, d-49009 Osnabruck, Germany

- *Index to Periodical Articles Related to Law,* University of Texas, 727 East 26th Street, Austin, TX 78705

- *Information Reports & Bibliographies,* Science Associates International, Inc., 6 Hastings Road, Marlboro, NJ 07746-1313

- *Information Science Abstracts,* Plenum Publishing Company, 233 Spring Street, New York, NY 10013-1578

- *Informed Librarian, The,* Infosources Publishing, 140 Norma Road, Teaneck, NJ 07666

- *INTERNET ACCESS (& additional networks) Bulletin Board for Libraries ("BUBL"), coverage of information resources on INTERNET, JANET, and other networks.*
  - JANET X.29: UK.AC.BATH.BUBL or 00006012101300
  - TELNET: BUBL.BATH.AC.UK or 138.38.32.45 login 'bubl'
  - Gopher: BUBL.BATH.AC.UK (138.32.32.45). Port 7070
  - World Wide Web: http: / / www.bubl.bath.ac.uk./BUBL/ home.html
  - NISSWAIS: telnetniss.ac.uk (for the NISS gateway)
  The Andersonian Library, Curran Building, 101 St. James Road, Glasgow G4 ONS, Scotland

(continued)

- *Konyvtari Figyelo-Library Review*, National Szechenyi Library, Centre for Library and Information Science, H-1827 Budapest, Hungary

- *Library & Information Science Abstracts (LISA)*, Bowker-Saur Limited, Maypole House, Maypole Road, East Grinstead, West Sussex, RH19 1HH, England

- *Library Digest*, Highsmith Press, W5527 Highway 106, P.O. Box 800, Fort Atkinson, WI 53538-0800

- *Library Hi Tech News*, Pierian Press, P.O. Box 1808, Ann Arbor, MI 48106

- *Library Literature*, The H. W. Wilson Company, 950 University Avenue, Bronx, NY 10452

- *MasterFILE: updated database*, EBSCO Publishing, 83 Pine Street, Peabody, MA 01960

- *Newsletter of Library and Information Services*, China Sci-Tech Book Review, Library of Academia Sinica, 8 Kexueyuan Nanlu, Zhongguancun, Beijing 100080, People's Republic of China

- *PASCAL International Bibliography T205: Sciences de l' information Documentation*, INIST/CNRS-Service Gestion des Documents Primaires, 2, allee du Parc de Brabois, F-54514 Vandoeuvre-les-Nancy, Cedex, France

- *Periodica Islamica*, Berita Publishing, 22 Jalan Liku, 59100 Kuala Lumpur, Malaysia

- *Referativnyi Zhurnal (Abstracts Journal of the Institute of Scientific Information of the Republic of Russia)*, The Institute of Scientific Information, Baltijskaja ul., 14, Moscow A-219, Republic of Russia

- *Sociological Abstracts (SA)*, Sociological Abstracts, Inc., P.O. Box 22206, San Diego, CA 92192-0206

(continued)

SPECIAL BIBLIOGRAPHIC NOTES

related to special journal issues (separates)
and indexing/abstracting

☐ indexing/abstracting services in this list will also cover material in any "separate" that is co-published simultaneously with Haworth's special thematic journal issue or DocuSerial. Indexing/abstracting usually covers material at the article/chapter level.

☐ monographic co-editions are intended for either non-subscribers or libraries which intend to purchase a second copy for their circulating collections.

☐ monographic co-editions are reported to all jobbers/wholesalers/approval plans. The source journal is listed as the "series" to assist the prevention of duplicate purchasing in the same manner utilized for books-in-series.

☐ to facilitate user/access services all indexing/abstracting services are encouraged to utilize the co-indexing entry note indicated at the bottom of the first page of each article/chapter/contribution.

☐ this is intended to assist a library user of any reference tool (whether print, electronic, online, or CD-ROM) to locate the monographic version if the library has purchased this version but not a subscription to the source journal.

☐ individual articles/chapters in any Haworth publication are also available through the Haworth Document Delivery Services (HDDS).

Pioneering New Serials Frontiers: From Petroglyphs to Cyberserials

CONTENTS

NASIG WORKSHOPS

NASIG Officers and Executive Board

1995/96

Officers:

Julia Gammon, President, University of Akron
Beverley Geer-Butler, Vice-President/President Elect, Trinity University
Susan Davis, Secretary, State University of New York, Buffalo
Dan Tonkery, Treasurer, Readmore, Inc.

Executive Board:

Jean Callaghan, Wheaton College
Bobbie Carlson, Medical University of South Carolina
Eleanor Cook, Appalachian State University
Birdie MacLennan, University of Vermont
Kat McGrath, University of British Columbia
John Tagler, Elsevier Science Publishing

—

1996 Program Planning Committee

Plenary

Karin Cargille, Co-Chair, University of California, San Diego

Pam Elsherbini, Pennsylvania State University

Cindy Hepfer, State University of New York, Buffalo

Sue Malawski, John Wiley and Sons, Inc.

Workshops

Ann Ercelawn, Vanderbilt University

Lisa Macklin, Georgia Institute of Technology

Bob Persing, University of Pennsylvania

Christa Reinke, Co-Chair, University of Houston

Pat Wallace, University of Colorado, Boulder

Bobbie Carlson, Board Liaison, Medical University of South Carolina

NASIG
Student Grant Award Recipients

Dana Marie Bellcher, University of Oklahoma

Loretta Crowell, Wayne State University

David W. Free, Clark-Atlanta University

Randall Hopkins, University of Maryland

Kimberly A. Maxwell, Catholic University of America

Maria Moff, Kent State University

Virginia Taffurelli, Pratt Institute

Richelle Van Snellenberg, University of British Columbia

Horizon Award Winner

Reba Leiding, Head of Acquisitions, Rensselaer Polytechnic Institute

ABOUT THE EDITORS

Christine Christiansen has worked at the Otto G. Richter Library, University of Miami, for seven years. She served as Head of the Serials Acquisitions Unit until 1990, when she was promoted to Assistant Head of the Acquisitions Department. Christine took "early retirement" in November, 1996, to assume her new role as full-time mother of two children.

Cecilia Leathem is currently Head of Serials Cataloging, Otto G. Richter Library, University of Miami. Cecilia previously has worked in the technical services area at the University of Rhode Island, SUNY at Binghamton, and the Martin P. Catherwood Library, Cornell University. Her most recent published work, entitled "An Examination of Choice of Formats for Cataloging Non-Textual Serials," appeared in 1994 in *Serials Review.*

Introduction

The eleventh annual conference of the North American Serials Interest Group met from June 20-23, 1996 at the University of New Mexico, Albuquerque, New Mexico, and was the largest conference yet organized by NASIG. The theme, "Pioneering New Serials Frontiers: From Petroglyphs to Cyberserials," attracted over 700 attendees, including 40 guests from abroad.

Attendees were rewarded with a series of challenging and stimulating papers delivered at the plenary sessions. The viewpoints of scholars, publishers and information providers brought new perspectives to the issues and problems facing those involved in producing, maintaining, and using journal literature. Not all speakers shared the same positive vision of cyberserials or the newer technologies, but all contributed to a lively exchange of ideas on where the world of serials "publishing" is heading and how it might get there.

Concurrent sessions addressed some of the methods for serialists to manage the ever-growing and increasingly complex arena of electronic serials. What does the serialist need to know about copyright issues and electronic product licensing? How does one evaluate and select Internet resources, and once selected, how are they cataloged and maintained? Publishers, research institutes, librarians and scholars all have a stake in these issues.

Given the concerns of all stakeholders, then, it was appropriate that two pre-conference programs offered attendees the opportunity to acquire specialized knowledge of standards for Electronic Data Exchange or to develop new skills as risktakers.

Nineteen workshops reinforced the diversity of issues facing serialists.

[Haworth co-indexing entry note]: "Introduction." Christiansen, Christine, and Cecilia Leathem. Co-published simultaneously in *The Serials Librarian* (The Haworth Press, Inc.) Vol. 30, No. 3/4, 1997, pp. 1-2; and: *Pioneering New Serials Frontiers: From Petroglyphs to Cyberserials* (ed: Christine Christiansen and Cecilia Leathem) The Haworth Press, Inc., 1997, pp. 1-2. Single or multiple copies of this article are available for a fee from The Haworth Document Delivery Service [1-800-342-9678, 9:00 a.m. - 5:00 p.m. (EST). E-mail address: getinfo@haworth.com].

From technical service concerns to customer relations, from management strategies to working with the Web, the sheer variety of workshop topics was proof that serialists must contend with and manage new formats, new standards, and new technologies.

This volume includes the six papers delivered at the plenary sessions, the presentations and discussions from the concurrent sessions and the summary reports of each of the preconferences and workshops. The editors anticipate that readers will gain insight, ideas, and some practical skills for dealing with the changing world of serials management.

The editors would like to thank Beverley Geer-Butler and Carol Pitts Diedrichs, our liaisons with the NASIG Board, and co-workers who provided advice and support. Special thanks to Maggie Horn and Tom McFadden, who prepared the index for this volume.

Christine Christiansen
Otto G. Richter Library
University of Miami

Cecilia Leathem
Otto G. Richter Library
University of Miami

PRECONFERENCE PROGRAMS

PRECONFERENCE 1:
EDI AND RELATED STANDARDS:
A PRIMER AND UPDATE
FROM THE FRONTIER

EDI Overview
(EDI: It's Not So Scary
After All This Time)

Tina Feick

Presenter

Meg Matthes Mason

Recorder

SUMMARY. The EDI (Electronic Data Interchange) Preconference was presented in six parts. It opened with a comprehensive overview of EDI, including its use within the library serials industry. The Pre-

Tina Feick is Sales Manager for North America, Blackwell's Periodicals Division.
Meg Matthes Mason is Serials Librarian, Einstein Library, Nova Southeastern University.

[Haworth co-indexing entry note]: "EDI Overview (EDI: It's Not So Scary After All This Time)." Mason, Meg Matthes. Co-published simultaneously in *The Serials Librarian* (The Haworth Press, Inc.) Vol. 30, No. 3/4, 1997, pp. 5-8; and: *Pioneering New Serials Frontiers: From Petroglyphs to Cyberserials* (ed: Christine Christiansen and Cecilia Leathem) The Haworth Press, Inc., 1997, pp. 5-8. Single or multiple copies of this article are available for a fee from The Haworth Document Delivery Service [1-800-342-9678, 9:00 a.m. - 5:00 p.m. (EST). E-mail address: getinfo@haworth.com].

5

conference was well-attended, attracting 170 people, including librarians, vendors, automation system representatives, and publishers. Tina Feick delivered the first, keynote presentation and laid the groundwork for the five talks to follow. *[Article copies available for a fee from The Haworth Document Delivery Service: 1-800-342-9678. E-mail address: getinfo@haworth.com]*

In this presentation, Tina Feick, Sales Manager for North America, Blackwell's Periodicals Division, focused her presentation on the following major points:

1. Definition of EDI; its key elements and history;
2. Benefits and requirements of EDI;
3. EDI standards;
4. Organizations involved;
5. Translation software;
6. Communication modes;
7. Match points-SICI;
8. SISAC X12 serials claim data elements;
9. EDI action for the future.

Feick began by offering a definition of EDI, introducing the following comparisons.

EDI is	**EDI is not**
An exchange of commercially-oriented information in standard electronic formats, between systems, and without human intervention.	Electronic mail MARC
A transmission in a standard syntax of unambiguous information of business or strategic significance between computers of independent organizations.	Z39.50 Bibliographic information

EDI was created by Edward Guilbert in 1948 and has been used by the transportation industry for over twenty years. The library sector is beginning to become involved in implementing EDI and creating EDI-compliant standards.

The key elements of EDI include business transactions (routine orders, claims, invoices, etc.); use of a standard format; cross-industry application (including transportation, retailing, banking, manufacturing); and computer to computer interaction with no human intervention or interpretation.

Feick then detailed the benefits of EDI. Computer to computer capability provides increased accuracy because there is no rekeying of information from library to agent to publisher. Some other advantages include cost-efficiency, as EDI replaces mail and paper claims; faster and improved service; staff reassignment to other projects; and better partnership relations. Feick noted that in order for the EDI computer to computer capability to work smoothly, there must be match points. Free text will cause the EDI transaction to drop from the trading partner's system and result in manual input. The need for match points led to the creation of SICI.

Some of the requirements for implementing EDI include extraction of information from the library automation system (output file), translation of information to the EDI standard, uploading of information to the trading partner's computer system, the trading partner's willingness and ability to receive the information, and industry-specific standards. The primary standards are ANSI ASC X12 for the United States and UN/EDIFACT, used in Europe. There will be a worldwide standard within the next few years, as the X12 standard is translated into EDIFACT.

Many organizations working with EDI are active in the serials industry. The BISG (Book Industry Study Group) has been the primary promoter within the United States. SISAC (Serials Industry Systems Advisory Committee), which is part of BISAC, has developed and published standards in X12 for invoice, claims, claim responses, and dispatch (journal issue shipment information). Other groups participating in the standards creation process are CBISAC/CSISAC-Canada and ICEDIS (International Committee for the EDI of Serials). Standards originally developed as part of the ANSI ASC X12 effort will now be translated into EDIFACT by a European working group, EDItEUR.

The communication modes can involve VANs (Value-Added Networks), the Internet, electronic mail, or FTP (File transfer protocol). The VAN mode handles data integrity verification, tracks messages, provides functional acknowledgment, sends/receives multiple items in a single transmission, and allows for restricted access. However, it is expensive if a library does not have a high volume of use and is difficult to implement, especially for academic libraries. The Internet mode currently provides free access, requires little training and is readily available.

The discussion led to many questions from the attendees concerning communication costs. Tina Feick suggested that, as EDI activity increases, the cost of using VANs should drop.

In the future, librarians, publishers and systems vendors need to sell the concept of EDI to their management, to put EDI in their RFP's (request for proposals) for library automation systems, to participate in SISAC and help create standards, to make users' groups a higher priority, and to create output files outside the automation system. The automation systems users' groups were encouraged to list EDI as a priority.

In conclusion, Feick read from a statement made by Dan Tonkery in 1991,

EDI
Everyone's discussing it
Everyone's deferring it
Everyone's doing it
EDI OR DIE!

During the question-and-answer period there was a variety of responses. Concerns included ways to motivate publishers to use the SISAC bar-codes, how to achieve standardization, and which translators work best on the Internet. A challenge was issued to the audience to spread awareness of EDI, to urge more publishers to participate in EDI and to make EDI a top priority in their individual institutions.

EDI and the Library

James Huesmann

Presenter

Mary I. Wilke

Recorder

SUMMARY. Following Tina Feick's informative and focused overview of what EDI is and is not, James Huesmann provided a broader
view, where EDI is defined as any commercial or non-commercial
transaction allowing information to be communicated electronically
without rekeying that information. Interlibrary loan, document delivery, and transmitting files using FTP are all examples of EDI in this
broader definition. Huesmann described his view of libraries and EDI,
as well as its specific use at his own library. *[Article copies available for
a fee from The Haworth Document Delivery Service: 1-800-342-9678. E-mail
address: getinfo@haworth.com]*

James Huesmann is the Head of Technical and Automated Services at
Linda Hall Library, where EDI has been evaluated and incorporated as a
part of their new Horizon system. Huesmann described the library as the
center of the universe. Radiating out from the library are six spokes representing two-way communication. The first spoke represents communication between the library and bibliographic utilities. EDI would include the

---

James Huesmann is Head of the Technical and Automated Services at Linda
Hall Library.
Mary I. Wilke is Head of Acquisitions at the Center for Research Libraries.

[Haworth co-indexing entry note]: "EDI and the Library." Wilke, Mary I. Co-published simulta-
neously in *The Serials Librarian* (The Haworth Press, Inc.) Vol. 30, No. 3/4, 1997, pp. 9-11; and:
Pioneering New Serials Frontiers: From Petroglyphs to Cyberserials (ed: Christine Christiansen and
Cecilia Leathem) The Haworth Press, Inc., 1997, pp. 9-11. Single or multiple copies of this article are
available for a fee from The Haworth Document Delivery Service [1-800-342-9678, 9:00 a.m. - 5:00 p.m.
(EST). E-mail address: getinfo@haworth.com].

importing of bibliographic and authority records extracted from a utility such as OCLC or RLIN into the library's local database. Conversely, bibliographic and authority records created, revised or updated at the Linda Hall Library are exported from their local database to the bibliographic utility.

The second spoke is the mutually beneficial communication between the library and the systems vendor. The library is responsible for conveying its priorities for EDI to the system vendor. Linda Hall Library achieved this by including EDI in its RFP. System vendors then have a dual responsibility: to develop EDI interfaces that are feasible and meet market demand, and to enter into a dialog with users to coordinate and implement those priorities. Huesmann cautions that if the systems vendor does not develop what the marketplace demands, the vendor runs the risk of being dead in the water.

The third spoke represents the financial or business office. Financial information such as exchange rates, current patrons (i.e., students), invoice information for vouchers, delinquent fees, etc., must flow to and from the library system and the financial office system. Presently, Linda Hall Library does not have EDI capabilities with their financial office.

The fourth spoke is the communication between a library and a document delivery source. At different times libraries can be customers for and then suppliers of document delivery. Requests for article photocopies, book loans, etc., as well as accompanying financial information, originating from Linda Hall Library need to be transferred from the library system into interlibrary loan and document delivery services. Incoming requests for items, financial and use data must then all flow into the library system from the interlibrary loan system. Linda Hall Library serves as resource library for document delivery vendors. Thus the library's holdings information needs to be exported from the Linda Hall Library system and transferred to the document delivery service's system. According to Huesmann, even the transference of the requested document is a type of Electronic Data Interchange when it is supplied via a system like ARIEL.

The final two spokes are the ones representing the serial vendor/publisher and the monograph vendor/publisher. Up and running EDI communication between Linda Hall Library and the serial or monograph vendor includes: X12 claims for serials, BISAC ordering of books, and SISAC barcode check-in. Possible future paths include such activities as invoicing (X12 and EDIFACT), X12 and claim responses. One of these possibilities, X12 claim responses for serials, will probably be implemented shortly after the NASIG Conference closes, as James Huesmann and Tina Feick were able to confirm on stage that each partner was willing and able to send or receive the X12 claim responses.

In the universe described by James Huesmann's broader EDI definition, many libraries are already using EDI to communicate. Libraries that supply interlibrary loan via ARIEL, libraries that FTP their orders, claims, or cancellations, and libraries that participate in bibliographic utilities and maintain their holdings in these utilities are all presently using EDI. The EDI picture taken from this perspective really does support the title Tina Feick gave to her overview, "EDI: It's Not So Scary After All This Time." It is difficult to be afraid of something one is already using on a daily basis. Huesmann emphasized that we remember the following important points: to push for marketable items, to use standards, and to be active.

EDI and the Publisher

Stephen Dane

Presenter

Marla J. Whitney

Recorder

SUMMARY. This presentation covers the issues, benefits and challenges involved in the implementation of appropriate EDI transaction sets and related standards from the point of view of the scholarly publisher. *[Article copies available for a fee from The Haworth Document Delivery Service: 1-800-342-9678. E-mail address: getinfo@haworth.com]*

From the publisher's perspective, there are three points to consider when implementing EDI (Electronic Data Interchange): Issues, Benefits, and Challenges. The business issues include obtaining management commitment for the development of EDI, finding trading partners, and planning strategies to ensure competitiveness and customer satisfaction. Technical issues include acquiring equipment capable of EDI transactions and software capable of translating data received; developing standards such as X12, EDIFACT, Z39.56 SICI; and choosing communication options.

Saving time, money and resources are the benefits of using EDI. These are achieved by eliminating mail delivery and paper production; reducing data keyboarding errors; and providing better service through a faster,

---

Stephen Dane is General Manager, Kluwer Academic Publishers.

Marla J. Whitney is Applications Specialist–Serials Acquisitions, CARL Corporation.

[Haworth co-indexing entry note]: "EDI and the Publisher." Whitney, Marla J. Co-published simultaneously in *The Serials Librarian* (The Haworth Press, Inc.) Vol. 30, No. 3/4, 1997, pp. 13-14; and: *Pioneering New Serials Frontiers: From Petroglyphs to Cyberserials* (ed: Christine Christiansen and Cecilia Leathem) The Haworth Press, Inc., 1997, pp. 13-14. Single or multiple copies of this article are available for a fee from The Haworth Document Delivery Service [1-800-342-9678, 9:00 a.m. - 5:00 p.m. (EST). E-mail address: getinfo@haworth.com].

more accurate trading cycle. One of the currently accepted standards is the MRO (machine readable order) which only handles renewals. The drawbacks of the MRO are the postage costs, time delays in the mail, and problems processing damaged tapes. Current X12 standards include dispatch information (transaction set 856), claims/claim response (transaction sets 869/870), and the price and sales catalog (transaction sets 832/846). The price and sales catalog helps agents by facilitating price information entry, a process that is currently very labor intensive and time consuming.

The largest benefit to the publisher is the use of dispatch data–current publication status of an issue–in reducing claims. Claims produce the second highest volume of processed data for the publisher and most of the claims (10 to 60%) are premature. Dispatch data can help reduce the number of premature claims by 30%.

The challenge is obtaining more publisher participation. Many publishers are not involved with EDI because they are in the middle of major system changes, or they may have other priorities such as electronic publishing. There is also a need for increased publisher awareness of EDI and the currently available standards. Lastly, there is the "chicken vs. egg" syndrome: everyone is waiting for potential trading partners to comply.

EDI and the Serials Vendor

Sandra Hurd

Presenter

Beth Holley

Recorder

SUMMARY. In an era when all parties strive to work more effectively, taking advantage of savings made possible by technology is imperative. Electronic Data Interchange (EDI) is one such technology available today. Sandra Hurd addresses the benefits and applications for subscription agents in their business relationships with libraries and publishers. *[Article copies available for a fee from The Haworth Document Delivery Service: 1-800-342-9678. E-mail address: getinfo@haworth.com]*

Sandra Hurd, Director of Automation, EBSCO Information Services, discussed the relationship of EDI to the serials vendor. In the library marketplace, the electronic loop consists of the library, ILS (Integrated Library System) vendor, publisher, and subscription agent. To take advantage of savings made possible by technology, it is imperative that all parties work together. The subscription agent, often viewed as the middle man, in reality is a partner in an endeavor which depends on everyone working together at a greater level than ever before.

The benefits of EDI for all participants are unquestionable, but the

---

Sandra Hurd is Director of Automation, EBSCO Subscription Services.

Beth Holley is Head of Acquisitions, University of Alabama Libraries, Tuscaloosa, AL.

[Haworth co-indexing entry note]: "EDI and the Serials Vendor." Holley, Beth. Co-published simultaneously in *The Serials Librarian* (The Haworth Press, Inc.) Vol. 30, No. 3/4, 1997, pp. 15-16; and: *Pioneering New Serials Frontiers: From Petroglyphs to Cyberserials* (ed: Christine Christiansen and Cecilia Leathem) The Haworth Press, Inc., 1997, pp. 15-16. Single or multiple copies of this article are available for a fee from The Haworth Document Delivery Service [1-800-342-9678, 9:00 a.m. - 5:00 p.m. (EST). E-mail address: getinfo@haworth.com].

obstacles that must be overcome are significant. Each subscription agent, publisher, library, and ILS vendor must determine its ability to participate in the development and implementation of standards, investments in equipment and software, re-engineering practices, and system rewrites. Since implementation is voluntary and each partner has different needs, getting the serials industry to comply will not be an easy task. However, standard groups such as BISAC, SISAC, ICEDIS, and others are working, either together or separately, on writing standards to bring us all closer to achieving this goal.

ASC X12, transaction set codes used in America, are being translated into UN/EDIFACT transaction set codes which are the European standard. These codes represent industry standards for business operations, and implementation varies by subscription agent, publisher, and ILS vendor. X12 standards for invoice (810), price/sales catalog (832), inventory inquiry/advice (846), ship notice/manifest (856), order status inquiry or claim (869), order status report or claim response (870), and functional acknowledgment (997) are all final standards. Purchase order for books and serials (850) and purchase order acknowledgment for books and serials (855) are in the early test phases for new orders only.

Other codes are being written and tested to fit library applications for business transactions. Initially, transactions will be transmitted among publishers, subscription agents, and ILS vendors. Ultimately, libraries will benefit through increased efficiency in business transactions and savings achieved through the ability to receive invoice information online from suppliers, transmit orders and claims online, and receive an online acknowledgment and/or response–all in less time and with greater accuracy. All participants will realize savings on paper, postage, staff time, a faster trading cycle, and strategic benefits such as an increase in customer loyalty and improved levels of service. In summary, EDI will provide faster, more accurate service for routine tasks now processed manually, freeing people to focus on the real problems.

EDI and Related Standards

Ted Koppel
Presenter

Marla J. Whitney
Recorder

SUMMARY. This presentation focused on the importance of the Serial Item and Contribution Identifier (SICI), its implementation and use in various types of serials transactions, and its relation to the SISAC Bar Code Symbol. Recent revision efforts are also discussed. *[Article copies available for a fee from The Haworth Document Delivery Service: 1-800-342-9678. E-mail address: getinfo@haworth.com]*

The ANSI/NISO Z39.56–1996 serial item and contribution identifier (SICI) was published in September 1996. SICI creates a serials contribution identifier record that is short but bibliographically unique. The identifier is used for SISAC Bar code symbols, EDI transmissions, contents, abstracting and indexing services, as well as to pay copyright fees, and to identify binary files appearing within the World Wide Web/URL (Uniform Resource Locator).

Some of the 1996 enhancements were developed to define the internal structure of the SICI into three distinct segments. These enhancements define specific external structure types for identifying Serial Item (journal)

Ted Koppel is Information Systems Manager, The UnCover Company.

Marla J. Whitney is Applications Specialist–Serials Acquisitions, CARL Corporation.

[Haworth co-indexing entry note]: "EDI and Related Standards." Whitney, Marla J. Co-published simultaneously in *The Serials Librarian* (The Haworth Press, Inc.) Vol. 30, No. 3/4, 1997, pp. 17-18; and: *Pioneering New Serials Frontiers: From Petroglyphs to Cyberserials* (ed: Christine Christiansen and Cecilia Leathem) The Haworth Press, Inc., 1997, pp. 17-18. Single or multiple copies of this article are available for a fee from The Haworth Document Delivery Service [1-800-342-9678, 9:00 a.m. - 5:00 p.m. (EST). E-mail address: getinfo@haworth.com].

versus Serial Contribution (article). They also provide for the ability to store and display the medium of distribution and refine the identification of derivative parts of a contribution such as the table of contents and index, changes to the title code algorithm length, and inclusiveness to make it as unique as possible. All fields are now mandatory, if available. The three distinct segments are the item, contribution, and control segments. The specific external structure types can use private numbering systems like PII (publisher item identifier).

Some important differences between SICI and PII are that SICI is for serials only, and only for published material. SICI is derivable from a citation or source document and explicit information about Medium Format and Derivative parts is stored in the control segments. SICI was designed to be unique based on title key, and includes information sufficient to identify a journal issue or article within a journal issue which includes the ISSN, volume, issue, page number, and date.

PII may be used for monographs or serials and may be assigned for pre-published or post-publication works. It may refer to a single medium and/or derivative part, but it is not evident from the PII string. The PII is unique if item numbers are properly and sequentially assigned. And finally, unlike the SICI, PII identifies a published entity but not a specific bibliographic citation.

EDI and the Integrated Library System

Sandra Weaver Westall

Presenter

Donnice Cochenour

Recorder

SUMMARY. The library today relies heavily on the EDI capabilities of its ILS system. Sandra Westall covers the implications, options, and realities of EDI development and implementation for the ILS vendor. *[Article copies available for a fee from The Haworth Document Delivery Service: 1-800-342-9678. E-mail address: getinfo@haworth. com]*

The final presenter for the EDI preconference, Sandra Weaver Westall, Vice-President, Innovative Interfaces, Inc., represented the Integrated Library System (ILS) vendor's perspective. She used the development of EDI for electronic claiming as an example of how an ILS vendor would create a new interface through product design, development, beta testing, implementation and on-going development.

Development begins with product design to define the purpose of the interface, determine the standard to be used, identify whether the data already exists in the ILS, and if so, is special coding required to structure

---

Sandra Weaver Westall is Vice President, Innovative Interfaces, Inc.

Donnice Cochenour is Serials Librarian, Morgan Library, Colorado State University.

[Haworth co-indexing entry note]: "EDI and the Integrated Library System." Cochenour, Donnice. Co-published simultaneously in *The Serials Librarian* (The Haworth Press, Inc.) Vol. 30, No. 3/4, 1997, pp. 19-20; and: *Pioneering New Serials Frontiers: From Petroglyphs to Cyberserials* (ed: Christine Christiansen and Cecilia Leathem) The Haworth Press, Inc., 1997, pp. 19-20. Single or multiple copies of this article are available for a fee from The Haworth Document Delivery Service [1-800-342-9678, 9:00 a.m. - 5:00 p.m. (EST). E-mail address: getinfo@haworth.com].

the data. Ms. Westall used the Serial Item Contribution Identifier (SICI) as an example of a code which might be derived from the ISSN in the bibliographic record and the enumeration and chronology in the checkin record.

Ms. Westall cautioned that the development process can be impeded if too many players are involved too early. Initially the ILS vendor may choose to work directly with the subscription agent and involve libraries only when the product is ready for beta testing. The choice of players for the beta test phase is dependent on these factors: (1) whether a particular library system has paid for the product, (2) the variety of hardware platforms and operating systems, and (3) the library's ability to fully test the product and give usable feedback to the ILS vendor. The number of participants is usually limited to keep distribution of changes to a minimum.

Ms. Westall emphasized that the ILS vendor must develop accompanying documentation and alert their clients of new releases so they can prepare staff for its implementation. A new EDI interface often requires staff training and changes in work habits, and may require the addition of new data elements to the database before the interface can be implemented. For example, staff can no longer include special notes to the agent in the structured EDI claim, and the subscription identifier (SID) or title number must be available for EDI claiming to work.

Ms. Westall concluded with several goals for any new development. The ILS vendor must make sure the new product:

- works,
- integrates into normal library workflows,
- integrates with other parts of the ILS,
- is attractive to the customer by ensuring ease of use, improved procedures, and a short learning curve.

Ms. Westall's summary of the ILS vendor's procedure was well organized. She gave those on the other side of the table a comprehensive picture of the approach used by an ILS vendor for development of an EDI interface or any new system function. A four-page handout summarized the slides used during the presentation.

PRECONFERENCE 2:
RISKTAKING FOR LIBRARY PIONEERS

Risktaking for Library Pioneers

Johann van Reenen
Presenter

Karen Dalziel Tallman
Recorder

SUMMARY. The abstract in the conference brochure promised that the workshop would explore the attitudes toward the resistance to, and the benefits of, risktaking, and why risktaking is imperative to individuals and work groups. Risktaking was seen as imperative at a time when librarianship and libraries are threatened by maintaining the status quo. Attendees were asked to participate in risktaking exercises and discussions in a confidential (safe) environment. At

Johann van Reenen is Director, Centennial Science and Engineering Library, University of New Mexico.

Karen Dalziel Tallman is Librarian, University of Arizona.

[Haworth co-indexing entry note]: "Risktaking for Library Pioneers." Tallman, Karen Dalziel. Co-published simultaneously in *The Serials Librarian* (The Haworth Press, Inc.) Vol. 30, No. 3/4, 1997, pp. 21-28; and: *Pioneering New Serials Frontiers: From Petroglyphs to Cyberserials* (ed: Christine Christiansen and Cecilia Leathem) The Haworth Press, Inc., 1997, pp. 21-28. Single or multiple copies of this article are available for a fee from The Haworth Document Delivery Service [1-800-342-9678, 9:00 a.m. - 5:00 p.m. (EST). E-mail address: getinfo@haworth.com].

the end of the session each person was asked to develop a Risk Action Plan in the context of a greater understanding of the potential for productive risktaking and the benefits of risktaking for themselves and their workplace. *[Article copies available for a fee from The Haworth Document Delivery Service: 1-800-342-9678. E-mail address: getinfo @haworth.com]*

PRELIMINARY QUESTIONNAIRES

About 30 registrants were asked via email by van Reenen to fill out two questionnaires prior to the workshop. The first questionnaire, entitled "Why Do You Want To Be a Risktaking Library Pioneer?", asked each person to consider: (1) their motivation for taking the workshop; (2) what they want to or should risk in the near future, stating the main goal or goals; (3) one reason for not doing #2; and (4) what risks could be taken now to reach the goal(s). The second questionnaire, entitled "Risktaking Or Security," asked each person: (1) describe what job security means to you and rate its importance from 1 (low) to 10 (high); (2) how often do you settle for security and safety? and (3) when you settle for security and safety there is a price to pay–list why you settle and the price you pay.

AGENDA AND GOALS

When registrants arrived for the preconference, an agenda and the goals for the workshop were posted in the meeting room. The ten-point agenda included: overview and goals, introductory exercise, what is risktaking? why risk at all? importance of risktaking for libraries, risk and conflict, risktaking goals, risk and security, motivation and risktaking, risktaking at work. The four goals included: understanding risktaking and its alternatives, changing attitudes to risktaking, encouraging constructive risktaking, and, at the very least, showing that risktaking can be an antidote to anxiety.

STRUCTURE OF THE WORKSHOP

Van Reenen used transparencies, handouts, flipcharts, breakout sessions, group participation and discussion during the course of the workshop. Almost all of the transparencies were available as handouts and there were some handouts that were not included as transparencies. Quotations from authors within and outside the library profession were included along with a list of the sources cited. At the beginning of the workshop van Reenen outlined what would not be covered, what specific areas individuals in a group setting might or might not be willing to share and risk, and the reason for personal confidentiality when leaving the session with information on what others shared.

INTRODUCTORY EXERCISE

In the introductory exercise each person was asked to share their answers to the first two questions on the first questionnaire. Responses focused on: career changes, organizational fit, changes in the work environment, anxiety to risktaking, asking administrators for information, viewing oneself as a risktaker, developing a Risk Action Plan, determining which risks might be better or might be unwise, staying in a position or at an institution, learning how to take risks, teaching or motivating others to take risks, becoming more open to changes in libraries, and moving from being a small risktaker to more radical risktaking.

DEFINITION OF RISKTAKING

Van Reenen then covered the definition of risktaking. Webster's definition for risk includes the possibility of loss, injury or danger. This negative view has led some people to avoid or resist risktaking. If one tries to intellectualize risktaking or make plans to circumvent the risk involved, artificial stops may be put in place. There is no safety net in risktaking. In order to get good at it, one has to be willing to take a lot of risks.

WHY RISK AT ALL?

Van Reenen next displayed a transparency with the following information: *My life can never be better than it is now if I do not take risks. It may not get worse, but it probably would. You hate your job now? You will probably hate it more next year. You fear technology and change? You will have more to fear next year.* Van Reenen next discussed the risk of not risking. For those who think big it becomes more of a habit to flex risktaking muscles. If your mother used to tell you, "Nothing ventured; nothing gained," what she really might have been saying was, "Nothing ventured, nothing lost." Once again if the process tries to intellectualize the consequences, the result may be to convince ourselves of failure and not take the risk.

IMPORTANCE OF RISKTAKING IN LIBRARIES

Van Reenen proposed that libraries and library schools do not really spawn risktakers. A common reaction after a discussion to introduce change or try something new is that there is not enough information to take action. But, in fact, what might be a better approach is to stop the talk, make a decision, and get on with it. Library staff and administrators seem to know what to do, what to start, but have trouble deciding what to stop.

Van Reenen used several transparencies with quotes from library educators to express positive opinions toward risktaking as well as the threats to and changes in librarianship. K. M. Cottam wrote, "Risk taking . . . can provide a way to break out of inflexible administrative structures and organizational predictability."[1] J. R. Euster stated, "Doing nothing is often the biggest risk of all, just as refusing to decide is also a decision. Breaking down a risk into component parts . . . helps to take the threat out of risks and make them more acceptable."[2] K. M. Cottam was quoted again, ". . . 'the opportunity for greatness' is usually centered on 'times of turbulence, conflict, innovation, and change.' . . . Such times require a willingness to step out and ahead, to envision what might come next, and to follow through with calculated action."[3] Other authors describe media futurists as intent on convincing university administrators that library schools are passe,[4] and that the characteristics of a successful librarian and leader today are different from those of 20 years ago.[5]

RISK AND CONFLICT

Van Reenen explored the area of risk and conflict by stating there cannot be risk without conflict. Someone has to stop doing something. Avoiding conflict leads us in circles. Van Reenen used a transparency to examine four different types or approaches to conflict. Agreeing with everyone produces resentment. Retreating from conflict produces appeasement. Pushing through conflict can result in attaining a goal and bonds people in the process. And constant conflict can produce change for the sake of change. Risktaking allows people to fail and displeases some people. For example, resources may be reallocated based on cost-efficiency data.

RISKTAKING GOALS

The next agenda item dealt with setting clear risktaking goals. A transparency contained a quote from J. Hagberg and R. Leider: "Many of us go through life not clear about what we want, but pretty sure that this isn't it."[6] Setting clear risktaking goals includes the following: (1) What do I really want? (2) Do I risk to gain, or to avoid losing? (3) What is stopping me from getting what I want? Van Reenen pointed out it is important that risktaking not be done for the wrong reasons–just to be "in," to get even, to get your way–but so the group wins. Van Reenen added the following rules to the list: (1) Never risk more than you can afford to lose; (2) Don't risk a lot for a little; (3) Consider your odds and your intuition!

TAKING THE RISK

For the next exercise van Reenen asked us to break into small groups of three. Each person was to think of a risk and do the following: (1) Describe the risk; (2) Give the reason you are prepared to take it and be clear about what's in it for you; (3) Explain how you think it might go; (4) Tell what you might learn about the risk, yourself, the other person(s) involved. The person describing the risk was asked to state just the facts. The others were instructed to just listen, not deny, defend or deflect the person describing the risk.

The larger group then discussed what we had learned. There is a continuous cycle for risktaking. Once you take a risk, you learn from the results, you think about the risk differently, you start making more effective decisions, you get better results, and then you start the cycle over.

RISK AND SECURITY

How secure is security? It is a myth that life is secure. Helen Keller said: "Security is mostly a superstition: it does not exist in nature nor do the children of man as a whole experience it. Security is no safer in the long run than outright exposure. Life is either daring adventure or nothing."[7]

The three main fears or risk inhibitors are: fear of failing, fear of disapproval from others, fear of uncertainty. If you "settle" for security, there are prices to pay. There is risk in not risking. If you know about the risks you don't take, you have more information with which to make a decision.

MOTIVATION AND RISKTAKING

The three key change motivators are crisis and shock, following the leader, and knowing about and choosing change. The first motivator is the primary cause for most change and the least productive in the long run.

The second motivator produces change that is scripted by someone else—your parents, teachers, supervisors. You are not the author. For the most effective change you must write your own story. The third motivator is the best way. You know who you are, where you are going, where you want to go. You can verbalize and write down what you are choosing to do. It is helpful and encourages success if you have people who know what you are doing and support your risktaking.

The most important personal motivators at work are feeling like you are making a difference or contribution, belonging, feeling good about yourself, followed by making money, and liking or loving the job.

THE CREATRIX

Van Reenen next used a transparency to discuss a risktaking matrix developed by R. Byrd called the Creatrix.[8] The Creatrix defines eight risk styles: repeater, modifier, challenger, practicalizer, innovator, synthesizer, dreamer, and planner. It lists the contribution and weakness of each. The matrix plots out the various styles ranging from low risktaking to high risktaking against production of few creative ideas to many creative ideas. It is important to know where you are on the scale.

RISKTAKING AND PIONEERS IN LIBRARIES

Van Reenen shared the following list of things to keep in mind when taking risks: Stick with core values, integrity, honesty. Be clear about what you will and will not do. Do what is desirable, rather than what is desirable not to do. Technical competence can be developed. Admit what you don't know and learn by asking. Take time to think above your current routines (needs, purposes, goals, objectives, procedures, tasks). Live with ideas and dreams and cultivate them in others. Share ideas, dreams, frustrations with co-workers. Speak up! Be assertive, not aggressive. Get involved! Balance impatience with experience. Involve other personality types. Celebrate successful risktaking. Success breeds success. We are all fallible. Risktakers learn from mistakes and rise above them. Watch for doing too much too soon, too much at one time, perfection, and too much detail. Focus on opportunities, not problems. Belief changes reality.

COMMONSENSE CONDITIONS FOR RISKTAKING WITHIN THE SYSTEM

The following conditions are important during risktaking: Take risks under the least embarrassing conditions for the other person. Take risks without name calling. Don't corner the person who has the power and authority. Measure your organization culture for openness. Don't take risks on paper. Don't take risks in social situations. Don't take risks during a crisis.

RISKTAKING AT WORK: A RISK ACTION PLAN

Van Reenen next discussed how to develop the following personal Risk Action Plan: (1) What's currently not working for me or needs improvement? List first priority. List second priority. (2) How do I feel about them? (3) If I take a risk, what results do I want to create? (4) How will I benefit from taking this risk? (5) What are the obstacles? (6) What support is out there if I take this risk? (7) What preparation do I need? (8) What is the next step? (9) How soon will I take it?

Van Reenen suggested that you write out the steps listed above and then share it with another person whose input you value. Check out your real fears or artificial stops. Tell someone what steps you will take. Sharing makes it more of a reality. The main purpose in sharing is to gain clarity, get support, and if you fail there will be someone to support you.

CONCLUSION

Van Reenen reviewed the goals at the end of the session to make sure that everything had been covered. Throughout the workshop he engaged the audience, provided an animated delivery of the material, and used a variety of approaches to stimulate participation and discussion. He encouraged questions and comments throughout the session. The group went away with a sense that the goals of the workshop were met and that all felt a little more informed about the benefits of risktaking.

At the end of the session van Reenen invited everyone to participate in one final risktaking experience. He asked each member of the group to rate the importance of their job security on a scale from 1-10 (not important to important) if they learned that their job was to end or be taken away tomorrow. Putting the question into the context of the information from the workshop he asked, "How devastating would this be?" The group marks ranged from 1-9 with the ratings fairly evenly divided. Most rankings had 3-4 votes; the highest number of votes (7) was given to number 6 on the scale.

NOTES

1. Cottam, K.M. "Professional Identity and 'Intrapreneurial' Behavior." *Journal of Library Administration,* Spring 1987; 8:29-40.

2. Euster, J.R. "Creativity, Innovation and Risktaking." *College & Research Libraries News,* Jul/Aug. 1987; 405-6.

3. Cottam, K.M. "Intrapreneurship and Risk Taking." In *Leadership for Research Libraries.* Scarecrow Press, 1988.

4. Woodward, J.A. "Auto Aces or Accident Victims: Librarians on the Information Superhighway." *American Libraries,* Nov. 1995 26(10): 1016-18.

5. Butcher, K., Hughes, J. and M.R. George. "Thoughts on Leadership: An Exchange." *College & Research Libraries News,* Oct. 1995 56(9): 636-8.

6. Hagberg, J., and R. Leider. *The Inventurers: Excursions in Life and Career Renewal.* Reading, Mass., Addison-Wesley, 1988.

7. Keller, H. *The Open Door.* Garden City, N.Y., Doubleday, 1957.

8. Byrd, R. *A Guide to Personal Risk Taking.* New York, N.Y., AMACOM, 1974.

PLENARY SESSION I: FROM PETROGLYPHS TO CYBERSERIALS

Reinventing Journals, Reinventing Knowledge

John Lienhard

SUMMARY. The invention of the alphabet just before 1000 B.C. created enormous change for the human race. The Gutenburg revolution meant far more than just increased availability of books. Now, as we ask about the future of the serial literature, we face far more than mere questions about information storage. The very meanings of words like "library" and "university" are about to undergo mutations too radical to conceive, much less predict. *[Article copies available for a fee from The Haworth Document Delivery Service: 1-800-342-9678. E-mail address: getinfo@haworth.com]*

John Lienhard is M. D. Anderson Professor of Mechanical Engineering and History, University of Houston.

[Haworth co-indexing entry note]: "Reinventing Journals, Reinventing Knowledge." Lienhard, John. Co-published simultaneously in *The Serials Librarian* (The Haworth Press, Inc.) Vol. 30, No. 3/4, 1997, pp. 29-40; and: *Pioneering New Serials Frontiers: From Petroglyphs to Cyberserials* (ed: Christine Christiansen and Cecilia Leathem) The Haworth Press, Inc., 1997, pp. 29-40. Single or multiple copies of this article are available for a fee from The Haworth Document Delivery Service [1-800-342-9678, 9:00 a.m. - 5:00 p.m. (EST). E-mail address: getinfo@haworth.com].

I shall begin with a personal story that I think you'll appreciate. The story began almost eight years ago–soon after I had begun doing my program, "The Engines of Our Ingenuity," on Public Radio. A publisher looked at my scripts and said, "I'm going to publish these in book form!"

So I went ahead and worked for a year with an artist, who was doing actual paste-up of pages. Meanwhile, nothing was happening with the publisher. Things slowed to a halt while we waited to be assigned a copy editor. Months turned to years.

Finally I learned that the publisher had sold his stock off to another book company. They'd taken only some of his books. The rest–mine included–were remaindered to a handbook company. Of course the handbook company had no interest in a book on creativity. They simply laid it aside.

But this fellow's journals–they were another story. The journals were sure money makers. None of them were remaindered.

Down through the '70s and '80s, publishers realized they could coin money by letting second-tier scholars start new journals. It made those professors' resumés look good. And it gave the rest of us more ways to pad our own resumés with papers.

So I had been gored by the very process that was making your work into some kind of academic reductio ad absurdum. The prices of periodicals were rising crazily. Meanwhile, the Citation Index showed that most of those papers were seldom used by anyone.

One of our library administrators goes to her director once a month to tell him he should cancel all subscriptions to journals. The use doesn't justify the cost. Well now: That's a bit extreme, but something does have to be done.

To sort this out, let's begin by asking, "What is the periodical literature, anyway?"

Occasionally, great advances in human knowledge do make their first appearance in that literature. But books are what contain the over-arching summa theologica statements of our thinking. Ideas with real permanence are transmitted in books.

The periodical literature is the early ferment. It is alive, bubbling, and unstable. Ideas get worked out in the serial literature. When a historian goes back to, say, the 18th century Proceedings of the Royal Society, it is to learn how ideas evolved–how arguments unfolded–what the intellectual forces and fluxes were. It is not to learn Newton's mechanics. You do that by reading a treatise or a textbook.

Now, it is this essential difference–the difference between the Proceedings of the Royal Society and Newton's Principia that I want to play with today. I want to explore what that difference means in your work.

First, a thought about technology. You librarians, and I–an engineer–are all technologists. We all work in the constructed world–a world of man-made systems.

You and I know what too many people don't understand–that we and our technologies drive one another. We form and shape each other. It is hard to find a line between what we are and the machines around us, because technology and culture are the same thing. For that reason, you and I both live very close to cultural bedrock.

And you will surely understand when I say that, for a technology to succeed, it must have a seldom-talked-about quality. For a technology to become a part of our lives, it must also be a part of our metaphorical substrate. Look closely at our cultural metaphors and you'll find most are technological.

I would like to use clocks to show you what I mean by that remark: The circular face of a sundial, with its shadow moving left to right; it was copied straight onto the faces of water clocks. They used hands moving around a 12 hour dial. Then, around 1300 AD, the tick-tock mechanical escapement radically improved clock accuracy. It made clocks smaller and cheaper.

But, changed as they were, clocks still had dials, bells, and gears. Medieval writers had almost nothing to say about the new mechanism inside, so historians still aren't exactly sure when that change took place. You see, the outward form, the clock face, could not change, because that's where the metaphor was expressed.

Around 1920, electrical timing elements used the steady oscillation of alternating current to replace mechanical escapements. Accuracy took another leap forward. But clocks still looked the same.

Now my quartz crystal desk clock not only has the circular face of a sundial or a water clock, it also has a second hand that moves in little jumps–as though it were controlled by an escapement mechanism. Designers understand, on a visceral level, that the meeting ground between user and machine should never change any more than it has to.

So what about digital clocks? They offer a more precise readout than analog clocks do. They are easier for children to read. Linear time–time as a sequence of rising numbers. That is pure simplicity. Of course it is simplicity in the same way a tree is simpler than a forest.

A circular dial paints a picture of Earth's rotation. It models our own experience of passing time. It is a lovely analog of reality. In a digital display, night never falls. Time just advances, without features, minute after minute.

The competition between analog and digital readout might seem to balance. But, what do you wear on your wrists? The fascinating truth is, the digital clock has already lost in that competition. Digital clocks simply can't compete with the metaphorical power and visual grace of the circling motion of an analog face.

Many technologies look good for a while, then they get left–Betamax, dirigibles, LP's, autogyros, and digital clocks as well. So what does survive, and why?

If you want to predict the death or survival of a technology you certainly ask: "Is it functional?" But that's never enough by itself. You have to ask if it is a metaphor for something more than function. Only after a technology has touched us in that deep visceral and emotional place will it find a way to persist from one generation to the next.

And so we come to another technology–to the book. Its story began in Pergamon–then one of the largest cities in the world. Now it is called Bergama, in Western Turkey–South of Istanbul and North of Izmir. It sits on a hill, 16 miles from the Aegean Sea.

Pergamon became Capital of the Attalid dynasty after 280 BC. It was one of two great centers in the cosmopolitan world that formed after Alexander died. The other was Alexandria, in Egypt.

The Attalids took their name from King Attalus who reigned until just after 200 BC. Attalus began an artistic Renaissance in Pergamon. His son, Eumenes, continued it. Eumenes set out to build the greatest library in the world. He meant to outdo the famous library in Alexandria.

What followed was the stuff of black comedy. His soldiers ranged the land stealing books. Book lovers buried what they could in secret hiding places. Pergamon scribes forged manuscripts. The library grew to 200,000 volumes.

Egypt didn't take all that lying down. She quit supplying papyrus to Pergamon. That could have ended Pergamon's pretensions. But Pergamon scholars had an ace up their sleeve. They had a rich wool industry. They had plenty of sheep. They had already begun writing on sheep skin, or vellum. They called the stuff, Charta Pergamene. That meant paper of Pergamon. The words Charta Pergamene mutated into parchment.

It is harder to roll parchment into a scroll than it is papyrus. So someone thought of folding parchment into rectangular pages and sewing those gatherings together. Someone invented the codex–the modern book.

Soon after that, both Pergamon and Egypt fell under Roman control. Then, in 40 BC, Roman soldiers in Egypt accidentally burned part of

Alexandria's library. Anthony, in his obsessive love for Cleopatra, did a remarkable thing. To repay the loss he gave her the Pergamon Library.

So we remember Alexandria and forget Pergamon. But out of that brief competition, Pergamon had given us the most efficient information storage technology ever known.

This was one of the few times a new user interface was good enough to introduce a new technological metaphor. But bear in mind: the scroll still survives, even to this day, as its own technological metaphor. The book–the codex–meanwhile became metaphor unto itself. It well may be the most powerful technological metaphor of them all–at least until today's electronic media.

Once a technology finds that place of metaphor in our psyche, its outward form will survive. The user interface will not be given up.

Remember what happened when Gutenberg began printing with movable metal type. He made print look just like the work of scribes. He counterfeited manuscript books. Even today, we still fold pages into gatherings, sew gatherings together, and lace them between hard covers. Movable metal type made books cheap and abundant. Yet we readers still receive information just as we did in Pergamon, 2000 years ago.

Friends ask me, over and over, "How much change will we have to undergo?" Well, where the user meets the machine is the one place we will not tolerate change–even though the machine itself is mutating into something so different as to redirect human history.

We do indeed bend ourselves to each new machine. But where the machine has become metaphor is where that process stops.

When I work at my personal computer, I use what is clearly recognizable as a typewriter keyboard. That awkward old QWERTY arrangement is over a century old. Once more, the place where I meet the machine, imperfect as it is, remains well-loved. It simply will not be abandoned.

Pianos evolved from harpsichord improvements. But they were soon something wholly different. Pianos are so different from harpsichords that you still need a harpsichord when you want to hear harpsichord music.

All the best technologies survive their replacements that way. Live concerts have survived recordings. Pens survive word processors.

Five years ago, everyone expected to be reading electronic books in some near future. Now the computer has already leapfrogged that technology. Before a decent electronic book could come into existence, the World Wide Web was on its way to providing everything we might ever hope to get from one: screen resolution and illustrations are improving, the supply of texts is rocketing upward. And now we have both sound and motion.

As we abandon the limitations of the paper book, its electronic equivalent is already unrecognizably different. And that is exactly why the paper book will have to survive, after all. Paper books will keep right on doing what they've always done so well. They take you into the author's mind. You give yourself over to her story-telling rhythm.

Your own mind frames the pictures and plays the music. You feel organic cloth and paper against your fingers. What the computer offers has as much in common with the paper book as the horseless carriage has in common with the horse.

Still, you can't help wondering what paper books have that computers won't soon have as well. If you fix the screen, fix the portability, find means for dog-earing your place, then what's left to fix?

Well, the answer lies in the metaphor. Not only has the book long since found its metaphorical place in our lives, but the computer has already found its metaphorical place as well.

The book is our metaphorical mentor.

The computer is our metaphorical servant.

We all switch between the roles of parent and child. We need some control over things around us. But we also need to submit to other people's knowledge. In some things, we should play the parent. In others, we had better know how to be a child.

And the child says, "Tell me a story." The story we choose might be a Gothic novel. It might be a math textbook. In either case we have to give ourselves over to the story-teller if we hope to profit from the story. We do that when we read a book, go to the theater, even listen to a concert.

Computer communications are quite another matter. The computer does our bidding. We say, "Go and do. Buy me an airplane ticket. Give me a stock quotation. Tell me if the library has a book. Pass this message to a friend." The computer dances to our tune. We are in control.

When you and I go to the computer for text material, it is to look things up. It is not to let words wash over us nor to touch and feel paper. The computer is far better than a book if you want to find things.

Insofar as paper books function as simple repositories of fact, they've already given way to computers. But the sort of book we submit ourselves to will have to remain written out and uncontrollable.

It is an important omen that the first books that appeared on computers offered their readers control over the story. It is no accident that the very first computer books were ones that let you dictate the course of the plot.

To learn, we become as children. We seek out our own ignorance. Now and then we follow the mind of someone who knows what we do not. We yield to the rhythm of the story-teller.

Printed books let us put control aside for a while. That's the wonderful Gift books offer. But the metaphor of the computer has already been set. Whatever we can do with electronic media, we simply will not use them as mentors.

Now, the dark side of all this: The emergence of a new technological metaphor means revolution, and revolution means trouble. Each major communication revolution has brought a new metaphorical substratum into our lives. But it has also brought with it terrible upheavals.

Let me trace a couple of those revolutions so you can see what I'm talking about. First, try the technology of writing itself. Let me ask: Is language about words? You see, there's a vast gulf between speech and writing. Breaking speech into words doesn't become really useful until we write language down.

A librarian friend chides my attempts to pronounce French. "John," he says, "You have to understand there are no words in spoken French, only phrases." His subtle point is, the way we cast speech into words is pretty arbitrary.

When Mark Twain's Connecticut Yankee uttered a bogus magic spell at King Arthur's Court, he used a gigantic German word: Konstantinopelitanisherdoodelsachspfifenmachersgesellschaft. That means an organization of bagpipe players from Constantinople. Now you tell me: Is that seven words or just one?

Egyptians, who did the first hieroglyphic writing, credited its invention to the ibis-headed god, Toth. They picture him writing with a reed pen. The Hindu god Brahma supposedly based letters on the shape of seams in the human skull. But: By the time the Old Testament took form, we took writing for granted. The Bible no longer treated writing as a Gift from God.

That's because the old hieroglyphic languages—the ancient petro-glyphs—had mystic meanings that lay far from human speech. Pictures are not the same as words. Early writing conveyed a sense of things, quite apart from speech.

Only gradually did we reduce speech directly into writing. To do that, we identified words as the least parts of speech with stand-alone meanings. The problem is, that doesn't work consistently.

For example: The word linger means to tarry. The preposition on means many things. If we say "The melody lingers on," we call out a small additional meaning. A person lingers, but a melody or an odor attaches itself to us. It lingers on. So: Is "lingers on" one word or two?

Signing for the deaf is a form of expression, remarkable for the way it blends words into continuous action. If you've ever watched a dancer incorporate signing, you've seen, dramatically, how artificial it is to break speech into separate words.

And a great trap opens before us. The linearity of written language can cloud our minds to the multidimensionality of human thought. Many of us have a hard time thinking without making recourse to words. Hamlet, asked what he read, replied hopelessly, "Words, words words." Imagination is far too complex to be hog-tied to anything so limited.

The very act of writing started a powerful shift in the very nature of human consciousness, but the worst was yet to come. The real fun began with the invention of the alphabet. By the way, the Greek word for alphabet is stoicheia. That is where chemists get the word stoichiometry–the science of combining chemical elements. For them, letters of the alphabet were the minimal elements of speech.

Early Sumerian cuneiform, in use 5000 years ago, only had some 300 characters. It lacked anything like the full expressivity of speech. Yet it evoked things that speech could not.

The invention of an alphabet was begun by pre-classical Greeks around 1400 BC, and finished by the Phoenicians in the 11th century BC. Alphabets now transcribed speech directly. All alphabets are phonetic. They reduce speech to their least divisible elements–to their stoicheia–to their atoms.

For 2000 years before the invention of the alphabet, writing gave us means for storing knowledge, but it stored it much as an etching or woodcut might. Then all that changed.

And the result was catastrophic. Psychologist Julian Jaynes has pointed out that it was just at this time–before 1000 BC–that humans developed analytical consciousness. In popular terms, we became very left-brain in our thinking. What followed was terrible social upheaval. Without the older and more mystical means of dealing with human behavior, leaders instituted the systematic use of cruelty. They took up slavery. Knowledge was once mystery, now it became power. We struck new poses of masculine domination.

Once writing turned into canned speech, we had means for watching ourselves think. In the long run that led to mathematics, philosophy, and literature. Perhaps the first great literature it produced was the Book of Genesis which begins by telling how we'd eaten the fruit of new and forbidden knowledge.

But don't for a moment forget the damage it did to us. A mid-19th century philologist, Henry Humphreys, saw the impact of the shift long before Janyes did. In 1853, he wrote,

> From the invention of letters the machinations of the human heart began to operate; falsity and error increased; litigation and prisons

had their beginnings, as [did] specious and artful language which causes so much confusion in the world.[1]

Alphabets altered human consciousness in wonderful and terrible ways. And the new 15th century printing presses altered it again. By the 16th century they had shifted our thinking to the external world. They had also called up all that was evil in the old classical world. We call that humanism. In fact it meant revivals of male-dominance, of slavery, and of a kind of egocentricity that had been under control in the medieval world.

Now computers are once more attacking the very metaphors for thought. They're providing inconceivable access to information. But what price do we pay! I will name just three domains of mischief: Pointillism, Memory, and Spatial Visualization.

First Pointillism: Computers do an odd thing with knowledge. Ask a question and, in a blink, they immediately highlight the precise answer—the citation, the definition. You're handed the answer with no context.

I have learned so much in the process of looking up something else—adjacent pages in a dictionary, sidetracks in books. With the computer, context becomes an avoidable waste of time. And that means far greater loss than we first imagine.

Next, Memory: When I used a slide rule, I had to do a lot of the calculation in my head. That meant memorizing decimal placements and roughing out the calculation as I went along. Now that dimension of thought is wholly gone. Once I had to memorize spelling, now the machine does that for me as well.

The problem is that creativity means recognizing a fact, an idea, out of context. Our dusty attic of randomly remembered stuff—names, dates, lyrics and melody—is what creativity feeds upon. Piece by piece, the computer is robbing us of that legacy.

And finally, Spatial Visualization: We've built the rules of perspective, geometry, and mathematical graphing into our computers. What we once did in our heads, the computer now does for us. We are simply handed the result on a two-dimensional screen.

Did you know that the builders of the great Gothic cathedrals did not even have working drawings? They built in their minds and then rendered in stone. Their achievement took an enormous capacity for seeing in their mind's eye. That seems so impossible to us, that we're hard-pressed to believe it ever really happened.

So the book will remain, but we will be changed. The metaphors we live by are being rewritten by this new technology. The electronic media are unthreading the culture we know. They are both serving and disrupting the human condition in ways we cannot yet conceive.

And we're back to the serial literature. At first blush, yours is a more restrictive problem. Yet everything I have said so far plays into it. My main purpose this morning is to pose what I believe is the primary question you face: "What is the metaphorical place of the serial literature? Is it a mentor or a servant? Is it something else?"

The serial literature is newer than books, of course. Let me draw your attention to one prototypical form that it takes. I mean the modern magazine—that sumptuous array of news, features, pictures, and stories. That medium is now 265 years old. The Arabic word "makhazin" means storehouses. Edward Cave invented the medium in 1731, and he called it *The Gentleman's Magazine.*

Cave was a commoner whose education had been cut short. He was brash and rough-hewn. He lacked social grace. Cave took up printing and he rode the crest of a new wave. Before the magazine, specialized news, political, and literary journals had already come into being. He was in the middle of all that.

Cave soon ran afoul of English law for publishing news of Parliament actions. That was strictly forbidden. After he'd narrowly escaped prison, Cave decided there might be more to journalism than contention. He hit on a new kind of journal.

He would include news analysis, but present both sides. He would include pictures and poetry. He would hold up a mirror to the public's interest.[2]

As his magazine matured, he began adding natural philosophy to his storehouse. In 1751, his press published Ben Franklin's new pamphlet on Experiments and Observations in Electricity.

Before he died in 1754, he had published the first description of an electric telegraph system. He had published an article on submarines. It gave the American, Bushnell, the design he tried to use against the British in 1776.

Today, *The Gentleman's Magazine* provides a window back into a rich time in history. We read obituaries of Johann Christian Bach and Robert Fulton. We read Ben Franklin on revolutionary theory three years before we declared our independence from Cave's England.

We emerge from this storehouse with a real sense of what it was to live in days when the whole world was being turned upside down. What Edward Cave gave us was a whole new means for sorting out who we are—and what we think.

But! No one sits by the fire with *The Gentleman's Magazine* today. You go back to it to find things—an obituary, a seminal idea, a famous writer's then-half-formed poem.

Last week, before we came here, my wife, who's an adept network surfer, spent some time showing me how she could download almost any magazine article. And I came away realizing that the network itself is already one vast magazine. It is a servant who will provide facts and pictures and articles as we need them.

Magazines are only a corner fringe of the periodical literature. But they are a defining corner. Periodicals range all the way from serial monographs to the *National Inquirer*. And in that spectrum a split must occur.

As you ponder the fate of the periodical literature, remember: When that literature really functions as a mentor, it will take its place with the printed book. When that literature is used as a repository of data, it is headed into the computer.

But it is no easy matter to know which is which. The answer doesn't lie in the length of articles. You will find it in the way readers use periodicals. Watch users in the field. For example, few scientists really read technical papers. Most scan papers looking for conclusions or for their own names among the references.

You will find that many important-sounding periodicals are hardly used at all. They are neither mentor nor servant; they are just data points on resumés. The fraction of your holdings that have real value in book form is shrinking.

In any case, you work at the nexus of the information revolution. If the modern library is being split into electronic and paper archives, the fault line comes right down through the serials department.

But don't forget: While you struggle with the problem of shaping the periodical literature, something larger is going on. The new electronic servant is altering us in profound ways. What we expect of our servants, and of our mentors, won't be the same—even ten years from now. And I can only wish you God Speed in carrying out the formidable task before you.

NOTES

1. Humphreys, Henry quoted in Drucker, J. *The Alphabetic Labyrinth: The Letters in History and Imagination*. London: Thames and Hudson, 1995.
2. Cave's advertisement for the 1st ed. gives the full title and clearly states his intentions:

> The Gentleman's Magazine; or Trader's Monthly
> Intelligencer: Being a Collection of all
> Matters of Information and Amusement:
> Compriz'd under the following Heads, viz.

Publick Affairs, Foreign and Domestick,
Births, Marriages, and Deaths of Eminent Persons, Preferments,
Ecclesiastical and Civil.
Prices of Goods, Grain and Stocks.
Bankrupts declar'd and Books Publish'd
Pieces of Humour and Poetry
Disputes in Politicks and Learning.
Remarkable Advertisements and Occurrences.
Lists of the Civil and Military Establishment.
And whatever is worth quoting from the
Numerous Papers of News and Entertainment, British and Foreign;
or shall be Communicated
proper for Publication.
With instructions in gardening, and the Fairs for
February.

By Sylvanus Urban of Aldermanbury, Gent.
Prodesse et Declectare.

Printed for A. Dodd without Temple-Bar. Price 6d.

BIBLIOGRAPHY

Carlson, C.L. *The First Magazine: A History of* The Gentleman's Magazine, Westport, CT: Greenwood Press, Pubs., 1938.

Gould, S.J., "The Panda's Thumb of Technology," *Bully for Brontosaurus: Reflections in Natural History*, New York: W.W. Norton & Company, 1991, Chapter 4.

Hansen, E.V., *The Attalids of Pergamon*, 2nd ed., Ithaca: Cornell University Press, 1971.

Kuist, J.M., *The Nichols File of* The Gentleman's Magazine, Madison: The Univ. of Wisc. Press, 1982.

Marshall, R.K., *Sundials*, New York: the MacMillan Company, 1963.

Miller, G.A., *The Science of Words*, New York: Scientific American Library, 1991.

Nangle, B., The Gentleman's Magazine: *Biographical and Obituary Notices, 1781-1819*, New York: Garland Pub. Co., 1980.

Nichols, J., *The Rise and Progress of* The Gentleman's Magazine, London: John Nichols and Son, 1821. (Reprinted in Literary London, [Stephen Parks, ed.] New York: Garland Pub. Co., 1974.)

Ogg, O., *The 26 Letters*, New York: The Thomas Y. Company, 1961, 1948.

Rohr, R.R.J., *Sundials: History, Theory, and Practice*, Toronto: University of Toronto Press, undated.

Sarton, G., *Galen of Pergamon*, Lawrence, KA: University of Kansas Press, 1954, Chapter II.

See also the Encyclopaedia Britannica article on writing.

PLENARY SESSION II:
PUBLISHING IN THE CYBER AGE

The Role of the Paper-Based Journal in an Era of Electronic Information

John Cox

SUMMARY. This presentation is a review of the changes in publishing methods that electronic publishing and distribution will involve. It presents a publisher's view of the methodology needed to exploit the potential that online and other electronic technologies offer. Included is a discussion on the role of the paper-based journal in an era of electronic publication, and the ambivalence of scholars and of learned societies toward electronic information. Additionally, the role of universities is examined, as they become partners of publishers in delivering published material to customers on the Internet: by hosting servers, by providing access to bandwidth, and by adding value through participation in the publishing process. *[Article copies available for a fee from The Haworth Document Delivery Service: 1-800-342-9678. E-mail address: getinfo@haworth.com]*

John Cox is Managing Director, Carfax Publishing Company, Abingdon, Oxfordshire, UK.

[Haworth co-indexing entry note]: "The Role of the Paper-Based Journal in an Era of Electronic Information." Cox, John. Co-published simultaneously in *The Serials Librarian* (The Haworth Press, Inc.) Vol. 30, No. 3/4, 1997, pp. 41-53; and: *Pioneering New Serials Frontiers: From Petroglyphs to Cyberserials* (ed: Christine Christiansen and Cecilia Leathem) The Haworth Press, Inc., 1997, pp. 41-53. Single or multiple copies of this article are available for a fee from The Haworth Document Delivery Service [1-800-342-9678, 9:00 a.m. - 5:00 p.m. (EST). E-mail address: getinfo@haworth.com].

This paper represents a cautious attempt to speculate about the future of electronic information provision, the future role of paper-based journals and the impact of this complex and changing world on publishers, libraries and on those in the academic community whom we both exist to serve. I am not an information scientist. I am no expert either on technological change or librarianship in general or on collection management in particular. Indeed, it would be both arrogant and indiscreet for a member of one profession to tell so many distinguished representatives of another what the future holds in store for them. But when has that ever stopped any of us?

We are beset by a constant process of change: electronic publishing experiments, new e-journals on the Internet, quality and reliability of information on the Net, document delivery, resource sharing leading to a single subscription where once there were half a dozen, shifts in journal circulation and subscription pricing, and the problems of information overload arising from the relentless rise in the number of research papers seeking publication. Data from the United States indicates that, during the period 1975 to 1990, funding for research doubled. The output of articles also doubled.[1] But library expenditure increased by only 40 per cent.[2] This pattern has been repeated throughout the developed world.

In the UK student numbers have increased by 15 per cent over the past three years, but funding per student has decreased by 30 per cent. There will be a further reduction of 10 per cent over the next three years. Both publishers and universities must work together to develop new means of doing business together in partnership.

This is what we think of as the "serials crisis." Yet these pressures and changes are paralleled with factors of continuity. All good academic publishers seek to serve both the producers and consumers of their products: the academic community itself. We turn the material output of academic life into value-added commodities which other academics want to have readily available. As publishers, we gain kudos and profit by applying high craft and professional skills. Successful publications obtain both tangible and intangible rewards for editors and for authors. The relationship remains truly a dependent partnership where both parties gain.

The technology developed in the last decade has given us the opportunity to handle masses of information with speed and economy. The promised speed of delivery, the elimination of paper, storage and transportation costs, and the ability to handle complex data tables, moving pictures and sound, are qualities which computer and telecommunications technologies bring to scholarly communication. The Internet provides an unparalleled opportunity for self-publishing. There is scarcely a publisher or university that does not have a Web Page. It is a symbol of institutional virility. Of more substance, the Internet provides a medium for the exchange of information within the scientific, academic and professional communities without the need for the traditional intermediaries—publishers and librarians. Information does not have to remain in the print dimension; images, sound and video can be incorporated as integral components.

Many publishers, both by participating in experiments in the scholarly community, and by utilising the experience of those already active in the mass market, know what can be done to produce journal literature electronically. They know that electronic publishing lends itself to modelling, moving graphics and manipulating data tables. However, they cannot see how they can price such products at a level that will recover the cost of peer review and of the multi-media and interactive features that will be needed both to complement the article text and to exploit the unique capacity of the medium. Moreover, multimedia and interactive components of research output present very real challenges to traditional notions of peer review which the academic community is properly reluctant to relinquish.

From the financial point of view, electronic publishing eliminates paper, printing, binding, physical storage and transportation costs. Nevertheless, it is just as costly to employ highly skilled editorial and technical staff to prepare data for electronic publication as it is for paper-based publishing. There are no obvious cost savings on marketing, as users still have to be identified and reached with information about the product. Moreover, the technology requires heavy capital investment in computer equipment that needs to be renewed every two or three years.

Most important are the views of academic researchers. In the experience of most journal publishers I know, academics are oddly ambivalent about changing the present system of research publishing based on the printed journal. For many years, tenure, promotion, and the grant of research monies has depended on the applicant's publishing record. Many are reluctant to abandon existing information sources. Many are simply intimidated by the technology, for which new techniques have to be learned. Few are prepared to devote the time and attention currently needed to download data from the Internet or from a CD-ROM. Indeed, the benchmarks used to measure acceptable on-screen response times the average user is prepared to tolerate are frighteningly short. A delay of more than four seconds is regarded as unacceptable in most business or office applications.

There is a constant demand for the establishment of new journals, as new frontiers of research are reached, and research funding patterns change. There is little demand for them to be published only as electronic journals. The printed word is still seen as being the authoritative medium and format for the publication of peer-reviewed research. The 'look' and 'feel' of the printed medium contribute to and reinforce the authority of the message. For many academics the electronically generated printout of their works devalues their impact. The bound volume provides a 'meta-value' which the photocopy and laser print lack.

But the printed word must have more substantive advantages than the present day perceptions of academics, which will undoubtedly change as older faculty retire and new blood is recruited. In our headlong enthusiasm for the new, we ignore some very real qualities which paper-based products will continue to offer:

1. The printed word is still the best medium for reading narrative text. Except for some–but not all–STM disciplines, most research papers are predominantly text. Reading text on screen is difficult. Paper is still the natural medium for this purpose.
2. Print also provides colour illustrations of a quality that is impossible to render with reliability on current technology. The most commonly used work station in many universities is still the VT100 dumb terminal.
3. Print accommodates mathematics and diacriticals much better than the Web can.
4. The printed product does not require any specialised equipment to access it. It is portable. It does not require a power supply. Moreover, it is a familiar technology that has 500 years of development behind it. It enfranchises everyone who has basic reading skills.
5. Paper-based publications have a 'fixity' that facilitates retrieval, citation, archiving and, ultimately, scholarship.

There is much debate within institutions about the cost-effectiveness of electronic journals from the user point of view. Even if they are free, on-line journals involve support costs. It is often less expensive to maintain a current print subscription than to support an on-line equivalent. At one American university we know, there is a debate between faculty who want to have access to journals on-line and information service staff who are more cautious, not seeing the need for an expensive and complicated service. At another university twelve on-line journals are on trial, but the library staff believe they will still have to maintain print subscriptions for archival purposes and for those patrons who refuse to use the electronic version. The complexity of networking on-line journals and the daunting nature of many license agreements have dissuaded many librarians from persevering with on-line versions when the printed version remains available. All the universities we have spoken to, in the United States, the United Kingdom and elsewhere, demand an assurance that continuing access to the on-line version should be maintained.

So what are publishers doing to meet the challenges of library budget constraints, electronic publishing, library consortium purchasing, quality control in the new media, and the uncertainty and complexity inherent in investing in and managing new technologies? I can only speak for my company, but I have no reason to believe we are untypical. The question for us is when and how the demand for publication is to be met in a multiple medium environment, and how we are to adopt new methods of working and develop new products without throwing away the considerable benefits of that somewhat older technology, the printed word.

We have put twenty-one journals on-line using the services of Catch-Word, an Internet publishing services company that has a truly global network of file servers. We have invested in better marketing to maintain our current level of printed journal subscriptions; indeed, many of our established titles have increased their circulations as a result. We have formed an alliance with a publisher who supplies specialist review journals and other medical information to the pharmaceutical and healthcare industries, in order to share in the development of the expertise needed to exploit the unique publishing features of CD-ROM and on-line media. We are changing our corporate view of ourselves. We are no longer merely a producer of printed artifacts; we are responsible to our authors for publishing their works in the medium or media most appropriate to the work itself and to the readership for which it is intended. As publishers, we have to respond positively not only to librarians' need for information in a form and at a price that can be accommodated within the budget, but also to the ambitions and concerns of researchers who need to publish.

We are not alone. Many publishers have Web pages to provide information both to subscribers and to authors. The Web is an ideal vehicle for disseminating general information. But it is not a publishing environment. So publishers have sought to create Internet publishing environments where researchers and scholars, and the libraries that serve them, have easy access to published scholarship and research, and where their own financial needs and duties to deliver quality services can be met. IDEAL, STeaMline, Ivy Binder, and CatchWord are all systems that attempt to do this.

Regardless of the medium of output, there is a range of publishing skills that will be needed to ensure material is presented and distributed well. Rarely does a paper reach a publisher in a state ready to publish. This is not to criticise authors, whose strengths lie at the cutting edge of research in their particular subjects. Authors often have strong views on the structure and layout of their works. That is quite different from expecting them to be expert in typographical layout or copy editing. Authors expect a reputable publisher to ensure the highest standards of readability and presentation in the published version.

Moreover, considerable skill and effort is required to ensure works are brought to the attention of their intended market. These are all skills the publisher brings to bear on the published work.

The scholarly publishing tradition has accumulated procedures and policies that have collectively become part of the culture of the research publishing process. It assumes deliberative and objective peer review, and the permanent availability of published papers as part of the library of all scholarly and research literature. There are three features in the tradition that argue for continuity rather than revolution. In these thoughts I am indebted to the ACM, which has widely published its policy papers on electronic publishing policy.[3] ACM has started a debate, and stimulated much further thought.

- A journal is created as an 'imprint' or 'brand.' Its editor and editorial board members are appointed, either by the publisher or by the society that owns the journal. These appointments are crucially important as the journal's authority, scope and content depend on them. For the specialist journal publisher, they are a matter of continual discussion between publisher, society, editorial board and editor.

- A journal paper itself passes through a number of processes: preparation and submission, peer review (and subsequent revision if required), editorial preparation, copy editing and proofreading, publication (including marketing and distribution), and archiving and indexing. Support for the review process, editorial preparation, copy editing and proofreading, and publication are the phases undertaken or managed by the publisher.

- Authors are expected to submit new research and scholarship that does not overlap significantly with papers previously submitted by them or by others. Authors should not distribute copies publicly until the paper has actually been published, and must give full credit to others who have contributed in any way to its preparation. The soundness, professionalism and uniqueness of the published work is established in this way.

In this scheme of things, it is noticeable that quality control is largely after the event of submission. It is likely that this process of validation will at least be speeded up, if not enhanced by broadening the scope of peer review, by using telecommunications.

Each journal seeks to gain prestige in its discipline by publishing only the most significant and well-grounded papers. Authors gain prestige in their community by having their works published in prestigious journals. This "quality imperative" drives a range of rankings. The best known are ISI's citation indexes. There are others. The Dutch Social Science Research Council, for example, maintains a five-point ranking of journal quality for 1200 journals, of which only 30 or so achieve the top rank. These gradings establish a particular journal as the most appropriate both to read and to submit to for particular types of research, topics or issues. The higher the grading, the greater its value to the author. It is every publishers aim to make his journal one of "first resort."

Publishers already use digital technology to prepare journals. Gone are the days when all a publisher needed was a typewriter to do business. Publishers need to be able to incorporate software, hardware and telecommunications into the publication process, in order to drive down costs and improve speed and efficiency. The hot-metal typesetter disappeared 15 to 20 years ago. Computerised typesetting and page layout software is commonplace. Journal articles are frequently submitted on disk; publishers apply their skills in quality management, presentation and layout to material already in machine-readable form. The printed product may look traditional, but it has been output from a system that our forebears would find unrecognisable. Moreover, that process creates datafiles from which output can be made in other media.

We must continue to use all the solutions offered by new technology, regardless of the medium of output of the published material. Authors are growing increasingly dissatisfied with delays in the traditional peer review process, often taking between 6 and 12 months to complete the review-revise phase, and another 12 months until actual publication. These delays can be reduced or eliminated by using the electronic media as a tool in our quality control processes.

My view as a publisher is that the paper-based journal will survive. It is convenient, portable, technologically indifferent, and astonishingly resilient to assaults from newer technologies. But it will no longer have the field to itself. Electronic products, particularly material delivered over the Internet, will become more important, when and where the unique features of the medium become important in relation to the research to be reported.

As we move into the twenty-first century, scholarly and research publishing will exploit different media for different purposes or user requirements. We need to clarify what exactly we mean by definitive publication, as works may well be stored not only in print but on databases offering access for browsing, downloading and printing. Databases will be maintained by publishers as a service both to authors and readers. There will be links between different works, serving both as citations and as points at which orders may be placed for copies.

"Publication" will mean that a publisher has declared the author's work acceptable after a review process. The copy of the paper placed in the publisher's database will, just as much as the printed version, be treated as the definitive copy of the work. The "Publisher" will be seen less as a producer of print products, and more as a custodian of intellectual property distributed in that medium that best suits the nature of the individual work and the needs of the readership.

"Journals" will become brands around which interest groups will coalesce, and in which appropriate papers will be placed. Libraries or individuals may purchase a subscription to a printed journal, or buy a right of access to a database on which that journal is held. They may purchase a site license, with usage rights tailored to their circumstances and requirements. Alternatively, they may simply shop on an ad hoc basis for documents as the need arises. They may register their profiles, to be notified when new items matching those profiles have been posted. Items may be supplied in print on demand, or electronically to a PC, or by fax. They will, in most cases, also be available in the printed issue.

There is much debate about the applicability of copyright to these new publishing models. Some are quite dismissive, and maintain that patents and copyrights should be abandoned, and that information should be as free as the air. The extreme position is that information should not be regulated at all, by obscenity, privacy, defamation, intellectual property or any other sort of law. This has only been tried once, during the French Revolution. The early revolutionaries argued that free communication was an absolute and precious right of man. The press and publishing were deregulated in 1789. The result was an explosion in seditious and pornographic material, and the collapse of quality publishing. In 1793 new legislation restored some order, recognised the rights of the author as creator, the printed work as property and the reader as a consumer.

There is an analogy with the current state of information on the Internet. There are few barriers to self-publishing on the Net–especially using the World Wide Web. Pornography and the weather sit side by side with the equivalent of a world-wide chat line. There is so much garbage that one cannot find the valuable contributions to research and scholarship that lurk there undetected. The publisher is needed to improve the quality of the works, and provide brand names recognised by the user as indicating quality and style. The publishers imprint or brand is needed as a mark of quality, so that material is not confused with the more informal information available on the Web.

In principle, copyright is an exclusive right belonging to the copyright owner. There are limitations on exclusivity that are referred to under US law as 'fair use' and in the UK as 'fair dealing.' Fair use is the great safety valve in copyright law. Unfortunately, in neither law is the concept clearly defined.

Under UK law, 'fair dealing' allows copying for the purposes of research or private study, criticism, review or news reporting–but not for 'educational' purposes–but must not undermine the economic rights of the copyright owner. Thus, no infringement takes place unless a 'substantial part' of a work has been copied. This is sometimes described in terms of 10 per cent of a work, or a chapter, or one article from a periodical.

Special provisions apply to copying undertaken by librarians for their readers. Librarians may copy journal articles or parts of published works if the reader signs a declaration that the copy has not previously been supplied to him or her, has not already been supplied to a colleague, and is solely for private study and research. Libraries may not keep copies requested through inter-library loan; they must be passed on to the reader who requested the material.

In the USA, the Copyright Revision Act of 1976 provides guidelines to, rather than definitions of, the kinds of use that are fair. The purpose and character of the use is relevant; leeway will be given if the use is not for economic gain. If its nature is educational–note the difference from United Kingdom law–or intellectual (e.g., political or scholarly debate) it is more likely to be considered fair. The amount copied is relevant, as is the effect of its use on the potential market for or the value of the copyrighted work. In the *Texaco* case, routine copying by researchers at Texaco was judged not to be covered by fair use, as copies were made in furthering Texaco's business, and that the practice deprived publishers of subscription income and revenue from licences that were available to it. On the other hand, recently in *Princeton UP v. Michigan Document Services,* the unauthorised copying of six works, varying from 5 to 30 per cent, for course packs was found on the evidence to be to obtain peer recognition and not for financial gain, and therefore within fair use. This is so unusual that it is likely to be appealed further. Clarity, especially in respect of academic use, continues to evade us.

In the world of on-line access to published material, transmission of a copyright work through a computer network must be regarded as a form of copying; it has the same effect as sending a photocopy. The recipient of a copyright work is simply not free to copy it and pass it on without the permission of the publisher, unless already licensed to do so. Copyright law is the best regime we have at this moment. It provides economic protection. It also provides a mechanism to protect published works from alterations without review and approval by the editor of the journal and by the author. And copyright is not going to go away, because there are too many other interests at stake: Hollywood, the music industry, photography, computer software, general publishing, video on demand and so on. If we believe that copyright, the currency in which all these industries trade, is going to be abandoned or weakened in a country like the United States where the export of intellectual property is the largest source of overseas trading income, we are simply deluding ourselves.

Many database publishers already seek to avoid the uncertainties of copyright law, particularly in the ill-defined area of fair use, by granting access to their products in the form of license agreements. The issues arising from a breach of a license will be much clearer and easier to settle. Indeed, the agreement of specific contractual provisions in relation to the use of intellectual property rights brings greater certainty and understanding both to publisher and to customer. Such licences have the advantage of securing remuneration for the publisher from libraries supplying copies of works either to their patrons or to other libraries on inter-library loan. They might restrict or extend fair use. The onus of combating restrictive license conditions is then thrown on the customer, who has to rely on the provisions of local law on the enforceability of unfair contractual terms.

What we as publishers ought to do is to ensure that site licences allow universities to use material in all the ways needed for both teaching and research at reasonable cost and without too much complexity. Site licenses are not the last gasp of neanderthal publishers concerned only with market share. They enable us to tailor usage rights to the needs of a dynamic and thriving academic community. We have to listen and respond to our customers; but they have to tell us what exactly is required. The evolution of appropriate licenses is bound to be an iterative process. In the United Kingdom, the e-Lib Programme comprises expenditure of some £16 million, or $25 million, over three years for a series of projects exploring the issues of copyright and license management involved in electronic reserves, on-demand publishing and course pack production, multimedia e-journals, and faculty and student usage of electronic resources.

It is in the developing electronic environment that the value of "moral rights" in copyright law becomes most obvious. Moral rights originated in France; the original principle underlying French copyright law was always concerned with the rights of authors: not only economic rights but also the right to have the personal relationship between a creator and his or her work recognised at law. Moral rights are now generally applied throughout the European Union. It should be noted that they are not recognised as such outside the EU, and do not form part of, for instance, US copyright law.

Moral rights provide methods by which published works may be protected from alteration without review and approval by the author. In principle, the policies and practices of any ethical publisher should already take account of authors' rights. But the too frequent occurrence of plagiarism, and the ease with which material can be adapted and used by others using modern technology highlights the need for the legal protection of the author.

There are four principal moral rights:[4]

1. *Paternity* is the right of an author to be identified with his or her work. Its duration is the same as that of copyright. It adheres to the author whether the author continues to own the copyright or has assigned or licensed it to others. It does not apply to works where copyright is first vested in the author's employer, or to newspaper or magazine articles, news reports or computer programs.
2. *Integrity* is the right of objection to distortion or mutilation or any action prejudicial to the reputation of the author. It covers translations, alterations and adaptations of the work.
3. *Non-attribution* is the right not to have a work falsely attributed to an author; this right lasts for the lifetime of the author plus 20 years only.
4. *Disclosure* is the right of a person commissioning a copyright photograph not to have copies issued to the public or exhibited or broadcast.

Moral rights are not transferable or assignable, even if the author may have assigned copyright in the work, say, to the publisher. However, they can be waived in writing. Breach of moral rights is actionable in court, and will normally result in the award of damages.

Copyright only gives us a basic roadmap. Within the scholarly community we need to establish the rules, protocols and understandings that will enable us to find our way. For example, electronic media provide means whereby readers can attach comments to an author's work, and authors can respond. These comments must not corrupt or alter the original. Indeed, by posting such comments to a database, their authors are formally attaching those comments to the work as part of a public discussion. These comments themselves should not be altered or withdrawn without formal annotation on the database.

In January 1996, a Conference on Fair Use (CONFU) working party began the process of developing practicable guidelines for fair use for the scanning and storage, reproduction and distribution of materials in an electronic reserve system.

The recommended guidelines[5] include the following:

1. Electronic reserve systems may include short items (such as an article from a journal, a chapter from a book or conference proceedings, or a poem from a collected work) or excerpts from longer items. They should not include any material unless the instructor, the library, or another unit of the institution possesses a lawfully obtained copy. The total amount of fair use material included in electronic reserve for a specific course should be a small proportion of the total assigned reading for that course. As a publisher, I believe that this needs further examination. How is 'lawfully obtained copy' to be defined? If it includes copies obtained on inter-library loan, that represents an extension of fair use that is unacceptable.
2. A statement of copyright should appear where users will see it in connection with access to the particular work; it should restate the elements of the primary copyright notice.
3. Electronic reserve systems should be structured to limit access to staff responsible and students registered for the course for which the items have been placed on reserve, for example using individual password controls or verification of a student's registration status, a password system for each class, retrieval of works by course number or instructor name (but not by author or title), or access limited to workstations accessible only to enrolled students or appropriate staff or faculty.
4. Permission from the copyright holder is required if the item is to be reused in a subsequent academic term for the same course.

Such guidelines will, when eventually agreed, be useful. While it is almost impossible to be precise about the line to be drawn between what is permissible under law, and what requires the permission of the copyright owner, it is clear that the circumstances in which small scale copying does not conflict with the normal exploitation of a copyright work, and does not unreasonably prejudice the legitimate interests of the copyright owner, are quite limited. The problem for publishers and libraries is that there is little case law on the basis of which we can be certain about the boundaries between fair use and illicit use. We need better definition and greater clarity.

Electronic publishing still has to marry its informality, economy and speed with the authority and authenticity given to the printed word. It is subject to the vagaries of archiving, the lack of indexing and the disdain of many in the academic community. The hypertext linked database that characterises electronic publishing may be wholly unsuitable for the linear progression or narrative character of academic argument in the humanities, social sciences and professional disciplines, in spite of its attractions in science and technology.

Electronic media have opened up a whole new range of possibilities for authors and readers of research literature. They have also opened up the opportunity for much closer cooperation between publishers—be they societies, university presses or for-profit companies—and the academic institutions they serve. Publishers add value to basic information generated in the academic community. Universities have access to huge band width on the Internet that should be available to any organisation serving the interests of academic research, upon mutually agreed terms. Scholarly publishers and universities have a symbiotic relationship that we should exploit together.

In exploiting the media, we must always remember that the author is the source of important and authoritative information. It must be easy to locate. It must not be lost in the noise of the Internet. Authors will continue to rely on publishers to provide an imprint or brand name that certifies the quality of the work and to locate readers. The publisher protects authors' interests by placing the imprint on his work so that readers can distinguish it from the mass of informal information and gossip on the Internet, by distributing the work widely and by making sure that it continues to be available from recognisable sources wherever the reader may be.

The publisher's contribution is to bring an assurance of quality, good presentation and, most important, an orderly infrastructure to research literature. It is true that any individual can offer for dissemination any work at low cost and with great speed. But without the publisher, there will be no structure or quality, no brand recognition, no order, only the noise of the rabble.

NOTES

1. National Science Board. *Science and Engineering Indicators.* (Washington, DC: The Board, 1991). SCISEARCH data from ISI, 1975-91.

2. Association of Research Libraries. *ARL Statistics.* (Washington, DC: The Association, 1975-to date).

3. Denning, Peter J. and Bernard Rous, "The ACM Electronic Publishing Plan (with interim copyright policies and an author's guide to those policies)," *Communications of the ACM* 38, no. 3 (April 1995).

4. *Copyright Designs & Patents Act 1988, UK,* Sections 77, 78, 80, 84.

5. Conference on Fair Use, Washington DC. *Fair Use Guidelines for Electronic Reserve Systems,* version dated 5 March 1996.

From Publishing Continuum
to Interactive Exchange:
The Evolution
of the Scholarly Communication Process

Richard T. Kaser

SUMMARY. Primary and secondary publishers have traditionally defined their role within the scientific communication process in terms of a model in which information flows in a neat, linear way from author/inventor to primary publisher to secondary publisher and back–either directly or through other intermediators and expediters–to the authors and inventors who need the information to support their own research. This "production orientation" model–closely tied to print technology, even though some of its forms are now electronic–continues to function. But these "channels" are increasingly being augmented by electronic alternatives that often defy definition under the production chain model. This paper will share the observations and thoughts of secondary publishers and information providers on trends, focusing on threats and opportunities for scholarly communication. *[Article copies available for a fee from The Haworth Document Delivery Service: 1-800-342-9678. E-mail address: getinfo@haworth.com]*

PREAMBLE

Publishing has become a business that confuses the imperative of making money, with its raison d'être.[1]

–Bela Hatvany, SilverPlatter

Richard T. Kaser is Executive Director, National Federation of Abstracting and Indexing Services.

[Haworth co-indexing entry note]: "From Publishing Continuum to Interactive Exchange: The Evolution of the Scholarly Communication Process." Kaser, Richard T. Co-published simultaneously in *The Serials Librarian* (The Haworth Press, Inc.) Vol. 30, No. 3/4, 1997, pp. 55-71; and: *Pioneering New Serials Frontiers: From Petroglyphs to Cyberserials* (ed: Christine Christiansen and Cecilia Leathem) The Haworth Press, Inc., 1997, pp. 55-71. Single or multiple copies of this article are available for a fee from The Haworth Document Delivery Service [1-800-342-9678, 9:00 a.m. - 5:00 p.m. (EST). E-mail address: getinfo@haworth.com].

55

My topic today is a difficult one to address without having someone in the audience tune me out. In the opening quote alone, I have already risked branding myself as one of the attackers of serials publishers . . . or one of the sympathizers with serials libraries.

Have publishers confused their imperative to make money with their purpose for being? Some perhaps. But I might as easily have opened with a statement such as, "Libraries have confused their imperative to SAVE money with their purpose for being" . . . or, "Scholars and researchers have confused their imperative to publish with their purpose for being." There is a bit of truth in each of these statements. But I am not here to take sides—rather, to step back and take a fresh look.

As the executive director of the National Federation of Abstracting and Indexing Services, I am, of course, not entirely without bias. I represent a group of leading database producers and information providers. They are organizations who have in their names (or at least their reputations) the words "abstract," "online," "CD-ROM"—as well as "print" and "microfilm." Many of these organizations have been involved in providing electronic information services for decades. They are pillars of the information and research community as it has existed in the past. And like everyone else they bring their own preconceptions—even their own vested interests—to a world that is rapidly changing.

And to prove that even they are not exempt from my reading of the situation, I will note that I might well have opened this address with a statement to the effect that, "secondary publishers have confused their imperative to cover the printed primary literature with their purpose for being."

The point is, it's time for all of us to step back and take a clean look at who we are and what we do. What is our purpose for being? What is our raison d'être? Is it to be money-making subscription sellers? primary literature coverers? information acquisition bargainers? prolific published authors? Or are we all about something much bigger?

THE LEGEND OF THE SCHOLARLY PRESS

Everything changes. Nothing exists without change.

—Teachings of Buddha[2]

Although publishers may, as a community, talk—incessantly it seems—about copyright protection, content ownership, security issues, piracy (be it from the photocopier or the interlibrary loan department) as their greatest concerns . . . and though the library community may appear fixated on the price of journals, the unseemly profit motives of commercial publishers, the dream of the digital library, or the infamy of a world without Fair Use . . . these are not the causes, but rather the symptoms of a system that is changing faster than our beliefs, conceptions, constructs, and ideals. The system that is changing is scholarly publishing. And the changes that are occurring are not because any great philosopher (or even a great administrator or great politician) sat down and thought it all through, but because external forces and internal pressures have changed the status quo.

Scholarly publishing, as we know it, evolved over several hundred years, first with the birth of primary journals, followed almost immediately with the invention of abstracting and indexing services.[3] Libraries have been around since the days of clay tablets and papyrus scrolls, but it was libertarian enlightenment that brought them and their private and public sponsors into their own during the Industrial Revolution. The Federal government has also played an active role, first in the young Republic's championing of a free press, in subsequently advocating literacy and education, and finally in promoting actively the advancement of science by directly funding pure, scholarly research. Still, for all its lofty ideals, the system is not immune from fundamental change.

As we think of it in retrospect, the pure and primordial system simply evolved from the need of learned individuals to communicate with one another. Since there was no grant money in those days, scholars did their work out of the love for it. Societies and academic presses evolved to publish it. Abstractors came along to summarize and index it. And libraries took on the mission of cataloging and housing the work not only for posterity but for the benefit of contemporary scholars. Everybody involved was dirt poor in quantitative terms, but for their wealth of knowledge and personal satisfaction they were rich in qualitative respects. Oh, all was Utopia. Until, like Adam and Eve in the Garden of Eden, they heard a snake speak. And it said: Publish or Perish. Everybody within earshot put on a fig leaf and started typing up footnotes.

It didn't take long for the system to outgrow the capacity of the letterset presses on campus. And next came what some have called an "unholy alliance" with commercial publishers to do the dirty, inky work—but it was really a mutually beneficial arrangement. The deal was this: The commercial publishers agreed to publish esoteric works of limited commercial appeal, given that authors would not get paid, in fact authors would donate their time to support the editorial process itself, and, furthermore, the colleges and universities would buy back the work in the form of printed subscriptions in enough volume to not only pay the printer but earn a profit for the publisher. It worked.

It worked—more or less—through the baby boom, the race for the moon, and more scientists and scholars than the world had ever seen before all living at one time and all publishing to beat the band. It had long been impossible for any human to digest all human knowledge, but now it also became a challenge for the publisher to publish it, the abstractor to cite it, the library to buy back if not also house it, and the scholar to find it. The old institutions labored under the strain, while—meanwhile—there was a new toy on campus . . . and it went by many names including ARPANET, NREN, and finally The Internet.

INSTITUTIONS IN TRANSITION

We can see a lag of from four to seven centuries between religious and secular architecture.[4]

–H. M. Worthington

In our consideration of the scholarly communication process, we need to recall that everyone involved—from author to publisher to library to patron—is a part of an institution. And we need to remember that institutions may not only tend to endure beyond the times and motivations that created them, but many tend to resist change.

The field of scholarly communication is no exception. Over the past two decades secondary publishers have undergone a progressive evolution from print publishing to electronic distribution; however, even after 20 years, print remains an important product of secondary abstracting and indexing services. Libraries, too, have shown a great determination and adaptability to preserve their role in an increasingly electronic information environment, even though they have not discarded their print and microform collections. But when library funding no longer supported comprehensive archiving, librarians themselves adopted computer networking to support interlibrary lending, for example. And no one can criticize them for not having a vision of the electronic future.

On the other hand, primary publishers—who play a pivotal role in the process, but are apparently conservative by nature—have been slower to adapt to changing conditions, and even today are still only "experimenting" with electronic distribution technologies. They too often paint the impression that they are determined to remain in the print subscription business forever, even though their customers keep telling them verbally and with their pocketbooks that paradigm is changing. New entrants to the arena, including many document delivery services, have filled some gaps. And others who used to act only as subscription agents have become "publishers" themselves of electronic databases. In some cases, a new breed of primary publisher–the authors themselves–has enjoyed some success in the new media, but–even with the World Wide Web–is not really enough to pose any immediate threat to the primary publishing community, which churns out between 50,000 and 60,000 print journals a year.

By now it would appear obvious to many that our times–and the specific roles we institutions play in the scholarly communication process–are changing. But our outmoded conceptual models remain deeply ingrained in our thinking about who we are and what we do.

You will often hear players in the field talk about the "information distribution chain," the "value-added" chain, or the scholarly publishing model. What people are referring to is a schematic diagram developed in the 1960s by mathematicians and information scientists. This model–which describes beautifully the way things were–shows research results passing neatly from an author to a primary publisher, where it is released in the form of a published paper in a scholarly journal. The journal is distributed either directly to a library, sometimes with the help of a subscription agent, or–I suppose there are still a few cases of this–directly to a researcher who maintains a personal subscription. At the same time, the journal is handed over to a secondary abstracting and indexing service in the hopes that one or more of the published papers will be selected on their merit for inclusion in the bibliographies, abstract collections, and deep indexes created by secondary publishers and which not only lend credibility to the work, but help would-be readers identify its existence. These secondary services, in turn, are purchased by libraries for the use of their patrons, who are authors themselves in many cases and will create new research based on the published literature to date. (See Figure A.)

It was a beautiful model that described very accurately a critical and well-established component of scholarly communication–the publication process, with its distinctive production orientation and division of labor that characterized our society's approach to things in the late industrial age. Scholarly communication, like everything else, was viewed as a production line, trailing up to and away from the means of the production, the printing press. But how this model has always differed from the conventional production line is that the process has never been driven by supply and demand economics.

FIGURE A. The Value-Added Chain

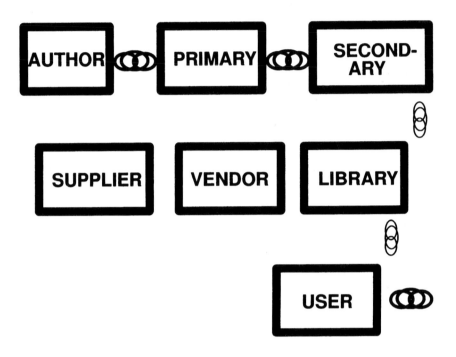

The scholarly press, as well as the research activities that produce the editorial output, has been subsidized from the very start. Federal or private grants, professional associations, or other backers have funded the research; authors, editors, and reviewers have donated their time; and academic budgets (some portion of which comes from donations and state or Federal subsidies) have paid to purchase and house the printed output, buy online access, obtain document copies, and otherwise maintain the overall scholarly publishing system.

Private corporations—who are often overlooked by the academy as being outside true scholarship—have also subsidized the process through their purchase of primary and secondary journals, their heavy use of online services, and their payment of royalties for the use of printed copies of research results for profit-making purposes and, of late, their private/public research partnerships. And of course, the governments of the world have been principal backers of this entire system, which could not function for long if it had to rely on the demand of a free-market economy. The information produced in this system—being technical if not also esoteric by its nature–is simply not of general interest to most people, though it may have a high value to some. Even among scholars, it has long been known that a large portion of the output of scholarly publishing is never cited by another researcher, never called from the stacks, and never ordered from the document supplier.[5] The philosophy has been that one cannot also tell what will be of use to future generations of scientists and scholars and therefore it is better to over-publish and over-house.

To put it bluntly, this entire system is propped up. It's propped up by, first, our ideals about the value of scholarly information to our society. Secondly, it's propped up by the willingness and wherewithal of sponsoring organizations to continue to sustain it by subsidizing it.

CRACKS IN THE VENEER

We're swept up in the politics of conflicting business and societal imperatives that at the stroke of a pen can change the direction of our communications systems; it can change the whole scholarly process.[6]

–Fred Spilhaus, American Geophysical Union

In my mind, the biggest change that has taken place in this community over the last 15 or 20 years is not–as some publishers believe–the advent of the photocopier, which though it does indeed diminish the leverage that comes of owning the printing press, does not in itself undermine subscriber bases. Nor is it what at times appears from outside to be the concerted and even consorted efforts of libraries to share subscriptions. But rather, as I noted early on, these are but the symptoms of a much more fundamental change in our society.

At a national level, we see the change in the form of emerging legislation that, by its nature, brings into question some of the premises and assertions that underlie scholarly publishing and the role that information has historically played in our culture.

As an aside, I would like to take this opportunity to thank the American Library Association for having so vigilantly defended the first amendment and free speech in court recently. Last week–just four months and four days after the Communications Decency Act was signed into law–the courts have restrained the Justice Department from enforcing it on the basis that it is patently unconstitutional and would chill free speech in the electronic environment. But the very fact that our legislature could pass into law a piece of legislation that on its surface was so much in opposition to our traditional ideals that the court was moved virtually instantaneously and unanimously to condemn it, leads me to be proud of our legal system, but also to wonder how long our old notions about information will hold up in an age when information is treated like a commodity rather than a resource.

Legislation recommended by the President's National Information Infrastructure Task Force is currently sitting in both houses of Congress. This legislation, if passed, would extend copyright protection in electronic environments to a degree that no print publisher has ever enjoyed in the past and that would conceivably allow for no fair use of copyrighted content. Meanwhile, CONFU–the Committee on Fair Use–attempts to reconcile this outstanding issue with content owners–but there is no guarantee fair use, as an intellectual concept, will follow us into the digital age.

With such fundamental concepts as freedom of speech on the line, are we then to believe that government funding for scholarly research, literature acquisition, and scientific advancement is sacrosanct?

CHANGES IN THE ACADEMY'S PRIORITIES

The increasing availability of information in new electronic formats allows libraries to be more efficient in meeting some of the information needs of students.[7]

–Kendon Stubbs (University of Virginia)

For almost a decade now I have been an outside observer of the ongoing debate between commercial primary journal publishers and academic librarians. But, though the impetus for this debate may be intuitively obvious to you in NASIG, I–as an outsider–just recently came to perceive that this debate is just a symptom and not the disease. An article in the *Philadelphia Inquirer* about escalating college costs raised my sights. In small part, the article reported that compared to 1980 there are now just 29 more students attending the University of Pennsylvania, but a whopping 1,820 more administrators and their staffs on campus.[8] This news hit me like a lightning bolt. Ah-ha! Academic libraries have clearly been forthright and honest in saying that they no longer had the funds to maintain current publishing levels. Why not? Not because their colleges and universities were underfunded, but because administrators had adopted other strategies and priorities than building comprehensive libraries.

Consciously or unconsciously college administrators had made business decisions to stop buying the complete journal literature, to stop having complete academic libraries housing and archiving the over-abundant output of their own research community and their own faculty-reward system. What did they want instead? A sidebar in the *Philadelphia Inquirer* reminded me: They wanted technology, fibre optic campus networks, state-of-the-art computers, and they fully expected that information in electronic form would be available on them.[9] All librarians were doing with their price comparisons and their consortia formation was responding in the best way they could to the business decisions that their administrators had made. And furthermore, they had responded brilliantly to the impossible challenge they had been assigned. I conclude: Publishers who believe that there is going to be a reversal in this philosophy–that perhaps, colleges will rip out their fibre optic networks in favor of going back to print–are sadly mistaken. And those who think they can coerce libraries into buying more subscriptions are barking up the wrong tree.

Why am I telling all of you this?

The scholarly publishing system can exist only as long as the values that support it exist . . . only as long as the funding is there . . . and only to the extent that the institutions and administrators involved desire it to continue.

The biggest irony of all is that a system which today is still driven by the need for publication to advance an academic career and that results in the over-publication of information is now increasingly being evaluated on the basis of how much the literature is used. Let me say that another way: A system which has nothing to do with supply and demand economics is suddenly being driven on the purchasing side by demand, while on the production side it is still driven by the ideal of publishing anything of any merit whatsoever. And to put it yet another way, what the academy as a whole seems to be saying is, everybody has to be published, but we only have to buy back the good stuff. College administrators can't have it both ways. But they're smart people, and I'm sure if they wanted to announce a new faculty evaluation system that does not depend on publication volume, they could do so as rapidly as they installed campus area computer networks in the 1980s. That's the other half of the equation they have already half-written on the board.

A WEAKENING IN GOVERNMENT SUPPORT

It is expected that future efforts to reduce federal spending will continue to put downward pressure on the dollars available to scientific and engineering research in the key mission agencies that traditionally support non-medical R&D.[10]

–American Society of Mechanical Engineers Report (1996)

As it has in the past, our government, as well as private organizations who have historically supported research, will also play a role in determining the future of scholarly publishing. Through the funding activities of federal, state, and local governments, the academy itself, and private sponsors, research studies result in the creation of the primary literature. Though a recent report by the American Society of Mechanical Engineers notes that the funding for academic research from all sources combined is one of the few areas where R&D spending has increased over the past decade–amounting to $16.3 billion in 1994 and showing real growth of 5% a year–there is no guarantee.

Under pressure to cut the budget, our legislature has been tempted to reduce–and in many cases has lowered–funding for government agencies where research has historically been conducted extensively, with information resulting as a by-product if not a principal output of the activity. Agencies affected thus far have been the Department of Defense, the Department of Energy, the Department of Commerce, the National Science Foundation, and NASA.

Warns the Society of Mechanical Engineers: "By the time it becomes apparent that the national science and technology infrastructure has been dealt a serious blow, those still involved in R&D will be faced with the prospect of trying to recover from the damage done. The recovery time may well be measured in decades." (We might say the same of the various pieces of pending content-ownership legislation in Congress!)

There was, of course, never a guarantee that agencies founded and initiatives launched during the Cold War and the Space Age would survive into the Information Age, even if information is their output, even if the advancement of science and technology was their aim, and even if we have all grown up believing in their importance. As government, along with every single industry and organization in the economy, reinvents itself based on current economic, social, and political conditions, old ideas come into question.

Few will maintain these days that the library is a repository for all human knowledge, or even should be–yet, not too many years ago that was the truth we lived by. Both primary and secondary publishers are still, in many cases, operating under the assumption that comprehensiveness of coverage is the ideal, even if it means wasted, unproductive and expensive human effort in publishing it all in the journal literature or abstracting and indexing it all, even the obscure.

Last year, members of the National Federation of Abstracting and Information Services created bibliographic records for more than 10 million documents, adding these on top of the nearly 160 million documents that they have already indexed, mostly in the past three decades. How long can it go on? Only as long as our beliefs and ideals encourage it. Only as long as our social structure supports it. Only as long as our economy can sustain it.

I do not imagine that anyone will sit down and consciously decide to quit publishing everything or to quit covering everything but that which users actually want to use. Rather policy changes, akin to the decisions college administrators and government officials have made and are making, will drive the decision. Above all else–and despite the fact that it is the academy we are discussing–market forces will prevail. Library consortia, through their increasing buying influence, will inevitably determine which primary and secondary journals are viable. The publishers (conceivably) will be forced to produce what sells. Users, as always, will decide what information is important to them . . . which leads me, at last, to the most important issue of them all . . . the new media.

THE NEW MEDIA

One of the things that happens when we have new and different communication media is that we have greater choices in the ways we communicate with one another.[11]

–Chet Grycz, Co-Author, *Official Internet Yellow Pages*

Though we may have labeled ourselves neatly in the past as to our role in the information distribution, value-added chain–we are "primary publishers," "secondary publishers," "libraries," and so forth–we must not confuse these labels with the role we play. Inherently and intrinsically, we are part of a process that has at its root nothing more complex (or less simple) than human communication. We–all of us–facilitate the exchange of information among scholars and researchers, wherever they live and work.

Though highly regarded and well respected in the past, the literature, after all, is not now and never has been the only recourse to information that researchers have at their disposal. What we used to call the "invisible college"–the personal network of scientists and scholars–has functioned alongside the literature since time immemorial, and in fact predates the literature. May I remind you that we are sitting today in a lecture hall, even though we have fax machines, phones, and access to voluminous information resources . . . even though this paper is going to be published. Faced with a question, there are two ways to get an answer: hunt it down in the literature or contact the expert directly. Anytime you want to you can reach me at nfais@hslc.org, or you can call me up at 215-893-1561, or you can fax me a request. And I'll probably respond. I probably won't spend as much time doing it as the effort I put into this paper, but the answer you receive may be more directly related to the issue that's important to you. Furthermore, as most of us know, it's often easier to ask someone who knows than to dig around for the answer yourself.

When people talk about the Internet–which I assume needs no introduction as a topic–they talk as if it's all in the future, this radical medium that is going to transform the way we do things. Perhaps for the average American that's true. Yet, who among you can deny that a revolution of sorts–at least in our part of the world–has already taken place? Over the past 25 years, it is, in fact, the scholars and researchers whom we serve, that have put networking technology to the task of facilitating informal (yet highly structured and often effective) direct communication. The invisible college–which used to depend entirely on meeting attendance, letters, and phone calls–is now hard-wired. Is it a new paradigm? Not really, at least not from a conceptual point of view. Scholars have always communicated directly with one another. But anyone who has been there knows, it *is* different. I personally regard the e-mail message as a distinct art form, in which many participants seem to be spending a considerable amount of time creating. It's current, timely, relevant and targeted at the needs of the moment . . . and a lot of it is, therefore, ephemeral.

But has it resulted–after even 25 years–in the diminution of the traditional scholarly literature?

This chart, which maps data from NFAIS members' coverage of the literature, indicates that the literature has not ceased growing over the last 25 years. (See Figure B.) Nor has the demand for it ceased, as indicated by the phenomenal volume of inter-library loans and document copies being produced these days. Since 1979, OCLC has arranged more than 66 million ILL's alone. The British Library is processing 4 million document requests a year. And the National Library of Medicine is handling another 4 million through their library network.[12] Both the traditional literature and the interpersonal, interactive Internet tools we have seem to be working in conjunction rather than in conflict, although there is no question in my mind that some questions which used to be taken to the literature to resolve are now handled more efficiently and as effectively through networking.

Researchers now have more options for handling their information requirements than they used to. They have more tools, but as Chet Grycz observes, this does not mean that the old media and methods will be abandoned, but more likely that the various media available will be used in conjunction with one another. I don't know what your office looks like,

FIGURE B. Total Abstracts Published

Selected Years 1957-1994, All Members

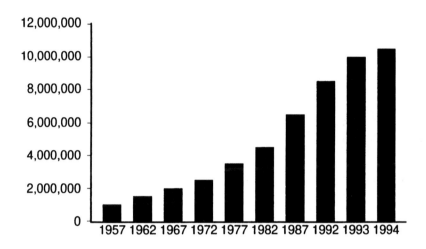

but mine contains a multimedia computer surrounded by filing cabinets, book cases, and stacks of paper everywhere.

MORE NEW MEDIA

Prolific and diverse electronic communications and publications consisting of messages, research discussions, pre-prints, and formal articles all in multimedia, run by scholars and scientists out of research labs and universities, may well have their day.[13]

–Ann Okerson, Yale

But even with 25 years under our belts, we are at a very early stage in our adoption of the new communications technologies. Everyone can cite examples of pioneering efforts by some editors who have now chosen the new media as their primary means of distributing journals, and by some accounts the number of such publications is doubling every year, though still measured only in the hundreds, or best single-digit thousands. Everyone can point to examples of forms of electronic publishing that go beyond our preconceived notions of what a journal should even be. But just because a technology is in place is no guarantee that it will be utilized to its full potential, at least not immediately and certainly not until we break our own well-ingrained habits about what solid research is and how one goes about conducting it, including the requirement for a literature search, complete with lots of citations.

I have, in fact, encountered of late several studies that, though they did not set out to prove so, conclude that the unwillingness of humans to use this media to its full potential is a major limiting factor. Raf Alvarado, commenting recently at the NFAIS Annual Conference, noted that his effort to build an innovative Internet resource through the collaboration of humanities scholars failed to be successful, because "intellectual property rights and social conditions for the production of reputation [for authors] are not yet assured." In a recent study published in the *Journal of Documentation,* Blaise Cronin and Geogrey McKim, of the University of Indiana, noted a whole host of barriers to scholarship on the World Wide Web, including the legitimacy of materials distributed over this medium as well as their archival uncertainty.[14] And Yitzhak Berman noted recently the virtual irrelevance of academic discussion groups to practitioners in some fields.[15]

Though publishers who want to remain print publishers may well breathe a sigh of relief over such declarations of the electronic media's inadequacy, it is not my intention to comfort them. I will quickly observe, such problems can and probably will be solved. But I do not see it happening over night, since the problems that are cropping up are not just technical challenges, but rather deep interpersonal challenges that go to the heart of our social conditioning. Many of us are not only old, but set in our ways, and there is a limit to our willingness and our ability to adapt.

NEAR TERM FORECAST

Incremental improvements will look pretty pathetic shortly after they have been started.[16]

—Bela Hatvany, SilverPlatter

I see several factors that will drive developments through the end of this decade. The first is library consortia, who in many respects are taking on the aspect of buying cooperatives. Through their powerful economic influence, they will continue to push for the development of electronic libraries—which as I have noted before, are their response to the challenges college administrators have given them. In this endeavor they will be limited by the independent decisions of primary publishers, whose journal collections are essential—at least right now—for the vision of digital libraries, but who have taken a cautious, conservative approach to the release of journal content in electronic form, due to economic concerns.

Recently, however, we have seen some rapid and progressive developments involving primary and secondary publishers in mutually beneficial partnerships. To these arrangements the secondary publisher brings knowledge and content useful in the efficient and effective search and retrieval of bibliographic records pertaining to the primary literature. By allying with primary publishers, some secondaries, such as the Institute for Scientific Information, are developing hybrid products that combine indexing and abstracting content with full electronic text of the primary literature. Clearly, users sitting at computers would like one-stop access to complete information, and these partnerships are one way that this desire can be met.

I regret however that for the short term, the researcher will be confined to what I think of as the "locked.doc." The digital image of a primary journal article is going to come to the user in a format that is fully secured and static. The very ability to retrieve a valid and verified copy of a journal article in electronic form, of course, will be a vast improvement for most users, who now must wait for inter-library loan or document delivery to achieve the same end. But in the long run, I do not believe that users will be happy with the locked.doc, since it will not permit them to do some of the things they would naturally like to do with such a document—for example link portions of it to other documents in their private database. But electronic document delivery of digital pages images is progress. And it is a good start.

These electronic materials will be delivered to libraries under a subscription agreement. Though this will not fulfill the complete vision of having materials purchasable on a demand-basis—and somewhat goes against the trends we have seen for collection building among affiliated libraries—again, it nonetheless will be an improvement. From the primary publisher's view, the subscription model is the prerequisite for providing the content in electronic form, because it is the only financial model that sustains the total publishing activity, even of materials that are infrequently requested.

Meanwhile we will continue to see new forms emerging on the Internet—some of them created by the same authors who write papers, moderate electronic discussion groups, or publish their thoughts in other ways than in traditional printed media. Some of these new forms will simply mirror the printed literature, but others will go beyond our conventional view of the journal–which by its historical development is constrained by the limitations of the printing press, restraints which no longer apply.

Some of these new forms of scholarly communication will compete directly–certainly indirectly–for the readership of traditional journals. Meanwhile, journal publishers will have gained more direct experience with the electronic media and at least some of them will start to innovate, once their initial fears are overcome and once they gain a better understanding of how their products are used in an electronic environment, or as importantly, how they can be reused.

Some secondary publishers are already taking the giant leap forward in the form of Web sites, one in particular being the Engineering Information Village–a service which goes beyond mere hypertext links and traditional constraints to take on a life of its own. As we move forward, I anticipate much more cooperation between primary and secondary publishers who, by working together, will be able to make things happen faster. Once a few show what can be done, the rest will follow. In the meanwhile, we will have to live with electronic document delivery.

In general, and despite any fears I may have raised, I predict we can look forward to a vibrant future for scholarly communication. But how the future unfolds is really out of the hands of any given player–be it a primary publisher, a secondary publisher, a library, or document supplier. But keep your eyes and ears open.

As I have emphasized in this presentation, entities outside the scholarly publishing community itself, such as college administrators and government officials, will also determine through their policies what happens. They already have had, in fact, a tremendous impact on the system as a whole and could effectively contrive to alter the way the entire system operates, knowingly or more likely unknowingly. Though I view this as the greatest potential threat to all of us institutions, I think it is unlikely to result in a sudden change. It is unlikely that administrators can or will abandon the publish or perish model of faculty evaluation all at once. I think it is unlikely that government will abandon all at once the underwriting of academic research–the scientific and technical community, as well as the academy, being a powerful lobby.

Neither should any of us prematurely abandon the good ship that has brought us primary journals, secondary services, fabulous libraries, and knowledge collections. For all our self-criticism of this ship, it still sails pretty well. And we are in no position to abandon it . . . quite yet.

NOTES

1. Bela Hatvany, "Redefining Ourselves for Strategic Advantage," *NFAIS Newsletter,* Vol. 38, No. 4-5, Apr/May 1996, p. 47.

2. *Teachings of Buddah* (118th rev.ed.), Tokyo: Bukkyo Dendo Kyokai, 1980, p.82.

3. The first scientific journal is generally regarded to be the French *Journal des scavans* (1665); however, it was really more of a digest than a journal. Around 1788 to 1790, we saw the birth of journals that more properly fit the primary publishing model as we know it, including *Chemisches Journal* (1788) and *Journal der Physik* (1790). Abstracting and indexing services emerged simultaneously. See: *Encyclopedia of Library and Information Science,* Vol. 22, p. 220-221. University of Pennsylvania: 1977. See also: Bruce M. Manzer, *The Abstract Journal, 1790- 1920: Origin, Development and Diffusion,* Scarecrow Press, 1977, Chapter 1.

4. H. M. Worthington, Prehistoric Indians of the Southwest; Denver, CO: Museum of Natural History, Denver, 1969. p. 64.

5. A recent study by the National Library of Medicine of the 2400 libraries in their network reported 2 million requests for 19,000 articles and other documents in 1992. Most of the articles (76%) were requested only once, and only 1% of the articles were requested more than 10 times. The library maintains a collection of 25,000 current serials and 80,000 in all, of these document requests represent a very small fraction indeed. See: *NFAIS Newsletter,* Vol. 38, No. 4-5, Apr/May 1996, p. 71.

6. Dr. Fred Spilhaus, "Unfettering Scholarly Communication," *NFAIS Newsletter,* Vol. 38, No. 4-5, Apr/May 1996, pp. 53-56.

7. Kendon Stubbs, "Service Trends Charted in Newly Released ARL Statistics," *ARL Newsletter,* #185, April 1996, p. 14.

8. Karen Heller and Lily Eng, "Why College Costs So Much," *Philadelphia Inquirer,* March 31, 1996.

9. "College Officials Defend Spending," *Philadelphia Inquirer,* March 31, 1996.

10. "The Impact of Budget Changes and Restructuring on Engineering, ASME, and the Public," The American Society of Engineers, Committee on Issues Identification, 1996, p. 2.

11. "Internet Publisher Gives Secondaries Advice," *NFAIS Newsletter,* Vol. 38, No. 4-5, Apr/May 1996, p. 51.

12. "Interlibrary Loan and Document Delivery Statistics Revealed," *NFAIS Newsletter,* Vol. 38, No. 4-5, Apr/May 1996, p. 71.

13. "Primary/Secondary Issues: Shifting Roles in Libraries," *NFAIS Newsletter,* Vol. 38, No. 4-5, Apr/May 1996, p. 75.

14. Blaise Cronin and Geoffrey McKim, "Science and Scholarship on the World Wide Web: A North American Perspective," *Journal of Documentation,* Vol. 52, No. 2, June 1996, p. 163-171.

15. Yitzhak Berman, "Discussion Groups on the Internet as Sources of Information: The Case of Social Work," *ASLIB Proceedings,* London: The Association for Information Management, Vol. 48, No. 2, February, 1996, pp. 31-36.

16. Bela Hatvany, "Redefining Ourselves for Strategic Advantage," *NFAIS Newsletter,* Vol. 38, No. 4-5, Apr/May 1996, p. 49.

How to Fast-Forward Learned Serials
to the Inevitable and the Optimal
for Scholars and Scientists

Stevan Harnad

SUMMARY. There is no conflict of interest between a trade author and a trade publisher. The trade author's product is his text, and the trade publisher produces and sells it for him, so they can both make a fair profit. Both wish to protect their product from theft; both wish to restrict access to those who have paid for it. Contrast this with the specialised scientific and scholarly research literature: The research has

Stevan Harnad is Professor of Psychology and Director, Cognitive Sciences Center, Department of Psychology, University of Southampton, Highfield, Southampton, United Kingdom.

[Haworth co-indexing entry note]: "How to Fast-Forward Learned Serials to the Inevitable and the Optimal for Scholars and Scientists." Harnad, Stevan. Co-published simultaneously in *The Serials Librarian* (The Haworth Press, Inc.) Vol. 30, No. 3/4, 1997, pp. 73-81; and: *Pioneering New Serials Frontiers: From Petroglyphs to Cyberserials* (ed: Christine Christiansen and Cecilia Leathem) The Haworth Press, Inc., 1997, pp. 73-81. Single or multiple copies of this article are available for a fee from The Haworth Document Delivery Service [1-800-342-9678, 9:00 a.m. - 5:00 p.m. (EST). E-mail address: getinfo@haworth.com].

been funded by a governmental research supporting agency or a public institution of higher learning and the results are meant to be made publicly available, especially so that other specialists can read and build further research on it. Through this cycle of research/report/research, all of humanity benefits from the fruits of learned inquiry. But because of the substantial real cost of producing print on paper in the Gutenberg era, research publication had to adopt the same economic model as trade publication: Researchers, who were not writing to sell their words, and would gladly have given them away to reach the eyes of their fellow researchers the world over, in their joint enterprise of broadening human knowledge, were forced instead to make the "Faustian Bargain" of transferring copyright to their publishers, who would then try to recover their substantial expenses plus a fair profit by selling those words as if they had been produced for trade. Research libraries the world over paid the hefty price, purchasing all the important journals so that each individual article could find its own small, scattered readership in perpetuum. This era is now potentially over: The much lower cost and much broader reach of electronic publication can free research from the counterproductive access boundaries imposed by the trade model. Research grants can now easily afford to cover the minimal marginal cost of electronic publication, making the research literature free for all, as it was always meant to be, with the growth of human knowledge no longer needlessly restrained by the Faustian Bargain and humankind the greatest beneficiary. *[Article copies available for a fee from The Haworth Document Delivery Service: 1-800-342-9678. E-mail address: getinfo@haworth.com]*

INTRODUCTION

Here are four recommendations to governments and institutions of research and higher learning, if they wish to help fast-forward learned serials to the inevitable and the optimal for scholars and scientists (Harnad 1995a,f; Odlyzko 1995):

1. Make sure to make and keep the Net free for researchers.

In the huge growth of the Internet the relative proportion of research use has shrunk to the size of the flea on the tail of the dog: All of humankind would benefit much more from giving the flea a free ride than from extracting a toll from it; let the much larger commercial use of the Net subsidise the continuing contributions of the Net's creator, Research.

2. Subsidise global electronic preprint archives in all learned disciplines.

This is a critical factor in accelerating the transition of the research literature to the Net. Paul Ginsparg's (1994) Physics Eprint Archive at Los Alamos (http://xxx.lanl.gov), now being generalised (Harnad 1995c) to the Cognitive Sciences at Southampton (http://cogprints.soton.ac.uk), should be the model for this. The start-up investment is tiny, the archives soon will be mirrored worldwide and virtually self-sustaining, and the dividends will be huge, as the entire research community in all disciplines will naturally adopt the new medium as its primary means of access to the learned literature.

3. Extend all research support grants to mandate and cover the page costs of publishing the findings in refereed electronic journals.

For less than 30% of the page cost of paper publication, this would make the refereed publication of research publicly available for free to everyone and would significantly hasten the transition of the entire literature to the electronic medium (Harnad 1995b; cf. Garson 1995).

4. Formally support electronic refereed publication in assessing the research publication productivity of universities to determine levels of support.

In assessing universities' research productivity, as in the UK's Research Assessment Exercises, giving full weight to refereed publication in electronic journals will be critical in ensuring researchers that full credit will be given for publication in non-paper journals.

SUPPORTING ARGUMENTS AND EVIDENCE

To understand why the transition of the refereed research journal literature to electronic form is both optimal and inevitable, one must understand the Faustian Bargain that researchers are currently obliged to make, and to understand why this bargain is Faustian, one must make a clear distinction between trade and non-trade publication. Unless one recognises and makes this distinction, one cannot make sense of either the profound conflict of interest that is inherent in the current means of publishing research findings, nor can one see why the ultimate outcome is both inevitable and optimal for researchers. Once it is apparent that the outcome is both optimal and inevitable, it will also be apparent that the only variable is time: Will it happen sooner or later? If it is recognised that the sooner the transition, the sooner the benefits–to research, to researchers, and to the ultimate beneficiaries of research: humankind–then it should also be clear that governments are now in a unique position to lead and accelerate the process.

Although the four recommendations are also applicable to research monographs and edited conference proceedings, they will be restricted to the research periodical literature; indeed, we will do our reckoning in terms of individual articles. It will become apparent why this is the right unit of reckoning shortly. But let it not be thought that this restriction means we are referring to a small literature: The primary scientific periodical corpus is huge, and growing. The approximately 7000 journals indexed in Science Citation Index are perhaps its core, but there are at least as many journals in its periphery; and if one includes the periodical literature in all other learned disciplines, in all languages, the numbers are still greater.

THE TRADE/NON-TRADE DISTINCTION

There is a very simple and reliable test of whether a text is trade or non-trade: (1) Did the author write it in order to sell his words? (2) Is there a market to buy them? For if the answer to both of these is yes, then the text is a trade text and the present proposal is completely irrelevant to it, to its author, to its publisher, and to its readership. If the answer is no, however, if, on the contrary, the author did not write the text to sell it–if he would, in fact, be happy to give it away, and would even go to the length of paying to have it reproduced and mailed (regular, snail mail) in the form of preprints and reprints to those who request it, and would even pay page-charges to have it published more quickly–then we are dealing with a piece of non-trade text.

THE FAUSTIAN BARGAIN

Why would an author want to give away his text, or even pay to distribute it? To understand this one has to understand why anyone would want to be a scientist or a scholar, rather than an author of best-selling novels, or perhaps a stockbroker, in the first place. One cannot answer such questions; but given that someone has chosen the path of learned inquiry, there is one critical consequence: Learned inquiry is not a solipsistic enterprise. One builds on the work of others, and one works in the hope that others will build on one's own contribution. For this to be possible, the work must be available, in perpetuum, to one's fellow scholars and scientists, present and future. Very few of them will ever want or need to read any given article (this is why it is so important to note that it is the article, rather than some other entity, that is the proper unit of reckoning), but for those few who might, wherever they might be, and whenever they might need it, the article must be accessible, ubiquitously, and in perpetuum.

Now in the Gutenberg Era of print on paper, the only way to ensure that an article reached its potential readership was to publish it in a paper periodical, which required a substantial investment by the publisher, as substantial as it would have been if the article had been written for trade. And in order to recover the cost of that investment, and to make a fair profit on it, the publisher had to protect it from theft. The author was accordingly required to assign copyright to the publisher, who would then charge for access to the text.

That was the Faustian Bargain: out of the necessity of reaching its small potential readership anywhere, at any time, the article's author had to collude in a restriction of access to those who paid, exactly like a trade author. Yet, unlike a trade author, the research author was not paid any royalties, nor would he have wanted to be paid; he would have been much happier to redirect those meagre revenues towards wider and less restricted access. Moreover, the market was for the most part not the small number of readers of that particular article, but a captive population of research libraries who had to subscribe to as many of the core journals as they could afford, to ensure that the research literature was available to their researchers. As periodical prices rose, the research author became more and more a victim of the Faustian Bargain, seeing access to his work become more and more restricted to the remaining libraries that could afford to subscribe to it, the rest trying to access it by the slow, cumbersome, and likewise expensive medium of interlibrary loan (usually in the form of mailed photocopies in the case of periodical articles).

It should be clear that if the goal of research PUBLICation is to make public one's research findings, then this goal was always ill-served by the paper medium, and has become increasingly so as the volume of research increases, and with it the price of research periodicals.

It is also important to note how small the readership of any given research article really is: This is a non-trade medium. If an article is read by only 10 or 20 specialists the world over, this is not a sign that something has failed the test of supply and demand: The research literature is an interaction among experts working for the benefit of us all. It is not necessary that their reports be candidates for a best-seller list. But if the means of dissemination denies access to even 10% of its tiny potential readership (and one must multiply this across all published articles), then the cumulative goal of research will have been disserved. Conversely, if a new means of dissemination could increase its readership by even 5 readers, that would be a 25-50% gain in such a small population!

There was no alternative to the Faustian Bargain in the Gutenberg era, because of the high cost and inefficient reach of print on paper. This era is now over: So why has research periodical publication not shaken off its Faustian shackles and taken to the skies of the PostGutenberg Galaxy (Harnad 1991, 1995d)? There are 4 main obstacles, and each component of the present proposal addresses one of them:

1. Researchers are afraid that eventually a price tag may be attached to their Net use, so they dare not become too reliant on it in their reading; nor do they dare to entrust their intellectual goods, their articles, to a medium that could become inaccessible to them and to their readership. This fear could be removed by an explicit intergovernmental commitment to keeping the Net free for researchers.

2. Researchers are reluctant to distribute their work electronically before publication for several reasons: (a) They are afraid it may be regarded as prior publication, so refereed journals will refuse to publish it. (Implementing recommendations 3 and 4 together with a clearer sense of the epistemic role of unrefereed preprints as opposed to refereed, revised, published reprints would fully assuage this fear.) (b) Given the anarchic quality of so much of the material on the Net, researchers are reluctant to consign their work to such a medium, akin to a global graffiti board. (Again, the remedy is implementing recommendations 3 and 4, increasing the number of Eprint Archives (2) and their coverage of the many different learned disciplines, and providing a reputable profile for Eprint Archives through systematic institutional support.) (c) Researchers fear that publicly posting their preprints may lead to plagiarism and loss of priority and credit for their work. (The remedy is again to strengthen and raise the profile of the Archives, providing password-protected date-stamping and permanent archiving to resolve any subsequent priority questions: With its powerful search and analysis tools, the Net can protect priority and detect plagiarism more powerfully than paper ever could. In general, it seems to have been the pattern so far that whatever new problem or vulnerability the Net breeds, it also breeds even more powerful means of remedying the problem and combating the vulnerability.)

3. Researchers are reluctant to submit their work to electronic journals because: (a) They are afraid they will not get credit for their work. (Rem-

edy is recommendation 4.) (b) They are afraid that the Electronic journals will not last and make their work available in perpetuum. (The remedy is again to support them, until their permanence becomes obvious; some common but completely unfounded worries about the permanence of the electronic medium itself, and its means of storage, are involved here; with distributed copies at many different sites, and mechanisms for backup and transfer to new storage technologies in place, the electronic medium can be made even more secure and permanent than paper, if we wish.)

4. Researchers are afraid that electronic publication will be seen as less prestigious than paper. (Competing with the established journals is a problem even for new paper journals: a new medium is working under an even greater handicap. But the solution is to implement these four recommendations, for that will ensure that the prestigious paper journals likewise migrate to the Net, bringing their editorial boards and their prestige with them. Implementing recommendation 4 will help to facilitate this.)

As their work is launched into the PostGutenberg Galaxy, scholars and scientists will discover yet another benefit of the optimal and inevitable medium for learned inquiry: interactive publication (Harnad 1992; see Hayes et al. 1992). I have dubbed this feature "Scholarly Skywriting" (Harnad 1990, Garfield 1991). The learned literature on the Net will be sectored into formal refereed publications (in a hierarchy of journals varying in the rigour of their peer review and hence their prestige, just as it is now in paper Harnad 1982, 1985, 1986, 1995b) and informal, unrefereed publications (Harnad 1995e). In BOTH sectors it will be possible to (respectively) publish and post commentaries and responses that will provide a rich source of feedback for researchers and (I have argued, on the basis of 19 years of editing a paper journal of Open Peer Commentary and 6 years of editing a similar electronic journal) a further dimension for the cumulative, self-corrective process of learned inquiry, to the benefit of scholars' and scientists' productivity (Harnad 1979, 1984, 1995c; Mahoney 1985). The main reason for this is that the Net has made it possible to reunite the slower, but more thoughtful and permanent medium of writing with the speed of human thought, which evolved in the service of on-line polyadic speech (see Harnad et al. 1976) rather than off-line monadic script (Harnad 1991).

For the background papers in support of this proposal, please see:

http://www.princeton.edu/~harnad/intpub.html
http://cogsci.soton.ac.uk/~harnad/intpub.html

In closing, let me add that if governments and research institutions do not support this transition, it will happen anyway, as a much more Net-oriented generation is coming of age, but the delay will be a pity for the current generation of researchers, who will not be able to benefit from the PostGutenberg Galaxy. Their research lifelines will be much shorter than they need have been, and we will all be the poorer for it. For them it is doomed to remain: so near and yet so far.

Publishers, too, would benefit from adapting to the inevitable, rather than trying to delay it at all costs. They can delay it for a while, but the price for that will be that they will lose their role entirely, for as they keep trying to defend an indefensible trade model, the rival non-trade model, with author page charges replacing subscription charges, will again be implemented by a new generation of electronic-only publishers who will simply recruit to the new medium the editors and the all-important referees who form the backbone of refereed periodical publication. Publishers would be much better advised to cooperate in the transition, adopting rather than rejecting the page-charge and subsequent free-distribution model that they find so unnatural and unwelcome. In the conflict of interest that exists under the trade model for research publication, it is inevitable that research will win and paper publishers will lose if they persist in making it a conflict rather than a collaboration.

REFERENCES

Garfield, E. "Electronic Journals and Skywriting: A Complementary Medium for Scientific Communication?" *Current Contents* 45 (1991): 9-11.
Garson, L.R. "Investigations in Electronic Delivery of Chemical Information." Paper presented at the International Conference on Refereed Electronic Journals: Toward a Consortium for Networked Publications, Winnipeg, Manitoba, Canada, October 1-2, 1993 (Proceedings in press).
Ginsparg, P. "First Steps Towards Electronic Research Communication." *Computers in Physics* 8, no. 4 (1994): 390-396. http://xxx.lanl.gov/blurb/
Harnad, S. "Creative Disagreement." *The Sciences* 19 (1979): 18-20.
Harnad, S. (ed.) *Peer Commentary on Peer Review: A Case Study in Scientific Quality Control.* New York: Cambridge University Press, 1982.
Harnad, S. "Commentaries, Opinions and the Growth of Scientific Knowledge." *American Psychologist* 39 (1984): 1497-1498.
_____. "Rational Disagreement in Peer Review." *Science, Technology and Human Values* 10 (1985): 55-62.
_____. "Policing the Paper Chase." (Review of S. Lock, A Difficult Balance: Peer Review in Biomedical Publication.) *Nature* 322 (1986): 24-5.
_____. "Scholarly Skywriting and the Prepublication Continuum of Scientific Inquiry." *Psychological Science* 1 (1990): 342-343 (reprinted in *Current Contents* 45: 9-13, November 11, 1991).
_____. "Post-Gutenberg Galaxy: The Fourth Revolution in the Means of Production of Knowledge." *Public-Access Computer Systems Review* 2, no.1

(1991): 39-53; also reprinted in *PACS Annual Review* Volume 2 1992; and in R. D. Mason (ed.) *Computer Conferencing: The Last Word.* Beach Holme Publishers, 1992; and in: M. Strangelove & D. Kovacs: *Directory of Electronic Journals, Newsletters, and Academic Discussion Lists* (A. Okerson, ed.), 2nd edition. Washington, DC, Association of Research Libraries, Office of Scientific & Academic Publishing (1992); and in Hungarian translation in REPLIKA 1994; and in Japanese in *Research and Development of Scholarly Information Dissemination Systems 1994-1995.*

_____. "Interactive Publication: Extending the American Physical Society's Discipline-Specific Model for Electronic Publishing." *Serials Review, Special Issue on Economics Models for Electronic Publishing* (1992): 58-61.

_____. (1995a) "Electronic Scholarly Publication: Quo Vadis?" *Serials Review* 211, no.1 (1995): 78-80 (Reprinted in *Managing Information* 2(3) 31-33 1995).

_____. (1995b) "Implementing Peer Review on the Net: Scientific Quality Control in Scholarly Electronic Journals." In: Peek, R. & Newby, G. (Eds.) *Electronic Publishing Confronts Academia: The Agenda for the Year 2000.* Cambridge, MA: MIT Press, 1995, 103-118.

_____. (1995c) "Interactive Cognition: Exploring the Potential of Electronic Quote/Commenting." In: B. Gorayska & J.L. Mey (Eds.) *Cognitive Technology: In Search of a Humane Interface.* The Hague: Elsevier 1995, 397-414.

_____. (1995d) "The PostGutenberg Galaxy: How To Get There From Here." *Information Society* 11, no. 4 (1995): 285-292. Also appeared in: *Times Higher Education Supplement. Multimedia.* May 12, 1995, vi.

_____. (1995e) "There's Plenty of Room in Cyberspace: Response to Fuller." *Information Society* 11, no. 4 (1995): 305-324. Also appeared in: *Times Higher Education Supplement. Multimedia.* June 9, 1995, vi.

_____. (1995f) "Universal FTP Archives for Esoteric Science and Scholarship: A Subversive Proposal." In: Ann Okerson & James O'Donnell (Eds.) *Scholarly Journals at the Crossroads; A Subversive Proposal for Electronic Publishing.* Washington, DC., Association of Research Libraries, June 1995.

Harnad, S., Steklis, H.D. & Lancaster, J.B. (eds.) "Origins and Evolution of Language and Speech." *Annals of the New York Academy of Sciences* 280 (1976).

Hayes, P., Harnad, S., Perlis, D. & Block, N. "Virtual Symposium on Virtual Mind." *Minds and Machines* 2 (1992): 217-238. ftp://princeton.edu/pub/harnad/Harnad/harnad92.virtualmind

Mahoney, M.J. "Open Exchange and Epistemic Progress." *American Psychologist* 40(1985): 29-39.

Odlyzko, A.M. ("Tragic Loss or Good Riddance? The Impending Demise of Traditional Scholarly Journals." *International Journal of Human-Computer Studies* (formerly *International Journal of Man-Machine Studies*), to appear. Condensed version to appear in *Notices of the American Mathematical Society,* January 1995. ftp://netlib.att.com/netlib/att/math/odlyzko/tragic.loss.Z Skywriting

Winners and Losers
in the Global Research Village

Paul Ginsparg

SUMMARY. I describe a set of automated archives for electronic communication of research information that have been operational in
many fields of physics, and some related and unrelated disciplines,
starting from 1991. These archives now serve over 35,000 users
worldwide from over 70 countries, and process more than 70,000
electronic transactions per day. In some fields of physics, they have
already supplanted traditional research journals as conveyers of both
topical and archival research information. Many of the lessons
learned from these systems should carry over to other fields of scholarly publication, i.e., those wherein authors are writing not for direct
financial remuneration in the form of royalties, but rather primarily
to communicate information (for the advancement of knowledge,
with attendant benefits to their careers and professional reputations).
These archives have in addition proven equally indispensable to
researchers in less-developed countries.

AN OVERVIEW

A major lesson we learn is that the current model of funding publishing
companies through research libraries (in turn funded by overhead on

Paul Ginsparg is a member of the Physics Research Staff, Los Alamos
National Laboratory. FAIR USE: I reserve the right to distribute this electronic
document in any way I so desire. It is publicly posted to the Internet on my server,
and anyone is free to establish a link to it from a subsidiary server (but not to copy
it for public posting on a remote server, since that could lead to an undesirable
proliferation of obsolete versions). It should not be reprinted for inclusion in any
publication for sale without my explicit permission.

[Haworth co-indexing entry note]: "Winners and Losers in the Global Research Village." Ginsparg,
Paul. Co-published simultaneously in *The Serials Librarian* (The Haworth Press, Inc.) Vol. 30, No. 3/4,
1997, pp. 83-95; and: *Pioneering New Serials Frontiers: From Petroglyphs to Cyberserials* (ed: Christine Christiansen and Cecilia Leathem) The Haworth Press, Inc., 1997, pp. 83-95.

research grants) is unlikely to survive in the electronic realm. It is premised on a paper medium that was difficult to produce, difficult to distribute, difficult to archive, and difficult to duplicate–a medium that hence required numerous local redistribution points in the form of research libraries. The electronic medium shares none of these features and thus naturally facilitates large-scale disintermediation, with the resulting communication of research information both more efficient and more cost-effective. A correctly configured fully electronic scholarly journal can be operated at a fraction of the cost of a conventional print journal, and could, for example, be fully supported by author subsidy (page charges or related mechanism, as already paid to some journals), ideally allowing for free network distribution and maximal benefit both to authors and readers.

Another lesson is that authors are unlikely to accept "electronic clones" of print journals (i.e., electronic versions identical in content, functionality, methodology and appearance, to paper versions), whether transmitted via CD-ROM or via the network. The electronic medium should not be constrained by any former print incarnation and, in particular, easily implemented quality appraisal mechanisms in the electronic realm will be dramatically superior to the binary (i.e., one-time, all-or-nothing) procedure employed by the print medium, which in turn frequently conveys inadequate signal. Moreover, authors and their funding institutions will be empowered to insist upon retaining the right to distribute electronic research documents and attachments in the format produced by the authors. Authoring tools already allow a highly sophisticated end-user format, including automatic network linkages, and will continue to improve.

The essential question at this point is not *whether* the scientific research literature will migrate to fully electronic dissemination, but rather *how quickly* this transition will take place now that all of the requisite tools are on-line. Secondary open questions include determining the most effective means of cost recovery for the disseminators of this information, what agencies will be responsible for insuring the long-term archival integrity, indexing, and cross-compatibility for the various research databases, and how peer review will be organized for those disciplines that depend on the value-added it can in principle provide.

Finally, I describe some of the major improvements, enhancements in functionality, and other expansions projected over the next few years for the existing archives.

INTRODUCTION

Electronic publishing in science has recently become the focus of an increasing number of workshops and conferences, typically including representatives from professional societies and other scholarly publishing concerns, and members of the library community, but only a small or vanishing participation from actual researchers. This is ironic since the average scientist provides the lifeblood of scientific publication on a daily basis as reader, author, and referee, frequently as editor, and also as organizer of conferences, schools, and workshops. Scientists consequently understand research publication from the inside-out as few non-researchers ever could, and many have grown frustrated at patronizing attempts to assure them that unthinking preservation of the status quo is in their best interest. It is clear that many traditional roles will be shifted by the electronic medium, and new roles will emerge, though precisely which players will acquire the competence to fill which roles, and when, remains to be determined.

In principle, the new electronic medium gives us the opportunity to reconsider many aspects of our current research communication, and researchers should take advantage of this opportunity to map out the ideal research communication medium of the future. It is crucial that the researchers, who play a privileged role in this as both providers and consumers of the information, not only be heard but be given the strongest voice. In particular, we need to dislodge definitively the curiously prevalent notion that the future electronic medium will strictly duplicate, inadequacy for inadequacy, the current print medium.

SOME HISTORY

Rather than relate here the full history of the "e-print archives" and whatever has occurred since mid-1991, instead I will concentrate only on some highlights that serve to illustrate the major lessons learned to date, and suggest their implications for the future. (For additional background information, see my article, "First Steps Towards Electronic Research Communication," *Computers in Physics*, Vol. 8, No. 4, Jul/Aug 1994, p. 390, originally adapted from a letter to *Physics Today*, June 1992. For some of the more recent publicity, see *Computers in Physics*, Vol. 10, No. 1, Jan/Feb 1996, p. 6; and *Science*, Vol. 271, 9 Feb 1996, p. 767.)

The first database, hep-th (High Energy Physics–Theory), was started in August of '91 and was intended for usage by a small sub-community of less than 200 physicists, then working on a so-called "matrix model" approach to studying string theory and two dimensional gravity. (Mermin ["Reference Frame," *Physics Today*, Apr 1992, p. 9] later described the establishment of these electronic research archives for string theorists as potentially "their greatest contribution to science.") Within a few months, the original hep-th had quickly expanded in its scope to over 1000 users, and after a few years had over 3800 users. More significantly, there are numerous other physics databases now in operation (see xxx physics e-print archives) that currently serve over 35,000 researchers and typically process more than 70,000 electronic transactions per day (i.e., as of 2/96; see the weekly stats for an overview of growth in World Wide Web usage alone at xxx.lanl.gov).

These systems are entirely automated (including submission process and indexing of titles/authors/abstracts), and allow access via e-mail, anonymous ftp, and the World Wide Web. The communication of research results occurs on a dramatically accelerated timescale and much of the waste of the hard copy distribution scheme is eliminated. In addition, researchers who might not ordinarily communicate with one another can quickly set up a virtual meeting ground, and ultimately disband if things do not pan out, all with infinitely greater ease and flexibility than is provided by current publication media.

It is important to distinguish the form of communication facilitated by these systems from that of Usenet newsgroups or garden variety "bulletin board" systems. In "e-print archives," researchers communicate exclusively via research abstracts that describe material otherwise suitable for conventional publication. This is a very formal mode of communication in which each entry is archived and indexed for retrieval arbitrarily at later times; Usenet newsgroups and bulletin boards, on the other hand, represent an informal mode of communication, more akin to ordinary conversation, with un-indexed entries that typically disappear after a short time.

While the high energy physics community did have a pre-existing hard copy preprint habit that had already largely supplanted journals as our primary communication medium, this is not a necessary initial condition for acceptance of an electronic preprint archive, as evidenced by recent growth into other areas of physics and mathematics, and even to computation and linguistics. The economics for all this remains favorable, with a gigabyte of hard disk storage currently averaging under $500 (i.e., roughly 25,000 papers including figures can be stored for an average of less than 2 cents apiece). Finally, politically correct elements typically fret over leaving the third world in the dust—but the reality is that less-developed countries are already better off than they were before: researchers in eastern Europe, South America, and the far East frequently report how lost they would be without these electronic communication systems, and how they can finally participate in the ongoing research loop. It will always remain easier and less expensive to get a computer connected to the Internet than to build, stock, and maintain conventional libraries–the conventional journal system had always been much less fair to the underprivileged.

To summarize, to date we've learned:

1. The exponential increase in electronic networking usage has opened new possibilities for formal and informal communication of research information.
2. For some fields of physics, the on-line electronic archives immediately became the primary means of communicating ongoing research information, with the conventional journals entirely supplanted in this role. Researchers will voluntarily subscribe and make aggressive use of these systems which will continue to grow rapidly. The current levels of technology and network connectivity are adequate to support these systems (though we anticipate the need for increases in transcontinental network carrying capacity to catch up with the recent explosion in non-academic usage–otherwise scientific usage will require either priority routing on the shared network or an independent network).
3. For some fields of physics, open (i.e., unrefereed) distribution of research can work well and has advantages for researchers both in developed and undeveloped countries.

SCHOLARLY VS. TRADE PUBLICATION

Before continuing, we must distinguish at this point between two very different types of publication, formerly grouped together only due to accidental similarities in their modes of production and distribution. Understanding this distinction is crucial to the future of scholarly publishing endeavors. My comments here have been strongly influenced by e-mail discussions with Stevan Harnad and correspondents, some of which are available at the following site:

ftp://netlib.att.com/netlib/att/math/odlyzko/tragic.lossz.

Other relevant discussions of electronic publishing issues by Harnad, with further references, are available at:

http://www.princeton.edu/~harnad/intpub.html
ftp://princeton/edu/pub/harnad

In scholarly publication (a.k.a. "Esoteric Scholarly Publication"), we are writing to communicate research information and to establish our research reputations. We are not writing in order to make money in the form of royalties based on the size of a paying readership. We have every desire to see maximal distribution of our work (properly accredited of course), and would fight any attempt to suppress that distribution. In trade publication, on the other hand, authors write specifically to sell their articles and books, and have direct financial remuneration in mind from the outset. It is consequently in their interest as well to maximize distribution, but at the same time to insure that each reader pays per view; for this the intermediation of a publishing company to maintain an infrastructure to exact money from paying customers and to root out bootleg distribution may well remain welcome.

So in scholarly publication, we have a situation wherein authors can joke that they would pay people to read their articles (N.B., this potential paucity of readership for any given article must not be used as an argument that support of basic research is intrinsically wasteful—it simply results from the naturally restricted size of a highly specialized community, and does not directly measure the ultimate utility of the research). So the essential point is now self-evident: if we the researchers are not writing with the expectation of making money directly from our efforts, then there is no earthly reason why anyone else should make money in the process (except for a fair return on any non-trivial "value-added" they may provide; or except if, as was formerly the case in the paper-only era, the true costs of making our documents publicly available are sufficiently high to require that they be sold for a fee). Now we are ready to consider the current role played by publishers of physics research information (at least in certain fields).

THE CURRENT ROLE OF PHYSICS JOURNALS?

It is ordinarily claimed that journals play two intellectual roles: (a) to communicate research information, and (b) to validate this information for the purpose of job and grant allocation.

As I've explained, the role of journals as communicators of information has long since been supplanted in certain fields of physics, so let's consider their other role. Having queried a number of colleagues concerning the criteria they use in evaluating job applicants and grant proposals, it turns out that the otherwise unqualified number of published papers is too coarse a criterion and plays essentially no role. Researchers are typically familiar with the research in their own field, and must in any event independently evaluate it together with letters of recommendation from trusted sources. Recent activity levels of candidates were mentioned as a criterion, but that too is independent of publication per se: "hot preprints" on a CV can be as important as any publication.

So many of us have long been aware that certain physics journals currently play NO role whatsoever for physicists. Their primary role seems to be to provide a revenue stream to publishers, a revenue stream invisibly siphoned from overhead on research contracts through library systems.

POTENTIAL PITFALLS

So this goes a long way to explaining how it could possibly be that a system whose primary virtue is instant retransmission is able to supplant entirely established journals as a credible information source in certain fields. (Though it is true that e-print archives are technologically somewhat ahead of what established publishers are offering in ease of use and functionality, and are likely to remain so for the foreseeable future.)

With an example of an electronic system that physicists will voluntarily and actively use in hand, it is illuminating to consider how a poor understanding of the properties and potentialities of the electronic medium can lead to badly mistaken implementations. An example of this was an American Physical Society (APS) "request for proposals" for an on-line version of Physical Review Letters back in autumn 1993. Its superficial problem involved asking that the electronic version be identical in appearance to the printed version–in other words to clone electronically every unnecessary artifact of the paper version. Its more profound problem is that the entire journal structure and organization needs to be reconsidered in light of the electronic format. In an era of instantaneous communication, why is there still a need for a letters journal with its draconian page limits and atavistic claims of rapid publication? As is well-known to potential physicist readers, artificial constraints result in articles too telegraphic to be useful either to experts or to non-experts.

While I have used familiarity with the situation within one small sector of physics publishing to illustrate these points, feedback from researchers in other fields indicates that there is a generic and growing frustration at the slowness of existing publishers to recognize that the needs of researchers can potentially be served in an electronic format in novel and creative ways. The current problem consists both of misguided selection criteria and of misplaced goals: publishers may measure the success of their journals by the number of pages published, whether certain artifactual and unnecessary constraints are met, and whether they're published "on time" (i.e., with regularity, not with speed). "Useful," "readable," "innovative" are not necessarily primary criteria in this established framework.

Even benign, nonprofit organizations and learned societies can easily become addicted to the amenities of scholarly publishing and lose track of their original mandate, thus placing the revenue-generating potential of their established publishing enterprises above the need to furnish creative intellectual services to their constituents. Until recently, there were few effective options for physicists or other researchers to break into an intellectually void closed loop involving only publisher and library systems. The resources necessary for production and distribution of conventional printed journals allowed publishers to focus on their mechanics, and avoid any pressure to rethink the intellectual content and quality of their operations.

PROBLEMS AND POSSIBILITIES

Why is it that the current implementation of peer review, as employed by paper journals, needs to be entirely rethought in view of new possibilities afforded by electronic publication and dissemination?

A most obvious problem in the current scheme is that as the number of researchers in any given field has grown (both due to global population increase and increased cold war funding for the sciences), the number of papers published in journals for any given field has vastly exceeded the ability of any one researcher to read and absorb. While perhaps there once was a time when a physicist could pick up a single journal each month and read it from cover to cover to remain abreast of all of physics, this idyllic state of affairs is not even a distant memory for any recent generation of physicists. Nonetheless, this outmoded methodology effectively remains the basis for many aspects of the current implementation of peer review, in physics and in other fields.

Once the mere fact of publication in a journal no longer gives a particularly useful guide, readers are forced to perform the majority of the selection on their own by some set of additional criteria, and their primary need is simply access to the information as quickly as possible. For this reason, a systematic preprint system was set up for high energy physics institutions in the early '70s and largely usurped the role of conventional journals as conveyors of topical information. This widespread preference for rapid access over the limited filtering provided by peer review was even more dramatically reinforced with the advent of the electronic preprint (e-print) archives in the early '90s, which quickly grew to supplant as well the conventional archival role of journals in many fields.

This is not, however, to argue that peer review cannot in principle provide substantial added-value to the reader. One of the foremost problems at present is the large amount of information lost in the conventional peer review process, with the end result only a single one-time all-or-nothing binary decision. Although this may somehow be adequate for the purpose of validating research for job and grant allocation, it clearly provides little benefit to the average reader.

A variety of superficial improvements can easily be implemented immediately in the electronic realm. Since there are no financial or physical barriers to widespread dissemination, we can imagine a relatively complete raw archive unfettered by any unnecessary delays in availability. Any type of information could be overlaid on this raw archive and maintained by any third parties. For example, the archive could be effectively partitioned into sectors, gradated according to overall importance, quality of research, or other useful criteria, and papers could be shifted retroactively as dictated by additional information or follow-up research. And rather than face only an undifferentiated bitstream, the average reader could benefit from an interface that recommended a set of "essential reads" for a given subject from any given time period. There could also be retroactively added descriptive information, "this paper was important since it drew upon a,b,c [hyperlinks to sources] and led to new developments x,y,z [more hyperlinks]" to provide a further guide to the literature. Or the interface could point to a specific paper as having been important, but warn the beginner to go first to a later paper by the same (or other) authors that subsumes, extends, or corrects the same results in a more understandable fashion; or this paper generated much attention but skip it since the fad played itself out and people returned to more serious pursuits. The literature need not be frozen in time as in the paper medium, but can remain as fluid as the research itself. Even interdisciplinary research (for example if I as a particle physicist wished to peruse the recent literature in biophysics or even biochemistry) can be easily facilitated by an interface that allows rapid identification of papers that provide pedagogic review material or are otherwise likely to be of specific interest to outsiders. Further possibilities such as moderated comments threads attached to specific points in papers together with more exotic features can be added in successive stages as desired.

WHO NEEDS IT?

Will the enthusiastic use of the instant communication provided by free access to un-reviewed electronic archives ultimately emerge only as an artifact, preferred only in isolated subsets of the scientific community? This is to a certain extent an experimental question, answerable only after all the bits have settled. But it is worthwhile to speculate on features that may characterize those scientific sub-communities most likely to find it practical and efficient in the future to sidestep the conventional peer-review structure for rapid access to new results, while still maintaining some form of electronic peer-review system to provide validation of and guidance to their archival literature. In other words, looking beyond current experience drawn from a well-defined and highly interactive community of voracious readers with a pre-existing hard-copy preprint habit, with a standardized word processor and a generally high degree of computer literacy, with a rational means of assigning intellectual priority (i.e., at the point of dissemination rather than only after peer-review), and with little concern about patentable content–all of which may be regarded as a momentary historical accident–is there some more abstract characterization of the required autonomy that allows a circumscribed community to flourish rather than suffocate in its own un-reviewed output stream? Again it will be easier to argue these issues in retrospect someday, but at least one noteworthy feature can be identified: in my own research discipline, the author and reader communities (and consequently as well the referee community) essentially coincide. Such a closed peer community may signal a greater intrinsic likelihood for acceptance and utility of free electronic dissemination of un-reviewed material.

Research communities comprised of a relatively small number of authors and a much larger number of readers could ultimately settle on a very different model, wherein the institutions that support the research assert copyright privilege, assume the role of publishers, and disseminate material produced in-house for a fee to those institutions that only consume it. Though this would upset proponents of free electronic access to all publicly supported research material, it would at least be a logical system, in which the real risk-takers–namely the institutions that support research by way of investment in salary and equipment–are able to profit from and protect the products of that investment. The current system, which cedes full copyright of high-quality content to low-risk publishers who step in at the last moment and provide at most a comparatively insignificant few hundred dollars of added-value (in most cases even selling it back at high prices to the initial sponsoring institution), has never been particularly sensible.

CLOUDY FUTURES

For the moment, conventional publishers have continued to express their unbridled enthusiasm for open electronic dissemination systems, despite an intrinsic potential for subversion. As long as their bottom line is unaffected, they can afford to be arbitrarily magnanimous in their desire for peaceful coexistence: "After all we have long been in the business of propagating research information, we would never dream of trying to suppress it in any way. . . . "

But ever financially pressed research libraries are poised for triage of their journal subscriptions. And as pointed out by Quinn (1994),[1] there's a potential explicit mechanism to encourage preferential cutting of subscriptions to physics journals: Libraries, faced with difficult choices, may decide that physicists already have an alternate information feed from the raw global electronic database; and physicists may well complain the least (or not at all) when their journals are threatened with cancellation. (Indeed this is already reported to be happening in India and other places with severely limited financial resources–as argued above, the less developed countries stand to benefit at least equally from recent technological developments.)

The physics and math archives now offer a variety of choices of high quality output formats (ex source, hyperdvi, gzipped hyperPostScript with choice of font resolution or type 1 PS, or pdf, . . .) and will be able to support higher level formats as they become available. With this aspect of end-user accommodation thus trivialized, the near-term concerns have shifted to the continued development of a robust global mirroring system, and to better means of handling meta-level indexing information. Additional mirror distribution sites and caching proxy servers will give better response times, especially to international users whose access is increasingly impeded during times of day when their national networks and transcontinental links suffer from the congestion caused by recent increases in non-academic network traffic. In the longterm, they also provide a global backup system resistant to localized database corruption and/or loss of network connectivity.

The problems of indexing and categorization of information in principle lie within the purview of the library and information science communities, but to date theirs has been a curiously low profile in the electronic realm, while various amateur brute-force indexing schemes are running dangerously amok. It would be remarkable if centuries of ostensibly relevant experience will find little applicability in the network context. We should also be alert to risks borne by authors who may find themselves prematurely encouraged to abandon "chemicals adsorbed onto sliced processed dead trees" in favor of an electronic-only archival format. There is a certain leap of faith involved here, since every once in a while one does after all get lucky and write a paper that could still attract readership a century from now. The physical format, with a worldwide system of institutional libraries serving as a multiply redundant distributed archive, has proven robust on the time scale of centuries to anything short of global cataclysm (in which case we'd probably have more pressing concerns). No current electronic format has proven similar longevity—for the simple reason that all have been in existence for little more than a decade, if that.

Few claim to know what will be the preferred electronic format a century from now, but I'm willing to go out on a limb and assert that it will be none of TeX, PostScript, PDF, Microsoft Word, nor any other format currently in existence. On the other hand, this is certainly not a fundamental problem of principle, and perhaps scientists will eventually come to rely on much-needed logistical assistance from future librarians in their role as archivists: just as endangered material on decaying acid paper is currently migrated to microfilm, automated translation to newer and more general electronic formats should always be possible during transition periods, provided there is an acknowledged need to prevent our living research archives from becoming data cemeteries.

One possibility is that some consortium of professional societies and institutional libraries will ultimately acquire the technical competence to provide umbrella sponsorship of the global raw research archive. Those societies that are as well non-profit publishers may continue to organize high-quality peer-reviewed overlays (though perhaps no longer as a means of generating income to subsidize other non-publishing ventures), and certain commercial publishers accustomed to large pre-tax profit margins on their academic publishing activities will probably have to learn to compete in more realistic marketplaces.

In the long term, it is difficult to imagine how the current model of funding publishing companies through research libraries (in turn funded by overhead on research grants) can possibly persist. As argued by Odlyzko (1994),[2] it is premised on a paper medium that was difficult to produce, difficult to distribute, difficult to archive, and difficult to duplicate—a medium that hence required numerous local redistribution points in the form of research libraries. The electronic medium shares none of these features and thus naturally facilitates large-scale disintermediation, with attendant increases in efficiency benefiting both researchers and their sources of funding. As described above, recent developments have exposed the extent to which current publishers have defined themselves in terms of production and distribution, roles which we now regard as trivially automated. But there remains a pressing need for organization of intellectual value-added, which by definition cannot be automated even in principle, and that leaves significant opportunities for any agency willing to listen to what researchers want and need.

NOTES

1. Frank Quinn. "Consequences of Electronic Publication in Theoretical Physics." (E-mail message to: cpub@math.ams.org from quinn@math.vt.edu. Subject: electronic publishing in physics) ftp://princeton.edu/pub/harnad/Psycoloquy/subversive.Proposal/who-pays piper. 14.quinn.peer-review-phy.

2. A.M. Odlyzko. "Tragic Loss or Good Riddance: the Impending Demise of Traditional Scholarly Journals," *International Journal of Human-Computer Studies*, in publication.
ftp://netlib.att.com/netlib/att/math/adlyzko/tragic.loss.Z

PLENARY SESSION III: PIONEERING NEW SERIALS FRONTIERS–PART 2

The Serials Revolution: Vision, Innovation, Tradition

James G. Neal

SUMMARY. The objectives of this presentation are to: outline important developments influencing the publication of scholarly journals, describe several electronic scholarly communication models now in development, summarize the goals and current status of Project Muse at Johns Hopkins, and share some preliminary findings and observations drawn from this experiment in scholarly publishing. *[Article copies available for a fee from The Haworth Document Delivery Service: 1-800-342-9678. E-mail address: getinfo@haworth.com]*

In 1991, the Association of Research Libraries published "Challenges Facing Research Libraries," which outlined key developments affecting future library priorities:

James G. Neal is Sheridan Director, Johns Hopkins University.

[Haworth co-indexing entry note]: "The Serials Revolution: Vision, Innovation, Tradition." Neal, James G. Co-published simultaneously in *The Serials Librarian* (The Haworth Press, Inc.) Vol. 30, No. 3/4, 1997, pp. 97-105; and: *Pioneering New Serials Frontiers: From Petroglyphs to Cyberserials* (ed: Christine Christiansen and Cecilia Leathem) The Haworth Press, Inc., 1997, pp. 97-105. Single or multiple copies of this article are available for a fee from The Haworth Document Delivery Service [1-800-342-9678, 9:00 a.m. - 5:00 p.m. (EST). E-mail address: getinfo@haworth.com].

1. dramatic increases in the cost, volume and formats of scholarly information
2. volume and diversity of information available exceeds capacities of current scholarly access systems
3. ability to develop and maintain comprehensive research collections threatened by soaring costs and lack of long-term resource sharing plans
4. deterioration in the physical condition of paper-based research collections and lack of a national preservation program
5. application, financing and impact of new information technologies
6. education, recruitment, continued development and effective use of library staff with new capacities and fresh energies
7. evolving nature of higher education, government policy, and public/ private funding presents a management/leadership challenge[1]

Five years later, these challenges persist and highlight a continuing crisis in scholarly communication characterized by the following factors:

- world production of published materials continues to increase
- cost of research publications continues to inflate at unprecedented rates
- acquisitions budgets have not kept pace with inflation, particularly for journals
- more expensive commercial publishers taking over from academic/ society publishers
- declining percentage of acquisitions funds invested in new monographs
- electronic production, storage and distribution of research information is of growing importance.

The overall result has been a general decline in ownership in North American research libraries. Recent data from ARL documents devastating trends over the past decade: a 138 percent increase in serial unit prices and a 106 percent increase in serials expenditures producing an 8 percent drop in number of serials purchased. Monograph unit prices have increased 58 percent and monograph expenditures 22 percent, generating a 23 percent reduction in number of monographs purchased. Serial price analysis for 1992-96 shows an overall increase of 50.6 percent, with a 14.7 percent rise last year. Projections for 1997 subscriptions point to an additional price growth of 9-11 percent.

Scholarly activity is the creation of knowledge and the evaluation of its validity, the preservation/archiving of information, and the communication of information to others. This process is being dramatically influenced by new technologies, new economics and new institutions. There are key factors in the information value-chain: creators/authors, sellers/publishers, intermediaries/aggregators, buyers/libraries, and users/readers.

The recent work of the Association of American Universities and the Association of Research Libraries (AAU/ARL) highlights the various functions performed across the scholarly communication process: information generation and creation, authoring, informal peer communication, editorial and validation activities, ownership, privacy, and security issues, distribution, acquisition and access, storage, preservation and archiving, information management, location and delivery, recognition, diffusion, and utilization of information. The work of libraries, traditionally focused in the core storage and service activities for students and scholars, is increasingly blurring across the value-chain.

The telecommunications network is expanding as the essential infrastructure for scholarly publishing, and the university is particularly positioned to be an influential player in this evolving environment. There is a common framework for interconnection, with a strong record of shared network development. There is enhanced connectivity and improved performance. There is rich horizontal integration across institutions on a global scale and technological diversity. There is a skilled population with expanding technical and information literacy. And there are higher levels of knowledge creation and use, a unique intensity of information production and demand. The ability to expand network use for access to scholarly publications will require improved capacity and reliability.

The AAU/ARL projects also highlighted a series of essential performance attributes for technology: ease of use, timeliness, responsiveness, accuracy, authenticity, predictability, adaptability, relevance, eligibility, cost, recovery, innovation, extensibility. These factors are similarly critical to the effective expansion of electronic scholarly publishing.

Several key principles/goals have accumulated around electronic experimentation in publishing:

- more kinds of information to be published quickly, easily and cheaply
- combine scholarly information with scholarly discourse through commentaries and moderated discussions
- primary source material can be used more widely and easily if digital and linked
- electronic scholarly publishing and academic rewards require support
- permission and use of material must be facilitated
- model site licenses and contracts should be designed to make materials readily available for all kinds of uses

- shift economic model to save money in production and distribution while continuing to maintain high quality editorial process.

New cooperative models for electronic scholarly publishing are developing. The academic server model proposes that universities obtain newly prepared research papers from their faculties and make them available over the network, perhaps through cooperative mounting of specialized discipline servers. The prestigious publishing model, based on scholarly societies (American Physical Society) and university presses (Project Muse and Highwire), seeks to bring quality electronic scholarly publishing into the mainstream. An important new initiative in discussion at ARL is the International Scholars Academic Network (IScAN). It is proposed as "a not-for profit, cost recovery consortium that creates, distributes, manages, uses and preserves networked scholarly and scientific communications and publications in a manner that is directly responsive to the interests of world scholarship and supports the teaching, research and service missions of the institutions served and which leverages resources and capabilities for the benefit of the scholarly community."[2]

These developments reflect important changes in the environment of scholarly publishing: the emergence of the Web as a distribution channel, the application of new dynamic data formats, the move of many mainstream publications to electronic distribution, new knowledge drawn from academic experiments such as Tulip, and significant movement among STM publishers to embrace electronic publishing. Important products such as OCLC's Electronic Collections Online and Elsevier's Science First will dramatically influence the emerging market, providing Web-based and centralized access and archives to large electronic journal collections.

Equally important is JSTOR, the Journal Storage Project spawned by Mellon and in development for fall availability. JSTOR seeks to create faithful electronic replications of the back volumes of core journals that will be of archival quality. It strives to improve dramatically, access to important journal literature by linking bitmapped images of journal pages to powerful search engines. JSTOR will enable libraries to study the effects of providing electronic access on the use of the back issues of journals across scholarly disciplines and in various academic settings. This initiative will address some of the pressing economic problems of libraries by easing storage problems and future capital costs, and by reducing operating costs associated with the retrieval and reshelving of journals.

Project Muse at Johns Hopkins University was launched in 1994 with the following objectives:

- make the 40 journals of the Johns Hopkins Press available electronically
- create a successful model for electronic scholarly publishing with attractive and liberal use policies
- increase access while decreasing serial costs
- provide a model for value-added information sources to the academic community
- encourage the use of network-based, non-proprietary interfaces
- maximize the ability of a campus to distribute and duplicate scholarly information
- involve actively librarians in designing electronic scholarly communication.

As Project Muse has advanced from prototype to production, it has brought the library, the press and academic computing into a strong cooperative relationship. Substantial three-year funding from the Mellon Foundation and the National Endowment for the Humanities has allowed the project to be launched successfully. Basic principles have guided early planning of the initiative: library-based subscription model; HTML documents to allow as many browsers as possible to view journals easily; ability to search individual titles or entire journal database, table of contents or full text with keyword Boolean capabilities; and support for unlimited simultaneous users.

Project Muse seeks to enable a variety of access models, with no linking of print and electronic subscriptions. There is free trial access enabling open exploratory searching of the journal databases. Single journal titles are set at ten percent less than the print price for full domain institutional access. Both print and electronic versions are available at 130 percent of print price. Both individual library and multi-campus/consortial pricing plans have been outlined. Access to subscribing libraries is provided through domain name and IP addresses. Currently, there are over 250 subscribers with approximately 1,000 additional in discussion. Early purchases indicate votes of support for the project and desire to create positive campus experience with electronic publications as primary motivators.

Project Muse provides expanded search and use capabilities. These attributes include the following elements:

- search individual title, groups of titles or entire database
- search table of contents or assigned subject headings of all articles
- search full text of all articles
- keyword and Boolean search capabilities
- search results show journal, volume, issue, author and title of all articles meeting search terms

- search results are relevance ranked
- hypertext links in the table of contents, endnotes, author biographies and illustrations
- text designed for on screen reading
- illustrations larger than print version, often in color
- ease of downloading or printing on demand
- earlier availability of electronic version, as much as four weeks

Project Muse has been designed with the fair use expectations and needs of library users at the core of license arrangements:

- no limits on number of simultaneous authorized users from a campus
- download, save and print articles for personal use
- download, print and distribute articles in multiple copies for classroom use as long as not sold for this purpose
- print out articles for hard copy inclusion in serials collection
- place unlimited articles on reserve, whether paper or electronic
- place listings and notices on the campus network to inform users of availability
- download and save materials on local domain server
- archive articles on CD-ROM or tape backup (libraries own the materials to which they have subscribed)
- interlibrary loan articles from the database using fair use guidelines via facsimile page systems.

Project Muse has involved careful consideration of technical options and directions:

- best viewed with graphical browser like Netscape and Mosaic, but also support text-only browser like Lynx
- seeking currently to conform to HTML 3.0-type specifications
- indexing each journal with SWISH (simple web indexing system for humans)
- shift in conversion methods and increased automation (abandoned Postscript to HTML) and working with software which plugs into mainstream typesetting packages
- in-house Muse scripts upgrade the quality and content to each HTML file
- comprehensive per article/per issue production checklists and tracking capabilities facilitate conversion, preparation, proofing of HTML documents by student staff
- investigating TEI (Text Encoding Initiative) headers and SGML content tagging (WYSIWYG freeware browsers and authoring tools)

- start-up technical support provided on server side, not on browser side
- tracking platform, browser and version of visitors and users
- dynamic allocation of most appropriate HTML/bandwidth pages to specific browser or browser class of user
- in-house and subscriber statistics presentation program (article hits, image hits, TOC hits, journal hits, ranking of articles used, ranking of subscriber activity)
- robust subscriber IP database, with robot investigations and updates nightly
- access denials and other server responses which might indicate error automatically logged and routed for staff investigation
- implementing open market secure commerce server to enable payment online and digital signature capabilities

Primary technical goals are the use of standard, non-proprietary software tools to enhance user support, and tools to advance innovation.

Project Muse short-term objectives include the following:

- complete implementation of all 40 Johns Hopkins Press titles (discussions proceeding with journal sponsors)
- expand significantly the subscription base
- expand access to backfiles prior to 1995
- secure more detailed understanding of the economics of electronic scholarly publishing
- collect and analyze reader feedback
- collect and analyze extensive use data (provided to subscribing libraries)
- monitor library collection development behaviors
- promote author awareness and creativity, including audio and video capabilities
- produce dependable income stream for journal sponsors
- monitor developments affecting SGML content tagging
- implement hypertext links to references and data sets
- establish permanent governance structure for project between library and Press
- add new journals to the project/subject clusters
- promote editorial experimentation
- individual subscriptions and document article delivery
- exploration of derivative works

The early experience with Project Muse enables a series of preliminary observations:

- subscriptions predominantly to entire database
- heavy consortial interest/few individual libraries
- libraries adding hotlinks directly to Muse from online catalogs
- expanding interest/contacts with current print journals about Muse distribution of electronic versions
- expanding interest/contacts with new electronic journals about Muse distribution
- significant new customer base for Johns Hopkins Press titles, most with low or no current subscriptions
- expanding international interest and access
- concerns about future identity of the journal title
- need for expanded technical support and customer service personnel at Press
- need among users for familiar journal elements, such as page numbers
- dynamic technical environment
- electronic journals used for different purposes than print versions because of searchability features
- appears that cost of electronic journal publishing is lower and start-up costs not as high as anticipated
- libraries indicate plans to cancel print journals, and this concerns journal sponsors
- Johns Hopkins Press experiencing more extensive involvement with customers to market, negotiate and implement
- Johns Hopkins Press experiencing culture shift and conflict as new electronic publishing team has grown
- need to promote use of electronic publications in the user community
- journal sponsors, associations and editors need to be convinced that Project Muse is a "good thing"
- societies focused on loss of members and revenues

The future of scholarly publishing will be dramatically influenced by the impact of initiatives like Project Muse. Success will depend, according to AAU/ARL, on the ability to:

- Foster a competitive market by providing realistic alternatives to prevailing commercial publishing options.
- Develop policies for intellectual property management emphasizing broad and easy distribution and reuse of material.

- Encourage innovative applications of available information technology to enrich and expand available means for distributing research and scholarship.
- Assure that new channels of scholarly communication sustain quality requirements and contribute to promotion and tenure processes.
- Enable the permanent archiving of research publications and scholarly communication in digital formats.

The scholarly journal had its origins in the information explosion of the 19th and 20th centuries and it has flowered as a core institution of research discourse. Its success in the past twenty years has been compromised by rampant expansion and specialization and as a tool of the academic reward structure. Under the impact of advancing technology, the journal will develop as a knowledge gateway and as a rich forum for learning and scholarship.

NOTES

1. Association of Research Libraries. Challenges Facing Research Libraries. Washington, DC, 1991.
2. Unpublished ARL working document on IScAN, created 1996.

CONCURRENT SESSIONS: AN ARRAY OF CHOICES

CONCURRENT SESSION I:
ELECTRONIC SERIALS CATALOGING

Electronic Serials Cataloging:
Now That We're Here,
What Do We Do?

Steven Shadle
Bill Anderson
Thomas Champagne
Leslie O'Brien

SUMMARY. Many aspects of electronic serials cataloging have not yet developed standard practice, or are still in transition. This article will explore some problematic issues in electronic serials cataloging

Steven Shadle is Serials Cataloger, University of Washington Libraries.
Bill Anderson is CONSER Specialist, Library of Congress.
Thomas Champagne is Serial Electronic Resources Librarian, University of Michigan.
Leslie O'Brien is Head of Technical Services, Virginia Tech.

[Haworth co-indexing entry note]: "Electronic Serials Cataloging: Now That We're Here, What Do We Do?" Shadle et al. Co-published simultaneously in *The Serials Librarian* (The Haworth Press, Inc.) Vol. 30, No. 3/4, 1997, pp. 109-127; and: *Pioneering New Serials Frontiers: From Petroglyphs to Cyberserials* (ed: Christine Christiansen and Cecilia Leathem) The Haworth Press, Inc., 1997, pp. 109-127. Single or multiple copies of this article are available for a fee from The Haworth Document Delivery Service [1-800-342-9678, 9:00 a.m. - 5:00 p.m. (EST). E-mail address: getinfo@haworth.com].

first by presenting current CONSER policy in these areas and then by examining the practices of three institutions who are cataloging electronic serials. For brevity, the term "electronic serial" will be used to mean "remote access computer file serial" unless the more specific term is needed for clarity. The five topics covered in this discussion are: Access and Location Information, Multiple Versions, Definition of Electronic Serial, Bibliographic Access Points and Display of Computer File Characteristics. *[Article copies available for a fee from The Haworth Document Delivery Service: 1-800-342-9678. E-mail address: getinfo@haworth.com]*

CONSER ELECTRONIC SERIAL CATALOGING POLICY AND PRACTICES

By Bill Anderson and Steven Shadle

The policies and practice that have been developed by CONSER for cataloging electronic serials are found in the CONSER Editing Guide (CEG) and the CONSER Cataloging Manual (CCM), Module 31 "Remote Access Computer File Serials." In addition, CONSER's home page[1] contains relevant documents in HTML format. These include an html version of CCM Module 31 and core record requirements for electronic serials, as well as links to OCLC's Internet Catalog and to electronic serial collections.

Recent changes resulting from format integration have been documented in the CEG. These include:

- the use of computer file fields previously not available in the serials format (538, 516)
- the addition of new computer file fields (computer file 007, 270, 856)
- the change in 008 used for electronic serials (from serial to computer file)
- the addition of the 006 fixed field to represent seriality in non-print publications

In addition, the CEG contains the newly developed core standard for electronic serials. Module 31 of the CCM contains CONSER practice and policy as of Fall 1995 for the cataloging of electronic serials. Besides covering the description of electronic serials using AACR2 and MARC, the module also discusses issues specific to electronic serials, including the definition of serial in an electronic environment, policies for multiple file formats and multiple sources of information, and location and access information. For information about the development of CONSER's current policies, an article about the module's development was published in PACS Review.[2] An update of the module is planned for late 1996.

Access and Location Information

The Electronic Location and Access field (856) is part of the CONSER core record for electronic serials. It is a repeatable field and there should be a single 856 corresponding to each mode of access (mail, http, ftp, gopher, telnet, dial-up) (see Figure 1). The 856 should represent an entire publication, not just a single issue, and must provide the complete information needed to locate an item. Commonly, the 856 will describe a main journal directory or home page. Generally, separate 856 fields are not supplied for different file formats because the organization of serial publications doesn't always allow for a distinct path to each format. CONSER prefers the use of the URL (subfield u) rather than having the same information broken into its component subfields in the 856, as the URL is used by systems which provide hot links to resources from their catalogs. Public notes (subfield z) are used sparingly and only contain necessary information not conveyed in other parts of the catalog record.

Library catalogs have the potential to display location and access information from the 856 field. In order to reduce redundancy (and therefore record maintenance), the Mode of Access note (538) contains general information. It always begins with the phrase "Mode of access:" and only records the access method (World Wide Web, Gopher). Often the 538 field provides more specific email subscription instructions since an email URL does not contain enough information to actually obtain or subscribe to an electronic serial.

MULTIPLE VERSIONS

Neither AACR2 9.2B nor the LC Rule Interpretations fully addresses the question of multiple versions (including multiple file formats), but a clear policy is necessary for CONSER catalogers using a common database. While discussions in the larger cataloging community did not produce uniform agreement, there was significant support for using one record for electronic serials published in multiple file formats, regardless of the type of formats involved or the extent of the differences between versions. However, because the paper and print media are so different, CONSER's current policy is to create separate records for a print serial

FIGURE 1. CONSER record in OCLC

```
OCLC: 22471982        Rec stat: c
Entered: 19901005     Replaced: 19951009      Used: 19951026
Type: m    ELvl:      Srce: d    Audn:     Ctrl:        Lang: eng
BLvl: s    File: d    GPub:                 MRec:        Ctry: ncu
Desc: a                          DtSt: c    Dates: 1990,9999
```

```
 1   010       sn90-3259
 2   040       NSD ǂc NSD ǂd NST ǂd NSD ǂd NST ǂd EYM ǂ MYG ǂ OCL
 3   006       [str1p      0   a0]
 4   007       c ǂb r ǂd c ǂe n ǂf u
 5   012       ǂi 9211 ǂl 1
 6   022       1053-1920
 7   037       ǂb Postmodern Culture, Journals Department, Oxford University Press,
2001 Evans Rd., Cary, NC 27513 ǂc Free (electronic mail) ǂc $30.00 (institutions,
microfiche or disk) ǂc $15.00 (individuals, microfiche or disk)
 8   042       nsdp ǂa lcd
 9   050 14    PN98.P67 ǂb P668
10   082 10    909 ǂ2 12
11   090       ǂb
12   049       DLCC
13   210 0     Postmod. cult.
14   222  0    Postmodern culture
15   245 00    Postmodern culture ǂh [computer file] : ǂb PMC.
16   246 3     PMC
17   260       Raleigh, NC : ǂb Postmodern Culture, ǂc c1990-
18   310       Three no. a year
19   362 0     Vol. 1, no. 1 (fall 1990)-
20   538       Mode of access: Electronic mail on BITNET or Internet, FTP, gopher,
and World Wide Web. For email subscription, send to: listserv@ncsuvm (BITNET), or:
listserv@ncsuvm.cc.ncsu.edu (Internet), the message: sub PMC-LIST [firstname lastname].
21   500       "An electronic journal of interdisciplinary criticism."
22   500       Description based on printout of online display; title from caption.
23   516 8     Electronic serial in ASCII and HTML formats
24   530       Issued also on microfiche and computer diskette.
25   650  0    Postmodernism ǂx Periodicals.
26   776 1     ǂt Postmodern culture (Microfiche) ǂw (DLC)sn 91019114 ǂw
(OCoLC)23234647
27   776 1     ǂt Postmodern culture (Diskette) ǂw (OCoLC)28863760
28   850       OU
29   856 0     ncsuvm (BITNET) ǂa ncsuvm.cc.ncsu.edu (Internet) ǂf PMC-LIST ǂh
listserv ǂi sub ǂz Email subscription
30   856 1     ǂu ftp://jefferson.village.virginia.edu/pub/pubs/pmc
31   856 7     ǂu gopher://jefferson.village.virginia.edu/11/pubs/pmc ǂ2 gopher
32   856 7     ǂu http://jefferson.village.virginia.edu/pmc/contents.all.html ǂ2 http
33   936       Vol. 6, no. 1 (Sept. 1995) LIC
```

and its online equivalent. CONSER is currently investigating, as an optional practice, the use of a single record for those publications that appear to be digital reproductions (i.e., digital conversions that replicate print publications).

Definition of Electronic Serial

The current definition of a serial has two components: the publisher must intend to continue to publish indefinitely and it must be issued in successive parts which are somehow numbered or otherwise uniquely identified. However, because of the ease with which material can be revised, it is often the case that an electronic version of a print serial may not meet the strict definition of a serial (distinctive issues or traditional designation). One example of this is MathSciNet, an Internet-accessible database (updated daily) which presents itself as the online version of two print serial publications. CONSER is currently investigating the definition of a serial in an online environment to determine if these items are best considered as monographs or serials and whether the definition of a serial in a networked environment needs to be changed to incorporate these not-exactly-serial versions.

Bibliographic Access Points

Multiple sources of information from the publication can be problematic for transcribing descriptive information from the publication. Cataloging rules instruct the serials cataloger to describe the first or earliest issue available, yet often an issue consists of multiple files or does not contain the type of descriptive information the cataloger is used to seeing. Catalogers may need to investigate and piece together information found online from a variety of sources. The chief source of information is the title screen or other "formally presented internal evidence." CONSER catalogers always note the source of the title and (if possible) take it from the first "issue." Both Designation (362) and Description Based On notes (500) are required as part of the core record if the information is applicable.

Name and related work added entries are the same as those for print publications. Currently CONSER catalogers are using an Additional Physical Form note and linking field (530, 776) to link records for electronic and print versions.

The Subject Cataloging Manual (SCM) does not provide a distinct form subdivision for electronic serials, instead using the subdivisions "Periodicals" or "Databases" as appropriate. An upcoming update to the SCM clarifies the use of these two terms in the context of electronic serials.

Computer File Characteristics

The computer file nature of the electronic serial is represented in a variety of places in the CONSER record. As mentioned earlier, recent changes to the MARC record have allowed for a more detailed description of the physical aspects of the electronic serial. CONSER is using a serial 006 field to describe seriality, computer file 007 field to record physical characteristics (i.e., remote access, sound, color), and computer file 008 field to represent the primary aspects (including Type of File 008/26). CONSER catalogers use the qualifying term "Online" in uniform titles used to distinguish online versions from their print counterparts. As instructed in AACR2, CONSER catalogers are using the general material designation (GMD) [computer file]. Other terms have been considered, but because there is no general consensus within the cataloging community for a suitable replacement term, CONSER is continuing to endorse the use of [computer file].

The MARC record has two fields containing information about the computer file: Computer File Characteristics (256) which is a field limited to recording whether a publication is a computer program or computer data, and Type of Computer File Note (516) which is a free-text note used to describe the nature of the computer file. CONSER catalogers currently do not use the 256 field as most electronic serials would be considered computer data. Instead, catalogers use the 516 field to note computer file characteristics, including file format, form, or other general information about the computer file.

The International Standard for Bibliographic Description of Computer Files (ISBD(CF)) is currently under revision. Among the proposed revisions is the development of more specific material designations (SMDs) which can be used in the 256. CONSER has made the following recommendations to the Review Group:

- In lieu of a commonly accepted GMD, continue to use [computer file]
- Abolish Area 3 (File Characteristics)
- Allow Area 5 (Physical Description) to contain information about physical characteristics associated with electronic serials (such as sound, color and the SMD "remote access")

Electronic serials have been on the CONSER agenda for several years and will likely continue to be a pressing issue. CONSER will continue to rely on discussion lists for feedback from the cataloging community to assist in the continuing development of cataloging policies as well as participation in ALA, NASIG, and CONSER meetings. The continuing evolution of electronic serials will likely compel CONSER to maintain its focus in this area for some time to come.

EXPERIMENTS IN BIBLIOGRAPHIC ACCESS TO ELECTRONIC SERIALS: ELECTRONIC SERIALS CATALOGING AT THE UNIVERSITY OF MICHIGAN

By Thomas Champagne

The University of Michigan is a NOTIS site, and we have named our implementation of NOTIS MIRLYN. We are also a CONSER member, and this has resulted in many of our practices already being closely aligned with national practice.

The University of Michigan began cataloging electronic serials in 1990. The decision was made at that time to catalog electronic serials independently of standard serials cataloging policies and procedures. In the beginning, Serials Cataloging staff chose which titles to catalog based on the *Directory of electronic journals, newsletters and academic discussion lists.* However, since last fall, collection development staff have been requesting the cataloging of collection-relevant electronic serials.

We do not acquire the titles we catalog, nor do we archive them in any manner. We only provide information on how to access these titles; we do not provide physical access to these titles. Each student at the University of Michigan has a computer account that gives them Internet access, and we are simply letting them know of the existence of these information resources. If they want to examine issues of a title, they have the capability to do so. Most titles cataloged during the early days were freely available.

Access and Location Information

We use as many 856 fields as are necessary to record most, if not all, access methods. We try to give at least one 856 for each major access method (email, FTP, Gopher, news, WWW). If there are multiple mirror sites outside the United States, we would probably not include them in the record. We do not have a firm policy on this, however, as each title is different and cataloger's judgment is often called for. Also, not all electronic serials are based in the U.S. and we always record the main site, wherever it may be. Sometimes the same title is available from different sites in different formats. In this case we will provide a separate 856 field for the individual sites and note the format (usually in the 856 ‡z). For example, a number of the more established electronic serials started in the ASCII era and are moving onto the WWW. The main site may remain strictly ASCII whereas another site might do more experimental work, converting the files to HTML, for instance, creating hypertext links between issues, etc. Examples of this practice are *Amateur computerist* and *EJournal*.

Although MARC does not prescribe a specific subfield order, generally we use the alphabetic order seen in MARC and CONSER documentation. The only exception to this is for email 856 fields where we put the fields in the following order:

856 0   ‒h processor of request, i.e., listserv
        ‒a host name, i.e., ncsuvm (BITNET) or ncsuvm.cc.ncsu.edu
        ‒i instruction, i.e., subscribe
        + [listname] [first name last name]
        ‒f Electronic name, or, the name of the list, i.e., PMC-LIST

856 0   ‒h listserv ‒a ncsuvm.cc.ncsu.edu ‒i subscribe [listname] [first name last name] ‒f PMC-LIST ‒z email subscription.

Hopefully, this makes for a little more legible public display of this information. Generally, we put 856 fields in order numerically by indicator 0-7, then alphabetically by mode of access within that arrangement (particularly with indicator 7 fields).

We do not generally put in a "System requirements:" note, unless special software for viewing or printing the title is needed (in instances where titles are in Adobe Acrobat, PostScript, or any of the variety of TeX, etc.). We do not use the "System requirements:" to let users know that they need a WWW browser, otherwise practically every record would have one resulting in wasted display space and wasted resources.

We use one "Mode of access:" note, listing all access methods (i.e., "Electronic mail, Gopher, Usenet . . . newsgroups, and World Wide Web.") For certain access methods, we will give fuller access information, particularly for email subscription instructions and WWW URL's. The 538/Mode of access note always displays in MIRLYN (the University of Michigan's implementation of NOTIS), whereas the 856 fields display only when patrons view the "long" display. The "brief" display (see Figure 2) is the default; patrons must choose to view the "long" display. Also, the current programmed display of 856 fields is less than ideal, rendering the fields as unlabelled strings of data. We are not sure that they are intelligible to patrons at all.

Giving this "additional" information in the 538 field makes sense in the case of electronic mail subscriptions, but you might be wondering about maintaining URL's in both the 538 and 856. Granted, this is one

FIGURE 2. NOTIS record in MIRLYN

```
Search Request: T=POSTMODERN CULTURE                    UMich Online Catalog
COMPUTER FILE - Record 1 of 7 Entries Found                     Brief View
-----------------------------------------------------------------------------

Title:          Postmodern culture [electronic serial] : PMC.


Published:      Raleigh, N.C. : Postmodern Culture, c1990-


Technical notes:
                Mode of access: Electronic mail on BITNET or Internet, FTP,
                gopher, and World Wide Web. For email subscription, send to:
                listserv@ncsuvm (BITNET), or: listserv@ncsuvm.cc.ncsu.edu
                (Internet), the message: SUB PMC-LIST [first name last
                name]. World Wide Web URL:
                http://jefferson.village.virginia.edu/pmc/contents.all.html.

SUBJECT HEADINGS (Library of Congress; use s=):
                Postmodernism--Periodicals.


------------------------------------------- + Page 1 of 2 ------------
STArt over      HOLdings                        <F8>  FORward page
HELp            LONg view                       <F6>  NEXt record
OTHer options   INDex

NEXT COMMAND:
4-                1 Session   141.211.144.98                      24/16
```

```
Search Request: T=POSTMODERN CULTURE                    UMich Online Catalog
COMPUTER FILE - Record 1 of 7 Entries Found                     Brief View
-----------------------------------------------------------------------------
Title:          Postmodern culture PMC

-----------------------------------------------------------------------------
LOCATION:              CALL NUMBER:                STATUS:
ELECTRONIC ACCESS      No call number available    Enter HOL 1 for holdings




------------------------------------------- + Page 2 of 2 ------------
STArt over      HOLdings                        <F7>  BACk page
HELp            LONg view                       <F6>  NEXt record
OTHer options   INDex

NEXT COMMAND:
4-                1 Session   141.211.144.98                      24/16
```

additional place where maintenance is needed when the URL changes. This can be accomplished very easily with two keystrokes in our Windows environment: one to delete the URL, another to paste in the new URL. As maintenance goes, this is one of the easier procedures, and it provides information that is important to the patrons without making them hunt for it. If we were to provide the URL only from the 856 display, then the patron would find it amidst a number of other 856 fields, along with potentially extraneous information that might prove to be confusing.

We verify all access methods listed in the bibliographic record during the cataloging process. If we are creating an original record, then we also re-verify all access methods just before inputting the record into OCLC. If the title sits for a while between the time we catalog it and the time the record finally goes into OCLC, then we may need to check the access methods a number of times. Currently, we are also verifying all WWW-accessible access methods (except mailto:) for each title weekly, using both manual and automated methods. As soon as we can verify a specific change in access method, we update both the MIRLYN and OCLC databases. However, it is not always possible to tell what is going on with a non-functioning access method. Some interruptions are temporary due to network traffic or the server being down, whereas others might be more permanent: the site has moved but they haven't yet let anybody know, the re-direct page has expired and been taken down, or at the other end of the spectrum the title has ceased and has been taken down permanently. Usually it becomes clearer with time what is happening—but not always. "Here today, gone tomorrow!"

Multiple Versions

We follow the current national standard here, using one bibliographic record to record all computer file versions, whether it be ASCII, Post-Script, HTML, etc. We use multiple records to record different physical versions (print versus computer file).

Definition of Electronic Serial

While we recognize that this is an issue, we have not cataloged any titles that did not fit the definition of a serial at the time of cataloging. A number of titles that originally adopted the print model of explicit volumes and issues have decided to do away with them in their online counterpart. One title, which we have not cataloged yet, even boasts of "obliterating the by-issue concept"! This is becoming more of a problem with time, however, as serials in the online environment "devolve" into article "databases," no longer requiring the batching together of articles into discrete issues for ease of distribution.

Bibliographic Access Points

A bigger issue is the evolution of any particular WWW page, and how the interpretation of the title may change with a redesign of the page. *JAIR*, the *Journal of artificial intelligence research*, is an example (and one that we chose not to include). Originally cataloged from the homepage with the title *JAIR* current cataloging using the redesigned homepage would transcribe the title as: *Journal of artificial intelligence research*, not *JAIR*. To highlight this, we now use a *Description based on*: note that reads: "Description based on: WWW display . . . " WWW homepages are very volatile entities, and basing a cataloging description on them can be very tricky. We try to follow print cataloging methods and record the title from somewhere on the earliest specific issue accessible online, but this is not always possible and sometimes we're forced to record the title from the homepage. WWW-accessible gopher sites are particularly problematic, being so menu-oriented.

Another lesson to learn from this: Be generous with variant titles! We now regularly add a 246 field for the HTML source title if it varies in any way from the bibliographic title. The HTML source title, when given, can be found between the <TITLE> and </TITLE> tags when viewing the source document.

It can be difficult to determine who really is publishing or is responsible for the title. Many electronic serials have a 260 field that consists of: [S.l. : s.n., . . .] because there is no formal publishing statement or statement of responsibility. However, sites usually provide at least an email contact that can be used for determining this information. We are finding that a greater percentage of titles are ending up under personal author main entry, and personal involvement is playing a greater role than is apparent for print serials.

We link to the print format when one exists. In the e-serial record, we use a 530 note "Issued also in print format" with a 776 field with indicator coded 1 giving the title and standard numbers for the print version.

We handle electronic serials in the same manner as print serials when it comes to subject analysis. We use standard subject headings, based on the subject content of the title. We do not use the form subdivision "–Databases" unless it is about databases. We use the form subdivision "–Periodicals" if it is a periodical.

We do not assign a call number to electronic serials. We assign a general classification number based on the subject analysis, but we do not cutter the number. The public display tells patrons that the title has "No call no." The classification number remains in the bibliographic portion of the record, and is not transferred to the copy holdings information as happens with print serials. We are still debating whether or not to classify electronic resources. Classifying them would make it possible to browse via the shelflist for these titles, providing an additional access method.

Computer File Characteristics

We generally follow national practice here in the use of 516, 538, 856 fields and the non-use of the 250 and 256 fields, but we vary from national practice in assigning the GMD. We feel that the GMD "computer file" is inadequate in this day and age, particularly relative to electronic serials. Patrons do not think of these titles as computer files, they think of them as "electronic journals." To aid in the identification of these titles as the entities they are, we use the GMD "electronic serial." We utilize the 516 field heavily, listing there all the different file formats we can identify from information presented within the publication.

We provide bibliographic information about these titles only. We do not have any physical holdings of these titles, therefore we have no holdings information. As a result all of the information displayed to the patrons comes from the bibliographic record.

CATALOGING REMOTE ELECTRONIC SERIALS AT VIRGINIA TECH

By Leslie O'Brien

When electronic journals first began to appear on the horizon, Virginia Tech's University Libraries formed the Task Force on the Electronic Journal to examine collection development and accessibility issues. Following the Task Force's report in early 1991, we began cataloging electronic journals. In the beginning, we cataloged six titles for which we paid a subscription fee; we then began cataloging some of the ejournals that were published as part of Virginia Tech's Scholarly Communications Project.

Access to these journals was then pretty cumbersome; it usually meant subscribing to a journal from a listserv or downloading text files, and this was all done on the campus mainframe. Many in the university community did not have ready access to the mainframe or to a computer. So the Task Force recommended downloading ejournals to the mainframe, archiving them, and providing free, anonymous access from terminals in the library.

For this reason, all of our early records had detailed directions in local notes for finding a mainframe terminal, locating the library menu on the mainframe, and going to the site from there. We felt that we should archive all journals we subscribed to, just as we would any print journal. When new issues became available, a staff member in serials cataloging was notified via email, she retrieved the files via FTP or other method, posted the files to the University mainframe (later, a library server), and updated the VTLS MARC holdings record.

We made the decision early on to use the record for the print publica-tion, if one existed, when cataloging the same title in an electronic format. We added mode of access notes to direct the patron to the online edition, and added free-text notes to our holdings records also. (We also followed this practice for microform versions of print items.)

We still feel pretty strongly about the use of a single record for serial titles, and I was interested to see that it was recently a discussion item on the INTERCAT list when Leanne McKinnon from the National Library of Australia wrote about that library's decision to use the "one record approach." I'm further encouraged by Jean Hirons's response that there should be more discussion of the topic. Since Virginia Tech is one library living with the "imperfect solutions" that Jean mentioned, I would like to hear further debate on this issue.

Access and Location Information

We list all the modes of access (web, telnet, ftp) that we know about, but don't include multiple mirror sites (see Figure 3). We list the 856 fields in order numerically by the indicator. When we archive a journal, we give our library server site. Our VTLS '94 OPAC currently has no hypertext link capability, so patrons must exit out of the catalog to get to the journals.

We don't usually use the system requirements note, unless special soft-ware is needed, and none of the titles we have cataloged fall into that category. However, we used to display detailed notes in 590 fields when we first started cataloging, telling patrons how to find a mainframe termi-nal, etc., as stated in my introduction.

We don't have a cataloging policy on verifying or maintaining addresses or access methods. Since we were archiving all issues, we were notified by Library Automation when the address of the server had changed, so we could go back and revise the 856 field. When we do develop a policy, I think it will state that we rely on the reference librarians to alert us to changes and we will try to use PURLs (Permanent Uniform Resource Locator) to reduce the amount of cataloging record revision. Editing on VTLS is somewhat cumbersome, since our catalogers aren't

FIGURE 3. VTLS record in VTLS OPAC

```
CALL NUMBER: PN98 P67 P67
       Title: Postmodern culture [computer file] : PMC.
   Published: Vol. 1, no. 1 (fall 1990)-
     Imprint: Raleigh, NC : Postmodern Culture, c1990-
   Frequency: Three no. a year
        Note: Mode of access: Electronic mail on BITNET or Internet, FTP,
              gopher, and World Wide Web. For email subscription, send to:
              listserv@ncsuvm (BITNET), or: listserv@ncsuvm.cc.ncsu.edu
              (Internet), the message: sub PMC-LIST [first name last
              name].
      E-mail: ncsuvm (BITNET) ncsuvm.cc.ncsu.edu (Internet) PMC-LIST
              listserv sub Email subscription
         FTP: ftp://jefferson.village.virginia.edu/pub/pubs/pmc
  Remote Acc.: gopher://jefferson.village.virginia.edu/11/pubs/pmc gopher
  Remote Acc.: http://jefferson.village.virginia.edu/pmc/contents.all.html
              http
        Note: Title from first screen of Table of contents file.
        Note: "An electronic journal of interdisciplinary criticism."
     Subject: Postmodernism -- Periodicals.
     Subject: Modernism (Literature) -- Periodicals.
 Added Title: PMC


   CALL NO: PN98 P67 P67
     TITLE: Postmodern culture [computer file] : PMC.
  LOCATION: Copy 1 UNIVERSITY LIBRARIES
      FREQ: 3 times a year

  v. 1  no. 1  fall 1990
  v. 1  no. 2-3  Jan.-May 1991
  v. 2  Sept. 1991-May 1992
  v. 3  no. 1-3  Sept. 1992-May 1993
  v. 4  no. 1-3  Sept. 1993-May 1994
  v. 5  no. 1-2  Sept. 1994-Jan. 1995

  This electronic journal is available for viewing at Internet
    workstations in University Libraries.  Please ask library
    personnel for specific locations of terminals.
```

using a Windows interface to the catalog, but all our catalogers have WWW access, Adobe Acrobat, and telnet software to view all files and verify access methods.

Multiple Versions

As I've already stated, we do not regularly enter multiple records for the same title in different formats. We distinguish between formats by adding MARC holdings records for each format. Since many of the early ejournals were just text versions of the printed journal, this practice seemed valid, but with the variation in forms of ejournals nowadays, and the fact that many print journals are being replaced by electronic formats, we may decide to follow CONSER policy and create new records.

Definition of Electronic Serial

All serials we have cataloged fit the definition of a serial. Many are just Internet-accessible versions of a print journal. However, as the other presenters point out, this will become more of an issue.

Bibliographic Access Points

We use the "Description based on" and "Title from" notes to record the source of the title used for the title proper and we record multiple variant titles. Our procedure for names and corporate bodies does not vary for ejournals from regular cataloging practice. Our November 1995 *Guidelines for Cataloging Electronic Texts* state that the publisher of an electronic text available over a network is the network provider.

Since we have been using only one record to catalog most of our ejournals, we would not add a linking entry to the print title. However, if we were cataloging on a separate record, we would add the linking entries for CONSER. The 530 and 776 fields don't display in our OPAC right now. Other linking entries do, but these are not indexed because they were deemed lower priority for public catalog displays. Like the University of Michigan, we assign subject headings following the same policies as we do for print serials. However, we do assign call numbers to ejournals. This is something we've always done, but we have started discussions about continuing to classify e-resources. I've read some debate on this, about whether or not it is convenient to assign some kind of phrase that can be used as a collocation device to see all the electronic resources in the catalog. I think it depends on the workload of the catalogers and public displays in the OPAC, and there is no one answer.

Computer File Characteristics

We follow the national practice of using the GMD [computer file]. We add a local note to all ejournal records to indicate the nature of the publication, but I'm not sure how obvious it is to our patrons that this is an electronic journal. The note is duplicated in a free text field on the holdings screen. We've chosen the location "University Libraries" to reflect the intangible nature of the title, or the "everywhereness" of it, which might be obscure to patrons. If the title has print holdings as well as online holdings (because we've archived the journal) the holdings records will show a specific location and the general location. If we decide to discontinue archiving, as I've a feeling we will, we'll need to come up with another method of indicating holdings and accessibility.

CURRENT STATUS OF THE INTERNET CATALOGING PROJECT AT THE UNIVERSITY OF WASHINGTON
By Steven Shadle

In 1992, the University of Washington installed a locally developed library catalog interface named Willow (Washington Information Looker-upper Layered Over Windows). It was originally developed to run in an Unix/X-terminal environment. Later editions of Willow were developed for an ASCII environment (WilCO or Willow Character Only) and for the Windows environment (WinWillow). The Willow software serves as a public interface to a wide variety of BRS-structured bibliographic and citation databases (including the Library's Catalog, LCAT). Willow serves only as a user interface to these databases. Maintenance of the library catalog is done using an Innovative Interfaces cataloging system. On a weekly basis, the Innovative MARC records are converted to BRS-structured records and the records are loaded into the Library Catalog. LCAT is the database the catalog user queries when using the public catalog. The example presented here is from an X-terminal OPAC available in a public service area. WilCO and WinWillow displays would look slightly different.

In December 1993, an Electronic Journals Group was assembled to investigate the feasibility of incorporating e-journals into the library's collection. At that point, twenty journals (mostly free publications available through FTP or Gopher) had been selected for inclusion in the catalog. However, before acquisitions and cataloging had been done for these items, the pace of World Wide Web development was such that it was deemed prudent to hold off implementation until more e-journals had been developed in this new environment. In May 1995, the Internet Cataloging Committee was formed to begin investigating the issues surrounding the incorporation of electronic resources into the Library's catalog. The Committee's charge was to contribute to the identification and selection of a "test" set of 100 remotely available electronic resources, provide bibliographic control for these resources through the Library Catalog, to gain experience and explore the issues involved in the application of existing bibliographic standards as to electronic resources, and to work with other Library efforts to develop local policy and procedure necessary to provide access to these resources through the Library Catalog. To date, we have selected and cataloged 62 Internet-accessible resources, 37 of which are serial publications.

Access and Location Information

Currently, we are following CONSER policy of creating one 856 field for each access method and creating a more general "Mode of Access" note. We are preferring to record a URL in 856 $u instead of partitioning the access information into its component 856 subfields, as when a hotlink is developed it will be plugging the contents of 856 $u directly into a Web browser. Currently, we are also transcribing the URLs into a public note in our checkin record, so that they appear in the brief display where our users normally look for holdings and location information (see Figure 4). Once we've established a field label in our displays for the URL, then the URL will be displayed directly from the 856 $u. At that point, we will no longer need to transcribe access information into our holdings.

We are reconsidering our decision to transcribe multiple modes of access for several reasons. First, our experience has been that the Web version of a title is either replacing or being used as a gateway to earlier issues or versions (e.g., gopher, ftp) of a title. Usually the most complete information about access methods is available from the homepage instead of an ftp or gopher readme file. Second, the Web version is the one which our campus community is most likely to use given the emphasis our campus computing services has placed on Web education and support. We also feel that a list of nearly identical URL's (e.g., http://foobar.edu; gopher://foobar.edu; ftp://foobar.edu) linking to the same information can be duplicative and can clutter up our catalog displays.

Multiple Versions

We follow CONSER policy of creating one catalog record to represent multiple computer file formats. We also follow the CONSER policy of creating separate bibliographic records for print and electronic versions.

Definition of Electronic Serial

We are using the traditional serial definition in determining the serial or monographic nature of a title. As a result, we have cataloged MathSciNet as a monograph. We are not linking monographs and serials, but we are providing title added entries so that users will retrieve the record for the

FIGURE 4. WILLOW record in LCAT

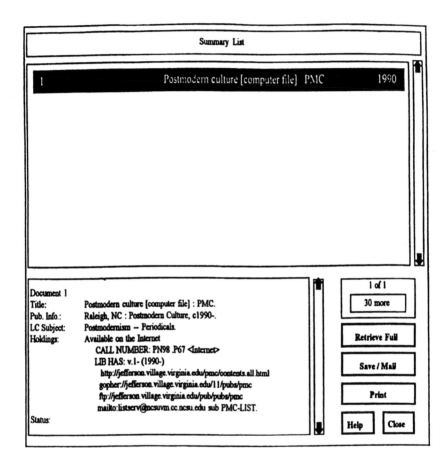

electronic version (whether monograph or serial) when searching on the print version title.

Bibliographic Access Points

We are following previously discussed national standards in terms of title and name added entries, subject headings and linking. We are making use of the subdivision "–Computer network resources" for titles that consist mostly of links to other network resources (electronic bibliography). As stated, we are also using title added entries in monograph records to provide access to differently titled versions, whether monograph or serial.

We are classifying our e-serials, but instead of using a main entry cuttering, we are cuttering with the phrase <Internet>. We felt it important to classify resources to facilitate call number browsing, but felt that a regular call number may foster the assumption that these resources are sitting on a shelf someplace. Since the angle bracket files before a letter in our system, one unintended consequence of this decision is that the Internet materials file before all other materials in call number browsing. A catalog feature in development is suppression of the call number. Once this feature is implemented, we will probably suppress the call number display so as to minimize any confusion about the nature of the publication.

Computer File Characteristics

We are following current CONSER practice in terms of where and how computer file characteristics information is placed in the bibliographic record. However, because our brief display consists of a small number of fields (author, title, pub. info, subject headings and local holdings) the only information from the brief display that would give any indication of the e-journal nature of the publication is the GMD [computer file]. Because our users are used to looking in the holdings information to determine location, call number/shelving title and issues held, we decided to customize this area to make it clear this is an electronic serial. The location code used for these materials is "Available on the Internet," the call number is cuttered by the phrase <Internet>, and the access methods (in the form of URLs) and any special system requirements (e.g., fonts, viewers) are noted there. In addition, for e-journals which don't appear to have an entire run of issues available, we have noted "Check the Internet for issue availability" in place of the usual holdings as we can't guarantee the holdings available at any particular point in time. Anecdotal evidence has confirmed that this is enough information to convey to catalog users the nature of the publication and how to access it. When we make use of the 856 field for display purposes, we will still display it in that same area since our users are used to looking at the bottom of the brief display for location information.

NOTES

1. http://lcweb.loc.gov/acq/conser/
2. http://info.lib.uh.edu/pr/v7/n1/ande7n1.html

CONCURRENT SESSION II:
ORDER OUT OF CHAOS:
COLLECTION DEVELOPMENT
AND MANAGEMENT
OF INTERNET RESOURCES

As World Wide Web home pages spring up faster than mushrooms after a rain, libraries are beginning to evaluate these and other Internet tools as information resources which should be available to patrons and staff. But how do you select and collect virtual resources? Are the traditional collection development principles we learned in library school still valid? Do we need new ones? How do you maintain a collection of resources that you cannot touch and that may change daily or move to another location? If the information provider discontinues the project, or we "cancel" the title, do we still "have" anything in the collection? This session explores these vital issues, as well as other issues which help make the development and management of an Internet-based collection a challenging new frontier for serialists.

Hunting and Gathering in Cyberspace: Finding and Selecting Web Resources for the Library's Virtual Collection

Margaret A. Rioux

Margaret A. Rioux is Information Systems Librarian, WHOI/MBL Library.

[Haworth co-indexing entry note]: "Hunting and Gathering in Cyberspace: Finding and Selecting Web Resources for the Library's Virtual Collection." Rioux, Margaret A. Co-published simultaneously in *The Serials Librarian* (The Haworth Press, Inc.) Vol. 30, No. 3/4, 1997, pp. 129-136; and: *Pioneering New Serials Frontiers: From Petroglyphs to Cyberserials* (ed: Christine Christiansen and Cecilia Leathem) The Haworth Press, Inc., 1997, pp. 129-136. Single or multiple copies of this article are available for a fee from The Haworth Document Delivery Service [1-800-342-9678, 9:00 a.m. - 5:00 p.m. (EST). E-mail address: getinfo@haworth.com].

The world of information is a world of chaos. It always has been. And the function of librarians from Alexandria and before until now and forever is to create and maintain islands of order (libraries) in that sea of chaos. The advent of the Internet and the World Wide Web doesn't change that function, it only enhances it.

Michael Gorman, writing about cataloging, sums up the situation:

> The net is like a huge vandalized library. Someone has destroyed the catalog and removed the front matter, indexes, etc., from hundreds of thousands of books and torn and scattered what remains . . . and the walls are covered in graffiti. . . . The net is even worse than a vandalized library because thousands of additional unorganized fragments are added daily by the myriad cranks, sages, and persons with time on their hands who launch their unfiltered messages into cyberspace.[1]

Over the centuries, librarians have pretty much gotten a handle on building collections of resources in the physical media like print and film. There are review journals, the publishing industry is well-organized, and subscription agents are always happy to help keep things neat and tidy. It's a little like agriculture, where the farmer/librarian goes into a well-tended field to harvest a crop of known type and quality. Developing a collection of Internet, especially World Wide Web, resources is another situation altogether. It's much more like foraging in the jungle: a trackless, vine-tangled wilderness full of unknown species, some of which look appetizing but may be poisonous and others of which look drab and unappealing but may well be the most nourishing. The librarian collecting electronic resources is not a harvester of cultivated crops but a hunter and gatherer of wild fruits and other treasures.

If collecting Web resources is so difficult, then the first question to be answered is "Why bother?" The answer to that one is easy: "We have to." The future of libraries lies in embracing the new media. Again quoting Michael Gorman, "It is possible to imagine future libraries in which it is as easy to locate, identify, and use electronic resources as it is to use books, scores, recordings, maps, videos, and all other library materials."[2] While not forgetting our more traditional collections, we also need to seek out new formats and types of information which will be of value to our patrons. More and more serials and other publications are appearing on the Web. Journals are being published in both electronic and print formats; some are even dropping their print versions and publishing electronically. Having electronic resources in our collection is a natural extension of having an electronic catalog. If we're engaged in bringing the catalog to the patron's desktop via the Internet, why not bring the collection (or at least part of it) along with it? Seeking out good quality electronic resources which are relevant to our libraries' users and including them in our collections provides valuable help to the patrons as they search for the "signal" in the "noise" of the Internet. While we may not have physical ownership of the materials, the act of providing access to particular sites "privileges" those sites as being of quality and value.[3]

Now that we're determined to add Web and other Internet resources to our collection, we're faced with another problem: How do we decide what to collect? In this case, the obvious answer is the best. Continue to collect in those subject areas in which you currently collect more traditional materials and collect in these areas at the same level as you do now. If you currently collect everything in print in a particular subject, such as history of early Twentieth Century American biology, you should also add to your collection all electronic resources of good quality that you can find which deal with this topic. If a particular subject is totally out of scope for your library, as English poetry would be for the author's, then it should remain out of scope for your electronic collection. In other words, the same basic principles we learned in library school still apply. Only the specifics and some of the tools are different.

As you begin selecting Web and other Internet resources for your collection, you should expand your collection development policy to include the electronic media you will be considering for the collection. Medium-specific criteria for selection, such as hardware required, specific format (SGML, html, image formats, etc.), functionality, availability of archives and method of access[4] will need to be added to the traditional list of criteria. However, the general criteria will remain the same:

- The item fills a gap in a subject area of importance to our community.
- The quality of scholarship is acceptable.
- The information is useful whether historical or current.
- It is in a language that can be used by the current or projected user community.[5]

If you use the RLG Conspectus to describe and define your collection development policy, you can continue to use it for electronic materials with some minor expansions in the language to account for access to as well as ownership of materials.

A somewhat more difficult problem encountered when expanding collection development to include Web and Internet resources is that of finding resources to add. There are a number of finding tools on the World Wide Web for locating resources. One might think of them as analogous to *Books in Print* and *Ulrich's*. Some, such as Yahoo (http://www. yahoo.com)

and the World Wide Web Virtual Library (http://www.w3.org/hypertext/
DataSources/bySubject/Overview.html) are directories which list sites in
hierarchical subject trees. Yahoo includes sites which Yahoo users have
submitted for consideration for inclusion. OCLC's InterCat
(http://www.oclc.org:6990) is a group of resources which have been cataloged by participants in the Internet Cataloging Project. Other finding
tools are search services which index Web sites. Lycos (http://a2z.lycos.
com), WebCrawler (http://www.webcrawler.com) and Digital's Alta Vista
(http://www.altavista.digital.com) use software which "roams" the World
Wide Web seeking links and indexing the documents it finds. In none of
these cases is there any attempt made to evaluate the quality of the sites
listed, beyond simply assuring that they actually exist.

Another Web site which can help the electronic collection developer
locate possible resources is NewJour (http://gort.ucsd.edu/newjour). New-
Jour is primarily an Internet mailing list for announcing "newly planned,
newly issued, or revised Internet-available" journals, magazines, newsletters and other electronic serials.[6] Subscribing to the NewJour mailing list
or searching its archives on the Web is a good way to learn about electronic serials, but again, this list makes no attempt to evaluate the offerings; it merely announces them.

Compared to the ubiquity of quality book review columns and journals,
there are very few reviews available of electronic resources. However, this
situation is changing rapidly. Both *American Libraries* and *Library Journal*
have recently added columns which review Internet and Web resources.
Internet World, published by Mecklermedia, is also a source of announcements and reviews. Although intended primarily for the individual Web
surfer, it includes a useful column called "Cyberlibrarian."

Another new source of professional quality reviews of World Wide
Web resources is the Infofilter Project (http://www.usc.edu/users/help/
flick/Infofilter). Subscribers to the working mailing list, including librarians and other information professionals, submit draft reviews of resources
to the list, following a template which outlines format and criteria. Following a comment period and possible revision, the review is posted to the
official home page where it is archived and can be accessed for viewing by
both subject keyword and resource name. The full text of reviews is also
searchable by keyword.[7] More and more professional review sources are
starting to appear, taking us beyond the "5 stars for coolness" type of
review and making the electronic collection developer's job a little easier.

Of course, in addition to these formal mechanisms for announcing,
locating and reviewing Web sites, there are also the informal mechanisms:
announcements or mentions of new sites in various email lists and news

groups, inclusion of Web URLs in advertisements, articles in magazines, mention of Web sites on the news and other television programs, and the sheer serendipity of finding a perfect gem while surfing the Web for something else.

Besides locating and reviewing Internet resources for possible inclusion in the library's electronic collection, there are a number of other questions which should be considered before beginning collection development on the Web. Most of these should be addressed in the library's electronic collection development policy, which needs to be in place before serious collecting begins.

The first of these questions is whether or not the library should add resources for which it has to pay an access fee and, if so, how should the access be granted and controlled. Some libraries don't like the idea of putting up resources on their Web sites or via other Internet access for which they have to pay a fee. They would prefer only to point to sites which are universally accessible without charge. The author's opinion is that this is too strict a limitation. There are a number of very useful electronic journals and databases to which the library's patrons should have access for which a fee is charged. For example, if you provide access to FirstSearch for your library users, you have added an electronic resource to your collection for which you pay a fee. Other databases, such as those from Cambridge Scientific Abstracts, are most easily searchable over the World Wide Web or other Internet connection at about the cost of subscribing to the CD-ROM version with a multi-user license. Considerations of relative cost for different media and delivery mechanisms should be part of your review process and the decision-making criteria laid out in your collection development policy.

If you are considering a resource for which a fee is charged, you also need to look at how access to that resource will be controlled. Obviously, if you're paying for access for your own patrons, you don't want them to be turned away because folk from somewhere else are tying up your connections; neither do you want to get a bill for services provided to someone who has no connection with your institution. If access is controlled by a username and password system, you need to determine how you will get the login information to legitimate users, but keep it away from those who shouldn't have access through your license. Is it possible to script the login sequence in such a way that only those computers in your network can run the script? Can you use a "dummy" server in some way as a gateway? Perhaps the particular publisher requires each user to register for their own account, but in order to do so, they need some sort of a "key" or account number from the library.[8]

The simplest method to restrict access to authorized users of a site is via

IP address checking on the server side. You supply the network portion of your institution's Internet addresses (e.g., 128.128 for the author's network) to the service provider and they set up their server to allow access only from addresses matching those you have given them. This is the simplest method, since all the work is done by the service provider. However, if you have users who regularly use your electronic library resources from home and they don't all access the Internet via your institutional LAN, this method will not allow those patrons to use these particular resources from their homes. Of course, you could always require patrons to access the service via a central site, such as logging in to the library's server, but this is difficult with Web resources and tends to limit patrons to character-based services only. Or if they have to physically visit the library to use some services, that negates much of the advantage of serving up library resources electronically to the patron's desktop.

Some services restrict access by requiring special software. In this case you would control legitimate access by giving out the copies of the software. However, this creates problems of distribution and maintenance. Access via the World Wide Web, on the other hand, allows patrons to use their own Web browsers to access the resources.

Whether the resource is freely available or restricted in access, you will need to consider the delivery mechanism. The resource may be delivered via the World Wide Web, telnet, gopher, or some other protocol. You will need to consider how your patrons will access it: Will they be able to go directly from their office or dorm room or will it require a special machine in the library? How will patrons learn about it? Will you be able to provide a link, or at least access instructions, in your online catalog or other electronic services menu? Perhaps you would be able to provide a direct link to the service from your library's home page on the Web. You may wish to "advertise" the resource in more than one way, including printed brochures.

Another criterion to be considered in choosing Web and other Internet resources for collection is the probable longevity of the resource. It is extremely easy for an individual, often a student, to put up a Web site on any computer running a Web server and make it known to the world. It is just as easy for a Web site to disappear overnight. Most of these ephemeral sites are not even worth adding to a bookmark list, let alone a library collection, but some of them do provide valuable information. Official institutional sites tend to be more permanent but many suffer from benign neglect after the first excitement of having a home page wears off. Electronic collection developers should be wary of pages whose URLs include the tilde character signifying an individual's home directory, although sometimes the value of the resource outweighs the risk of its sudden disappearance. Some very valuable "official" online resources had their starts as student projects. Collection developers should also look closely at the date a page was last updated, especially if it contains the type of materials which need to be modified and added to regularly.

There is one more issue which we tend to take for granted with more traditional media, but which must be explicitly considered in the collection of Web and Internet resources: that of provenance and integrity. This is actually a very old issue. Before the advent of printing and the development of the publishing industry, it was difficult to know for sure that a document was really what it claimed to be. Anyone could make a manuscript which purported to be a valuable information resource. In addition, errors could (and frequently did) creep in with successive copies, thus making the integrity of a work automatically suspect. This is one reason geography and science didn't truly flourish until after the invention of printing, which at least ensured the integrity of the copies, if not the accuracy of the original work. Today, in printed books and serials, the reputation of the publisher stands behind the work itself and is an important and reliable criterion for collection developers to use.

In cyberspace, and particularly on the World Wide Web, the world has come full circle. The distinction among public relations, advertising and vanity publishing has become blurred, making it difficult to evaluate Web sites for credibility and integrity.[9] Also, the procedure for registering domain and node names does not concern itself with the external world of commerce so that a name which seems to belong to a particular company or individual may actually have no connection with the apparent owner. It may just mean that someone else got there first. To illustrate the need for caution in evaluating Internet resources, Don E. Descy, an associate professor of library-media education at Mankato State University, has created a fake Web site for the city of Mankato, Minnesota (http://www.lme.mankato.msus.edu/mankato/mankato.html).[10] A quick visit to this home page is all it takes to make you realize that a healthy dose of skepticism is important when reviewing sites for your electronic collection! A close look at the URLs sometimes helps as well. The real City of Mankato Web site (http://www.ic.mankato.mn.us/mankato.html) has a geographic domain name, while the fake one is in the edu domain. Another point to remember when evaluating provenance and integrity is that you tend to get what you pay for. If you're paying for access to an electronic publication or resource, you can be fairly sure where it's coming from and who stands behind it.

There are many considerations to be taken into account in making decisions about an electronic collection. Most of them are the same principles and considerations used in traditional collection development. The rest are more or less common sense and professional judgment extrapolated to the new medium. The underlying principle is to keep the best from what we already know, but also to be careful not to ignore the ways in which the world is changing rapidly.

In building our cyberspatial collections, we need to always keep in mind that we are in the information business, not the "serials on paper" business. We need to use all the resources we can to bring needed information to our patrons in the formats which are most convenient and useful to them, whether it is on paper in the library stacks or from the Web to the computer on their desktop. We must never be afraid to try new things. Hunting and gathering in cyberspace can be a great new adventure and, most of all, a lot of fun.

NOTES

1. Gorman, Michael. "The Corruption of Cataloging." *Library Journal* 120:15 (September 15, 1995), 34.
2. Ibid.
3. Buckland, Michael. "What Will Collection Developers Do? *Information Technology and Libraries* 14:3 (September 1995), 155-159.
4. Ferguson, Anthony W. "Interesting Problems Encountered on My Way to Writing an Electronic Collection Development Statement." *Against the Grain* 7:2 (April 1995), 18.
5. Ibid.
6. NewJour Welcome page (http://gort.ucsd.edu/newjour/NewJourWel.html), viewed May 28, 1996.
7. Gilson, Tom. "From the Reference Desk: Reviewing the Internet: The Infofilter Project." *Against the Grain* 8:1 (February 1996), 58.
8. This technique is sometimes used to provide free access to the electronic version of a journal to patrons from an institution whose library purchases the print edition.
9. Lynch, Clifford. "Integrity Issues in Networked Information." Talk presented at "Evaluating the Quality of Information on the Internet," program presented by the American Society for Information Science, New England Chapter, 6 September 1995, Cambridge, Mass.
10. "On Line." *Chronicle of Higher Education* XLII:32 (April 19, 1996), A27.

Keeping the Jell-O® Nailed to the Wall: Maintaining and Managing the Virtual Collection

Betty Landesman

Following Maggie's advice, we have decided that we will collect electronic resources, and we have used our professional hunting and gathering skills to select the resources appropriate to our users. *NOW WHAT??!!*

One of the most important roles a library has always had is to provide access to the materials in their collections. In recent years, this role has expanded to include information that may not be in the collections themselves but which supplements them. In order for the library's users to take advantage of this information, it must be organized and bibliographically controlled–a.k.a. cataloged–so that users know that it exists, why they would want it, and how to get it.

Michael Gorman has likened electronic resources to an "uncharted wilderness":

> The net is like a huge vandalized library. Someone has destroyed the catalog and removed the front matter, indexes, etc., from hundreds of thousands of books and torn and scattered what remains . . . and the walls are covered in graffiti. Surfing is the process of sifting through this disorganized mess in the hope of coming across some useful

---

Betty Landesman is Coordinator for Systems Planning, Gelman Library, George Washington University, Washington, DC.

[Haworth co-indexing entry note]: "Keeping the Jell-O® Nailed to the Wall: Maintaining and Managing the Virtual Collection." Landesman, Betty. Co-published simultaneously in *The Serials Librarian* (The Haworth Press, Inc.) Vol. 30, No. 3/4, 1997, pp. 137-147; and: *Pioneering New Serials Frontiers: From Petroglyphs to Cyberserials* (ed: Christine Christiansen and Cecilia Leathem) The Haworth Press, Inc., 1997, pp. 137-147. Single or multiple copies of this article are available for a fee from The Haworth Document Delivery Service [1-800-342-9678, 9:00 a.m. - 5:00 p.m. (EST). E-mail address: getinfo@haworth.com].

fragments of text and images that can be related to other fragments. The net is even worse than a vandalized library because thousands of additional unorganized fragments are added daily by the myriad cranks, sages, and persons with time on their hands who launch their unfiltered messages into cyberspace.[1]

The best of the growing number of Internet "catalogs" (like Yahoo) and "search engines" (like Alta Vista) do not use a controlled vocabulary or support field searching in the same way that our catalogs and indexes do. Even with developments in relevancy ranking, and with the most skillful Boolean qualification, a search for information using an Internet search engine often yields a vast number of hits, many of which are not what the searcher wants or needs. This is akin to the patrons who approach our online catalog terminals and perform a keyword search on "United States," and who then scroll through thousands of index entries happy that they are finding so much information. And we have actually *selected* the material in the catalog, so that this (albeit vast) subset of the knowledge universe is at least comprised of material that we thought would be "good" in terms of supporting our users' needs. When out on the net, they are happily finding all this STUFF and may not have the information literacy skills to determine what is good. It is our responsibility to point them in the direction of the "good" stuff.

Increasingly, libraries are creating or contributing to directories of selected Internet resources on gopher servers or World Wide Web home pages. These are often organized by subject. A few examples of the many that are available are those of North Carolina State University (URL: http://www.lib.ncsu.edu/disciplines; go to the section called "Internet Resources Organized by Subject"); the University of Pennsylvania (URL: http://www.library.upenn.edu/resources/subject.html); the University of Buffalo (URL: http://wings.buffalo.edu/libraries/e-resources/ejournals); and the University of Tennessee, Knoxville (URL: http://www.lib.utk.edu/Electronic-Journals/ejournals.html#subject). These all represent titles organized by subjects assigned by the library staff, rather than pointers to subject lists organized by other agencies, e.g., the WWW Virtual Library (URL: http://www.edoc.com/ejournal). Of the sampling above, only University of Tennessee, Knoxville's had a description of the provenance or content of many of the titles at the time of writing this paper. A simple title entry in these subject lists is more the norm. The CIC Electronic Journals Collection does have bibliographic records cataloged by the member libraries; I will discuss this collection in greater detail later.

However, the library gopher or web site is not the same as the library online catalog. Libraries which have electronic resources onsite—mostly

CD-ROM databases, but also electronic journals which have been loaded on a local server–have usually included these titles in their catalogs without hesitation. These titles are part of the collection; they are physically *there*. The question of whether or not to provide catalog records for electronic resources that are housed on a remote computer, somewhere "out there," has generated a great deal of discussion as to the technical, staffing, and philosophical issues involved.

As Martha Hruska puts it, "It is a challenge to determine how to manage something the library does not own, something that does not come in a container that can be controlled. It is most challenging to determine how this type of electronic digital entity can be physically described in a bibliographic record in the OPAC."[2] Thornier than the literal questions of how to formulate a bibliographic description for this type of material, and of envisioning the nature of catalog maintenance in this context, has been the bottom-line question of whether the catalog *should* contain records for material the library does not own. Is it an inventory of the library's collections, or a gateway to global information?

Hruska's article is one of five contributions to a "Balance Point" column in the winter 1995 issue of *Serials Review* entitled "Cataloging Remote-Access Electronic Serials: Rethinking the Role of the OPAC." Eric Lease Morgan redefines the catalog as a finding aid, "a tool designed to help a defined set of people locate information in a comprehensive collection of data."[3] Since there is an increasing amount of useful information available via the Internet, libraries need to provide access to it in order to best serve their users. Allison Mook Sleeman states that Internet materials selected by library staff should be considered as part of the collection, and therefore made accessible through complete catalog records with subject headings.[4] Wayne Jones echoes both views: although the library is unable to exercise the same degree of bibliographic and archival control over titles maintained at a different site as it would for titles it holds within its walls, the quantity of information on the Internet and the lack of good searching tools make the catalog "an even more important means to help users dig in those mines."[5]

Regina Reynolds, however, analyzes the potential pitfalls of this approach. If the library is not accessing sites linked to on a regular basis, changes that are not detected will cause retrieval failures and threaten the credibility of the catalog. The title on a remote gopher menu may not be the one the local cataloger would use when working from the chief source of information. A catalog is different from a bibliography; the catalog "has to serve not only the patron's needs but the library's own need to know what it holds."[6] While acknowledging the inevitability and indeed the need to shift from the catalog-as-inventory to the catalog-as-gateway approach, Reynolds cautions wisely that we need to make clear in our records which titles we have control over and which we do not.

Despite these valid concerns, I believe that it is necessary to provide catalog records for the electronic resources to which we choose to steer our patrons. We all subscribe to indexes that include citations to journals we do not have. Many of us now have these indexes tapeloaded into our online systems. We are also increasingly providing links to external databases such as UnCover and FirstSearch. When a patron walks up to a public terminal in our libraries, or dials in to the library's online system, s/he sees a menu of database choices. Only one of these is the literal catalog. But to the patron, the "catalog" is what they see on the menu screen. We have put these additional databases up on our "catalogs" in order to provide more information to our users. There are sometimes problems with remote servers, or with the Internet, that impede access to some of these databases. Few of our patrons understand the distinction, and hold us accountable for service to everything "in the catalog." We put them on the menu, nevertheless, because it is in the best interests of our patrons. I submit that we have already breached the wall. We understand the distinction between our catalogs and the other items on our system screens, but our patrons neither understand it nor care to. So when we consciously select an electronic resource, we should proceed to "do it right" and provide a level of bibliographic control that will benefit both our users and ourselves.

The electronic resources to which we provide access are no longer limited to freebies, some of which may have uncertain reliability. Libraries are increasingly paying for subscriptions to commercially-published electronic journals, which include as part of the price some level of accountability on the part of the vendor. If we pay for a journal subscription, we should catalog the journal. Furthermore, we may now have both print and electronic versions of the same title, or the electronic version has superseded the print. If the records for the print and electronic version are not in the same place, we cannot provide the necessary explanatory links between the versions to allow our patrons to find what they need.[7]

Following the standard cataloging practice we employ for bibliographic records in our online systems provides us with an opportunity for fuller description and more precise and controlled retrieval than is typically available through an Internet search engine. We use controlled subject headings. Patrons can use existing OPAC searching techniques, and we can supply information on how to get to the resources. The inclusion of specific, selected electronic resources in the catalog helps library staff identify titles that patrons will ask about. We are catalog users, too!

The library's catalog should be a center of research. If we do not provide access to all the information our users need, they will either miss out or they will bypass us. Most of us are in a transitional stage regarding our online systems' capabilities and hardware requirements: we are moving towards a graphical catalog environment, but still have many text-based terminals. Likewise, our patrons are increasingly Internet-connected but not necessarily there yet. At present, most of our users can access our catalogs remotely with relative ease; not all can get at the Web. And if we do not provide our patrons with the information they need, someone else will.[8]

Libraries need to keep up with changing times and technology. Our users expect it, and we expect it of ourselves. While few installed catalogs currently support "hot links" (the ability to find an Internet resource in the OPAC, click on a hypertext link provided in the record, and be taken directly to that resource), most will, and soon. We want to be ready when the capability is there–and that means making sure the appropriate records are in the database.

Now that that's settled, just do it! Seriously, though, the enabling infrastructure for cataloging electronic resources is at last moving from anguished debate into implementation. Cataloging guidelines are available. CONSER has developed policies for cataloging remote access computer file serials; Module 31 of the *CONSER Cataloging Manual* is accessible via the Internet.[9] OCLC also developed guidelines for cataloging Internet resources as part of its InterCat project.[10] Individual libraries have made their internal cataloging policies and procedures available for consultation by others.[11]

Necessary changes to the MARC format have also been made. The 856 field has been defined for the description of electronic location and access. Furthermore, it has now been implemented by the bibliographic utilities and many local systems, so that it can be used in cataloging records. Format integration means that we are no longer required to choose between the serial and computer file formats in order to catalog a title, and are finally able to have a 538 "System Details Information" note in a serial record.

We are also seeing the contribution of shared cataloging records to national databases. The Committee on Institutional Cooperation (CIC) has an Electronic Journals Collection which is cataloged by librarians of the member universities. The cataloging records are contributed to OCLC.[12] OCLC itself has sponsored the Internet Cataloging Project to create Inter-

Cat, a catalog of Internet resources that have been selected and cataloged by OCLC member libraries participating in the project.[13] These shared databases are in their formative stages. They are still far from the critical mass of records which would enable libraries to mainstream electronic resources into their regular copy cataloging process. But they are an excellent start.

This is not to say that no improvements are needed. I spoke earlier of the ability to use a controlled vocabulary in subject analysis. Our familiar Library of Congress Subject Headings, however, are not always sufficient to describe the material we have been cataloging in the past. The length of time it takes to add terms to the LCSH makes it problematic when applied to the swiftly moving target of the Internet.[14] Some recommended changes to AACR2's Chapter 9, for example the expansion of the list of descriptors of file characteristics to include terms such as "electronic journal" and "bibliographic database," have not yet been approved.[15] The values defined in the first indicator of the 856 field for the access method are: Email, FTP, Remote login (Telnet), and "Method specified in subfield 2" –i.e., "Other." The access methods defined do not represent the majority of the resources we are cataloging today.

Nor, possibly, do the cataloging rules and guidelines fit all our needs. There is only one GMD authorized for electronic resources: [computer file]. The words "computer file" do not necessarily evoke the nature of what we are cataloging. I have already seen at least one institution make the decision that the term does not meet their users' needs; they are using the GMD [electronic serial] instead and this GMD is in their contributed OCLC records. The cataloging guidelines provide for the use of a single bibliographic record for an electronic resource, with multiple 856 fields to accommodate multiple forms of access. The record for the electronic version is nonetheless separate from the record for the print version. This perpetuates the difficulty facing our patrons in locating a desired issue of a title into the new environment. Some libraries are already making the decision to add the electronic version as another "copy" of the print in their online catalogs, for the benefit of their own patrons. This will have long-term implications for shared bibliographic databases, as libraries will have to continue to choose between following rules they believe provide a disservice to their own users, cataloging one way for their local system and another for the world at large, or cataloging only one way and choosing the local system as the higher priority. It is difficult for the cataloging rules to evolve as quickly as the medium.

The final improvement needed is not a cataloging issue but a hardware and software issue. In order to take the fullest advantage of online catalog records for Internet resources, our systems vendors will need to support the "hot links" to those resources from the OPAC. And, probably more difficult to achieve, we will need to replace all of our text-based "dumb" terminals with graphically-capable microcomputers to be able to execute those links. This will require a considerable investment of money for equipment, telecommunications, and computer support. I hope that the potential for providing a new dimension of user service—predicated of course on the availability of those hot-linkable records in our catalogs—can help leverage the necessary funding for this investment.

Providing records in the catalog for electronic serials has the same pitfalls for the inexpert researcher as providing records for print serials: the patron thinks that going to the journal whose title s/he found and browsing through it is how to do research on that subject. This behavior has always challenged our user education skills, and will continue to do so. One of the biggest payoffs to having serial records in the online catalog has been the ability to link to those records from locally mounted indexes— the "hook to holdings" where a user finds a citation and can see if the library has (or in this case, provides access to) the title and issue being cited. Abstracting and indexing services are not yet picking up electronic resources to any great degree. As for the issue-specific information, I think it unrealistic to try to provide detailed holdings unless the library is down-loading each issue. This may not be permissible for all journals, and in any case is a labor- and space-intensive effort. It is likely, therefore, that we will be providing open-ended holdings statements instead of detailed Z39.44 Level 4 holdings.

As the indexing of electronic resources increases, however, I would like to encourage librarians and the A&I database vendors, whose customers we are, to think about the traditional online "hook" using the ISSN. Even though our records for print, microfilm, and microfiche holdings are separate, they share a common ISSN. Therefore the user can see whether the library has the journal being cited, no matter what format it is in. The electronic version of the same title is considered a different "edition," and will have a different ISSN. If the library has the electronic version of a serial being cited, and not its print equivalent, how will the user know the library has it?

One more consideration in following our standard practices is in the area of resource sharing. Traditional cataloging workflow typically includes adding the library's holding symbol to a record in a bibliographic utility to promote resource sharing. If the holding symbol is not added, the library is in violation of its participation agreement with the utility. On the other hand, we probably don't want our holding symbol appearing for titles we are unable to lend. This conundrum, along with the multiple record question and the detailed holdings question and the ISSN question and many other questions, provides areas for consideration as we try to adapt traditional practices to the not-yet-traditional electronic environment.

Just like our more tangible collections, the virtual ones require maintenance. If the library has decided to check in each issue, staff need to know that a new one is out there to be checked in. Sometimes there is an alert sent via E-mail; sometimes staff will need to monitor assigned sites to see if there is anything new. There is some, but not a great deal of, automated assistance in the monitoring process. Eric Lease Morgan developed a software program called "Mr. Serials" which extracts bibliographic information from incoming electronic serials and adds it to the library's locally maintained archive.[16] However, the program only handles serials received via E-mail, and does not address serials accessed via other methods such as gopher or the World Wide Web.

Claiming of missing issues is not qualitatively different from claiming print journals–staff do not see those either! The difference is perhaps in how they go about identifying them. The maintenance of the virtual serials collection requires a great deal of staff time, certainly, but even more important is the different skill set required of a check-in clerk. Accessing URL's; downloading binary files; following links–these require an entirely new dimension of training. One of our biggest concerns is ensuring the integrity of the links to resources that we "collect." Addresses of remote servers are prone to change, and links must therefore be checked on a regular basis. There is some software available to assist in this process. One list of "validation checkers" is available via Yahoo (URL: http://www.yahoo.com/Computers_and_Internet/Software/Data_Formats/HTML/Validation_Checkers), and another from Webreference (URL: http://webreference.com/html/validation.html). Most of these programs validate HTML coding, but some do checking of links. Nevertheless, this is largely a process that needs an investment of staff time and training, and is likely to remain so. A benefit of integrating electronic resources into the library's online system is the ability to utilize the same acquisitions tools (e.g., reports triggered by a library-specified action date) as are available to assist us with maintenance of the print collection.

In order to perform the new level of tasks required to maintain electronic resources, library staff will require not only training but a computing and telecommunications infrastructure to support the work they now have to do. Good, fast, Internet-connected PC's will have to replace "dumb" terminals in staff areas, or staff will be unable to perform their jobs effectively. The need to maximize staff productivity can, I hope, help to leverage the hardware investment required to provide the necessary working environment in technical services.

Since locations can change so readily, standards developments are under way to provide more persistent links than the URL. The Uniform Resource Identifier Working Group of the Internet Engineering Task Force (IETF), which defined the URL, is now working on a standard for a Uniform Resource Name (URN). The idea is to define a text string that unambiguously identifies an Internet resource independent of its location. This string would then be used by a resolution service, which would accept the URN and return one or more URL's.[17] OCLC has developed the PURL (Persistent Uniform Resource Locator, or Persistent URL), which points to an intermediate resolution service instead of the URL itself. This external administrative component, maintained by OCLC, then finds and returns the URL associated with the PURL.[18] According to the PURL home page, 6460 PURL's had been created as of June 16, 1996.

The final, and probably thorniest, maintenance concern that I will address is that of archiving. Who has the responsibility for maintaining the archives of an electronic title?

If the journal is freely available or our subscription terms permit, library staff can download and store the issues. I have already mentioned storage and staff time issues associated with doing this. The library is then dependent on potentially obsolete hardware and software to provide access to the archive in the future.[19] And just as our print and microform collections are subject to physical deterioration, there are preservation issues for electronic media. As Neavill and Sheblé point out, "Neither magnetic nor optical media are considered to be of archival quality. The lifetime of digital storage media is measured at best in decades. . . ."[20]

Some journals have backfiles available on diskette or microfiche. *Postmodern Culture* is one example. This is not, however, widely available.

Publishers can maintain archives for their publications. But there are potential problems here as well. Publishers can change. The direction of not-for-profit organizations can change. The editors and publishing responsibilities of smaller societies and professional organizations can change.[21] The economics of electronic publishing are only now being determined, and I think a topic for future discussion will be what the incentive would be for publishers to maintain the archives.

Cooperative projects have been developed. The CICNet consortium is a major one. What we are looking at when we access the CIC Electronic Journals Collection is an effort by and on behalf of the CIC member universities. While the collection is currently available to everyone, its maintenance takes an enormous amount of work and there is no guarantee that the CIC will be able to continue to provide access to outside users.[22] New partnerships are developing between publishers and libraries. In the case of the Scholarly Communications Project at Virginia Tech, the publisher *is* the library; Project Muse is an example of an alliance between university presses and libraries.[23]

Neavill and Sheblé present the possibility of libraries establishing cooperative archiving on a national or international level, similar to the establishment of bibliographic utilities for cooperative cataloging.[24] They acknowledge that this is a concept for the future.

These archiving questions are very real, and their resolution is not at all clear. Likewise the bibliographic questions and the staffing and training issues involved in providing access to and maintaining our collections. In the rapidly changing environment of electronic resources, the questions may change before any answers are proposed. Despite the lack of answers, libraries have already embarked on the electronic path. In order to provide the best service not only to our users but to ourselves, we must do our best to manage our virtual as well as our literal collections. It is our responsibility to nail that slippery Jell-O to the wall.

I would like to conclude this paper by resuming the quotation from Michael Gorman with which I began it:

> Current attempts to control this chaos (Mosaic, the World Wide Web, etc.) are, when compared to the established structures of bibliographic control, inadequate. The alternatives are stark. We can either resign ourselves to terminal Information Anxiety or we can clean up the mess. Librarians . . . are uniquely qualified to tame the electronic wilderness—"If not us, who? If not now, when?"[25]

NOTES

1. Michael Gorman, "The Corruption of Cataloging," *Library Journal* 120, no. 15 (1995), 34.

2. Martha Hruska, "Remote Internet Serials in the OPAC?" *Serials Review* 21, no. 4 (1995), 68.

3. Eric Lease Morgan, "Adding Internet Resources to our OPACS," *Serials Review* 21, no. 4 (1995), 70.

4. Allison Mook Sleeman, "Cataloging Remote Access Electronic Materials," *Serials Review* 21, no. 4 (1995), 72.

5. Wayne Jones, "We Need Those E-Serial Records," *Serials Review* 21, no. 4 (1995), 75.

6. Regina Reynolds, "Inventory List or Information Gateway? The Role of the Catalog in the Digital Age," *Serials Review* 21, no. 4 (1995), 76.

7. Hruska, 69.

8. Morgan, ibid.

9. Melissa Beck, *Remote Access Computer File Serials*. CONSER. URL: http://lcweb.loc.gov/acq/conser/module31.html. For background on the development of Module 31, see Bill Anderson and Les Hawkins, "Development of CONSER Cataloging Policies for Remote Access Computer File Serials," *The Public-Access Computer Systems Review* 7, no. 1 (1996). URL: http://info.lib. uh.edu/pr/v7/n1/ande7n1.html.

10. Nancy B. Olson, ed., *Cataloging Internet Resources: A Manual and Practical Guide*. OCLC, 1995. URL: http://www.oclc.org/oclc/man/9256cat/toc.htm.

11. Two examples are the University of Virginia Library's *Cataloging Procedures Manual (Computer Files Cataloging, Part D) (Online)*, 1994 (URL: http://www.lib.virginia.edu/cataloging/manual/chapxiid.html) and Wei Zhang's and John Blosser's *Interactive Electronic Serials Cataloging Aid (IESCA)* for the Northwestern University Library (URL: http://www.library.nwu.edu/iesca/).

12. URL: http://ejournals.cic.net/index.html.

13. URL: http://www.oclc.org:6990.

14. Morgan, 71.

15. Priscilla Caplan, "Controlling E-Journals: The Internet Resources Project, Cataloging Guidelines, and USMARC," *The Serials Librarian* 24, nos. 3/4 (1994), 105.

16. Morgan, "Description and Evaluation of the 'Mr. Serials' Process: Automatically Collecting, Organizing, Archiving, Indexing, and Disseminating Electronic Serials," *Serials Review* 21, no. 4 (1995): 1-12.

17. For background and description of Internet resource naming standards see Caplan, "U-R-Stars: Standards for Controlling Internet Resources," *The Serials Librarian* 28, nos. 3/4 (1996), 239-246; William Arms et al., "Uniform Resource Names: A Progress Report," *D-Lib Magazine* (February 1996) (URL: http://www. dlib.org/dlib/february96/02arms.html); and LC's Network Development and MARC Standards Office's "Naming Conventions for Digital Resources" (URL: http:// lcweb.loc.gov/marc/naming.html).

18. URL: http://purl.oclc.org.

19. Donnice Cochenour and Tom Moothart. "Relying on the Kindness of Strangers: Archiving Electronic Journals on Gopher," *Serials Review* 21, no. 1 (1995),72; Gordon B. Neavill and Mary Ann Sheblé, "Archiving Electronic Journals," *Serials Review* 21, no. 4 (1995), 16.

20. Neavill and Sheblé, 15. See also Maynard Brichford and William Maher. "Archival Issues in Network Electronic Publications," *Library Trends* 43, no. 4 (1995), 706.

21. Cochenour and Moothart, 72-73.

22. Cochenour and Moothart, 72.

23. Cochenour and Moothart, 73.

24. Neavill and Sheblé, 19.

25. Gorman, ibid.

CONCURRENT SESSION III: THE ELECTRONIC PHYSICS LITERATURE AT THE FOREFRONT OF CHANGE

Journals and the Electronic Programme of the Institute of Physics

Alan Singleton

SUMMARY. The paper offers some personal reflections on journals based on twenty-five years' experience. All IOP (Institute of Physics) journals have been available electronically on the World Wide Web since January 1996. The paper charts the history, current status and near future development of IOP's electronic journals programme, including some previously unpublished results of a large scale international survey of physicists. *[Article copies available for a fee from The Haworth Document Delivery Service: 1-800-342-9678. E-mail address: getinfo@haworth.com]*

Alan Singleton is Journals Director at the Institute of Physics.

[Haworth co-indexing entry note]: "Journals and the Electronic Programme of the Institute of Physics." Singleton, Alan. Co-published simultaneously in *The Serials Librarian* (The Haworth Press, Inc.) Vol. 30, No. 3/4, 1997, pp. 149-161; and: *Pioneering New Serials Frontiers: From Petroglyphs to Cyberserials* (ed: Christine Christiansen and Cecilia Leathem) The Haworth Press, Inc., 1997, pp. 149-161. Single or multiple copies of this article are available for a fee from The Haworth Document Delivery Service [1-800-342-9678, 9:00 a.m. - 5:00 p.m. (EST). E-mail address: getinfo@haworth.com].

INTRODUCTION AND BACKGROUND

At its best, a scientific journal is an expression of *a* community, and *of* community. It helps to bind and identify that community, and, Janus-like, both differentiate it from other communities and integrate it with communities of which it is a part. It will have its own codes, practices and guidelines; it will be a curious mixture of the fashioned and the serendipitous, all giving it a recognizable character and standing. It will be much more than a random collection of articles loosely linked by subject definition. It will not, mostly, have the 'mentoring' characteristics described by Lienhard at this conference, and to that extent the format, be it hard-copy or electronic, is secondary. But it *is* an entity, shaped by design and circumstances, with 'information transfer' as only one of its functions. We should not lightly cast it aside.

However, at its *worst*, you could say that a journal is a conspiracy of ambitious academics with their superfluous outpourings, egged on by vain editors and greedy publishers, supported by blind and bureaucratic funding and evaluation bodies–and purchasers would have to take some of the blame, too.

Of course, most journals fit somewhere between these two extremes. Many start off hoping to be the 'best' type, then gradually transmute or turn out to be nearer the 'worst'–a problem for us all is that the 'worst' *need* to fail, not stagger on in some expensive limbo, curiously supported by the subscriptions of a handful of libraries. One of the best things we could do together would be to lobby for quality rather than quantity in research and researcher evaluation and funding.

If journals are to survive, it will require a balance, or at least a correlation, between the amount of legitimate research, and consequential research output. Without this, arguing for funds for the support of its publication, whether at the point of the author or user, becomes indefensible.

But, to return to the nature of journals: perhaps unsurprisingly, your views on this can be much affected by where you interact with them. My own varied (some would say chequered) career includes spells as an engineer, an information scientist, a technical indexer, a researcher, a commercial publisher, and with a subscription agent, as well as a long spell at the Institute of Physics. I've always been struck by how my own attitude has changed, depending where I sat. Here are a few examples:

As a physics undergraduate, I had no contact with the primary journals at all. To the extent that I was aware of them, they were places for leading edge research, far beyond my ken. My world was books, labs, and lectures.

To some extent, that is how it should be. I'm reminded of what an eminent physics professor said to me a few years ago: "*Books* are where the science is, not journals. Journals are where you see the *process* of science recorded, mistakes and all–they are the lifeblood of science, *not* where you look for the established consensus." This is of course consistent with modern philosophies of science, but here merely serves to point out part of the complex nature of the journal–that it is indeed a formal archive (and not, for example, part of the informal network of science) but an archive of potentially transient findings and perspective, not of science itself.

When I was an information scientist, I worked in a library and handled technical enquiries, searches, book selection and cataloguing, etc. Here I developed the approach or attitude that the journals–or, rather, journal *articles*–were information resources because I had client needs. So I did the searches and tried to find relevant articles–it didn't matter to me which journals they were in, as long as I had ready access. In a sense, the journal was simply a given, another part of 'documentation' and I used it to meet some user demands.

Then I did a three-year stint as a researcher on physics communication. This gave me a shock. Physicists had a totally different view on communication and on what a journal was. Here, all the emphasis tended to be on creation, not the use. The journal paper was more often the end point, not the beginning of their thinking, and almost superfluous in the first communication of ideas, even if critical as record. As John Ziman has put it, a scientific paper is as a baby brought into the world, but one that then to a large extent has to make its own way. The journal in which it appears (and of course an author normally has a range of options on where to submit) provides some kind of environment, or context.

I then went into publishing, as a commissioning editor at a commercial publisher, and saw another side. Again, here the emphasis was on creation–shaping journals, starting new ones, conducting market research– but, crucially, amongst the authors, who were assumed to be the consumers too. Never, then, the librarians. Exposure to the detailed economics of journals changes attitudes also–how much needed to be invested in a launch, the relation between costs and circulation. A little more detail on all this kind of thing can be found in Singleton (1994): the problems if it goes wrong, but the very favourable economics for a successful journal, the prospect of which goes some way towards explaining the great proliferation of titles and commercialization of journals in the wake of post-World War II economic and research expansion.

This was all so intriguing I spent the next five years back in research, looking at all the players in research communication, and all the types of communication–including electronic journals (this was in 1980–Singleton 1981). Here I became very aware of the different types of publishers– learned society and commercial–and how this differed from country to country, and, particularly, how interdependent many of them were in jour- nal publishing. I even did a study of subscription agents and then went to work for one.

As a subscription agent you are critically aware of financial aspects, since the margins are often very low even though apparent turnover can be very large, because so much money goes, more or less, straight through them. But here the actual journals themselves, in a sense, become almost a side issue since the focus is, quite rightly, on customer (library) service and publisher discounts.

For the last eleven years I've been totally immersed, once more, in publishing, but this time at a learned society which, as a registered charity, has dissemination and education as key parts of its charter. Here you see journals somewhat as the commercial publisher does, but also as an inte- gral part of the society's raison d'être.

This somewhat long-winded recitation is not, or not just, an ego trip. It's just meant to illustrate in a very personal sense that what you see depends upon where you stand; that, indeed, the journal is multi-faceted; that we would do well to think hard before we cast it aside–especially in favour of some centralized undifferentiated collection, or even a differen- tiated collection, but one where the journal entity is lost. Creating it after a discontinuity would likely be a painful and expensive process.

And yet it is clear that it is no longer (it never was, really) good enough for us publishers, commercial or learned society, to pontificate about 'add- ed-value' and what we bring to journals. If we wish to survive, we need to start *demonstrating* and *delivering* it.

And now, at last, to our electronic journal programme.

ELECTRONIC JOURNAL PROGRAMME

After some initial experiments (Rowland, McKnight and Meadows, 1995), the programme really started in *September 1994* with the full-text launch of our journal *Classical and Quantum Gravity* on three types of server–list, gopher and World Wide Web.

The decision to go electronic in this way was, no question, editorially driven. The journal is highly theoretical and mathematical, and most of the community were already using the TEX system to compose their papers; we at IOP had been taking TEX manuscripts for some years; the Ginsparg e-print system at Los Alamos, which many of this community use, takes TEX. So we made the full-text available in TEX.

At first, usage of the list and gopher servers was dominant, but within a few months WWW usage took over to such an extent that we turned off the other servers.

This was a lesson for us when we came to launch our next service, *Physics Express Letters* which consists of all the research letters from 12 of our journals, in May 1995. We were now looking for better presentation quality. We had to determine whether to do it ourselves, or, for example, use an intermediary with a proprietary interface. Our experience in mounting a journal at all, and the evidence of WWW usage—even I could use it!–determined that we should do it ourselves. This we did, this time with full-text in HTML and quite elegant full-rendering of maths in position. This service proved to be extremely popular.

To bring us up to date, these experiences, and our surveys, gave us the courage to "go for it" so we decided, in mid-1995, to launch all our 31 journals on the Web from January 1996.

Importantly, we also made the decision that a full-rate subscription to the hard copy would entitle anyone at the subscribing site to electronic access, *at no extra charge*. We are committed to this policy and have no plans to change it.

This we did, using HTML for bibliographic information and abstract, and Postscript and Adobe Acrobat® pdf as options for full-text.

Although we did this in a short space of time we do proceed by trying to find out what people want, using, amongst other things, two standing Library Advisory Councils (one in North America and another in Europe), focus groups of librarians and physicists, and surveys.

I'd like to turn to one of the surveys we did, almost a year ago. We sent out very fat questionnaires to over 13,000 physicists world-wide. Some 3,500 were completed and returned. We asked them all sorts of things in their roles as authors, referees, readers, influencers, and purchasers. I'll give some of the findings, which I hope are useful (not too useful to competitors!), and interesting when you are either considering launching electronic products or following the debate on electronic journals, refereeing or e-print systems.

What kind of equipment do physicists use?

There are significant geographical differences in our sample, with UK and continental Europe significantly heavier users of PC's. (See Table 1.)

There were also some significant variations across the subfields of physics.

On network connectivity, virtually everyone (98%) was on e-mail and, in mid-1995, just over half had WWW access, and virtually all expected to have it by mid-1996.

On refereeing, we thought we should ask, not just whether they thought it was a good idea, but something a little more quantitative on whether, in their opinion, it made a difference. Since, at IOP, we administer the refereeing system we already know that, in one sense at least, it certainly does. First, 30% or so are typically rejected. Then, of the rest, 60% to 70% are revised, sometimes substantially so.

We asked, for the papers they refereed, how often a *material* improvement resulted? The results, which are fairly unequivocal, are given in Table 2.

We then asked, slightly differently, what the effect had been of refereeing on their *own* papers, with the results in Table 3.

You may be right if you think you can detect a subtle difference in the view of refereeing as it refers to their *own* papers, but even here these findings offer strong support for the concept. Importantly, there were no significant differences in these findings across the subfields of physics. Of course, those who advocate, in the literature and elsewhere, the complete abandonment of refereeing are few and far between, and for the most part may be considered extremists. But there are many more who suggest surrogate systems, perhaps based on open-peer commentary, open recommendations, access and comment, even bald usage data. All of these seem, to me, to have several drawbacks for science, even if they do save time,

TABLE 1

Equipment

	UK	USA	Continental Europe
PC	60%	33%	45%
MAC	18%	32%	25%
Unix	22%	37%	32%

TABLE 2

Refereeing

How often has material improvement resulted in the papers you have refereed?

Never	< 1%
	8%
	34%
	44%
Always	14%

when compared with the advantages and apparent effectiveness of the single- or double-blind peer review system.

We asked them about e-print servers, which at that time already existed in most major sub-fields of physics. Just over half (54%) did not know whether there *was* one in their field, but over three quarters of these (and those who thought they didn't have one) said they'd like one.

Perhaps of more interest was their opinion of what should happen to an e-print when a 'final' version was published. Forty-four percent thought it should be deleted immediately, 56% disagreed. So we also asked questions of the "If not now, then when" variety and a significant proportion of the 56% thought it *should* be deleted later.

As you might expect, we asked a number of questions about electronic journals. Table 4 lists the top five features they wanted to see, all having very similar ratings. Perhaps 'searchability' of abstracts is a little surprising in this list. More surprising, at least to me, were the features rated *least* important (and these really did get low ratings). These are listed in Table 5.

These are the kinds of things much hyped in the literature as key 'added

TABLE 3

Refereeing

What % of your articles materially improved?

Percentage improved		Response
0	→	8%
1-25	→	36%
26-50	→	24%
51-75	→	17%
76-100	→	15%

TABLE 4

Electronic Journals: Top five important features

- Searchability of abstracts
- Printout locally
- Browse TOC
- Full peer review
- Typeset quality maths

TABLE 5

<u>Electronic Journals: Least important features</u>

- Video
- Colour
- Simulations
- How articles are added (e.g., by issue or incremental)

value' items. Sometimes electronic journals are much criticised if they are mostly 'versions' of paper journals. Perhaps this is just, and we certainly need to interpret such findings with care, if the respondents are not familiar with their potential advantages. At the moment, however, it is clear (confirmed by surveys that we have done in areas more apparently 'ripe' for multimedia) that a significant number of the community will consider such features as a 'gimmick' with the potential to distract from the important core function of a journal paper. Time will tell whether this is a manifestation of the 'horseless carriage' syndrome, or something more lasting.

Two thirds of respondents said that their research departments now subscribed to some of their own journals. Rather fewer subscribed to journals personally, although the percentage that did was significantly greater in the USA than elsewhere.

Most said they had some influence over the purchasing decisions of the library. Since they don't actually sign the cheques, it may well be that the physicists have a distorted view of their influence. See what you think of these findings, a selection of which is given in Table 6.

As you can see, there was significant geographical, and, in one case, subject variation. I imagine if we had asked the librarians at these same institutions, we may have received a different view!

At the conference, the remainder of this paper talked about near-term developments, illustrated with Web pages, where colour is more easily rendered than on paper. That and the transient and the more informal nature of a presentation makes it unsuitable for repetition here (which itself can be fuel for discussion!), so I will summarize the position.

First, the easiest way to see what we are up to is to come into the Web site (http//:www.iop.org) where there are numerous free and fee-based services. As you would expect with a learned society, there are pages devoted to our educational activities, our conferences—including on-line registration, representations made on behalf of physics, a free jobs service; PEERs—a fully authorised 'white pages' of thousands of physicists' e-mail details, including their URL's if they have them.

TABLE 6

Selecting journals for the Library: Who has the most influence?

UK/Continental Europe

1	Head of Library Committee	44%
2	Head of Department	32%
3	Library staff	16%

U.S.A.

1	Head of Library Committee	48%
2	Library staff	30%
3	Head of Department	14%

Biophysics/Medical Physics

1	Head of Department	41%
2	Head of Library Committee	31%
3	Library staff	20%

We are currently engaged in a considerable Web redesign. This particular one will be complete in July 1996, but it is really an ongoing process as usage patterns and services change, and we learn more. The current redesign aims to make presentation clearer and navigation simpler and, in particular, ways of orienting yourself within the server so you know where you are. We always welcome feedback which you can, of course, give us via the server.

We are also introducing some modifications to our electronic journals, perhaps the most obvious of which will be the introduction of 'Home Pages' for each journal, suitable for subscribers and non-subscribers alike (and, perhaps, for those who wish, a URL which could be included in on-line catalogues). Apart from offering more news about the journal and another route to electronic access, this page will also contain "Featured Articles." These will be one or more research letters, reviews or papers that have been selected by the Editor of the journal on criteria such as topicality, general interest, popularity with subscribers, even importance or quality. These will be *freely available* to all in both Acrobat and Post-script, and will change over time.

The other important modifications in electronic journals this year are, in response to requests, more tailoring of the system to an individual's needs. For example, we have introduced a *'Filing cabinet'* where researchers can privately file articles of their choice, with comments; they can personalise their 'main menu' of journals so that only those that are of direct interest to them are displayed; we now have a *'journal alerting'* feature which, when enabled, will e-mail the user with a new table of contents of the journal of choice when it is mounted–and other such features.

There are already multi-media journals on the net. Despite the reservations I've mentioned, we believe that these features will be valuable in some journals where a majority of the associated community are in favour and, indeed, are already generating simulations, video clips, etc. *Multimedia features* will be introduced on some IOP journals in 1997. They raise interesting questions of refereeing, authoritative archive, etc., which is already the subject of debate. For a variety of reasons, we currently view the hard-copy version to be the authoritative archive. Clearly, this can be a difficult view to maintain if we accepted multimedia versions which were essential for the understanding of the paper. We don't expect that in the early days.

Next year we will introduce *'incremental' publication* for our lower frequency (bimonthly and quarterly) journals–this simply means that, when accepted, and all bibliographic information is known, including pagination, it will be mounted and accessible. This will mean that neither authors nor readers need be inconvenienced by delays in conventional publication. There will be exceptions, however. In keeping with my argument earlier, journals are not just ad-hoc collections of papers and there will often be cases of special issues, ordered sections, etc., which will not lend themselves to incremental publication.

One of the most interesting and taxing innovations to electronic journals, which we *know* users would love, is citation linking, i.e., the ability to jump from a reference to the referenced article. Since no journal I know of cites itself more than all others, and typically references go back many years, it is tough to make this anything near comprehensive. We will start with *self-citing*, and try to work on *interciting* (i.e., between journals and, maybe, publishers) on an experimental basis. We will also be able to *forward* or *future-cite*, e.g., a 1996 article that is cited by a 1997 article can be annotated and linked.

We plan, also, an improving mixture of informal and formal areas centred around our journals–you may be familiar with some similar offerings on other web sites. All in all, we see an ambitious and exciting programme which will more than keep us busy.

Lastly, I wanted to return to some more general issues on economics and electronic journal publishing. There has been a lot of debate, in print and at conferences, about the relative costs of electronic and hard-copy journals. In fact, large-scale studies on this issue go back 20 years and more (e.g., King and Roderer, 1978). The debate should be able to be more realistic now but in fact sometimes gets stuck on such issues as the 70:30 argument–e.g., does it save 30% of costs to do electronic only, or 70%? Apart from huge problems of definition, this particular argument is largely irrelevant. What we are really talking about, as I believe such as Harnad and Ginsparg know, is the publishing paradigm. I can illustrate this in two ways.

First, Bob Marks of the American Chemical Society recently published an article in *Serials Review* (Marks 1995) which tackled an important part of the issue. Table 7 summarizes his main illustrative costings. What he basically says here is that, *within the current publishing system*, most of the costs are associated with getting to the first copy, and even if it were possible to remove all production costs in electronic form, it would save little.

Discussion of first-copy costs can lead so naturally into the plausible but not entirely convincing arguments for the page-charge system, effectively taken up again by Harnad, that I can hardly resist the digression, but I will, save to refer the reader to the most interesting exploration of the issue by Conyers Herring and others many years ago (e.g., COMSAT 1970, National Academy of Sciences 1972).

TABLE 7. Publication Cost Analysis
Reprinted with permission from *Serials Review*, © 1995, Robert H. Marks.

Production Step	Range of Costs Per Page
(1) Editorial Management	$14 to $50
(2) Editorial Mechanics	$20 to $35
(3) Electronic Production	$20 to $80
(4) Illustrations	$5 to $20
Total First-Copy Cost	$60 to $185
Percent of Total Cost	86% to 82%
(5) *Printing, Paper and Binding	$10 to $40
Percent of Total Paper Cost	14% to 18%
(6) Total Print on Paper Cost (100%)	$70 to $225

* Note – Journal print run in the range of 1,000 to 10,000 copies

Within the current publishing paradigm, therefore, the issue is, or should be, not so much production *cost* but journal *price*. I can illustrate this in a simplistic fashion in Figure 1.

Here, 100% of the price of a standard, established journal is represented by the total of A, B, and C. A represents profit. The exact position of the dotted line will vary according to journal and publisher, but it's normally pretty much in that sector. Now there's a legitimate area for debate–should there *be* a profit? What is its justification? Is it any more justified if it's used in support of the relevant subject community? Is it still justified or justifiable if it goes to shareholders unconnected with the community? There are points to be made on each side of each of the above questions.

C represents production and distribution cost. Again it's down in this sector, and saving 70% or 30% of this, even if it were possible, would not make a great deal of difference to the price.

So what is B? It's simply '*Publishing,*' that's all, and it's the biggest part. That should be the focus of any debate.

And that *is* the part that the Ginspargs and Harnads attack on several fronts. For Harnad, it represents an inappropriate 'trade' model; for Ginsparg and others, a lot of it is either unnecessary or already or potentially automatable–or, can be funded in other, smaller, relatively painless ways (e.g., by authors).

So what *is* in there? In our case, at IOP, there's my salary, for example. This is not intended to be a trivial point (even if it's a trivial *amount*), since it illustrates that I and colleague publishers have a strong vested interest– it's our *livelihood*, and we can be expected to defend its legitimacy come what may. This might well mean that an argument from this quarter might

FIGURE 1

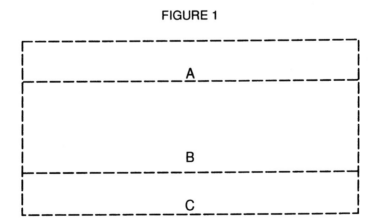

be distrusted, but we should at least hope that it would not be *discounted*, but judged on its merits.

Also, in B, for IOP, are the 20 or so staff we have administering the refereeing system (with all the associated computer equipment and costs) which we have seen is still so valued by physicists. Also in there is a similar number of production staff, still needed to intervene in authors' electronic files, helping to clarify their English (whose native language it often isn't–leading to just such infelicities of style as this!) and prepare for conventional and electronic production; then there are fulfillment and order processing staff–still necessary if you charge *anything* for the journal; finance department, computer services, marketing, building services, rent and rates, etc. Altogether we have nearly 100 staff working on journals–all for the trade model? All automatable? Maybe, and maybe not.

We, of course, like to think we are doing something worthwhile, and that we are in a good, if not the best, position to take advantage of any economies and value-added benefits we can offer. To a considerable extent the market mechanism, and having competitors who have to compete in the same way–unsubsidised, not state-funded, helps us do that.

The danger for us publishers (incidentally) and scholarship (importantly) is that we all learn that B in Figure 1 *is* important, but that we have to pass through an expensive discontinuity–losing it–before we, expensively again, recreate it.

BIBLIOGRAPHY

Committee on Scientific and Technical Communication. *Report of the Task Group on the Economics of Pricing Publication* (National Academy of Sciences, Washington, DC, 1970).

King, D. W. and Roderer, N. K., *Systems analysis of scientific and technical communication in the United States: The electronic alternative to communication through paper-based journals* (King Research Inc. 1978; NTIS PB 281 847-PB 281 851).

National Academy of Sciences. National Research Council, *Physics in Perspective*. Vol 1. Chapter 13, *Dissemination and Use of the Information of Physics* (Washington, DC, 1972), p. 890-966.

Rowland, F., McKnight C., and Meadows, J. *Project ELVYN: An experiment in electronic journal delivery–facts, figures, and findings* (London: Bowker-Saur, 1995).

Singleton, Alan K. J. 1981, *The electronic journal and its relatives, Scholarly Publishing,* Vol.13, no.1, pp. 3-18.

Singleton, Alan, *"Information UK Outlooks. Present trends and likely futures– their impact on library and information services,"* The Scientific Journal, no.7 (June 1994).

Digital Archiving
in the Physics Literature:
Author to Archive and Beyond–
The American Physical Society

Robert A. Kelly

SUMMARY. The American Physical Society (APS) has long recognized as its goal the diffusion of the knowledge of physics. For the past 100 years, the society has used a paper-based, print-oriented publishing process in support of this goal. This paper describes the strategies and projects, being developed and implemented, that will enable the exploitation of the emerging Internet and electronic publishing technologies in support of the Society's goal. The transparencies used in this presentation are available on http://publish.aps.org/ RAKELLY/rakelly.html. *[Article copies available for a fee from The Haworth Document Delivery Service: 1-800-342-9678. E-mail address: getinfo@haworth.com]*

INTRODUCTION

The primary journal family of the American Physical Society is the *Physical Review.* Since its inception in 1893, the journal has twigged into six primary journals, *Physical Review A* through *E* and *Physical Review*

Robert A. Kelly is APS Director, Journal Information Systems.

[Haworth co-indexing entry note]: "Digital Archiving in the Physics Literature: Author to Archive and Beyond–The American Physical Society." Kelly, Robert A. Co-published simultaneously in *The Serials Librarian* (The Haworth Press, Inc.) Vol. 30, No. 3/4, 1997, pp. 163-170; and: *Pioneering New Serials Frontiers: From Petroglyphs to Cyberserials* (ed: Christine Christiansen and Cecilia Leathem) The Haworth Press, Inc., 1997, pp. 163-170. Single or multiple copies of this article are available for a fee from The Haworth Document Delivery Service [1-800-342-9678, 9:00 a.m. - 5:00 p.m. (EST). E-mail address: getinfo@haworth.com].

Letters. The Society also publishes a review journal, *Reviews of Modern Physics.* I estimate that by the end of 1996, we will have published approximately one and a half million pages of physics.

At the start of our journey into electronic publishing, in the summer of 1993, the APS adopted three unique, at the time, approaches to the journey. For starters, we decided to take a systems view and consider publishing as a process that starts with the researcher (author), passes through peer review, production, distribution, an archive and then onto another scholar (the reader).[1] The process most likely is repeating itself, with research building upon research, in a continuing cycle from 1893 into the future. Our strategy was, and is, to apply electronic publishing technologies and the use of the Internet to this physics publishing process.

Our second approach was to change the paradigm from the printing of articles to one of archiving and then distributing physics information. We were early adopters of SGML and the use of ISO12083 as a DTD. In 1994, we migrated *Physical Review Letters* (PRL) from a TROFF based composition system to a production process based on SGML. This enabled APS not only to reduce costs in the composition of the PRL print journal but also to offer the journal on-line. In July of 1995, we launched *Physical Review Letters-online* (PRL-o), via the OCLC Guidon interface. In August of 1995, we launched an HTML and subsequently a pdf version, also through OCLC, of PRL-o. Both of the on-line versions were made possible by the use of SGML in the production process.

We also recognized that much of the innovation in this new era would come from the researchers, the authors and the readers. Paul Ginsparg's e-print server is a prime example of user innovation being brought into the process. I'll talk more on e-prints later.

Four strategic goals were developed:

- Provide access to articles–past, current and work-in-progress.
- Facilitate the author-to-reader process, by making it faster and less costly.
- Prepare for the introduction of new technologies–appletts, multimedia, etc., that will expand beyond the technical capability of the paper article.
- Prepare for the introduction of new electronic services: inter-journal citing and linking, discussions, editorial reviews of articles, etc.

Over the past three years, our goals have been formed in response to technology and business challenges. The business challenges include rising costs, declining funds for subscriptions and the internationalization of the process.

The business challenges will continue. However, it is time to explore the new media as a new way of scholarly communication and research. In his book, *Film Style and Technology: History and Analysis,*[2] Barry Salt posits that the basic format of a stage play, possibly enhanced, has been carried over into the cinema. It was the introduction of technology that enabled the director to change the theatrical viewing perspective by moving the camera. It was the introduction of technology that enabled trick effects leading to the current film releases exploiting special effects.

Our efforts, to date, have been to replicate the print journal, with its supporting infrastructure, on-line. There are differences between a paper being presented at a conference, an article in a journal, or a paper on an interactive bulletin board on the Internet. The same "information" could be communicated through any of these forms, yet the treatment of the information is quite different in the way that the reader interacts with it. The role of the "reader," on the Internet, has been replaced with that of "user." Assuming the continued explosion of the Internet technology, what can happen to the journal structure and process? We have recently set up a journals research group to answer this question.

PROJECTS

In anticipation of answering the above question, The American Physical Society has created four major project categories as an umbrella for experimentation and implementation of our strategic goals: E-Print, Re-engineering the Editorial Process, Archiving and Distribution. The future direction of these projects will be guided by the work of our research group. The remainder of this paper will be to describe these projects.

APS E-PRINT SERVER

For years physicists had been communicating current research with their colleagues through a process known as pre-print. This was the distribution of articles in advance of the article being submitted for peer review. The World Wide Web was created at CERN as a tool to facilitate this communication. In 1991, the pre-print process evolved into an e-print archive, at Los Alamos National Laboratory. For the first time, physicists had a place to store their papers so that others might retrieve them. The process changed from one where the article was pushed to the reader to one where the reader pulled the article. The paradigm shift of push to pull is an important distinction in the evolution from print to e-publishing.

The American Physical Society had followed the e-print archive phenomenon with great interest. The APS sensed that it might have an important role to play at this critical juncture. In the summer and fall of 1994, the APS conducted an on-line forum and on October 30, 1994, a workshop,[3] at Los Alamos National Laboratory, to assist in the formulation of APS policy concerning e-print archives. Observations from the workshop are the following:

1. The landscape of scientific publishing is changing rapidly.
2. We can use technology not only to accelerate the process but also to improve it and add value to it.
3. A "one size fits all" paper-based policy is obsolete. We can craft a process that fits the different needs of many users.
4. Author tools and education are necessary.
5. There is a place for e-prints in the current and probably future APS publishing policy.
6. The definition of future processes should be explored through small experiments.
7. We should establish a collaborative effort with universities, libraries, and other societies; representatives from all of these were present at the workshop.

On July 1, 1996, APS launched a prototype e-print server.[4] The APS server will complement the XXX server at Los Alamos. Testing and development is scheduled to be complete for this first version by October 1, 1996. The APS e-print archive will be freely available to all physicists, without regard to discipline or journal of ultimate publication. Authors, if they so choose, will be able to submit papers, from the e-print archive directly to APS for review. In addition to allowing authors to make their preprints readily available, the service is intended to help with the exploration of new Internet-based technology for submitting, refereeing, editing, and publishing papers in the *Physical Review* journals.

Articles submitted for information sharing purposes should be in a readable format. We prefer postscript, pdf or HTML. Articles submitted for eventual submission to an APS journal should include the source material for the article. ReVTeX, LaTeX are preferred. We hope to accept SGML in the future.

For the future, we are considering the development of a web-based SGML authoring tool, similar in concept to NetScape Navigator Gold. Using JAVA appletts, the tool would guide an author through the creation of a manuscript, following an SGML DTD. The resulting article would be available in pdf and PostScript with a SGML source file that parses to an arbitrary DTD. In addition to preparing the article for future archiving in a database, the tool could provide services such as verifying references and creating web links.

RE-ENGINEERING THE EDITORIAL PROCESS

In an article titled "Re-Engineering Peer Review" in the magazine *The Economist*,[5] the author states "The Internet was developed by scientists for scientists, but many now fear that its anarchic style could endanger the quality of research. The threat is an opportunity in disguise." We believe that it is a major opportunity to reduce costs and improve the cycle time of the peer review process. We also believe that once our entire process is using web-based technology, it will be easier to change the paradigm of peer review.

It is our intent to build a web-based Intra- and Internet process to manage our editorial and peer review processes electronically and with electronic manuscripts. This system will service users who are authors, referees, editors and readers, scattered around the planet. An example of the services we will provide is in our recently implemented Author Status Inquiry System (ASIS). The system, accessed through the World Wide Web, enables an author to pinpoint the progress of a paper in peer review.

Our target is to convert accepted articles into SGML and archive them for subsequent use. Currently we archive *Physical Review D, Physical Review Letters* and the Rapid Communications sections of all of our journals in SGML. We use ISO 12083 as the standard for our DTD. I anticipate that all of our journals will be in SGML format by year end 1997. All of our journals are composed electronically, producing postscript for the printed issue. This gives us the opportunity to distill pdf files from the PostScript files. We are conducting our e-journal experiments using these pdf files.

ARCHIVE

APS, like most publishers, started composing journals electronically in the early 1980s. The first steps were a combination of electronic keystrokes of text and math that created a single-column camera-ready copy that was then cut and pasted with figures into mechanicals. We saved all of these keystrokes which have become the nucleus of our archive activities. Currently the archive is a hodgepodge of formats; from TROFF to TeX to

Xyvision to SGML. By the end of 1997, I hope to have all future content in SGML, our theory being that an SGML database will provide us with the greatest reusability and data base options.

In 1994 we started an experiment at Los Alamos: *Physical Review On-Line Archives* (PROLA).[6] The goal of the project is to see if we can use the saved keystrokes and integrate the various composition formats used over the past ten years. Image and pdf will be used for display and the keystrokes for searching, linking and other navigation techniques. We have been successful and the project is being tested by physicists at Los Alamos. Our immediate goal is to have an archive from 1985 through 1995 that can be linked to from our e-journal offerings. We are seriously considering bringing the archive on-line back to 1893, the beginning of *Physical Review*. This archive will be a component of future offerings.

E-JOURNAL OFFERINGS

The paradigm shift of push to pull is an important distinction in the evolution from print to e-publishing. The current STM publishing process, from a reader's point of view, is a push process. The peer reviewed articles are packaged by a publisher, into a journal, and pushed out, to the readers. With the introduction of web technology it is possible for a reader to interact with the publisher's system and pull the information. The publisher need only make the URL of the content available and the reader can obtain the article with a web browser.

The American Physical Society has several ongoing experiments where the reader comes to the content. On July 1, 1995, we launched *Physical Review Letters-on-line* through OCLC. As of July 1, 1996 we will have three volumes of this weekly letters journal, on-line, covering from January 1, 1995 to July 1, 1996. The journal is available on the web with the articles in pdf format. The journal is also available through the OCLC Guidon interface.

On July 1, 1996, we launched *Physical Review C on-line* (PRC-o) and *Physical Review B Rapid Communications* on-line (PRBR-o). Both of these offerings are web-based and deliver pdf files of the articles. PRC-o is available to institutions and members of the APS. PRBR-o is only available to members of the APS.

We have several experiments where we deliver content to institutions for subsequent use. The TORPEDO project at the Naval Research Laboratory[7] is an example of a subsequent-use archive customized for an institution. APS supplies unbound copies of *Physical Review Letters* and *Physical Review E* to NRL for availability to the NRL researchers. The journals are scanned into an image format and are available to the researchers. In 1997, we plan to assist NRL in migrating this system to an SGML database-oriented system with pdf copies of the articles.

The University of Illinois at Urbana-Champagne, was one of the winners of the National Science Foundation grants for the Digital Library Initiative.[8] One of the goals of this project is to develop the technologies and processes to integrate the SGML (ISO 12083 compliant) files from several publishers into a database that will provide on-line access to the journals at the University. The APS is supporting this effort by contributing SGML created for the distribution of the paper and on-line editions of *Physical Review Letters*. We are using the same SGML process and files to feed the paper, on-line, and DLI.

CONCLUSION

In conclusion, the American Physical Society is committed to exploiting emerging technologies to develop a full-electronic infrastructure, setting the stage for innovation in scholarly communication and research. Our immediate goal is to improve the cycle time of the process and reduce costs.

AUTHOR NOTE

The visions, strategies and projects described in this paper are not the product of any one individual but the sum of numerous conversations, debates, and meetings with many physicists, librarians, the APS Electronic Publishing Committee, the APS Editorial staff, and the Journal Information Systems staff of the American Physical Society.

NOTES

1. One of our first public discussions of our strategy was presented at the Association of Research Libraries conference on November 6, 1994. A copy of the paper is on http://publish.aps.org/RAKELLY/arl.html

An even earlier presentation is included in my testimony before the Joint Committee on Printing, US Congress, "New Technology and the Government Printing Office," July 24, 1991.

2. Salt, Barry. *Film Style and Technology: History and Analysis*. London: Starwood, 1983.

3. The workshop proceedings are available at http://publish.aps.org/EPRINT/eprthome.html

The observations are in the REPORT TO COUNCIL ON E-PRINT ARCHIVE WORKSHOP, LOS ALAMOS, OCT. 14-15, 1994 B. Bederson at http://publish.aps.org/EPRINT/losa.html

4. The APS E-Print Archive can be found at http://publish.aps.org/artintro.html

The description of the service, in this paper, is extracted in part from the above URL.

5. *The Economist*, June 22, 1996, page 79.

6. A paper on our archival thinking is available at http://www.c3.lanl.gov:8077/papers/apsPlan.html

7. NRL Library Home Page-InfoWeb, http://infonext.nrl.navy.mil/

8. Illinois Digital Library Initiative Project, http://surya.grainger.uiuc.edu/dli/

CONCURRENT SESSION IV: ISSUES IN ELECTRONIC LICENSING

Navigating the Electronic River: Electronic Product Licensing and Contracts

Nancy L. Buchanan

SUMMARY. Electronic products are now a staple of libraries. CD-ROMs, online services, Internet databases, diskette products, and other electronic resources provide library users with vital information in new and useful formats, but they can pose problems for the library staff attempting to essay the confusing, deep, and quickly changing waters of electronic product licensing. The purpose of this paper is to provide a practical overview of the licensing process for electronic products, focusing on the information library staff need to know in order to deal with vendors and contracts accurately and effectively and highlighting major areas in licenses that may be problematic for libraries. *[Article copies available for a fee from The Haworth Document Delivery Service: 1-800-342-9678. E-mail address: getinfo@haworth.com]*

Nancy L. Buchanan is Coordinator of Electronic Resources, University of Houston Libraries.

[Haworth co-indexing entry note]: "Navigating the Electronic River: Electronic Product Licensing and Contracts." Buchanan, Nancy L. Co-published simultaneously in *The Serials Librarian* (The Haworth Press, Inc.) Vol. 30, No. 3/4, 1997, pp. 171-182; and: *Pioneering New Serials Frontiers: From Petroglyphs to Cyberserials* (ed: Christine Christiansen and Cecilia Leathem) The Haworth Press, Inc., 1997, pp. 171-182. Single or multiple copies of this article are available for a fee from The Haworth Document Delivery Service [1-800-342-9678, 9:00 a.m. - 5:00 p.m. (EST). E-mail address: getinfo@haworth.com].

There is a commercial currently on television that shows a businessman trying, repeatedly, to use a copy machine. A voice-over states, "In business school they never told you about paper jams." That's what I have sometimes felt like over the past three years as I have worked with contracts and licenses for electronic products. When dealing with such issues as authorized users, remote access, and legitimate use I have been known to moan, "They didn't tell me about this in library school."

In my position as the Coordinator of Electronic Resources for the University of Houston Libraries, I have dealt with all the contracts and licenses for our public-use electronic databases for the past three years. We have an Electronic Publications Center with over 100 networked workstations and over fifteen specialized and stand-alone workstations. In this area we make available almost eighty electronic products, and forty-five of them are also available remotely. Working with licenses for this many products has been sometimes challenging, sometimes frustrating, but always a learning experience. My goal is to share with you what I have learned, and to make your future experiences in this area easier.

Before I begin, I want to clearly state that I am providing a librarian's perspective on electronic product licenses and contracts. I am not providing legal interpretation or advice. Also, I am using the words "license" and "contract" interchangeably.

Libraries must deal with a product's licensing from the beginning. A library shouldn't wait until it has decided to buy an electronic product; it should start when it's just considering the product. Before a product is brought in for evaluation, the library needs to ask licensing questions. The best person to query is the appropriate sales representative at the vendor company. If the library does not know who its representative is, it can call the information or general number for the company and ask.

There is a caveat, however. One can't always believe the verbal answers one receives. If possible, the library should get a copy of the license. While it does not happen frequently, it is not unheard of for libraries to be given incorrect verbal licensing information from vendors. Sometimes the problem is that the sales representative does not have the newest version of the license. Sometimes it is due to difficulty in interpreting problematic contract clauses. One is most likely to get incorrect information when one isn't dealing with the appropriate representative, but with a vendor's informational phone operator. These operators may be good sources of flyers and price lists, but may not have copies of licenses and are probably not trained in interpreting them.

When the library decides to bring an electronic product in for trial, it definitely must get a copy of the license. Just because no one has to sign a license, don't assume the library is not bound by one. These licenses and contracts can take a variety of forms. Some require a library signature only, some require a library signature and a vendor signature. Some require no signature, but come packaged with the product or with an acknowledgement of an order. Some are shrink-wrapped to a physical product, such as a CD-ROM. Some are printed on the back of subscription or renewal forms. The one certainty is that there will be a license or contract; make sure the library has it.

In addition, some contracts are in effect permanently once they begin, while others are subject to change when the library renews a subscription or service. When using a renewal form that has a license printed on it, read the license very carefully. It may or may not be the same as the previous year's license. Also be alert for changes to licenses throughout a subscription period. It is not uncommon for a vendor to send out notices of license changes, usually with a notation that the change is in effect as of the sending (not receipt) of the notice. One of the most difficult aspects of such notices is making sure that they are received by the appropriate library staff. For physical products, such as CD-ROMs, such notices are typically sent with a product update. In most libraries, the person receiving the shipment is not the person who needs the notice. Serial departments, systems departments, and everyone else who might receive or handle a product shipment must be on the alert for such notices. For services, these notices are usually sent to the billing address or the vendor's contact at the library. It is also not uncommon for vendors to replace an existing license with a totally rewritten one. Sometimes these new licenses are sent to customers and sometimes they are not. If the library is concerned about a license clause for an existing product, it is a good idea to contact the vendor to make certain the library has the newest version of a contract. On several occasions I have done this, only to find that the new license, which had not been sent to me, addressed the very issue about which I had questions.

Once the library has the contract, the next step is to read it. This is the simplest-sounding step, but the most vital. Whether the license is two or twenty pages long, read the entire thing. And when reading it, be sure to pay close attention to the definitions. One can't assume one knows what the license means when it uses common English words. They often have very different meanings in different licenses. Some of the most problematic words are "site," "organization," "campus," "remote access," "dial-in," "network," "local area network," "wide area network," "authorized user," and "affiliated." Note how the following definitions from actual contracts give clearly different interpretations of what a "site" is:

- For purposes of this agreement, "sites" are defined as locations governed by separate boards or governing bodies.
- "Authorized Site" means a single designated campus for academic institutions, and one or more offices within a single ZIP code or postal range for corporate organizations.
- Site: all facilities of Licensee within one city.

When reading a license, an understanding of the definitions is the first vital step. Once one has a clear understanding of them, it is time to examine the entire license. There are several topics that are commonly addressed in licenses and are commonly problematic. These areas, which must be closely examined, are legitimate use, users, location of use, remote access, technical considerations, terms of payment, and legal considerations.

Legitimate use is an area new license-readers may not expect to see in a license agreement. After all, one would think, we're libraries, so any product we're sold would be acceptable for library use. However, it is not uncommon for electronic product contracts to have definitions of legitimate use of the product that some libraries cannot accept. The most common legitimate use clause deals with commercial use vs. noncommercial use, with only the latter being allowed. This is not problematic for most libraries. However, some legitimate use statements also cover specialized library uses, such as interlibrary loan and cataloging. Some products have tight restrictions on printing and downloading. And some licenses put restrictions on what an organization can do with old versions of physical products, such as CD-ROMs. Some allow the library to keep and use an older version within the institution, such as at a branch library, while others require that they be destroyed or returned. And if the library cancels its subscription, it may or may not be allowed to keep the last version of the product.

The following is a typical legitimate use clause from a contract. It addresses the concern over commercial use.

- You may use the software only in the internal activities of your institution or organization . . . You may not make the software and databases available for any other use by any pass-through, loan, rental, service bureau, external time-sharing or similar arrangement.

The phrase "internal activities" is common in contracts, although a good question is what it means for libraries who allow the general public to use their resources.

The clauses below demonstrate the kinds of restrictions that licenses can put on printing and downloading. While the intention is clear and totally reasonable–the vendors want the databases to be used as searching tools, and do not want people copying significant parts or all of the databases for future use–the wording used in some licenses poses problems. Some restrictions are rather unrealistic in a library environment, while others are impossible to monitor or control. A typical contract may allow a library to:

- [M]ake a very limited number of hard copies of any search output that does not contain a significant segment of the Database which copies may be used by the customer only internally but may not be sold.
- The Licensee may print out data or copy it to a computer disk, provided that such copy is for his/her own personal use or internal corporate or institutional use only, and provided that such data is bona fide the result of searching the database with the software.
- [M]ake one copy of any search output in electronic form, i.e., diskette, hard disk, or tape to be used for editing or temporary storage only.

A very problematic section of this clause is the requirement that output be "temporary," since libraries have no way of ensuring whether users erase downloaded files or not. The clause below also addresses this, plus has some other problematic parts. For example, how can libraries keep users from sharing data, and for some common uses, such as group projects, why would they want to? However, this clause does contain a rare and appreciated exception to the commercial use prohibition relating to consulting relationships.

- Each Authorized User may view screen displays of the data . . . and may make one (1) copy per screen display of any portions of such data being viewed by that person for that person's internal or personal, noncataloging and noncommercial purposes. In addition, such copies of limited portions of such data may be transferred or sold as an incidental part to the attorney-client, consultant-client or similar relationship, or used for ordering or interlibrary lending purposes, where the principal purpose is not the distribution of data. Screen displays of such data may be electronically downloaded and temporarily stored in machine-readable form by the person so viewing the data solely as required for the person's use and/or copying of the data . . . provided that such machine-readable copies of data shall be erased after such temporary use and/or copying and shall not be transferred, shared or accessed by any other person.

Another common licensing problem area concerns users. The most problematic user issue is who is an authorized user. According to the license, who can use the product? This is a very important area in which to read the definition of "authorized user" or "legitimate user." These vary tremendously from license to license. Who would need to use the product who does not fit the definition? The general public? Alumni? Donors? Friends of the library? Retired faculty and staff? Courtesy card holders? Out-of-area card holders? Anyone not registered at the library or organization? This issue gets quite complicated if one is dealing with a consortial license, as the different libraries comprising the consortium may provide different levels of access to and use of electronic products to different groups of people. Here are some different descriptions of authorized users from actual licenses:

- Access to the Service is intended for the exclusive use of Subscriber's employees at the location(s) specified below, and such access shall not be shared with others.
- The users must be . . . either employees or registered patrons.
- If Licensee is an academic institution, then Affiliates are the registered students and faculty of the institution. If Licensee is a Public Information Service Organization, then affiliates are those individuals of the general public who utilize the information services provided by the organization (for example, public library patrons) . . . Public Information Service Organizations: public libraries, educational institutions, government agencies or nonprofit entities that provide, as one of their primary functions, no-charge public access to information.

With the first two clauses, an enormous number of typical library users are left out. The final clause begins problematically for academic libraries, but when one refers to the definition of "public information service organizations" it becomes quite reasonable.

Who counts as an "authorized" user is not the only important user issue to look for in a license. Also vital is how users are counted. For a networked product, is the library allowed a number of simultaneous users that are defined by how many are using the product at a given time, or are the users counted not by actual users, but by potential users? If the first, does the library have software capable of controlling this properly? If the second, what does "potential users" mean? If this term is used, or if the license refers to authorized or legitimate or counted "workstations," then the product is probably limited to being on a network with a limited number of workstations. For example, at the University of Houston we have a network with 104 networked terminals. If we license such a product, we have to pay for 104 potential users or workstations, even though we have software capable of limiting the actual use to any number of users we specify.

Another clause to look for is any mention of counting uses instead of users. Some services are designed with this as an up-front option. Just be clear about exactly what constitutes a "use." Is it a search? If a search is limited or refined, does that count as another use? Is a "use" every time the enter key is pressed? Does displaying, printing, or downloading a record count as a use? How about accessing the help function? And hard as it is to believe, there are a few CD-ROM products that count both simultaneous users and total uses. With these, a library has the rights to have up to a certain number of people simultaneously use the product for the length of the subscription period, but the library is also limited to a certain number of searches, prints, and/or downloads. These are monitored by the product's software, and when the library uses up its allotment, it must either stop searching, printing, and/or downloading, or pay the vendor additional money for more uses.

The third often tricky license area is the location(s) where the library can use the product. Don't assume that a library can use its new resources wherever it wants in its library or library system. Most contracts are very explicit about where a product can be located and used. The location may be defined by: a physical building or buildings; a campus with clear geographic boundaries; a campus defined not geographically but administratively; a school system; a library system; city or county boundaries; or a combination of these. A license's allowed location(s) may be too restrictive or not give a library the type of access it needs, or it may be a restriction that works well for one type of library but not for another type. If it is not acceptable, does the license provide the option of adding more locations or types of locations for an additional fee?

The different definitions of "site" noted above are good examples of varying location clauses. Below are two contract clauses that very specifically define where a product can be used. They even require specific buildings to be listed.

- Licensee may use the Product on a single user workstation or on a multi-user local-area network within the single building where the CD-ROM discs are physically located. The address of this building is . . .

- You may use the software program and databases on a multi-user network and/or optical file server at the Licensed Locations(s) specified on the reverse of this form, providing that the multi-user network and/or optical file server permits no more than the following number of users to access [the database] simultaneously in each specified building . . . You may not move the program or the database from the Licensed Location or any other location without the prior written consent of [the vendor].

In today's computing environment, many libraries want to make their electronic resources available remotely. Unfortunately, this can be a major problem area in licensing. First of all, not all licenses allow remote access. If it is allowed, the library must determine what methods of remote access are allowed (dial-in via modem, telnet, etc.). What security must be in place to insure that only authorized remote users can use the product? Does the vendor require a password system, restriction by IP address, or another means? If a password is required, are there restrictions on what methods the library can use to disseminate the password? Who are authorized remote users? They are rarely the same people who qualify as on-site authorized users. And, once all these have been determined, does remote access cost extra? Remote access fees can vary from zero to six times the annual database subscription fee. The following remote access contract sections point out some of the pitfalls:

- "Dial-In Access" means access to the Licensed Product by modem or other remote access device.

This clause makes one wonder why it's called "dial-in," a very misleading use of the phrase. These next clauses address who may use the product remotely:

- Dial-In Access from outside the Authorized Site is only permitted for Users whose primary work location is within the Authorized Site.
- [T]he Customer may provide remote access but only to employees or registered patrons who are normally physically resident at its site or to registered students who are enrolled in "distance learning" courses.

The intent of these clauses seems to be to very reasonably ensure that the whole world does not get remote access to the product, but the language used can cause problems for libraries. The first clause, for example, would be very troublesome for a public library. "Primary work location" also raises interesting questions regarding university students who also have full-time off-campus jobs, such as business people pursuing MBAs and teachers returning for advanced work. It is also not uncommon for libraries to have legitimate users, such as students, who are not registered library patrons (at least until they need to check out books). However, the note about distance education students in the second clause is much appreciated and, in today's educational environment, very necessary.

Another type of clause to be alert for deals with technical considerations. Technical concerns do not wait for when the Systems Department is ready to load a database. Clauses in the contract will determine what the library can do with a database from a technical perspective. How can the resource be mounted, loaded, or accessed? Can the software or data be adapted or changed by the organization? What are the technical options if a product will not function when installed according to the directions? And does networking or any other means of access cost extra? The following clauses show how much these issues can vary:

- The Licensee may only copy the software in accordance with the installation procedures supplied with the Product, and may not alter the software in any way.
- For the purpose of improving network performance, you may download abstract-and-index databases to hard drives on the network . . .
- The Customer may not . . . transfer the Database or the Software to hard disk unless authorized by [the vendor].

The first one forbids a library to do anything not spelled out in the installation instructions. This might be a problem if the library's computing environment requires slight adaptations to make products function properly. The last two address the same issue, but are in direct opposition. This next clause has a very restrictive, outdated definition of what an allowable network is:

- [T]he customer may provide access to the Database in a single site by means of a local area network whose terminals are physically linked together by cable within the organizational premises for up to that number of simultaneous users for whom the fee has been paid.

The following two clauses point out that a license may explicitly state that there is no guarantee that a product will work at all:

- The Licensor does not warrant that the Product will function properly in every hardware/software environment.

- [The vendor] makes no representations or warranties, expressed or implied, relating to the ability, or capacity, of your multi-user network and/or optical file server to accept the number of simultaneous users specified above, nor does [the vendor] make any warranties, expressed or implied, regarding your system's performance or response time when used by the number of simultaneous users mentioned above or any lesser number of simultaneous users.

Another area of contractual concern is more familiar to libraries: terms of payment. Not all licenses and contracts specify these, but those that do may well specify terms that are not acceptable to an institution. Does the license state when the library will be billed? When payment is due? If payment must be within a certain number of days after an event, is that event the date of invoice, receipt of invoice, or something else? Date of invoice and receipt of invoice can easily vary by two weeks, so this is an important difference. If payment is not made on time, are there late payment penalties? The following clauses are typical of payment-related specifications:

- . . . said amounts to be due and payable upon execution of this Agreement.
- . . . and Licensee agrees to provide Licensor with full payment therefore within thirty (30) days from the date of Licensor's invoice.

These are not problematic if the organization is prepared to pay upon signing license, as opposed to receiving an invoice, and the organization has no difficulty with paying within thirty days of an invoice date. If the library cannot agree to these terms, they are major problems.

Another consideration is legal in nature. Most contracts have a clause stating under what state's laws or courts a dispute relating to the contract will be settled or in which city or state arbitration will take place. The named state or city is almost always where the vendor company has its headquarters. This is not so much a question of what an individual or a library is willing to agree to, but whether this is something the organization is allowed to accept. Some institutions, usually those that are publicly supported, are required to settle all legal disputes according to the laws and in the courts of their home states. I have seen only one contract that states that disputes shall be resolved in the state or city in which the customer is located.

Depending upon the institution, there may be additional payment, procedural, and legal considerations with which one needs to be concerned. The person dealing with licenses must become as familiar as possible with the rules governing his or her organization and make sure that any contract or license conforms to them.

When the license reading process is finished, a library may want to or be required to change one or more clauses. This is the time for negotiation. A library can always try to negotiate. It may not always get what it wants, but it never hurts to try. A library will definitely not get any contract changes if it doesn't ask. The first rule of negotiating is to work with the appropriate vendor sales representative. The library should have been doing this from the beginning, so the representative is hopefully aware of any concern by this stage. Explain the library's concerns, focusing on the reasons why something is a problem instead of just repeating that it is. Explain why the library's situation means that it cannot agree to a license with the objectionable clause. Does it violate organizational policies? Does it require the library to keep one of its user groups from using the product? Would it be impossible to provide the type of remote access security specified? If the vendor understands why a clause is problematic, he or she can work with the library to find a solution. But be honest about the importance of an issue. Don't present something as a make-or-break issue if it isn't. If the clause does not get changed, and the library purchases the product anyway, it has put itself in a very bad position with that vendor. He or she will not take future concerns seriously after the library has once cried wolf.

When the library is ready to purchase or subscribe to a product or service and has agreed to a contract or license, the contract must be approved by all involved parties. If it is a signed contract, the library absolutely must get a copy of it after it has been signed. If there are changes to the contract, those must be in writing, signed by an authorized person at the vendor company. No one should ever accept license changes, additions, or questionable interpretations verbally only. There is a great deal of turnover in sales representatives. A new sales representative will not know what the previous one agreed to verbally. And if a representative is not willing to put something in writing, he or she probably does not have the authority to make that change anyway.

The experience of dealing with a product's contract or license will go smoothly at times, be problematic at others. This will partially be determined by several vendor characteristics. First is whether the vendor is the data producer, the software producer, or just the vendor. The best of all possible worlds occurs when one company plays all three roles. That kind of company has the best knowledge of the product, the greatest understanding of the license, and the authority to change the license. The process is the most difficult when all three roles are played by three different companies. Then the vendor generally has the least understanding of the product and frequently must go to one or both of the other companies to make contract changes.

The size and experience of the vendor company also makes a difference. Generally speaking, the more experience the vendor has in dealing with electronic products and the more electronic products the company handles, the greater the understanding the company has of the issues involved and the more they usually realize that not all libraries can abide by the same terms and conditions. Companies new to the electronic product field may be willing to work with libraries, but there is usually a significant learning curve involved.

In addition, vendors who focus on libraries (or the licensee's type of library) as their target market and have libraries as their usual customers are generally easier to deal with. They have a better understanding of library needs going in, and have a vested interest in learning how to work effectively with libraries or a specific type of library. Some of the most difficult companies to deal with are those that may be very large and quite experienced in electronic products, but deal primarily with the home consumer market. Not only do they not understand why some license clauses are totally inappropriate for libraries, they often have little interest in investing the time it would take to learn about the library market and make appropriate license changes. One such company I dealt with could not even refer me to a sales representative I could work with. At such companies, the sales representatives may deal exclusively with wholesale and retail companies, not actual users.

While it may be a tad depressing to contemplate the pitfalls of electronic product licensing, the point is not to discourage but to inform. Libraries need electronic products, and we need them to have acceptable licenses. Those who deal with these licenses need to know what to be alert for and what questions to ask. By going into the process with as much information–and forewarning–as possible, a library can acquire a good product governed by a good license. And if in the process a vendor learns more about libraries and what is and is not acceptable to them, the procedure should be that much easier the next time around.

Site Licenses:
A New Economic Paradigm

Rene Olivieri

SUMMARY. Over the past decades librarians have been variously outraged and resigned to budget cuts and spiralling prices, leading to the decimation of their holdings. A wholesale move to a pay-per-view pricing system or to online access over the Internet presents technical and administrative difficulties with which libraries are ill-equipped to deal at present. In short, the situation appears unstable and unsatisfactory; yet it survives in the absence of something better, such as a win-win scenario in which publishers, librarians and researchers could all benefit. *[Article copies available for a fee from The Haworth Document Delivery Service: 1-800-342-9678. E-mail address: getinfo@haworth.com]*

INTRODUCTION

What I have to say today can best be seen as signposting to a new paradigm. Like me, however, I suspect you have seen more than your share of second-rate journal articles which advertise their ephemerality by starting with 'Towards a theory of X.' Site licenses are not a new phenomenon. They have been with us for a long time in other contexts; it is only in the serials environment that they can be considered a relatively new phenomenon. Indeed, I would argue we can learn much from examining the experiences of the software industry.

Rene Olivieri is affiliated with Blackwell Publishers.

[Haworth co-indexing entry note]: "Site Licenses: A New Economic Paradigm." Olivieri, Rene. Co-published simultaneously in *The Serials Librarian* (The Haworth Press, Inc.) Vol. 30, No. 3/4, 1997, pp. 183-190; and: *Pioneering New Serials Frontiers: From Petroglyphs to Cyberserials* (ed: Christine Christiansen and Cecilia Leathem) The Haworth Press, Inc., 1997, pp. 183-190. Single or multiple copies of this article are available for a fee from The Haworth Document Delivery Service [1-800-342-9678, 9:00 a.m. - 5:00 p.m. (EST). E-mail address: getinfo@haworth.com].

Today I will try to put the site license in its proper context. In the first instance I will deal with the economic background that has made site licenses a possible way out of the current vicious cycle of price rises and subscription decline. I will then try to build an economic model to show what's happening. I will next talk about how that model is effected by technical change. At that point I'll come back to site licenses relating them to this model. I will talk about the UK site license scheme in general terms; and, finally, I will give you some arguments for the necessity as well as the desirability of site licenses.

THE REAL PROBLEMS ARE LEGAL AND COMMERCIAL NOT TECHNICAL ONES

Site licenses are just one of the ways of getting a better deal for consumers. Their advantages are greater in electronic formats, but you can have a site license for a hard copy format as well. Indeed, this goes to the heart of the first fundamental point I would like to make. The real problems today are not technological but commercial and legal.

What the UK site license scheme does is test the commercial and institutional viability of doing things differently. Electronic versions make site licenses more valuable and add a new dimension which I will address in a moment. However, you can have a site license to a hard copy journal and the economic and organizational benefits of licensing versus copyright should not be ignored. The point is that the real issues are not about electronic delivery; they are about copyright and value for money.

Many Internet enthusiasts believe that information should be free. I take it as a given that no good is ever free for very long. Where are we headed as far as intellectual property rights are concerned? What will governments do? Will they want to defend intellectual property rights? To answer these questions let's turn briefly to the American White Paper which was produced by a federal panel, called the Working Group in Intellectual Property Rights. The fact that it is chaired by the Assistant Secretary of Commerce might give us a clue as to its leanings. In brief, the Paper comes down squarely on the side of commercial exploitation. It recommends the minimum adjustment possible to existing law. Furthermore, one of the most interesting suggestions coming from the White Paper is that copying devices designed to break the law, to allow unauthorized copying, should be made illegal themselves.

Why this unequivocal support for commercial exploitation? Cynics might say it's because governments are in the pockets of big business, and I do not mean academic publishers. Far more important than academic

TABLE 1. The Average Cost of a Periodical

	1989	1994
HUMANITIES AND SOCIAL SCIENCE	£ 51	£ 88
MEDICINE	£ 124	£ 226
SCIENCE AND TECHNOLOGY	£ 214	£ 403
AVERAGE GREAT BRITAIN	£ 115	£ 214
AVERAGE US AND CANADA	£ 147	£ 266

(NOTE that amounts are in Pounds)
SOURCE: British Library Research and Development Department

research are the entertainment and software industries. Others might see the marketplace as the only alternative to government sponsorship and control. Is it realistic to expect government to intervene when everywhere else it is pulling back from interference in the economy? A more straight-forward explanation is that where there is commercial activity, there are taxes to be paid.

Many who are dissatisfied with the current copyright system are not looking for gradual change but for revolution. By holding themselves aloof from the system, trying to overthrow it rather than work within it to effect change, they are actually helping to sustain a commercial environment which is doing a very poor job of satisfying its customers.

The figures cited in Table 1 are by now a familiar story. With more titles being published, prices are rising at rates well above inflation. Library budgets have been capped and are declining in real terms. Money that used to be spent on books is now being spent on journals. Money that used to be spent on the social sciences and humanities is getting siphoned off to pay for ever more expensive science publications. Note the differences in prices by category. There is no reason that the average science journal should cost four times its social science and humanities counterpart.

THE VICIOUS CYCLE OF RISING PRICES AND DECREASING USAGE

As a publisher, I cannot believe that it is good for a business to see the increase in its revenues coming from an increase in prices ahead of inflation. A lot more is being published but the average customer has access to a decreasing proportion of that growing pool of knowledge. This is not a very healthy picture for publishers or their customers or for the industries–

learning and research–which they both ostensibly support, especially when the prices of electronic media appear to be dropping.

We publishers are chasing our tails. With each drop in unit sales we try to recover the gross margin and satisfy the imperative for profit growth with a rise in prices. The questions we must ask ourselves are: "Is this a self-fulfilling prophecy?" "Are we selling fewer units because the demand is falling or because prices are rising?" "What is cause, what is effect?"

ECONOMICS

The traditional economic model of supply and demand holds that as price goes down demand goes up, the relationship is inversely related. Where demand and supply curves intersect is the so-called equilibrium point where a deal should be struck, a market made. Of course, this assumes that the customer does not have to buy the product, and that they have a choice between competing products.

Academic journal publishing differs from the traditional economic model in that there exists what is called inelasticity of demand. Demand is more or less fixed and does not fall with a rise in price. The equilibrium point shifts as publishers scrabble to take advantage of this 'sticky' demand by raising prices and thereby revenues. In a truly competitive market, you might expect demand to decline roughly in proportion to the price increase, leaving the publisher with the same revenues. Here the publishers can raise revenues, just by raising prices, at the customer's expense, of course. Moreover, if one publisher starts this trend and gets away with it, other publishers follow suit to avoid losing market share.

In traditional publishing we know that there are fixed costs, what you spend to make the first or 'camera' copy, and variable costs, what you spend to physically manufacture each unit. With longer print-runs the average manufacturing cost declines gradually but flattens out, as does the proportion of fixed costs in each unit. As volume declines, the proportion of fixed costs in total costs increases; publishers lose economies of scale.

In electronic publishing the origination costs may well be higher but the cost of replicating the camera-copy is much less. The average unit costs fall more quickly than in traditional publishing. Economic theory predicts that in a truly competitive market the selling price will eventually end up somewhere close to the marginal cost of production. In the case of the electronic format this should be well below the traditional price and close to zero. If a customer wants both the hardcopy and the electronic versions, the two together are going to cost slightly more than either separately.

In a fully electronic environment, the cost of satisfying each additional customer falls off rapidly.

The implications are:

1. To the extent that there are additional unsatisfied customers out there, their demands can be met even if these customers are price sensitive. The trick is for the publisher to distinguish between the essential and nonessential purchase.
2. Another way to look at it is that, once the master has been created, once the camera-copy has been prepared, it costs almost the same to satisfy 20,000 customers as it does 200. So, in theory, publishers would be no worse off if they gave all their titles to all their customers in electronic formats. Of course, the consumers would be incomparably better off.

I have tried to explain in economic terms how publishers can turn the current system on its head, lowering prices and giving customers better value for their money. The site license makes theoretical sense of this analysis. It is a kind of bulk deal which takes advantage of economies of scale. It also has lots of practical advantages to recommend it. Please note that I realize that in the electronic environment some other costs to libraries, particularly work stations, hardware, and training, may increase.

ADVANTAGES OF SITE LICENSES

Empowerment–Fair use and copyright are fuzzy and subject to national and international law. In contrast, it only takes two 'consenting adults' to make a contract. Psychologically it can be liberating not to think you have to pay each time you use something.

One Transaction–The purchase price and/or subscription fee eliminates transaction or monitoring costs.

Apparent Fairness–Electronic site licenses can be geared to the technological infrastructure and the size of the customer's universe. If copyright is 'one size fits all,' contracts can be tailor-made. This should help the 'little guy.' At present a journal/book costs the same to a university with 20,000 students, 10,000 PCs and 20 sites as to an institution a tenth of that size. There is nothing to stop the smaller institutions from banding together to get better terms and increase their holdings where none might have existed before.

Reproducible Models–Publishers are used to managing with lots of slightly different contracts already; they are called authors' agreements. Some may worry that the cost of negotiating each sale will be too high. Models will emerge, I predict, to make this easier.

Precedents–Models for rights/pricing already exist in the software industry which we can draw on.

Predictability–The budgetary infrastructure to deal with site licenses already exists within institutions. People do not have to worry about overspending. This is the way most institutions are already set up; it does not require massive re-engineering.

Renewability–If publishers can rely on a continuing income stream they will provide better support and ongoing development.

NATIONAL SITE LICENSE FOR GREAT BRITAIN

Higher education in the UK is financed by the central government. As of yet there are no tuition fees. The Higher Education Funding Councils for England, Scotland, Wales and Northern Ireland have a budget in the billions. They have allocated substantial sums of money for specific innovative projects. One of these is a site licensing scheme for journals.

The pilot involves three publishers over three years and affects 220 institutions. The three publishers are: Academic, the Institute of Physics, and Blackwell Publishing. The scheme for each publisher is slightly different. In the Blackwell case, the councils provide a subsidy which means we are now worse off than we were before. But the libraries get three things which make them better off:

1. Hardcopy for 60% of the UK hardcopy subscription price.
2. Electronic versions where available. (By next year this means our entire list.)
3. Unlimited copying privileges for all members of their institution in both hardcopy and electronic versions, including photocopying for course packs.

The purpose of the scheme is to provide better value for money, to enable institutions to both buy more and use what they buy more freely. It is not primarily about electronic delivery. That's a means to an end, not the end itself. Consequently, the measure of success will be if material is more readily accessed and copied and if the unit price of consumption falls.

OPEN QUESTIONS

Getting the packaging and pricing right is difficult, but this is always the case. Experience and negotiation are the best guides. Customers often can't tell a producer exactly what they want until they see a prototype.

There is also the problem that in the short run we will still have to deliver hardcopy and electronic copy to most libraries so there are not the dramatic costs savings you get from purely electronic reproduction and delivery.

There is concern that decision-making will become more centralized. In my view, collaborative bargaining is already emerging and will give the consumer greater power in the relationship with producers.

There is a genuine concern that societies will lose their members if the journals they publish are available electronically on a campus network. Societies will have to think hard about the individual's needs and concerns and offer new services to keep them on board.

And of course, there is real concern that publishers will get librarians to pay by the bushel-load. A site license price unrelated to usage but just to the number of titles or articles will simply encourage publishers to push out more titles and accept more articles, fueling the information explosion and doing nothing to ease the financial strain on libraries.

WHY SITE LICENSES ARE INEVITABLE

- Because we are making little headway on the copyright side. When they are talking something as global as copyright law, publishers are going to take the most conservative position. If they are making a deal with the University of Keele, they may take a more relaxed view of 'fair use,' knowing it's not opening up floodgates world wide.
- Because the customers I have talked to think, given that information is not going to become a free good tomorrow, site licenses are the lesser of three evils, with the current system and some form of 'pay per view' being alternatives.
- Most importantly, I think once a few publishers have taken the plunge and are succeeding in getting their stuff much more widely available thanks to site licenses, other publishers will be forced to follow suit, or risk losing the best articles to others. They will not stand by and watch other publishers employ site licenses as a tool for gaining competitive advantage.

THE VIRTUOUS CYCLE OF FALLING COSTS AND GREATER ACCESS

From the dynamic just stated, I see a virtuous cycle replacing the vicious one. The publisher using site licenses will be:

- pricing to encourage use, and subscriptions
- allowing much freer use and distribution of their titles
- thereby gaining more readers because of the increased availability
- which in turn will lead to more citations and a higher profile
- which in turn should lead to more and better submissions
- which in turn will gain more readers.

CONCLUSION

Site licenses are not a panacea. Customers' needs are different. The models of the future for delivering information will be a mixture of pay per use, site licenses, individual document delivery, etc. What I am suggesting is that a world where consumers are better off is within our grasp and does not require major structural change but practical problem solving and negotiation. Radical change, 'revolutions,' occur not just because things are bad, but because people have an expectation that things should be better. Unfortunately, revolutions do not always bring about the results desired by their instigators. I have tried today to acknowledge that the expectations of librarians are not unreasonable, that they deserve better than they are getting, that there is a peaceful way out of our current predicament, if we as producers and consumers—publishers and librarians—will only seize it.

CONCURRENT SESSION V: THE CIC ELECTRONIC JOURNALS COLLECTION PROJECT

The CIC Electronic Journals Collection Project

Bonnie MacEwan
Mira Geffner

SUMMARY. The Committee on Inter-institutional Cooperation (CIC) is an academic consortium of thirteen large research institutions in the midwest with its own regional network, CICNet. The CIC libraries and CICNet are building a managed electronic journal collection out of the content and collection experience of the CICNet E_Serials Archive–a collection of over 800 freely distributed electronic serials. The libraries have developed and endorsed a broad collecting policy for the new collection, the CIC Libraries Electronic Journal Collec-

Bonnie MacEwan is Collection Development Coordinator, Pennsylvania State University Libraries.

Mira Geffner is Project Manager, CIC Electronic Journals Collection.

[Haworth co-indexing entry note]: "The CIC Electronic Journals Collection Project." MacEwan, Bonnie, and Mira Geffner. Co-published simultaneously in *The Serials Librarian* (The Haworth Press, Inc.) Vol. 31, No. 1/2, 1997, pp. 191-203; and: *Pioneering New Serials Frontiers: From Petroglyphs to Cyberserials* (ed: Christine Christiansen and Cecilia Leathem) The Haworth Press, Inc., 1997, pp. 191-203. Single or multiple copies of this article are available for a fee from The Haworth Document Delivery Service [1-800-342-9678, 9:00 a.m. - 5:00 p.m. (EST). E-mail address: getinfo@haworth.com].

tion (CIC EJC). CIC Librarians are selecting a complete, authoritative and permanent collection of electronic journals to be shared by the CIC libraries. The collection will be actively managed, cataloged and maintained by CIC libraries and CICNet staff. Some titles from the E-Serials Archive are being selected for the EJC, and many new journals are being included as well. Catalogers from six CIC institutions are creating bibliographic records for each selected title. The records will be entered into OCLC and made available to each CIC library's online catalog. This paper focuses on the specific problems encountered in creating the managed collection: locating all issues of each title, cataloging the collection, providing access and managing the collection as a long-term cooperative resource for all the CIC-libraries, and making it accessible to the scholarly research community at large. *[Article copies available for a fee from The Haworth Document Delivery Service: 1-800-342-9678. E-mail address: getinfo@haworth.com]*

INTRODUCTION

The Committee on Institutional Cooperation (CIC) libraries are presently engaged in collaborative development of the largest, fully managed collection of electronic journals available on the Internet. The CIC Electronic Journals Collection (CIC EJC) is online now in prototype form, with 49 titles included in the collection. This project directly addresses the growing need to develop, test, and implement networked information tools and resources which utilize collaborative, multi-institutional efforts. In this paper, we will describe the CIC, the consortial context in which the EJC has developed, and we will outline the development of the EJC, including the history of the collection, its current status and our plans for its future. We will also touch upon the role this project could play in the developing future of scholarly communication.

The EJC emphasizes the role that a large consortium of major universities can play in building electronic resources. The collection can demonstrate the potential of collaborative work, the impact that changing patterns of scholarly communication can have on these institutions, and their role and responsibility in taking leadership in shaping those changes. These institutions take seriously the opportunity and obligation they have to experiment with new ways of acquiring and distributing digital information and the technologies that make this distribution possible. Much of our work in adjusting to and developing new uses for information technology has centered on defining the roles of technologists and librarians in managing information. Librarians have needed to engage technologists in the development of access tools that enable scholarly use of electronic information, and similarly, technologists have relied on librarians' experience with organization of information.

WHAT IS THE CIC?

CIC stands for the Committee on Institutional Cooperation, a 35-year old consortium which now unites the University of Chicago, the University of Illinois, the University of Illinois at Chicago, Indiana University, the University of Iowa, the University of Michigan, Michigan State University, the University of Minnesota, Pennsylvania State University, Purdue University, Ohio State University, Northwestern University and University of Wisconsin-Madison. Today, there are over 75 distinct cooperative activities operating under the aegis of the CIC.

The CIC is comprised of the provosts of these 13 universities, who meet four times annually. The office of the CIC is currently located at Champaign-Urbana. It is professionally staffed, with a director and 9 FTEs. Its current operating budget is slightly in excess of $4 million. In order to understand the context of this paper, it is important to emphasize that there is core financial backing to the philosophical concept of the Committee on Institutional Cooperation Additional funding, from member dues, research grants, and the usual host of other sources, exists for most of the initiatives which have evolved under the umbrella of the office of the CIC.

Collectively, the CIC universities account for more than 17% of the Ph.D.s awarded annually in the United States, approximately 20% of all science and engineering Ph.D.s, in excess of $2.5 billion in externally funded research annually, and over 17% of the holdings of the Association of Research Libraries. They represent an aggregate total in excess of 500,000 students, 33,000 faculty, and 60 million volumes within their libraries.

Like all the nation's major institutions of higher education, the CIC universities depend on the availability of reliable, high quality resources of all kinds, ranging from those available through their libraries and faculties to the most advanced technologies in their laboratories, computing environments, and related teaching and research facilities. The many initiatives within the CIC which depend on a reliable and advanced networked infrastructure and on staff, facility and financial investments focused on true programmatic cooperation make the CIC unique. Collaborative initiatives which require stable inter-institutional technical standards and support mechanisms have evolved over the life of the consortium, increasing the availability of shared, reliable information resources and services. There are now some initiatives which might not be possible without such infrastructures.

The CIC is governed by its three founding principles:

1. That no single institution can or should attempt to be all things to all people;
2. That inter-institutional cooperation permits educational experimentation and progress on a scale beyond the capability of any single institution acting alone, and;
3. That voluntary cooperation fosters effective, concerted action while preserving institutional autonomy and diversity.

These principles are critical to the successes of our programs. Among consortia, the nature of the CIC institutions' collaboration is outstanding: individually these are some of the most competitive institutions of higher learning in this country. They are driven by different missions, governed by separate boards and obtain their funding from a variety of separate sources. They are all clearly autonomous organizations with no central funding or administrative body. Further, each of these universities has unparalleled academic and research programs in a variety of fields; they sometimes compete fiercely for funding, students and stature. Yet, cooperatively, they have been able to become an impressive force in higher education.

CIC OFFICES: COORDINATION AND LEADERSHIP

Two offices which have evolved under the umbrella of the CIC are CICNet, Incorporated and the CIC Center for Library Initiatives.

CICNet, the regional TCP/IP network founded by the CIC in 1988, serves the Internetworking needs of the CIC universities, other academic institutions, not-for-profit organizations, and businesses. CICNet has had a strong interest in the design and deployment of networked information services, and is currently involved in several major National Science Foundation-funded projects to provide networking and online services to educational projects in the Great Lakes region. Funding for CICNet is primarily from three sources: the National Science Foundation, commercial activities, and the member institutions including the universities of the CIC.

The CIC Center for Library Initiatives (CLI) was established in September 1994, to support collaborative efforts specifically among the CIC libraries. Cooperative resource sharing has long been a practice among the CIC libraries, and the CIC has an enviable record of successfully funded R&D projects. Most notably, the CIC libraries are now engaged in a Virtual Electronic Library (VEL) project, funded through a United States

Department of Education grant. The VEL project will develop the technical infrastructure required to provide seamless interconnections among a range of OPAC systems within the CIC libraries, and demonstrate its applications through user-initiated interlibrary loans and document delivery throughout the CIC. The VEL will enable more than one-half million faculty, staff, and students to explore and take advantage of the vast resources within the CIC. Inherent to the VEL project is the addition of an expanded set of electronic resources to the VEL pool. The Electronic Journal Collection is a key piece in the plans to build this collection of electronic resources.

The general framework for collaboration lies in the strong support at the highest levels of member university administration as evidenced by the existence of the funded office of the Committee on Institutional Cooperation and its subsidiaries. Relevant initiatives in support of the missions of the member universities flow from within this framework. The CIC Electronic Journals Collection is one such case, involving the CIC Center for Library Initiatives and CICNet, Inc.

PROJECT BACKGROUND

The CIC Electronic Journals Collection has its roots in the CIC libraries' and CICNet's early work with electronic serials. In 1991, the CIC Collection Development Officers asked CICNet to create an archive of the freely redistributable electronic journals many of them had begun to collect locally but had no long-term means of archiving. CICNet went beyond this original charge: archiving e-journals available at CIC member institutions, and sweeping the Internet to collect all e-journals that could be obtained through mirroring, an automated FTP process. The CICNet E-Serials Archive represented an early effort to provide the CIC library community with collaborative access to electronic serials. Establishment of the CICNet E-Serials Archive also coincided with widespread implementation of Gopher, which CICNet used to provide access to the archive. The archive was an undifferentiated collection of some 800 titles in varying depths of retrospective coverage and completeness, housed on a CICNet server. At the peak of its usage it was accessed 35,000 times daily by Internet users.

The automated collection process we used for the E-Serials Archive was valuable in illustrating the range of materials available, but it soon became clear that no entirely automated process could produce a collection that would satisfy the needs of most scholars. We could only use the mirroring process to gather those items available on FTP servers. Since many new electronic journals are published via Gopher and World Wide Web servers, the collection has become incomplete and out-of-date as result of these technological changes. Additionally we have learned that it is not possible to build an academically useful collection of electronic materials without librarian and technical support staff managing the collection. An uncataloged, unsearchable collection like the E-Serials Archive, whose contents were not examined regularly by collection staff, could not be of widespread, long-term or consistent value to scholars because it offered no assurance that the collection is complete, current and worthy of preservation.

The E-Serials Archive is no longer available to the public although it has been preserved on tape for researchers interested in the development of online resources. The Archive is best thought of as a snapshot of materials available at a particular time in the history of the Internet rather than a comprehensive resource, but the frequency of its use clearly indicated the need for a reliably managed collection of e-journals.

The content management issues described above challenged us to move from the automated collections process of the E-Serials Archive to the EJC model. Answering the questions raised in the transition from a relatively unmanaged collection to a fully managed one has presented technical development problems for the collection managers. Building and maintaining a full archive of electronic serials require new and innovative uses of Internet technology as publication of e-serials shifts from FTP to Gopher to HTTP. The advanced formatting and more labor-intensive file transfer of Gopher and the World Wide Web demand a more sophisticated and responsive approach. Archiving materials on the World Wide Web requires more intelligent tools than the mirroring jobs CICNet ran to collect the e-serials.

To address all these issues, the Task Force on the CIC Electronic Collection was charged by the CIC Library Directors to explore the management and use of shared electronic resources and to consider relevant issues for the CIC libraries including specific recommendations on collection policy, organization, bibliographic control, and access policies for electronic journals and full-text electronic collections. The Task Force responded with a complete plan for building a managed electronic journal collection, the CIC-EJC. The Task Force, which includes representation both from CICNet and the CIC libraries, planned the collection from selection to maintenance. This process identified key areas of collection management: selecting an interface (WWW), cataloging, publisher contact, and archiving. CICNet staff then developed a prototype system based on the recommendations and input from the Task Force. The prototype system is available on the World Wide Web at http://ejournals.cic.net/ as an illustration of the collection the CIC university librarians and the CIC-Net staff plan to build.

WORLD WIDE WEB FRONT END

The collection opens to a descriptive World Wide Web home page which provides subject, title and keyword searching; the ability to view titles in the collection listed either alphabetically or by subject; and bibliographic records for all titles in the collection including hotlinks to the originating journal servers. From these hotlinks, the user can move directly to the electronic journal. The EJC's links and holdings records are updated weekly.

CATALOGING

Six CIC universities participate in the collaborative cataloging of the journals held in the CIC EJC. The cataloging libraries are: Indiana University, University of Michigan, University of Wisconsin-Madison, Ohio State University, University of Illinois at Chicago, and University of Minnesota. All titles are cataloged in MARC format, using the new 856 field. Records are then contributed to OCLC (the CIC symbol is YNT) and to the CIC OPACs. CIC universities with local systems capable of using the 856 field can hotlink directly to the journals through the OPACs. Users then have the option of the serendipitous search afforded by the collection as a whole, or simply moving directly to the title of interest. The bibliographic records currently appearing in the collection are improvised, and will be replaced with MARC records once we have a critical mass to load from OCLC.

PUBLISHER CONTACT

Access to all journals in the collection is provided by pointing directly to the publisher's site. CICNet staff contact each publisher for prior approval before any journal is added to the collection. This initial contact is important in building publisher/library relationships and in maintaining user confidence in the site.

ARCHIVING

Pointing directly to the publisher's site ensures that users see the publications exactly as intended, but does not ensure a permanent record of the publications. Therefore, CICNet is also building a full archive of all the titles in the collection. The titles are presently stored on a disk and backed up to tape weekly. This archiving process is being discussed and reviewed by the CIC Task Force on Preservation and Digital Technology, in concert with CICNet technologists, in order to identify a long-term archiving solution. The archive is intended to serve as a permanent record, to be used in the event the original site is discontinued; therefore, the archive is not available as a "public site." This model is consistent with traditional archiving efforts, in which (for instance) original microform copies are stored, with public access provided through copies. The CIC is committed to planning and implementing long-term preservation of these materials while the distributed model of viewing the collection contents through links provides for ready access.

We hope that our work will serve as a model for individuals and organizations wanting to create similar repositories of electronic information on the Internet. Our effort to engage both technologists and librarians in building and professionally managing this collection is especially useful. We will identify and document those areas where librarians can contribute to the increasingly difficult task of managing Internet resources, while technologists design sophisticated access, retrieval, and archiving tools and processes. To this end we are fully documenting the development process and making this documentation available via the World Wide Web. There is initial technical documentation about the collection available at http://ejournals.cic.net/ej.doc.html. We invite comments, questions and criticism from any interested parties including electronic publishers, librarians, patrons and authors.

FUTURE PLANS

Our long-term goal is to create a significant collection of public domain electronic journals on the Internet, which will provide access via the World Wide Web to scholars, libraries, and individuals around the world. All of the journals in the collection today are free and in the public domain. In the future we plan to work with publishers and authors in the important areas of distribution, use, copyright and security for titles distributed by paid subscription or license.

The CIC also plans to begin running a Persistent URL (PURL) server, using the new OCLC software for maintaining consistent URLs. The PURL server is OCLC's implementation in response to the URN discussions.

CONSORTIAL WORK:
BUILDING PROCESSES FOR COLLABORATIVE EFFORTS

There are tremendous benefits in shared expertise, material resources and time to be gained from collaborative efforts in journal management.

Sharing these resources requires an initial investment in working out the approach and methodology. Because the EJC is run consortially from selection to cataloging to providing access and archiving, the project provides the CIC with an opportunity to build and demonstrate success with this level of cooperation. However, it should be noted that cooperation on this level requires a significant investment of time and resources. It is essential to build a common knowledge base and to spend the time necessary to work toward agreed-upon procedures and approaches. Descriptions of the various working groups and copies of their reports can be found on the CIC web site, http://cedar.cic.net/cic/.

The Task Force on the CIC Electronic Collection has laid out a collaborative acquisition process for all electronic library resources acquired by the CIC as a consortium (additional information can be found at the CIC website). As selectors from the individual universities request materials, they use an established procedure to survey their CIC colleagues for interest in collective buy-in and to put forth a formal proposal. The CIC Center for Library Initiatives takes the lead in negotiating with vendors and facilitating the process. Each step in the process is recorded on the CIC Web server so that all participants can easily check on the status of the various projects and so that each step is carefully tracked as it works its way through the complexity of consortial action.

The level of consortial activity needed to build the EJC and other aspects of the electronic collection is quite complex. Each institution has a unique organizational structure and decision-making style. Because there is no common position at each institution to whom the responsibility would naturally fall for seeing through the local review of each proposal, the Task Force on the CIC Electronic Collection requested that each library director appoint an Electronic Resources Officer specifically charged with this responsibility. The need for this assigned responsibility was identified through experience and was not obvious at the beginning of our efforts.

Similarly, the participating cataloging institutions are sharing training and expertise in electronic resources cataloging through their joint work on the EJC.

WHO IS IT FOR?
CHANGES IN SCHOLARLY COMMUNICATION

There is little doubt that the nature of the scholarly journal is changing. What we don't know is what the future of this kind of communication will look like. There are many interests in shaping this future–scholars, librarians, academic presses, commercial presses, academic associations, and even copyright lawyers are just a few with a strong interest in the future of the scholarly journal. The EJC is an attempt to mesh traditional library support for scholarly communication with the changing nature of that communication. Some of these issues are explored in a recent book published by the Association of Research Libraries, *Scholarly Journals at the Crossroads: A Subversive Proposal for Electronic Publishing.*

The subversive proposal in question was posted by Stevan Harnad, then of the Princeton University Cognitive Science Laboratory, and refers to an idea he posted to the electronic libraries discussion list VPIEJ-L. Harnad suggests that for esoteric scholarly publication (those works whose authors wish only to reach an audience of their peers and not to make any money from their publication), the most effective approach is for individual authors to publish freely on the Internet and make their works available via public FTP. Harnad argues that paper publishing interferes with the rapid communication of esoteric (no market) scholarship.

Charles Hamaker in a recent article in the *Newsletter on Serials Pricing Issues* was equally provocative. His research suggests that it may be more cost effective in many cases for libraries to purchase individual articles from document suppliers rather than maintain costly subscriptions. His research and conclusions go further and even suggest that it may be a disservice to our users to continue these expensive titles, since he discovered in a number of cases the investment in these resources had been an impediment to acquiring the titles actually used by local scholars. Both of these works and many more suggest that the nature of the journal as the primary means of delivering scholarly information, particularly scientific information, is changing.

Just as there are many interests in the future of scholarly communication, there are many models available for the publication and distribution of scholarly material online. One example is Paul Ginsparg's High Energy Physics pre-print server which began as a means of supporting pre-print publication by providing a centralized server and technical support. Scholars can use e-mail to access and read preprints, and to publish their work. Although providing preprints in this way lacks many of the features of an established refereed journal, Ginsparg has described this project as supporting the lowest common denominator—the necessary underpinning for raising the level of quality of electronic publication across the board. Ginsparg's service is supported by the National Science Foundation and the University of California and is free to the scientific community.

Several professional societies and publishers who support their activities to some degree with subscriptions are also entering the Internet arena.

The American Mathematical Society charges subscriptions for its print publications, and publishes the *Bulletin of the American Mathematical Society* online free of charge; the Association for Computing Machinery follows this model as well. Other online publications like *Matrix News* publish only electronically, and charge subscription fees for their online publications.

We believe that the CIC should play a role in this changing environment and that the EJC should provide an opportunity for us to experiment and build a knowledge and resource base from which to play this role.

The CIC is uniquely positioned to deliver a high level of access and management to scholarly journals. The CIC's consortial work gives it a level of collective resolve that can be used to build and complete a project of this scope. The combined strength of the CIC institutions' faculties, collections, etc., positions us to be in the forefront of shaping this aspect of the future of scholarly communication. The CIC has both the opportunity and the obligation to use its strengths to be among the first experimenters with this sort of technology. Once the EJC is fully operational we will be able to explore these and other issues.

A VITAL COLLABORATION: THE CHIEF INFORMATION OFFICERS AND LIBRARIANS

If we have learned anything through our efforts it is that collaboration must occur locally and at the consortial level. One collaboration that is essential is between librarians and information technologists. Much is to be gained locally, consortially, and for the information world as a whole by bringing together the expertise of the CIC librarians and technologists. On some campuses this is already a thriving and healthy relationship (in fact on at least one campus the library director and CIO is the same person), on others the work to build this relationship on the local level is just beginning. At the same time efforts are underway to bring the CIC CIOs and librarians together as a group and to build a working relationship between both groups and the CICNet technologists.

In March of this year, the Task Force on the CIC Electronic Collection organized a meeting between the Library Directors and the Chief Information Officers to explore networking and computing needs associated with major electronic text projects. The meeting was held on the University of Michigan campus and centered on presentations of the University of Michigan Digital Library, TULIP, JSTOR and the Humanities Text Initiative. The purpose of the conference was to talk about the specific requirements of transmitting and presenting information of various sorts—text images, visual images, encoded text and metadata. Both the CIOs and Library Directors came away with a clearer understanding of the level of communication that needs to happen both consortially among resource sharers and locally between resource and access providers. This meeting is only one example of the many discussions and meetings we need to have to get the job done.

This is a necessary working relationship because Internet technology is increasingly the preferred medium of scholarly communication and publication. However, the promise of the new technology won't be fulfilled without the skills in selection, content management, archiving, and organization of information brought by the librarians. At the same time it is clear to the librarians that they need the skills of the technologists to identify and build the technological tools to fully exploit and access the vast and varied information resources needed by library users.

CONCLUSION

The EJC project was developed as a response to an identified need on the part of several CIC libraries. As they began to collect public domain electronic journals the complex issues around collecting, making accessible and maintaining these collections quickly became obvious. It also seemed obvious that the solutions to these problems would have to be replicated at each institution as they began to collect and make available these resources. The EJC was developed as a response to the need for the CIC libraries to approach this new challenge with the technology and expertise available from CICNet, Inc. Although the project is a response to the needs of the members of the CIC it is clear that it has implications far beyond the consortium.

The EJC is an opportunity for the CIC Libraries and CICNet to work together to create the solutions needed by all libraries to the challenges created by emerging changes in information. The vast resources and skills of the technologists and librarians in the two organizations allow for experimentation, and exploration that might be beyond the resources available in the individual institutions or outside the consortium. In this sense the EJC can serve as a research project with the information learned of benefit to all of the member institutions and to everyone interested in the changing nature of scholarly communication.

Of course the EJC is more than a research project, it is also a product with the concrete goal of meeting the information needs of scholars at the thirteen member institutions. Mechanisms for selection are in place to ensure that the collection will reflect the information needs at each of the institutions. However, it is our expectation that a collection sufficiently varied and rich to meet the needs of the many scholars of the CIC institutions will also be useful to libraries which either lack the resources or choose not to develop local resources.

BIBLIOGRAPHY

Ginsparg, Paul H. "@XXX.lanl.gov: First Steps Toward Electronic Research Communication," Los Alamos Science 22:156-165 (1994).

Hamaker, Charles. "Access vs. Ownership at LSU: Response to Dana Roth in No. 153," *Newsletter on Serials Pricing Issues* 154 (February 12, 1996). http://sunsite.unc.edu/reference/prices/1996/PRIC154.HTML#154.1

Lewin, David I. "An Interview with Paul Ginsparg: How a Physicist Helped to Launch a Revolution," *Computers in Physics,* 10:6-7 (January/February 1996).

Okerson, Ann (editor). *Filling the Pipeline and Paying the Piper: Proceedings of the Fourth Symposium.* Washington, DC, Association of Research Libraries, Office of Scientific & Academic Publishing, 1995.

Okerson, Ann and James O'Donnel (editors). *Scholarly Journals at the Crossroads: A Subversive Proposal for Electronic Publishing.* Washington, DC, Association of Research Libraries, Office of Scientific & Academic Publishing, 1995.

Taubes, Gary. "Electronic Preprints Point the Way to 'Author Empowerment,'" *Science* 271;767-768 (February 9, 1996).

CONCURRENT SESSION VI: THE GREAT DEBATE OVER COPYRIGHT IN THE ELECTRONIC ENVIRONMENT

The Great Copyright Debate: Electronic Publishing Is Not Print Publishing–Vive la Différence

Carol A. Risher

SUMMARY. This session focused on new electronic publishing models and demonstrated how they differ from print models. Copyright protection for electronic publishing and how the library and fair use exemptions should be applied were also explored. As publishing changes, the impact of the law also changes. To try to fit old concepts on new models creates tensions and conflicts. Perhaps when people realize that the information model is different, they will also understand the need for different patterns and practices of behavior. *[Article copies available for a fee from The Haworth Document Delivery Service: 1-800-342-9678. E-mail address: getinfo@haworth.com]*

Carol A. Risher is Vice President for Copyright and New Technology, Association of American Publishers.

[Haworth co-indexing entry note]: "The Great Copyright Debate: Electronic Publishing Is Not Print Publishing–Vive la Différence." Risher, Carol A. Co-published simultaneously in *The Serials Librarian* (The Haworth Press, Inc.) Vol. 31, No. 1/2, 1997, pp. 205-210; and: *Pioneering New Serials Frontiers: From Petroglyphs to Cyberserials* (ed: Christine Christiansen and Cecilia Leathem) The Haworth Press, Inc., 1997, pp. 205-210. Single or multiple copies of this article are available for a fee from The Haworth Document Delivery Service [1-800-342-9678, 9:00 a.m. - 5:00 p.m. (EST). E-mail address: getinfo@haworth.com].

The theme of this eleventh NASIG Conference–"Pioneering New Serials Frontiers: From Petroglyphs to Cyberserials"–is not that different from the theme for next year's twelfth NASIG conference–"Experimentation and Collaboration: Creating Serials for a New Millennium." The papers and speeches will be different but only because every day we are pioneering new frontiers as we all live through an incredible transition period. It is this transition period that underlies our concerns and our enthusiasm for the new millennium.

Serials publishers and serials librarians (as well as all publishers and all librarians) are being forced to reinvent ourselves "on the fly," "as we go," and without a clear idea of when we will reach a place where we can slow down and take stock. The changes affecting us all are advances in computer technology, communications technology, information delivery, information formats, and the educational process. The changes are also driven by many different forces. What I'd like to do today is sketch out a few of the changes we are being asked to address and then focus on the ongoing Conference on Fair Use–CONFU (in which both Laura Gasaway and I are participants) because the dynamics of the CONFU process will probably help to describe why publishers and libraries are perhaps not in the same place on some of these issues. I will then conclude with a recommendation from the International Publishers Association (IPA) 25th Congress, held two months ago in Barcelona, and urge all of us to take to heart the theme of next year's NASIG–experimentation and collaboration–because by joint projects we will prepare for the new digital age.

CHANGES AFFECTING PUBLISHERS AND LIBRARIES

Network delivery makes it possible to provide digital content direct to a reader at a desktop, in an office or home when the information is requested. Because it is possible to receive information almost immediately, the readers are demanding more content and faster delivery. They are also asking for only the relevant information–not the entire journal issue, but only the article–not the article, but only the pertinent excerpt of the article that answers the current question. Faster networks and decreased storage costs create a demand for more and more content in digital form–both the archival materials and the newly published, and an expectation that the economics or cost to purchase and use the materials won't change, or will be less.

However, publishers have found that providing the same materials in both print and electronic form doesn't take advantage of the technology to its fullest. So, many of the new digital products are being designed with increased functionality–hyper links, powerful search engines, pointers to later publications, more frequent updates of sources and references. In point of fact, the new electronic products currently being designed are very different from their print-only forebears. But, the marketplace for electronic products is also not monolithic but instead has computer equipment of all ages and sophistication levels from pre-286 Intel chips to high-powered pentiums, with connection speeds from a mere 2400 baud to T-3 lines. A publisher cannot today provide only one format, and it is too early to shift from print-only to digital only. This means not the expected economies when paper, print and binding are no more, but rather increased costs of production. It frequently requires additional staff and production efforts, sometimes running two separate operations.

The technological revolution is also changing the expectations users place on libraries, but I don't need to tell you about those.

CONFU

During the early discussions on the National Information Infrastructure, Commissioner Bruce Lehman, chairman of the Working Group on Intellectual Property of the Information Infrastructure Task Force, stated his firm belief that the doctrine of Fair Use would still apply in the digital environment. He called on authors, publishers and other copyright proprietors to meet with representatives of educational institutions and libraries to attempt to negotiate voluntary guidelines on how to apply fair use in the digital environment. These meetings have been taking place for almost two years–first in monthly plenary meetings of about 80 participants, and then for the last four months or so in more intensive working group meetings focusing on five specific guidelines. As I noted earlier Laura Gasaway and I are among the CONFU regulars and I am almost sure that I can speak for Laura as well as myself when I say that this process has been extremely valuable.

In September 1994, each organization presented its statement of principles–we came to the table prepared to defend our positions. What changed was not a diminution in our resolve but a better understanding of the technology and how people envisioned it being used.

We learned about the extent of Distance Learning taking place in this country and abroad from kindergarten to graduate school. We learned about libraries' on-line public access catalogues and the requests from users at remote sites for materials cited in these OPACs. We learned about the vast collections of visual images that schools have assembled over the last thirty or more years and how these slides are used today. We learned about second graders making multimedia works as class projects and graduate students submitting electronic multimedia dissertations. We learned a lot, but we also shared with librarians and educators the new digital book products and services under development, and we reminded everyone that the Fair Use provisions in the Copyright Law are fact specific. A finding of fair use depends on the facts when the given use is made. Among those facts is the effect of the use on the potential market for or value of the work. If new ways to provide a product are developed, such as by-the-piece, in response to a market that wants to purchase articles by-the-piece instead of by the bound journal, then the effect on the market of not paying the requested fee is directly relevant.

The movie industry's shift to a reliance on licensing income is easy to document. Originally the costs of production were made back during the theatrical release of a film. Such is no longer the case. The movie industry relies on multiple revenue streams to recoup investment before profit is possible. Similarly, the printed sheet music industry is no longer viable on sales of sheet music. Some music is not sold but leased along with the requisite performance rights. Commercial exploitation changes to accommodate usage patterns. Many print publishers of journals are similarly concerned that their business model will be shifting–this is what makes these discussions so interesting but also so important. We must negotiate the rules of the road for uncertain vehicles riding on uncertain terrain.

The Guidelines most likely to emerge from the CONFU process are the ones for teachers and students who wish to use portions of copyrighted materials for making multimedia works for non-profit educational purposes. These guidelines include portion limitations, time limitations, and protection from unauthorized network access or re-distribution.

Another set of guidelines that I fully expect to see in place this fall are the guidelines for image archives to permit lawfully acquired slides to be converted to digital form and used under certain circumstances. An example of the give and take of the negotiation process here might prove instructive. The issue was whether under any circumstances it would be fair use to digitize copyrighted prints and slides acquired after January 1, 1997 and available for purchase or license in digital form. Companies such as Corbis have licensed electronic rights to large collections of photographs and fine art. Digital versions of many of these images are available on the Internet today. In addition, organizations such as the American Society of Media Photographers, Picture Network International, Presslink, and Kodak, are in various stages of creating online licensing services and some even provide the digital version of the image electronically instantly. Already, today, there are at least a half dozen home pages where photos can be viewed and rights to use them obtained.

If it is possible to obtain a license or purchase the digital version of the work from the copyright holder, and these systems were set up to accommodate the very needs in which the schools are interested, are there any uses without permission that would be fair use or not infringing that would cover digitizing the image from a book or magazine?

What we worked out seems eminently fair and acceptable to all sides. It borrows the concept of spontaneity from previous guidelines. A teacher decides to use an image from a book. The teacher can digitize that image and use it in the class. However, this is a one-time use. If the teacher wishes to use the same image again or to add it to the collection of the school, permission must be sought or a license obtained or a digital version purchased. The guidelines detail a full inquiry for subsequent uses that include determining if the image is available in usable, digital form or for license for the educational marketer, or is from a known source where permission can be requested. The concept of one-time use provided both a fair use window and a recognition of the evolving market for digital images. It was also a realistic solution.

Distance Learning guidelines to expand the rights of public performance and public display of copyrighted works provided in the existing copyright law for face-to-face classrooms were negotiated to cover remote classrooms under certain circumstances. These are close to completion for non-networked use but have a ways to go on networked uses.

"Interlibrary Loan," now referred to by the combined term "Interlibrary Loan/Document Delivery," is a more difficult area. The working group reached a very quick agreement that it was premature to try to draft guidelines for the digital delivery of digital originals because the products and services are still in development and it is not clear how they will evolve nor how libraries will want to use them.

Electronic Reserves represents an even thornier problem. Librarians claim to be applying technology to a traditional library function but publishers point out that scanning print into digital form is changing the nature of the work (and making a copy), and the portions requested are far beyond permitted fair use copying. If a work has a value to the market, that value should be recognized. In fact there are multiple electronic systems for providing the very functions that the e-reserves seek to achieve: selected excerpts assembled in digital form for print on demand. University of California-San Diego and Case Western Reserve University are just two examples of schools that have developed automated electronic reserve systems with permission for including copyrighted materials and payment for usage built into the systems. These systems are being used for electronically facilitated course packs–an established market for copyright holders.

Fair Use was intended to permit limited, occasional, non-systematic copying in certain proscribed circumstances. In many countries, broad licenses for elementary and secondary schools cover the copies made on a day-to-day basis and the principle of respect for copyright is maintained, while the needs of the user community for timely copies is also met. In the United States, we agreed to some educational use without permission where the use does not interfere with the normal exploitation of the copyrighted works. The guidelines that we have developed in the CONFU process show that such arrangements can be developed for the electronic environment in some areas but not as easily in others.

EXPERIMENTATION

During the IPA Congress, a paper on publishers, libraries and the electronic environment was presented. It made the points that digital is different from print and its impact is thereby different, that document delivery is one of the new primary services that publishers are planning to offer, and that publishers recognize the changing role of libraries. The paper called on publishers and libraries to work together on pilot projects and experimentation as we both prepare for the digital age. I urge you to consider such projects. Many AAP journal publishers are already involved in collaborations with libraries. We have also received a new proposal from a college for a project to digitize a specialized collection of print journals for electronic delivery to students and teachers at their desks. We are eager to consider other projects that let us explore with libraries as partners. This is a fertile time to explore. As the title of the Conference says, "We are all pioneers" on the new serial frontiers. Let's cooperate and not just try to import old concepts from the print world that are no longer applicable in the electronic. I look forward to next year's NASIG where you will discuss "Experimentation and Collaboration."

The White Paper, Fair Use, Libraries and Educational Institutions

Laura Gasaway

SUMMARY. Libraries and educational institutions strongly believe that the continuance and expansion of fair use is critical in the digital environment. Libraries bridge the gap between the information haves and have-nots. Only if copyrighted works continue to be subject to fair use can copyright law satisfy the Constitutional mandate to "promote the progress of science and the useful arts." *[Article copies available for a fee from The Haworth Document Delivery Service: 1-800-342-9678. E-mail address: getinfo@haworth.com]*

Scholars, researchers, librarians and college and university administrators fear that the fair use of copyrighted works for teaching and scholarship is under serious attack. Fair use is an important doctrine in copyright law in that it preserves the right to reproduce copyrighted works for certain purposes, among them the typical uses that students, teachers and researchers make of these works which are so valuable for education. The U.S. Constitution grants to Congress the right to enact copyright laws . . . "To promote the Progress of Science and the useful Arts, by securing for limited Times to Authors and Inventors the exclusive Right to their respective Writings and Discoveries."[1] There are three interests that are served by copyright law. First, authors are served by the existence of copyright

---

Laura Gasaway is Director of the Law Library and Professor of Law, Law Library, University of North Carolina, Chapel Hill.

[Haworth co-indexing entry note]: "The White Paper, Fair Use, Libraries and Educational Institutions." Gasaway, Laura. Co-published simultaneously in *The Serials Librarian* (The Haworth Press, Inc.) Vol. 31, No. 1/2, 1997, pp. 211-220; and: *Pioneering New Serials Frontiers: From Petroglyphs to Cyberserials* (ed: Christine Christiansen and Cecilia Leathem) The Haworth Press, Inc., 1997, pp. 211-220. Single or multiple copies of this article are available for a fee from The Haworth Document Delivery Service [1-800-342-9678, 9:00 a.m. - 5:00 p.m. (EST). E-mail address: getinfo@haworth.com].

laws that award rights to authors who produce original works of authorship that are fixed in tangible medium of expression now known or later developed.[2] To encourage the creation of new works, Congress awards copyright to authors who own the rights in works they create absent a transfer of those rights. Second, the interests of publishers are served by copyright law. Publishers take the literary work from the author, reproduce it in copies and distribute it to libraries and bookstores. Publishers' rights must be protected if they are to perform this very useful facilitation function which delivers copyrighted works to the public. This is done through the transfer of rights from the author to the publisher.[3] The third reason that we need copyright law is to ensure the public's right to use copyrighted works in certain ways. Through the copyright law, Congress has attempted to balance the rights of these groups.[4] This balancing among these interests and rights creates a tension in copyright law.

Despite support from the U.S. Supreme Court that copyright exists to serve the public interest,[5] in recent years it appears that copyright law no longer serves that interest as it was intended but too often is viewed as a welfare provision for publishers. Fair use[6] and the library[7] and nonprofit educational exemptions[8] in the Act permit certain uses of copyrighted works and strike much of the balance between the rights of users and copyright owners. The library and education community seek to preserve fair use in the electronic environment to include browsing of material in digital format and to ensure that the right to read not be converted into a right to "pay-for-view." Additionally, educators seek to continue the current wide uses of copyrighted works in nonprofit educational institutions (the classroom exemption) and to extend that exemption to distance learning. Librarians are concerned that access to information for the poor and disabled be ensured. The Clinton administration is interested in furthering the electronic environment through the National Information Infrastructure (NII). A Task Force on the NII was formed in 1993, and it studied intellectual property rights for the NII and recently issued a report on the subject. The report, commonly referred to as the "White Paper," appears to have taken the position that what is good for the publishing community is good for the country regardless of what its recommendations do to the existing balance between creators and users of copyrighted works. The recommendations contained in the White Paper have now been embodied in Congressional bills.[9]

While publishers and librarians share many of the same interests, they also have some competing interests in the copyright arena. Publishers understandably want to maximize profits and stay viable in the digital age. Librarians believe that they are the representatives of the public in their quests for information. They want to ensure that the public's access to information not be further hampered. Libraries purchase copyrighted works for multiple users to access, and librarians cannot stand idly by and see fair use converted into a licensing arrangement in which all access must be pay-for-view.

THE WHITE PAPER

In 1995, a report entitled *Intellectual Property and the National Information Infrastructure* was issued by the Task Force on the National Information Infrastructure.[10] The White Paper was preceded by a draft called the Green Paper.[11] While neither version pays adequate attention to the reason that copyright law exists, i.e., for the public good, the Green Paper contained considerably more recognition of that than does the later White Paper. For example, the following statement appears in the Green Paper:

> The Copyright Act exists for the benefit of the public. To fulfill its constitutional purpose, the law should strive to make the information contained in protected works of authorship freely available to the public. "Freely available," of course, does not necessarily mean "available free." . . . Public libraries and schools, and the access to information that they provide, have been important safeguards against this nation becoming a nation of information "haves" and "have nots." We must ensure that they continue to be able to assume that role.[12]

Unfortunately, this statement disappeared in the final report. One can only speculate why even the minimal emphasis on the public's interests in the Green Paper was changed or dropped in the White Paper. It is fairly obvious that the sometimes subtle (and other times not so subtle) changes sacrificed acknowledgment of the public good to emphasize the commercial interests of the content providers. The Green Paper contained this statement:

> Our intellectual property regime must (1) recognize the legitimate rights and commercial expectations of persons and entities whose works are used in the NII environment . . . and (2) ensure that users have access to the broadest feasible variety of works . . . [13]

The statement reflects the parallel nature of two important concepts: fulfilling legitimate commercial concerns and expectations and ensuring broad access to users. The White Paper changed those equal statements into the following:

> An effective intellectual property regime must (1) ensure that users have access to the broadest feasible variety of works by (2) recognizing the legitimate rights and commercial expectations of persons and entities whose works are used in the NII environment.[14]

Now, clearly, the access of users is subservient to the commercial interests of the copyright holder community. In fact, the White Paper appears to state that the only way to further the interests of the public is to maximize the rights of the publishing community over the rights and expectations of users of copyrighted works. The two equal clauses are no longer equal. Another recognition of the public's rights is also found in this statement from the Green Paper:

> As more and more works are available primarily or exclusively on-line, it is critical that researchers, students and other members of the public have opportunities on-line equivalent to their current opportunities off-line to browse through copyrighted works in their schools and public libraries.[15]

This statement, too, disappeared in the final report.

RECOMMENDATIONS CONCERNING THE LIBRARY EXEMPTIONS

Concern over the lack of attention to the public's rights is not to imply that libraries are unhappy with all of the White Paper. It does contain some important recognition of the fact that libraries will engage in digital copying as technology now permits. This will involve both copying from print to digital format and digital to digital reproduction. The reasons libraries will do such copying include preservation of existing print and other analog materials, reproduction of copies for users under § 108(d) and (e) of the Copyright Act and interlibrary loan copying.

The White Paper's focus on digital copying by libraries appears in the discussion of interlibrary loan:

> While it is clear that § 108 does not authorize unlimited reproduction of copies in digital form it is equally clear that § 108(g)(2) permits

"borrowing" in electronic form for interlibrary loan in the NII environment, so long as such "borrowing" does not lead to "systematic copying."[16]

A brief description of the licensing systems that publishers may develop to make their works available is also included in this discussion. Because of the existence of the systems in the future, the White Paper takes the position that it will be difficult to define "subscription or purchase of a work" and difficult to apply the existing interlibrary loan guidelines to all electronic transactions.[17]

The White Paper makes three specific statutory recommendations concerning libraries, each to amend the library exemptions:

> (1) to accommodate the reality of the computerized library by allowing the preparation of three copies of works in digital form, with no more than one copy in use at any time (while the others are archived), (2) to recognize that the use of a copyright notice on a published copy of a work is no longer mandatory, and (3) to authorize the making of digital copies for purposes of preservation.[18]

While these are important and worthy recommendations, the pending bills actually cause some problems due to the misplacement of the proposed "three copies" amendment. The bills would alter the exemption found in § 108(a) that permits libraries and archives to make and distribute a single copy of copyrighted works under certain conditions by changing it to three copies; but libraries would be allowed to distribute only one of those copies.[19] Since the need to reproduce three rather than one copy of the work is for preservation and replacement purposes, and it deals with the requirements of national microfilm standards requirements, only two sections of the Act are implicated, not the whole of § 108. Section 108(b) currently allows libraries and archives to reproduce facsimile copies of unpublished works for purposes such as preservation, security or deposit for research in another library. Section 108(c) permits libraries to replace copies of lost, stolen, damaged or deteriorating copies of works after the library first tries to obtain an unused copy of the work at a fair price. The three-copy limitation is more properly placed in these sections than in § 108(a). The pending bills also insert the word "digital" into these sections.

Library associations have proposed that this matter be corrected and the three-copy limitation on reproduction and the one-copy restriction on distribution be placed in §§ 108(b)-(c) where it more properly belongs.

TRANSMISSIONS AS DISTRIBUTION

Another important recommendation of the White Paper is that transmissions of copyrighted works via digital means be recognized as a distribution of a copyrighted work which falls within the exclusive rights of the copyright holder.[20] Many copyright scholars already believe that the distribution right includes the transmission right whenever there is any commercial transmission of the works. However, making all transmissions fall within the exclusive rights of the copyright holder, even those that are of a non-commercial nature, is of serious concern to libraries that want to deliver copies of requested copyrighted works to their users via electronic means. It also could have unfortunate consequences for the performance of copyrighted works for distance learning. The pending bills propose to amend § 106 of the Act to adopt the White Paper's proposals on transmissions.[21]

Library associations and education associations do not oppose the redefinition of the distribution right to include transmission so long as the fair use section of the Act also is amended to indicate that there may also be fair use transmissions of a work. Currently, the fair use section of the Act reads:

> Notwithstanding the provisions of section 106 and 106A, the fair use of a copyrighted work, including such use by reproduction in copies or phonorecords or by any other means specified by that section for purposes such as criticism, comment, news reporting, teaching (including multiple copies for classroom use), scholarship or research is not an infringement of copyright.[22]

The amendment offered by library and education associations would insert the word "transmission" into the above wording to read: " . . . the fair use of a copyrighted work, including such use by reproduction in copies or phonorecords, by transmission, or by any other means . . . is not an infringement of copyright."

FIRST SALE DOCTRINE

The first sale doctrine in copyright law permits one who purchases a copy of a copyrighted work to dispose of that copy through sale, lease, lending, etc., with no payment of royalties to the copyright holder.[23] In other words, the copyright owner is entitled to royalties only on the initial sale of the copy of the work. The first sale doctrine permits used book-stores to sell pre-owned copies of books with no payment to the copyright holder; it also permits libraries to loan materials in their collections. The White Paper proposes that the first sale doctrine be eliminated for digital works on the theory that the electronic environment changes the conditions so substantially that the doctrine is inapplicable.[24]

The reasons given for this proposal are somewhat strained. To many experts it is perfectly possible for the owner of a digital work to erase or delete the work from his computer and to give it either on disk or through transmission to a second person. According to the report, this cannot happen since, in the print world, a purchaser of a copy of a book can actually dispose of that copy. In the digital environment, however, even if the first owner of the copy deletes her copy, the copy received by the second party is not the same one held by the first owner but is instead another copy of the work.[25] This peculiar reasoning fails to recognize that there are no more copies in existence after the first owner deletes his copy and sends it to a second party than existed in the print environment.

Should the bills be enacted that eliminate the first sale doctrine for digital works,[26] then one who purchases a digital work would be prohibited from disposing of it via sale or transfer to another party without paying a royalty. This is contrary to most views of what ownership of copies of works means, and it is opposed by library and educational associations.

COPYRIGHT MANAGEMENT INFORMATION AND DECRYPTION DEVICES

There are copyright management information systems currently under development that will embed into a copyrighted work a digital signature or "watermark." This copyright management information can be very useful to the users of works since it will indicate who owns rights to the work, where to go to obtain permissions, and perhaps watermarks will specify the fees for use. The White Paper proposes that such systems be protected by punishing anyone who fraudulently removes such information from a work.[27]

There are many published works, however, that contain both protected material along with public domain information. Yet, copyright management information can be placed on the entire work or even on the equivalent of every digital "page." It is not infringement for one to reproduce public domain works, and thus removal of copyright management information from that portion of the work should not invoke penalties for a user.

A similar problem exists for decryption devices. The White Paper recommends penalties for the production of devices that have as their primary purpose the decryption of copyrighted works.[28] But what if the works decrypted or the portions decrypted are within the public domain? Decryption of a public domain work is not infringement. Works encrypted might also be a combination of protected material and public domain information. So, punishing one who develops devices that may be used to decrypt public domain works should not be an acceptable solution.

ONLINE SERVICE PROVIDER LIABILITY

Another major concern of libraries and educational institutions is the White Paper recommendation that online service providers be liable for copyright infringement by subscribers to the online service.[29] It is a daunting prospect for libraries and colleges and universities that maintain online systems to realize that they may be held liable for infringing acts of the users of their systems. It is well-accepted that one who directly infringes a copyrighted work via an online system should be liable for that infringement just as she would be in the print world. The question of whether the online service provider should be liable is a much more complicated issue, however. What types of filtering systems would have to be employed to detect copyright infringement in a large university-maintained or supported network?

Many scholars have suggested that online service providers should be liable only if they first are notified of the infringement and then fail to take action within a reasonable period of time to remove the infringing work from the system and stop the infringement. These suggestions are summarily rejected in the White Paper.[30] The pending bills are silent on this issue based on the White Paper's position that the current law indicates that the online system provider would be liable.[31]

Since the publication of the report, a recent case has taken the opposite view. In *Religious Technology Center v. Netcom On-Line Communications Service*,[32] the only case to deal directly with this issue, the federal district court held that the service provider was not liable for the posting of copyrighted materials from the Church of Scientology by a subscriber.[33] The White Paper, however, simply states that the answer to the question of online service provider liability should be yes, and one of the reasons stated for this position is because of the business relationship that exists between the provider and the subscriber.[34] If this is indeed the reason, then perhaps libraries and educational institutions that maintain online systems will be able to opt out of liability since there is no business relationship between the provider and the user of the service.

CONCLUSION

Librarians and educators should have serious concerns about the future of fair use in the electronic environment. The development of technological means to control and license access may well convert the present system of free public libraries to a pay-for-view system. Although there will still be a role for fair use even in such a system, the access portion of fair use will be preempted. The remaining role will be restricted to what one can do with the copyrighted work after the work is accessed.

In the face of such licensing systems, librarians and educators must ask themselves whether the balance that existed between users and copyright holders was good for society or whether a licensing system is better. What level of use should be permitted before incurring a fee? Who will pay the fees? Will such licensing systems further divide rich from poor in this country? Is this the society we as a people want?

If the answer to this last question is no, then we must take action to see that Congress recognizes the full implications of the recommendations contained in the White Paper and the pending legislation.

NOTES

1. U.S. Const. art. I, § 8, cl. 8.
2. 17 U.S.C. § 102(a) (1994).
3. Id. § 204(d).
4. Some writers maintain that the public has no "rights" in copyright. See INTELLECTUAL PROPERTY AND THE NATIONAL INFORMATION INFRA-STRUCTURE: THE REPORT OF THE WORKING GROUP ON INTEL-LECTUAL PROPERTY RIGHTS 73 (1995). But Professor L. Ray Patterson states that fair use is a right of the user of the copyrighted work in L. Ray Patterson & Stanley W. Lindberg, THE NATURE OF COPYRIGHT: A LAW OF USERS' RIGHTS 191-200 (1991). Professor Paul Goldstein refers to fair use as a "privilege." See Paul Goldstein, 2 COPYRIGHT LAW § 10.1 (2d ed. 1991). When one searches for the meaning of the word "privilege" in BLACK'S LAW DICTIONARY, one finds "privilege" defined as a "right." See BLACK'S LAW DICTIONARY 1077 (5th ed. 1979). So, perhaps it is merely a matter of semantics whether fair use is a right or a privilege.
5. See *Feist Publications, Inc. v. Rural Telephone Service Co.*, 499 U.S. 340, 349-50 (1991).

6. 17 U.S.C. § 107 (1994).

7. Id. § 108.

8. Id. §§ 110(1)-(2).

9. NII Protection Act of 1995, H.R. 2441 & S. 1284, 104th Cong., 1st Sess. (1995) [hereinafter H.R. 2441].

10. INTELLECTUAL PROPERTY AND THE NATIONAL INFORMATION INFRASTRUCTURE: THE REPORT OF THE WORKING GROUP ON INTEL-LECTUAL PROPERTY RIGHTS (1995) [hereinafter White Paper].

11. INTELLECTUAL PROPERTY AND THE NATIONAL INFORMATION INFRASTRUCTURE: A PRELIMINARY DRAFT OF THE REPORT OF THE WORKING GROUP ON INTELLECTUAL PROPERTY RIGHTS (1994) [here-inafter Green Paper].

12. Id. at 133.

13. Id. at 9.

14. White Paper, supra note 10, at 13. 15 Green Paper, supra note 11, at 133.

15. Green paper, supra note 11, at 133.

16. White Paper, supra note 10, at 89.

17. Id.

18. Id. at 27.

19. H.R. 2441, supra note 9.

20. White Paper, supra note 10, at 213-14.

21. H.R. 2441, supra note 9.

22. 17 U.S. C. § 107 (1994).

23. Id. § 109(a).

24. White Paper, supra note 10, at 92.

25. Id.

26. H.R. 2441, supra note 9.

27. White Paper, supra note 10, at 191-94.

28. Id. at 231.

29. Id. at 114-24.

30. Id. at 114.

31. Id. at 122.

32. 907 F. Supp. 1361 (N.D. Cal. 1995).

33. Id. at 1372-73.

34. White Paper, supra note 10, at 122.

CONCURRENT SESSION VII: PARTNERSHIPS: HOW MANY FORMS, HOW MANY ISSUES?

Digital Library Partnerships: The Issues and Challenges

Jacqueline H. Trolley

SUMMARY. This session established a global overview on digital libraries and partnerships. The focus then centered on a corporate research and development initiative and a library/public agency collaboration. In both cases the scope and background of the projects were outlined and such issues as implementation and ongoing support were discussed. The Institute for Scientific Information and Thomas Jefferson University concentrated on ISI's Electronic Library Project which has been designed to test and validate electronic access to bibliographic data and images of a large corpus of scholarly journal literature. The Cornell Mann Library/USDA collaboration,

Jacqueline H. Trolley is Director of Corporate Communications, Institute for Scientific Information.

[Haworth co-indexing entry note]: "Digital Library Partnerships: The Issues and Challenges." Trolley, Jacqueline H. Co-published simultaneously in *The Serials Librarian* (The Haworth Press, Inc.) Vol. 31, No. 1/2, 1997, pp. 221-226; and: *Pioneering New Serials Frontiers: From Petroglyphs to Cyberserials* (ed: Christine Christiansen and Cecilia Leathem) The Haworth Press, Inc., 1997, pp. 221-226. Single or multiple copies of this article are available for a fee from The Haworth Document Delivery Service [1-800-342-9678, 9:00 a.m. - 5:00 p.m. (EST). E-mail address: getinfo@haworth.com].

which makes available via the Internet nearly 300 USDA electronic publications, will discuss the goals and challenges of implementing this new service. *[Article copies available for a fee from The Haworth Document Delivery Service: 1-800-342-9678. E-mail address: getinfo@haworth. com]*

There has been an escalating interest in electronic libraries over the past few years, as evidenced by the increasing number of new products, new projects, and new players around the world who are engaged in their development or release. But there is still much confusion about these "libraries" and the terms being used in conjunction with them. Some people might say that we, as an industry, are in a "state of chaos"; others might argue that we are on the verge of a revolution.

Many of these recent developments relate to the electronic availability of audio and visual materials. This paper, however, will focus on the electronic delivery of analog materials–printed information and works of art–and the players involved.

Who is involved in developing these electronic libraries? The list is long: technology companies, primary publishers, subscription agencies, associations, service providers, publishing technology providers, networking suppliers, non-profit organizations, libraries and library consortia, governments, and private individuals.

Very few of these organizations are working independently. Rather, partnering is the predominant approach. The reason for this appears to be rooted in a fundamental consideration: economics. The technology investments in these projects are costly.

However, the measure of success in these "partnerships" must go beyond economics. Not only must we share the costs, it is imperative that we share a common vision or goal in the design and testing of these endeavors.

This shared vision or goal can be a blend of for-profit and not-for-profit objectives. The for-profit objective often belongs to the partner or organization that brings technological expertise to the project. This is evident in the development of the electronic or digital libraries whose primary purposes are archiving and preservation. Examples include the 1987 project in Madrid, in which the IBM Digital Library Team helped the Spanish government digitize papers that chronicled Columbus's voyage to the new world, and the more recent Brandywine Project, the purpose of which was to scan and electronically store ten thousand works of Andrew Wyeth.

The technologies developed in these partnerships are interesting. The IBM Watson Laboratory developed a digitized camera, imaging software, and search technologies with the overall aim of ease-of-use. The digitized camera developed uses of a CCD sensor chip akin to the sensitive light-gathering devices used in telescopes.

In the Vatican Library Project, a more recent initiative, a team using two of these cameras scanned about one-hundred-and-sixty images per day. The first phase of this project involved the scanning and archiving of approximately thirty thousand manuscript pages, which can now be viewed by scholars at ten individual workstations. The Vatican would eventually like to make this material available through the Internet.

Other cameras are being used to digitize holdings at the Lutherhalle Wittenberg museum in Germany, the National Gallery of Art, the Library of Congress, and the Smithsonian Institution in Washington, DC.

Partnering is also evident in the journal-based initiatives coming from the publishing industry, associations, and universities. Content providers are partnering with technology companies. Funding, in some cases, is provided by private and government sources. Let's look at some examples:

- The Ideal Project, in which a primary STM publisher, Academic Press, has partnered with Fujitsu to test the delivery of documents over the Internet using Adobe Acrobat.
- Project Muse, a University Press initiative that will offer approximately forty-six titles via the World Wide Web. This subscription-based project is the result of a collaborative effort by Johns Hopkins University Press, The Milton S. Eisenhower Library at Johns Hopkins, and Homewood Academic Computing. It has benefited from private and governmental funding.
- CORE (Chemistry Online Retrieval Experiment) involves a partnering of the American Chemical Society, Cornell University, Sony of America, Digital Equipment Corporation, Sun Microsystems, and the Cornell Theory Center.

Some of these "libraries" are accessible now; some are still in the planning phase. Few are witnessing an exchange of money.

The issues and the costs remain complex; the parameters, "loose." Each project still requires a great deal of cooperative effort. Because while the technology problems are being resolved, we are just beginning to discuss other issues we are facing, such as archiving, electronic preservation and restoration responsibilities and costs, all of which remain unresolved.

Designing, implementing, and testing these electronic library initiatives and offerings requires flexibility, communications, and attention to myriad technical and managerial details. It is therefore imperative that we extend these partnerships to the users, the library and technology managers, the content providers, and the technological organizations, all of whose input is invaluable.

After all, we still know so little about such issues as security, actual usage, library and technology support and maintenance. We still need to solve integration, delivery, and storage concerns. In fact, many systems still have not addressed the fundamental question as to what defines a print journal in electronic form. For instance, is it just the article or is it all items within that issue? Does it encompass all advertising, including employment notices?

And these partnerships require an honest look at a basic issue: costs. In some quarters, the expectation for the future is that costs will decline. However, libraries have had to invest in the technologies necessary to even view the results of these electronic initiatives and products. The cost of one computer has been multiplied many times over to allow for access by many, and that is compounded by the costs of networking and the infrastructure needed to support it.

In terms of development, costs for these initiatives and products are in the billions of dollars. While a cost savings in delivery of information via electronic channels may appear "cheaper," the cost of designing and supporting these systems has been dramatic.

Before even looking at the impact of an electronic library, consider the costs involved in this scenario. Forty years ago, the Institute for Scientific Information launched the first Current Contents print edition. ISI now supports seven editions and four electronic formats of this product alone, is involved in three distributorships, supports technical help desks on three continents, employs software and new product developers, uses two replicating houses, has invested in a company that has transformed data processing plants in two different countries to scanning and imaging facilities, and continues to invest heavily in staff training and development of new technologies. And ISI still supports a print edition and delivers it internationally.

The Institute for Scientific Information recently extended the parameters of its table-of contents database to include the delivery of the images of the primary journals themselves. The ISI Electronic Library Project, a corporate research and development effort, is testing the feasibility of delivering the bibliographic information and abstracts of one edition of Current Contents–Life Sciences–and the images of the source journals for which publishers have given permission.

Fundamental to the ISI Electronic Library project has been partnering. ISI needed to plan for a model that would provide flexibility for current–and future–product initiatives.

Short-term and long-term goals needed to be considered. Costs in terms of development time and currently employed skill sets were important.

Therefore, ISI chose a technology partner: the IBM Digital Library Group at Almaden, experts in relational database management and high-volume storage, retrieval, and delivery of information in a distributed environment.

One challenge ISI brought to IBM was the need to plan for the storage and delivery of large amounts of imaged data. The solution: a hierarchical storage management system that would efficiently maintain and archive this large amount of data on tape, optical media, or hard disk, while offering the fastest access at the lowest cost. ISI is now using ADSM, IBM's hierarchical storage management system, which was developed at the Almaden Research Lab.

ADSM enables ISI to employ cache management for the storage and delivery of huge amounts of imaged data. For the Electronic Library Project, ISI stores electronic subscriptions at its central server and delivers the full images from the most recent issues to the proprietary ISI server at the pilot site. The local server then delivers the images to the user at his/her workstation with little degradation of retrieval time and at a large cost-savings for the site.

If the ISI Electronic Library is launched commercially, authorized sites could opt to purchase, install, and configure their own server according to the simple server configuration guidelines that ISI has designed.

Future possibilities may also include the ability for the end-user to receive images directly from a publisher's digital archive.

Another challenging issue was rights management and security in an electronic environment. The electronic delivery of copyrighted material offers the potential for unauthorized distribution and even alteration of information. It was therefore essential to the Project's success to develop alternate ways of protecting data without impeding access.

Partnering again came into play, saving time and money. IBM and ISI created new technologies for rights management that protect the information content owners, as well as the end-users of the system.

These encryption techniques are incorporated at every point in the system, from the encryption of the actual image at ISI to the authentication of digital signatures through the ISI viewer at the workstation. As a result, data is secure from the time it leaves ISI's central server until it reaches the workstation. Images are only accessible to authorized users at a pilot site, and only at sites where a subscription has been purchased. Additional security measures include watermarking techniques, copyright statements, and user passwords.

The ISI Electronic Library Project involves other technology partners: IBM Global Network, Lotus Development Corporation, and Lexmark International, Inc.

Another key partnership in the development of the ISI Electronic Library Project involves over three-hundred-and-fifty scholarly, international publishers who produce the journals indexed in Current Contents/ Life Science. More than one-hundred-and-twenty of these publishers have agreed to participate in this project. Their greatest concern has been pricing. Their greatest interest lies in learning about the economics involved, the models needed for the future, and researchers' reaction to this electronic medium.

The pilot sites have also been key to this endeavor. These partnerships provide a critical assessment: user, and library and technical management evaluation of the value of an imaged electronic library. ISI chose sites that represented a challenging mix of academic, corporate, and public library institutions: Purdue University, Thomas Jefferson University, University College London, SmithKline Beecham Pharmaceutical R&D, Glaxo Wellcome Research and Development, and The New York Public Library. Each presented a new challenge; all have proved to the ISI Electronic Library Team the need for flexibility, communications, and attention to technical and managerial issues.

These pilot sites have had to address some interesting issues. Paula Lynch, Thomas Jefferson University, will detail one especially relevant challenge: the collection and development methodology used to build an electronic library at their site.

Partnering to Provide Electronic Access to Life-Sciences Serials: The Experience of Journal Selection for the Electronic Library Project

Paula M. Lynch

Located in Center City Philadelphia, Thomas Jefferson University (TJU) is the second largest private health sciences academic institution in the United States. Academic Information Services and Research (AISR) oversees and directs Scott Memorial Library (SML), and supports a broad spectrum of services to the three colleges of Thomas Jefferson University. Scott Library's journal collection consists of over 2,300 current subscriptions and 100,000 bound volumes.

Changing social and economic trends in the health care industry have complicated the provision of core collections to the entirety of our expanding customer base. The Jefferson community no longer consists solely of on-campus constituents who need only walk across a street to use the Library's collections. Today, our customers include persons in rural Pennsylvania communities, various U.S. states, South America and Central Europe. Health care information providers must now satisfy the increasing call for point-of-service access to journal literature via workstations installed in nursing and clinical units, emergency rooms, and urban and

Paula M. Lynch is Collection Management Librarian, Scott Memorial Library, Thomas Jefferson University, Philadelphia, PA.

[Haworth co-indexing entry note]: "Partnering to Provide Electronic Access to Life-Sciences Serials: The Experience of Journal Selection for the Electronic Library Project." Lynch, Paula M. Co-published simultaneously in *The Serials Librarian* (The Haworth Press, Inc.) Vol. 31, No. 1/2, 1997, pp. 227-233; and: *Pioneering New Serials Frontiers: From Petroglyphs to Cyberserials* (ed: Christine Christiansen and Cecilia Leathem) The Haworth Press, Inc., 1997, pp. 227-233. Single or multiple copies of this article are available for a fee from The Haworth Document Delivery Service [1-800-342-9678, 9:00 a.m. - 5:00 p.m. (EST). E-mail address: getinfo@haworth.com].

rural physician and health care (i.e. physical/occupational therapy, etc.) offices. These changes also affect allied health educators as medical schools are now providing new educational models which involve computer-based learning (CBL) and distance learning with an increasing focus on continuing education.

In the early 1990s, AISR created JEFFLINE (http://jeffline.tju.edu), the main route of electronic access to information services for the University, Hospital, Health System, and affiliated members of the TJU community. JEFFLINE integrates a variety of both global and locally-based electronic information resources, the library catalog (THOMCAT), and a variety of specialized subject home pages for Jefferson academic departments and research endeavors.

Over the past two years, serialists have watched the growing trend of medical and scientific publishers exploring dissemination of printed journal literature in electronic formats. At the same time, serials librarians have been struggling to sort out the various interfaces, multiple formats, and creative price structures ("to fee or not to fee?") which accompany the experimental electronic formats.

An electronic journal might be part of a collection of electronic resources, like Academic Press's "IDEAL," or may be the sole title released by a publisher. A title may consist of a simple representation of the table-of-contents, with or without abstracts, like Elsevier's EPIDOC service, or a full-image or full-text title, with or without pictures and graphics, such as *Nucleic Acids Research* (Oxford University Press). The electronic resource may consist of supplemental information to the print journal, for example the American Chemical Society titles. The electronic journal may require specific hardware or software for access; for example, Adobe Acrobat is frequently required to display images or whole articles. With so many choices of format, and a growing demand for electronic access, librarians are faced with providing traditional print journal collections, while adapting policies, technical areas, training, and fiscal structure to the demands of electronic resources.

WHAT IS THE ELECTRONIC LIBRARY PROJECT?

In order to meet the changing needs of the Jefferson community, AISR accepted the Institute for Scientific Information's (ISI) invitation to participate as the initial installation site of the Electronic Library Project (ELP). The two-year project provides access to electronic delivery of *print* journal literature, rather than electronic delivery of electronic journals. It is the encapsulation of electronic delivery of print journal literature.

For the duration of this project ISI adds to its traditional role of second-ary publisher the roles of coordinator, subscription agent, publisher, and archivist. ISI partners with cooperating publishers to produce a database of scanned full-text journal articles from selected titles indexed in ISI's *Current Contents–Life Sciences* (*CC-LS*). Where other projects like Adonis must build an index of journal citations, projects like ELP and Ovid's full-text collections add value to a product currently in existence.

SML's partnership responsibilities include testing the viability and quality of the ELP database and its delivery mechanisms to SML's part-ners, our local and remote community of information service customers. SML and ISI will explore the economic viability of the Electronic Library Project pricing structure by comparing the cost and use of the electronic subscriptions in relation to their paper counterparts. User preferences and training issues will also be examined during the project.

The primary attraction of this project for Scott Library is the opportu-nity for expanded access to titles currently held in our collection and to enhance that collection by providing access to titles not held. The project also provides an opportunity for SML staff to explore collection develop-ment issues in the electronic environment by evaluating and testing reac-tion to the Electronic Library Project.

METHODOLOGY

A project team of four librarians, the Director of Collection Manage-ment (project leader), the Collection Management Librarian, the Director of Public Services, and the Document Delivery Services Manager, designed an intensive study of Scott Library's collection of *CC-LS* titles and a project implementation plan.

The first stage of the project matched a "project list," a selected sub-set of journal titles indexed in *CC-LS* to the collection of titles available for electronic subscription via ELP, and determined hardware and software specifications. The second stage will consist of library staff training and marketing of ELP. The third step will promote on-site user access, training and use of ELP document delivery at specific workstations within the Library and will explore ELP as a possible supplement to traditional document delivery services. During the fourth stage, selected Jefferson academic departments and research groups located outside the library building will be invited to test ELP's delivery of journal literature to various remote locations. This paper reviews the first stage of the project, specifically the journal and user selection portion of the study begun in

April of 1995. Unless otherwise stated, all results reported are based upon data from July 1994 to April 1995.

Keeping in mind that SML was entering into a two-year test, the project team strongly believed the journal titles on the "project list" for the ELP collection should reflect a broad selection across the life sciences, yet should complement and enhance the current SML print collection. The Scott Library journal collection concentrates on English language publications and a broad base of STM titles which support patient care, research endeavors and study. In FY94/95, SML held 41% of the 1350 *CC-LS* titles. Due to the experimental nature of the project it was determined that no print subscription would be cancelled because of the ELP.

In order to arrive at the sub-set, or project list, of *CC-LS* journal titles, the project team analyzed three criteria commonly used for journal selection:

- internal and external circulation data,
- cost-per-use data, and
- interlibrary loan/document delivery data.

The primary criteria for journal selection were the circulation and cost-per-use data. In selecting possible offsite research groups, the main factor was frequent use of the ILL and document delivery service. However, network connectivity and hardware capability also are significant factors for any offsite group to partner in the Electronic Library Project.

FEASIBILITY:
INTERNAL AND EXTERNAL CIRCULATION DATA

The single most important criterion for continued provision of serial titles at SML is the evaluation of internal and external circulation use data. The library system compiled internal statistics from bound and unbound journal issues scanned as they are reshelved by library staff. External statistics are gathered as bound journals circulate outside the library. The system reported circulation statistics sorted alphabetically by title and in rank order of highest use to lowest. It could not report zero circulation by title. This report was the primary criterion for selecting titles for the project's target list.

Each journal title in the *CC-LS* index was analyzed individually for length of SML holdings, including title changes within the previous three years, and considered whether or not a "dead," or non-current, title was cancelled.

The title that earned the number one rank in FY94/95 for highest combined internal/external circulation (2,924) and highest internal circulation (2,839) was *New England Journal of Medicine*; however, *Journal of Biological Chemistry*, which was third in overall circulation, had the highest external circulation at 132 uses.

Circulation usage was preliminarily analyzed by rank. Titles were selected for the project list if the circulation rank was between #1 and #50 (from 2924 to 512 circulations-per-year), resulting in a sub-group of 43 titles. It was determined that this list was too short, and the subject coverage not broad enough. The circulation criteria were broadened to include titles in the SML collection which had circulated more than ten times during the first three-quarters of FY94/95 (rank down to 322). Subsequently, the initial sub-group list grew to approximately 220 titles.

As part of the circulation data analysis, the project team compiled a list of previously cancelled titles demonstrating high use. Of the eleven titles which circulated more than twenty times, four titles demonstrated significant high use. The project team added these four to the project list reasoning that the titles could essentially be "reinstated" or resubscribed to via ELP.

COST-PER-USE DATA

At SML, cost-per-use information is the second criterion used to evaluate possible adjustments to the journal title list. Cost-per-use is calculated by dividing the subscription cost by the fiscal year internal and external circulation (use) for a given title. Because the subscription price does not include overhead costs such as staff time, bindery fees, or system and physical plant costs, the derived figure is understood to be an approximate dollar figure.

One expectation of the project is to explore the feasibility of the ISI economic model. The project team collected the cost-per-use data as an indicator of which print titles might be better subscribed to on a per-article basis. For example, if a title had low circulation and therefore did not make the initial project list, a high cost-per-use calculation suggested that a subscription to electronic access with a specified number of article reprints should be considered in lieu of subscribing to the title in print.

Data in this project showed that the top three highest cost-per-use titles indexed in *CC-LS* for FY1994/95 were:

1. *Growth Regulation* ($257.00)
2. *Synapse* ($240.50)
3. *Pathology International* ($209.50)

The lowest cost-per-use title for the same time period was *New England Journal of Medicine* at less than a nickel per use. Average cost-per-use for the *CC-LS* titles held in the SML collection was calculated to be $4.40.

Of the *CC-LS* titles in the study with a cost-per-use of more than $50.00, 47% have holdings that begin after 1990, and of the titles with a cost-per-use greater than $100.00, 83% have holdings beginning after 1990. Not surprisingly, then, SML added two of the three above high cost-per-use titles to the print collection in 1994, and the third in 1995. A title which has just gone through a title change or which is in its "childhood" and consequently not well-indexed will naturally have lower circulation, and therefore higher cost-per-use, than a long-established or highly revered title. The project team had to consider the length of holdings when evaluating cost-per-use data on specific titles.

From this data, the project team considered adding five titles with cost-per-use over $25.00 to the target list.

INTERLIBRARY LOAN DATA

As a health information provider, SML uses the National Library of Medicine's Docline system, equipped with extensive reporting capabilities, as the primary Interlibrary Loan (ILL) system. As a regular step in evaluating journal titles for new subscriptions, the Collection Development Policy outlines that ILL request data be reviewed annually. As recommended by CONTU guidelines, ILL request and copyright data for the previous year is evaluated for the most recent five years of each journal title.

The project team analyzed ILL and local document delivery data for each journal title indexed in *CC-LS* to determine which of our constituents frequently submit requests. The Docline data showed high volume titles, potential gaps in the SML collection, and which departments and research groups were possible partners for the ELP. The Copyright Clearance Center supplied copyright fee data for the high volume titles. Since Scott Library pays 75% of the costs associated with document delivery activity, could the Library supplement the print journal collection with ELP titles for lower cost than providing ILL service?

The ILL data demonstrated interesting results. This study indicated that an estimated 29% of all ILL activity can be associated with *CC-LS* titles. Of the fifty *CC-LS* titles to which SML does not currently subscribe, one had ceased, ten were held in the SML collection (requests were for missing volumes/issues), and five were out-of-scope as outlined by the SML Collection Development Policy. The remaining thirty-four titles were added to the project team's list and were also submitted to the Serials Committee for possible subscription in the upcoming renewal period.

Further analysis of the Docline data was performed to select departments and research groups with a high ILL request rate, which might be interested in becoming focus or test groups for ELP. Each of the five groups selected will be approached with an invitation to experiment with desktop access to the selected ELP titles.

CONCLUSION

Analysis of three criteria, circulation, cost-per-use and interlibrary loan data, resulted in a compilation of over 250 titles which the project team considered for subscription via ISI's Electronic Library Project. Comparison with the ISI's preliminary list of titles available for subscription, released in July of 1995, matched three of the titles on the project team's title list. Since that time, 44 titles have been added to Scott Library's ELP subscriptions. The data analysis also supplied a group of five departments within the Jefferson community actively utilizing document delivery services. These five groups will be approached to participate in the Electronic Library Project.

This project has allowed the Scott Library project team to explore collection development issues in an electronic environment, to enhance the print collection by providing alternative access to journal literature using a common interface, and to respond to current trends in health science information service by providing access to journal literature in electronic format.

The USDA/Mann Library Partnership: A Collaboration Between Public Agencies and an Academic Library

William J. Kara

One of the key benefits of a partnership is that by working together each partner can realize some benefit towards fulfilling his goals. Those goals can differ widely and they can include a for-profit motive or not. Although public and academic libraries are rarely engaged in for-profit activities, enhancing their services and collections as cost-effectively as possible is a powerful motive for investigating cooperative opportunities with producers and vendors. The goals of any partnership have much to do with the mission and needs of each organization.

The partnership between the Albert R. Mann Library and three agencies of the U.S. Department of Agriculture helps illustrate one type of partnership. This initiative between an academic library and publicly funded agencies illustrates many elements of a successful collaboration. In Rosabeth Moss Kanter's article "Collaborative Advantage: The Art of Alliance," she discusses many aspects of a successful partnership.[1] These include both partners contributing something of value in the partnership, each partner benefiting by being able to accomplish something they would not be able to do on their own, and the importance of good communication, trust, and flexibility during the collaboration.

William J. Kara is Acquisitions Librarian, Albert R. Mann Library, Cornell University.

[Haworth co-indexing entry note]: "The USDA/Mann Library Partnership: A Collaboration Between Public Agencies and an Academic Library." Kara, William J. Co-published simultaneously in *The Serials Librarian* (The Haworth Press, Inc.) Vol. 31, No. 1/2, 1997, pp. 235-242; and: *Pioneering New Serials Frontiers: From Petroglyphs to Cyberserials* (ed: Christine Christiansen and Cecilia Leathem) The Haworth Press, Inc., 1997, pp. 235-242. Single or multiple copies of this article are available for a fee from The Haworth Document Delivery Service [1-800-342-9678, 9:00 a.m. - 5:00 p.m. (EST). E-mail address: getinfo@haworth.com].

The partnership between the Albert R. Mann Library and three economic agencies of the U.S. Department of Agriculture is already in its third year. These agencies are the Economic Research Service (ERS), National Agricultural Statistics Service (NASS), and the World Agricultural Outlook Board (WAOB). The result of this collaboration was the creation of the USDA Economic and Statistics System, which is a significant collection of agricultural economics information produced by these agencies, but made available to the public through the Internet by Mann Library.

THE USDA ECONOMICS AND STATISTICS SYSTEM

The USDA Economics and Statistics System was introduced to the public at the end of 1993.[2] At that time the System contained approximately 150 different datasets and full-text reports on various aspects of the production, cost, and trade of agricultural products. The USDA System is not only a collection of titles, but it also includes an important service component. Since these files are available to the public and many questions arise regarding their use and content, the System provides online information to assist users and contact information for those needing additional help.

In April 1995 the System was expanded significantly with the addition of time-sensitive commodity reports as an important feature of the service. With the addition of these reports, there are now over 300 different titles in the collection. Users can access these reports and datasets by title, subject, agency, or keyword search. Figure 1 shows the initial screen that one sees after logging into the USDA Economics and Statistics System.[3]

The use of the USDA System has steadily increased. In May 1996 there were over 12,000 logins to the System. Users can use the WWW, gopher, telnet, or ftp to access the USDA System. In addition, since the commodity reports contain time-sensitive information of economic value, many researchers want access to this information immediately after it becomes available to the public. Individuals can subscribe to one title or groups of titles and automatically be sent a copy of any new issue posted to the USDA System by Mann Library staff. Since these reports are published on a preset schedule, researchers don't need to wait, check the time, and log onto the system to see if a new issue has been added. There are now over 1,600 unique subscribers who, as a group, maintain almost 10,000 subscriptions. Interest in individual titles varies considerably. For example, there are over 300 subscribers for the latest data on wheat production, but a mere 23 for walnut production.

SCREEN 1

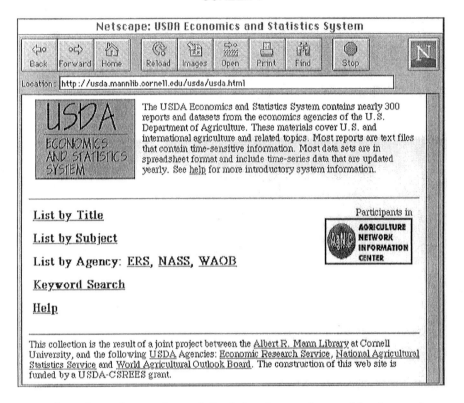

The USDA Economics and Statistics System is possible due to the commitment of resources and staff by both partners. Although many libraries would have an interest in providing up-to-date agricultural information, few would take the significant step to set up and maintain a system. It is important to understand the goals and roles of each partner.

MANN LIBRARY

The Albert R. Mann Library is the second largest library in the Cornell University Library system. It has approximately 700,000 volumes and supports over 20 departments in the NYS College of Agriculture and Life Sciences, the NYS College of Human Ecology, and the Divisions of Biological and Nutritional Sciences. It has one of the preeminent research collections in the field of agriculture.

Mann Library is also the largest of the state-funded land grant libraries at Cornell. This land grant designation is an important factor in how the Library interprets its mission and goals. Not only does the Library serve the faculty, students, and staff of Cornell University, but it endeavors to provide varied services to the citizens of New York state. As the Library increasingly developed its collections of online resources, it was clear that contractual limitations for most commercial or proprietary resources would restrict use of those items to the Cornell community or provide limited access to in-Library use of the resources to the general public.

The Library also has a large networked electronic collection which can be accessed through what is called the Mann Library Gateway (http://www.mannlib. cornell.edu/catalog/). The Gateway is a single point of access to over 550 networked titles, including bibliographic, numeric, and full-text files and it is widely used by the Cornell community.

In the early years of the Gateway, most of the files available were bibliographic databases, such as BIOSIS and AGRICOLA, but there was a growing interest in developing online collections of full-text and numeric files. The need to build a core collection, a critical mass that would be useful for researchers, was also recognized. If the Gateway continued to contain only sparse collections in numerous fields, it would not effectively meet researchers' needs. In 1992 library staff had already begun to investigate potential sources of research-quality resources to add to our online collections.

THE USDA ECONOMIC AGENCIES

The U.S. government collects an enormous amount of statistics and is in turn a huge publisher. The USDA economic agencies are no exception to this phenomenon. Among these agencies are the Economic Research Service (ERS), the National Agricultural Statistics Service (NASS), and the World Agricultural Outlook Board (WAOB). As economic agencies they collect data on numerous aspects of agricultural economics, whether on the production, cost, and trade of specific products, or about related topics such as farm labor, land prices, weather conditions, or use of fertilizers. Many of these statistical compilations were well-suited for publication and use in electronic form. By 1993 these agencies already had a catalog of approximately 150 electronic products for sale on diskettes. With the addition of new titles and the time-sensitive, full-text commodity reports, there are now approximately 300 titles available in electronic form. Many of these titles are also available in print, and Mann Library continues to receive them through the Federal Depository Program.

Together, the 300 titles create a core collection in agricultural economics. The titles do, however, vary considerably in regards to their size, format, and frequency of updates. For example, there are large datasets containing historical and current time series data that need to be used with a spreadsheet program, such as Lotus 1-2-3, and there are many full-text reports that vary considerably in length and coverage. Some reports are updated infrequently or never, yet many are published on a regular schedule. As in any serials collection there are annuals, quarterlies, monthlies, and weeklies. Some titles are published only during the growing season.

A brief sampling of titles includes the very large *Crops County Data* and the *World Agricultural Supply and Demand Estimates* to more unusual titles such as *Poultry Slaughter,* and *Catfish Processing.* Occasionally supplements are also received, such as *Sheep and Goats Predator Loss.*

THE PARTNERSHIP

As with many things in life, this partnership began with an informal discussion over coffee. Mann Library's Government Information Librarian, Gregory Lawrence, was in Washington, DC, attending a conference. There, during a coffee break, he chatted with Jim Horsfield, who is Branch Chief for the Research Support and Training Division at ERS.

The ERS and other agencies were interested in better disseminating their information electronically but had not yet developed the infrastructure to do it. Mann Library had the interest, the experience, and an online system, the Gateway, which could be expanded to include these publications.

The two organizations shared a vision to make a core collection of agricultural information freely available to the public as widely as possible. With that in mind, Greg, Jim, and others in both organizations discussed details about what could be done. A Memorandum of Understanding was signed which outlined the objectives of the partnership, listed the obligations of each party, and set a time line for developing and implementing the system.

Both partners were full participants, and each brought resources to the partnership that the other needed or wanted. The economic agencies supplied the datasets and full-text reports; they also supplied start-up funds. The agencies were looking for a cost-effective means to better disseminate their information. Contributing to the further development of Mann Library's online system, the Gateway, was less expensive than starting from scratch. The agencies also remained the authority on the data. If there were questions regarding the content of the reports, staff in each agency could be contacted.

Mann Library had the experience in providing access and user support to online resources. Its online system, already developed, could be expanded to include the USDA reports. The Library also brought other skills to the partnership, such as organizing and cataloging the collection. In addition, public services staff would field questions by phone or electronic mail from users nationwide about how to use the system and download the data. Help guides were also written and included in the system. The Library would maintain the collection and would keep an archive of the reports.

Both partners not only contributed essential resources and skills, but they were complementary. Together the partners could develop and maintain the system; independently it would take much greater effort and resources.

THE IMPACT ON ACQUISITIONS

Two other features of successful partnerships–communication and flexibility–are best demonstrated by examples of processing reports and maintaining the system. Communication and flexibility aren't only essential at the beginning, planning stages, but are necessary components to any ongoing relationship. The reports and datasets that comprise this collection of USDA resources are processed in the Acquisitions Unit at Mann Library. Early on in Mann Library's evolution to an increasingly electronic library it was decided that staff in all the units had skills and experience to contribute to its development. It was in the individual units that specialized skills for acquiring materials, organizing the collection, and providing user support already existed.

New issues and new titles are uploaded to a locally maintained server by staff who usually process print monographs and serials. Unlike earlier initiatives with electronic resources, where the Unit only handled the contracts and payments for new online collections, the USDA System also required that the Acquisitions Unit develop the skills and procedures for retrieving and uploading files. Designing the procedures and routinely handling new files produced by the USDA economic agencies have demanded considerable flexibility on the part of staff within the Unit and good communication between Mann Library and the agencies. The need for effective communication is clear when one looks at who is involved in the service. At each of the three USDA agencies there are two or three staff members involved in the preparation of the reports or administrative details. At Mann Library, staff throughout the library are involved. In the Acquisitions Unit, the Government Information Librarian, the Acquisitions Librarian, and three staff members participate in processing the reports.

Approximately 10-15 new reports are received each week. For the time-sensitive commodity reports staff work from a preset schedule and know the date and time when a new issue is expected. Staff will usually have reports posted to the server and accessible to the public within 5-10 minutes of their availability. There are sometimes delays and due to the importance of handling these reports quickly, the staff need to contact the appropriate agency to determine the status of the reports. Sometimes a delayed report will require a staff member to stay later than scheduled or add a message online about the status of the report. This type of ongoing communication is both routine and essential.

A partnership is not static; things change, and there are unforeseen developments or snags. Flexibility is very much tied to good communication and it is important for both the big issues and small details. For example, Mann Library entered into a 3-year agreement with the USDA agencies and during this time technology developed considerably. Mann Library made the system available via the WWW earlier this year; that development could not have been foreseen in 1993.

CONCLUSION

Working with the USDA not only provided an opportunity for Mann Library to develop its own online collection, but also helped the library fulfill part of its land grant mission to serve users outside the Cornell community. It took thought, effort, and planning and also required new skills from the staff, but it is a successful effort that staff have pride in.

By working with the Economic Research Service, the National Agricultural Statistics Service, and the World Agricultural Outlook Board, Mann Library was able to develop a System that helped serve the needs of all the partners. The partners brought complementary skills and resources to the collaboration. Although most libraries would not have an interest in developing and maintaining an online collection in agricultural economics, this field is central to the mission of all the members of this partnership. By successfully making these resources freely available to the public, the goals and purpose of the partnership and the individual partners are well-served.

NOTES

1. Rosabeth Moss Kanter, "Collaborative Advantage: The Art Of Alliance," *Harvard Business Review* 72, no. 4:96-108 (1994).

2. For more information on the USDA System, see: Gregory Lawrence, "U.S. Agricultural Statistics on the Internet: Extending the Reach of the Depository Library," Journal of Government Information v. 24, no. 4:443-452 (1996).

3. Access instructions to the *USDA Economics and Statistics System*:
World Wide Web: URL: http//usda.mannlib.cornell.edu/usda
Gopher: Host = usda.mannlib.cornell.edu
Telnet: Host = usda.mannlib.cornell.edu
- User ID = usda <lower case>

FTP: Host = usda.mannlib.cornell.edu
- User ID = anonymous
- Password = <your e-mail address (optional)>
- After logging in, change the directory with the following command: cd usda

NASIG WORKSHOPS

Finding the Missing Link:
How Cataloging Bridges the Gap
Between Libraries and the Internet

Pamela Simpson

Workshop Leader

Patricia Banach

Recorder

SUMMARY. Information from government sources is being added to the Internet at an ever-increasing rate. Catalogers at Penn State are working with AACR2, OCLC's Internet Cataloging Project (Intercat), and the creators of the Penn State Libraries' World Wide Web

Pamela Simpson is Serials Cataloging Librarian, Pennsylvania State University. Patricia Banach is Head of the Cataloging Department, W.E.B. Du Bois Library, University of Massachusetts, Amherst, MA.

© 1997 by the North American Serials Interest Group, Inc. All rights reserved.

[Haworth co-indexing entry note]: "Finding the Missing Link: How Cataloging Bridges the Gap Between Libraries and the Internet." Banach, Patricia. Co-published simultaneously in *The Serials Librarian* (The Haworth Press, Inc.) Vol. 31, No. 1/2, 1997, pp. 245-249; and: *Pioneering New Serials Frontiers: From Petroglyphs to Cyberserials* (ed: Christine Christiansen and Cecilia Leathem) The Haworth Press, Inc., 1997, pp. 245-249. Single or multiple copies of this article are available for a fee from The Haworth Document Delivery Service [1-800-342-9678, 9:00 a.m. - 5:00 p.m. (EST). E-mail address: getinfo@haworth.com].

Home Page to include both Internet sites and electronic publications in the library's online catalog. The use of cataloging records to show relationships between Internet resources and the printed materials that they supplement or replace is demonstrated. *[Article copies available for a fee from The Haworth Document Delivery Service: 1-800-342-9678. E-mail address: getinfo@haworth.com]*

In this workshop Pamela Simpson, Serials Cataloging Librarian at Pennsylvania State University, described a project in which she and a Documents Librarian, Dena Hutto, explored the possibility of providing better access to government documents Internet materials by creating cataloging records for Penn State's online catalog. The impetus for this project was two-fold: (1) the desire to provide access in the catalog for the Internet resources already available on the Penn State Libraries Documents homepage, and (2) the announced intention of the U.S. Government Printing Office to discontinue paper publications in favor of electronic format by 1998.[1] As an 85% depository library, Penn State had many government documents titles in paper format already cataloged and present in their catalog. The prospect of losing access to these titles when they switched to electronic format was not appealing. Furthermore, Federal Depository Libraries are mandated to provide access to depository materials.

SELECTION

Although Penn State did have experience cataloging non-print formats and had been routinely adding records to their OPAC for CD-ROMS, computer files, and electronic media for some time, they had not dealt with the broad array of issues presented by the cataloging of Internet resources until April 1996, the start of the project described by this workshop. The first consideration was what selection criteria to use in determining which government documents sources to catalog. These criteria for electronic resources should be very much the same as the criteria for print resources.

Since the library is, in effect, providing a quality filter for the Internet, Ms. Simpson emphasized the importance of selecting authoritative sources. With finite cataloging staffing available, it is essential to focus their efforts effectively. In implementing this selection criteria, the library chose to include in the project those Internet resources already listed on the library's Documents homepage, as well as document titles whose print versions were ceasing.

CATALOGING ISSUES

Ms. Simpson presented several examples of cataloging records for titles from the project and discussed some of the cataloging decisions that had to be made concerning them. One concern was how to deal with the fact that the Penn State OPAC does not yet display or provide a "hot-link" from the 856 field which includes the URL (uniform resource locator). The solution was to add a 538 field which displays the Internet address in a note, appropriately labelled "Internet Address." Providing access to a passworded web site posed another challenge. In this case, the solution was to add a 506 field which displays a note labelled "Local access: Password available at Documents Reference Desk." The question of whether or not to add a holdings statement for Internet resources was decided in the negative. Ms. Simpson's rationale was that a holdings screen is intended to provide information on materials actually *held* by the library. In the case of Internet resources, the library does not actually hold the materials and the prospect of maintaining an accurate holdings statement in an ever-changing environment is too daunting.

CASE STUDIES

To underscore the full extent of the cataloging options possible in various situations, Ms. Simpson presented the workshop audience with two case studies and asked them to consider how they would catalog these titles. The first case study was the *Debates of the House of Commons of Canada (Hansard)*. Since the individual online issues lack a title, Ms. Simpson chose as the cataloging title the information included on the title screen of the homepage and cited that source in a 500 note. Two 538 notes were included in the record showing "Mode of access: World Wide Web" and the "Internet address" detailing the Web address. For future "hot-link" capability, a non-displaying 856 field was also added. No attempt to show beginning date of publication, or date specific holdings information was made because of the uncertain nature of the online file, which can change. Instead, Ms. Simpson added a 530 note to the record for the paper edition, stating "Current issues available in an online edition," and a 776 field in the record for the paper version, linking it to the entry for the online version.

A somewhat different challenge was posed by the second case study which focused on the multi-section title *Current industrial reports.* In this case, the paper version, which was cataloged separately for 135 individually named sections, was summarized on one record for the online version. The labor-intensive nature of creating and *maintaining* 135 separate records for the online format was considered prohibitive. Instead, a 520 summary note was included in the record for the online version, and each of the records for the paper versions was modified to add a 787 linking field for the online version. A 580 linking note was also added to each of the records for the paper format stating "Information for 1992–available via Internet at this address: [followed by the Internet address]."

AUDIENCE DISCUSSION

Ms. Simpson's workshop was well-attended, the first session having 126 registrants and the second 76. Throughout the workshop, considerable audience discussion and participation occurred as NASIG members grappled with the cataloging problems posed by this new format. Ms. Simpson's cataloging solutions, while not totally orthodox according to the cataloging rules, seemed well-received by the audience. One new proposal, currently under discussion in the serials cataloging community, was the possibility of allowing the addition of an 856 field for the URL to be added to the record for the paper version of a title that is switching to electronic format. Whether this proposal gains wider acceptance is still under consideration, but it was clear that a number of members of the audience favored it as a practical solution.

While the discussion was wide ranging, two basic concepts received considerable attention. One was the concept of identification vs. description. It was suggested that catalogers consider the option of attempting only to adequately *identify* the nature and scope of online sources rather than attempting to exhaustively describe them in an environment where change is the norm. The second concept that was explored during the exchange with audience participants was the question of whether it was sufficient to provide one cataloging record to uniquely identify the intellectual content of a title rather than attempting to catalog all of its manifestations separately.

CONCLUSION

It was clear from the interest and level of attendance and participation that the challenges posed by cataloging of Internet resources is a topic much on the minds of today's serials catalogers. One comment from an audience member provided a thought-provoking admonition to those present, and, by extension, to the serials cataloging community at large: we are the ones who made the serials cataloging rules and we are the ones who need to creatively re-examine them in order to provide both a useful and realistic approach to providing information access in a new information environment. This workshop was an effort to do just that, and it was, by all criteria, a successful effort in that regard.

NOTES

1. *Administrative Notes: newsletter of the Federal Depository Library Program,* v. 16, no. 18 (Dec. 29, 1995).

Untangle the Web:
Introduction to Browsers and HTML

Donnice Cochenour

Workshop Leader

Sarah Tusa

Recorder

SUMMARY. Cochenour designed this workshop for serialists who have had little or no experience with Internet browsers. After defining essential concepts and functions of browsers, the presenter and two assistants led the sixteen participants in a series of exercises in Netscape Navigator. Attendees learned to customize a Web screen, assign HTML markup tags to text, and incorporate images and links to other Web sites into a home page. Ms. Cochenour provided two handouts, which contained not only basic information about browsers, but several pertinent references as well. *[Article copies available for a fee from The Haworth Document Delivery Service: 1-800-342-9678. E-mail address: getinfo@haworth.com]*

Donnice Cochenour provided a hands-on introduction to basic concepts and functions of Web browsers in her tutorial-style presentation, which was held in room 254 of Zimmerman Library. The sixteen attendees, all librarians, sat in pairs at the eight personal computers residing in the room.

Donnice Cochenour is Serials Librarian, Morgan Library, Colorado State University.

Sarah Tusa is Serials Acquisitions Librarian, Lamar University, Beaumont, TX.

[Haworth co-indexing entry note]: "Untangle the Web: Introduction to Browsers and HTML." Tusa, Sarah. Co-published simultaneously in *The Serials Librarian* (The Haworth Press, Inc.) Vol. 31, No. 1/2, 1997, pp. 251-254; and: *Pioneering New Serials Frontiers: From Petroglyphs to Cyberserials* (ed: Christine Christiansen and Cecilia Leathem) The Haworth Press, Inc., 1997, pp. 251-254. Single or multiple copies of this article are available for a fee from The Haworth Document Delivery Service [1-800-342-9678, 9:00 a.m. - 5:00 p.m. (EST). E-mail address: getinfo@haworth.com].

Two handouts were provided to each participant. One was a thirty-eight page reproduction of the workshop slides and exercises. The second handout was a double-sided page that contained an "HTML Quick Reference Guide" on one side and "Entering HTML text (in a Windows environment)" on the reverse. Two assistants opened Netscape Navigator at each PC workstation and continued to oversee the progress of each participant throughout the session. The workshop objectives were stated as follows: to understand the basic setup and operation of a Web browser; to understand the basic HTML markup elements used to create a Web page; and to create a simple Web page. Attendees were directed to follow along on the prepared diskettes, which were loaded onto the Netscape browser. Following the outlined objectives for her presentation, Ms. Cochenour began with a functional definition of a Web browser as "a software program which allows one to connect to computer servers available on the Internet." As explained in the workshop, a Web browser belongs in the "client" category of the "client/server" model frequently referred to in the context of the Internet. Within this framework, Ms. Cochenour explained that while typical functions of the "server" are to provide storage, retrieval, and links to electronic files, the functions of the client have to do with screen display, printing, and downloading of documents. The client interprets mouse and keyboard commands and thus serves as the tool with which one performs Internet searches and manipulates the retrieved data. The term "browser" originated specifically in connection with the World Wide Web, but Ms. Cochenour pointed out that some browsers can connect a user with the Internet through gopher sites, FTP sites, and via telnet, and some even enable e-mail communication. Ms. Cochenour then explained that HTML tags are the means by which the browser "interprets the structure of the text" for a Web page and partially determines "how the text is formatted."

The presenter then explained the function and structure of uniform resource locators (URL's). The URL is a machine-readable code that allows an Internet browser to "send a request to the appropriate Internet address and retrieve or access the resource." The structure of a URL, as presented in one of the workshop slides, consists of two parts. The first part identifies "the protocol required to communicate with the host server." A prevalent example is "http" (hypertext transfer protocol), which signifies a link to the World Wide Web. The URL for a gopher server, on the other hand, uses the protocol designation of "gopher." The second part of the URL provides the Internet address for a given information source. The address in turn is comprised of the network address and the filename of the source, including pertinent directory paths where applicable. Attendees also learned that the appearance of a tilde in a URL designates a personal home page. However, it is important to remember that personal home pages need to be updated periodically in order to provide accurate information. In the longer handout Ms. Cochenour provided a few sample URL's to sites of particular interest to NASIG members.

The presenter then turned to the topic of home pages. The home page constitutes a starting place for individuals, organizations, and companies who wish to provide access to information via the Internet. Typically, a home page provides information about the provider and/or links to favorite or relevant Web sites. Included in the slides and handout was a list of sample Web sites of interest to serialists and Web users in general, including sources for guides to HTML use. The sites are listed in the handout under the following categories: organizations, style guides, search engines and indexes, HTML/Web standards, HTML tools/tutorials, and other interesting/fun sites. The workshop disk even provides active links to each site listed.

To illustrate the browser's function of controlling the display of Web text, the presenter demonstrated how to customize one's screen in Netscape by using selections under the "options" menu. For example, under the category of "general preferences" one can select different display colors for items such as background, links, followed links, and text.

After a demonstration of how to use other items on the menu bar, the HTML exercises began. Ms. Cochenour prefaced the exercises with a concise overview of hypertext markup language (HTML). She explained that because Web browsers cannot interpret word processing commands, HTML tags are necessary to control the appearance and formatting of text for the Web. Each markup tag was presented individually, and a separate exercise was conducted for each tag. The handout titled "HTML Quick Reference Guide" contained a number of essential tags listed in categories according to function. Participants then performed a series of exercises on the 3.5" disks provided. The exercises included attaching document structure tags to pre-existing text, to applying formatting tags, creating lists, and creating "anchors" (links to a location within a document or to another Web site).

For the first exercise, participants were instructed to assign HTML structural tags to a brief unformatted text. To this end, Ms. Cochenour demonstrated how to toggle between the text editor program "Notepad" and the browser display to view the HTML page by holding down the "alt" key and tapping the "tab" key on the computer keyboard. After inserting the appropriate tags (e.g., <HTML>,</HTML>), the group learned to reload the text into Netscape and view the altered text. The next exercise entailed formatting headings by use of the <H> . . . </H> commands with various assigned levels. Each level is designated by attaching a numerical value to the tag, where the digit "1" produces the largest heading font. In the next exercise, the fledgling Web enthusiasts applied "empty" HTML elements to produce line breaks <BR>, paragraph breaks <P>, and horizontal lines <HR>. As Ms. Cochenour cites in her handout, "because these tags indicate a spacing action and do not apply to specific text, they *do not* require a closing tag." Similar to headings, horizontal lines can also be assigned a number to designate thickness.

Because Web browsers do not recognize word processing commands, as stated earlier, character style tags constituted yet another exercise. While tags for boldface, underlining, and italics were presented, it was nevertheless pointed out that the Netscape browser does not recognize the underline tag <U>. It disregards this tag, no formatting takes place, and the text is left plain. Similarly, other browsers do not recognize various tags and ignore their occurrence. Another important thing to remember is that the <pre> tag preserves the spacing exactly as it exists in the text bracketed by the beginning and ending tags <pre> and </pre>. No formatting takes place within said text. In earlier versions of the HTML standard, this was the only way to create columns and control spacing between text.

The participants then learned and practiced creating unordered and ordered lists, before advancing to the final exercises, in which they created links to other Web locations and incorporated images into HTML text. To this end, participants learned to create "anchors" or "hotlinks" to other resources available on the Internet. Due to technical difficulties with one of the workstations and to a few missteps in completing the previous exercises, the task of creating inline images was left to be completed at home. Participants were also encouraged to experiment with creating their own Web pages. In addition to the "HTML Design Tips" included in the handout, a number of the home pages cited in the longer handout and on the diskette provide further instruction on browsers and Web page design.

The target audience for "Untangle the Web" was beginners, and the level of experience of the 16 attendees ranged from minimal experience with Web browsers to none at all. There were a few occasions during the presentation and the exercises where one or more participants had a little difficulty keeping up because of the time constraints, but in general the ambience of a successful classroom prevailed. One comment offered by the presenter seemed particularly well-received because it provided a trace of familiarity to an otherwise new experience. Those participants who remembered earlier versions of word processing nodded in recognition when Ms. Cochenour pointed out the similarity between HTML tags and commands used in early word processing programs. Participants also expressed appreciation for the distribution of the workshop diskette and the practical nature of the handouts.

Serials Management in Special Libraries: Present and Future Relationships Between Libraries and Vendors

Georgia Briscoe
Paul Wakeford
Anne McKee

Workshop Leaders

Phoebe Timberlake

Recorder

SUMMARY. The management issues facing those who deal with serials in special libraries may be common to all special libraries, unique to the particular discipline, or shared by all libraries struggling to deal with serials in the 1990s. A law librarian and a medical librarian described the history, nature, and use of serial literature in their respective subject areas, and discussed important customer issues facing their libraries, including the financial aspects. They

---

Georgia Briscoe is Associate Director and Head of Technical Services, University of Colorado Law Library.

Paul Wakeford is Coordinator, Resources Management, University of California, San Francisco.

Anne McKee is Territory Sales Manager, The Faxon Company.

Phoebe Timberlake is Chair of Resource Coordination, Earl K. Long Library, University of New Orleans.

[Haworth co-indexing entry note]: "Serials Management in Special Libraries: Present and Future Relationships Between Libraries and Vendors." Timberlake, Phoebe. Co-published simultaneously in *The Serials Librarian* (The Haworth Press, Inc.) Vol. 31, No. 1/2, 1997, pp. 255-260; and: *Pioneering New Serials Frontiers: From Petroglyphs to Cyberserials* (ed: Christine Christiansen and Cecilia Leathem) The Haworth Press, Inc., 1997, pp. 255-260. Single or multiple copies of this article are available for a fee from The Haworth Document Delivery Service [1-800-342-9678, 9:00 a.m. - 5:00 p.m. (EST). E-mail address: getinfo@haworth.com].

were joined by a vendor's representative who summarized the similarities and differences in these library situations from a vendor's
perspective, including the opportunities and limitations of the ven-
dor/special library relationship. *[Article copies available for a fee from
The Haworth Document Delivery Service: 1-800-342-9678. E-mail address:
getinfo@haworth.com]*

The unique aspects of legal and medical serials, how the patrons of
these special libraries use their serials, and the serious financial and organizational issues facing law and medical libraries provided the focus for
this workshop which concluded with a description of the vendor/special
library relationship. Georgia Briscoe, Associate Director and Head of
Technical Services, University of Colorado Law Library, began by stating
that she had wanted to open her presentation with a joke but realized that
"there is nothing funny" about legal serials. The law changes daily with
each new case or statute. "Administrative regulations breed like rabbits."
Because the law changes constantly, serials are the best way to monitor the
changes, and therefore they dominate law libraries (accounting for 80% of
the materials). Legal serials grow exponentially, are usually chronological
in nature, supersede each other, and require exact indexing. They are
published in many formats, including pamphlets, looseleaf, advance
sheets, supplements, pocket parts, interim bound volumes, and permanent
bound volumes. Removal of superseded/outdated material is as critical as
providing access to the current. Patrons may need to work from a broad
overview of a topic explained in one of the multivolume legal encyclopedias (*American Jurisprudence* or *Corpus Juris Secundum,* both updated
annually or semiannually) to the latest law or court decision in a set of
codes (statutes in a subject arrangement), digests (cases annotated in a
subject arrangement), a treatise, a restatement, or a periodical index. All of
these materials are issued in serial format.

Although a number of different publishers print the same court decisions or laws, legal publishing is dominated by a relatively small number
of publishers. Some of them, such as Lawyers Cooperative Publishing and
West Publishing Company, date back to the late 1800s. There is also a very
small group of vendors who specialize in legal materials: Fred B. Roth-
man, William S. Hein, and William W. Gaunt & Sons.

In terms of financial management, prices for law books and serials have
been compiled annually for twenty years by law librarian Bettie Scott and
published in *Law Library Journal.* This year's price index was issued as a
separate publication, available from the American Association of Law
Libraries. In comparison to some other subject areas, prices have not
inflated as drastically, ranging in recent years from less than 1% to almost

18%. Briscoe stressed how fortunate this has been because law librarians find it very difficult to eliminate titles when all cases are citable and all laws must be accessible. In 1969, an article in the *American Bar Association Journal* caused the Federal Trade Commission to investigate the law book industry and to ultimately issue guidelines for them, the only area of publishing to be given this treatment. (The guidelines are published in Title 16 of the *Code of Federal Regulations.*) The findings addressed complaints such as putting new titles and bindings on old books and adding local names to books that were not truly local. Even with the guidelines in place, what Briscoe called "oversupplementation" or the issuing of unnecessary supplements remains a major problem. There may also be financial consequences of the continuing buyouts of one publisher by another. With the most recent agreement, Thompson Corporation will own West Publishing Company, giving them control of 100% of the national legal encyclopedias, 76% of state legal encyclopedias, 100% of commercial U.S. Supreme Court reporters, and 100% of the Supreme Court digests. With every merger, competition decreases and library expenditures increase. Briscoe concluded her presentation by acknowledging that "It's an interesting time to be a law librarian, and if you're a law librarian, you're also a serials librarian."

Paul J. Wakeford, Coordinator, Resources Management, University of California San Francisco Library, then described the characteristics of medical serials and the serials management challenges found in his medical library. In the early years of medical literature, there were no commercial publishers, just scientists and societies exchanging information and correspondence, and recording the transactions and proceedings of their meetings. Between the 17th and 20th centuries, however, publishers appeared, and the number of journals doubled approximately every thirty years, resulting in the journal literature expanding to 10,000 titles by the 1900s. A very common occurrence became the proliferation of titles by the splitting of established journals into multiple parts or sections. The immediacy or currency has always been important to medical library patrons, but as the number of titles increased, the need to index and retrieve specific information quickly helped bring about the development of abstracting and indexing services such as the National Library of Medicine's *Index Medicus,* and eventually, Medline. Another important characteristic of the literature is the frequent use of illustrations, and that has encouraged the use of more expensive, glazed or glossy paper which renders those illustrations more faithfully.

The financial picture painted by Wakeford is a library materials budget which is now 80% serials and 20% books, moving toward a probable 95%

to 5% split by the end of the century. Demands placed on the budget by serials inflation are so great that it is difficult to maintain a return rate acceptable to any vendor for a book approval plan. Wakeford's institution competes with several other similar institutions for federal funds but now finds itself having to do this with a diminishing number of periodical titles, down from 4500 titles five years ago to an expected 1500 next year. Generally, the research faculty are the high-demand users, rather than the clinicians, and electronic journals, remote access, and document delivery are some of the ways in which medical libraries increasingly will be rendering service to their users. The shelflife of medical journal literature is generally three to five years, with use falling off rapidly after the first year or two, and this factor must be considered in purchasing decisions. Fortunately, medical libraries have a long history of resource sharing with the National Library of Medicine leading the way. In the 1960s, a network of regional medical libraries was established as a means of getting information to the clinicians, and that continues, while enhancing collections through exchange programs has pretty much disappeared. Another factor the medical librarian must consider is that patrons do a lot of photocopying with approximately a half million copies being made each month or six million copies per year. This behavior must be examined when the possibility of providing journal literature in another form is considered. Most of their foreign language subscriptions have already been canceled, and while many of the remaining journals are published in Europe, the articles are written by researchers in the United States.

Wakeford's library has been involved in the Red Sage Electronic Journal Library and Alerting System, a partnership with AT&T Bell Laboratories and Springer-Verlag to make approximately seventy-five journals in molecular biology, radiology, and general medicine available on the Internet. Bell Laboratories RightPages software provides a graphical interface enabling users to browse, search, read, and print articles. Links have been established from *Index Medicus* to the articles in the journals database. As the project concludes its third year, a means is being sought to greatly expand the number of titles included.

Another development with potential for affecting libraries and vendors is the Subscribe software developed by Rowecom. Wakeford's library is one of about a dozen using this Internet-based product for ordering, claiming, and even transferring funds through EDI. With Subscribe, on a base of approximately 75 titles, he estimated his saving at about 5-8%. Wakeford closed by suggesting that all libraries are facing the questions of "Vendor Who? Who publishes what and who sells it to whom?"

As the final presenter, Anne McKee, Serials Specialist with Blackwell's

Periodicals, spoke from the vendor's viewpoint. Serials were originally handled by book suppliers, but as serials became more numerous, interest increased in working exclusively with this kind of material. However, within the industry, the 1960s saw a push to automate services, the beginning of the slide in publishers' discounts to agents, and many closings, mergers, and buyouts of smaller agencies. Currently, serials vendors assist libraries in managing ordering, claiming, and payment operations. They also maintain current bibliographic and pricing information on tens of thousands of journals. By consolidating the invoices for many subscriptions, they eliminate the cost of cutting thousands of checks. Vendors are also providing increasingly specialized services to libraries including electronic options such as electronic ordering, claiming, invoicing, and various kinds of collection management reports, either standard or customized. They are also expanding the services they can offer in the way of "outsourcing" activities, including making the library's materials shelf-ready upon arrival. Vendors continue to serve publishers by handling many orders for the same title, combining payments, securing renewals, and performing preliminary work on claims.

Vendors accustomed to dealing with law libraries understand that most law serials are considered "core," leaving little that can be canceled. Law libraries rarely subscribe to foreign titles. The libraries are usually smaller, with fewer staff, and those staff often have broader, more varied responsibilities than at other libraries. Their travel budgets may be completely consumed by travel to specialized meetings such as those of American Association of Law Librarians, denying them the opportunity to send staff to American Library Association or other "mainstream" conferences. Their publications are constantly changing and appear in various formats, and the libraries will probably have to purchase all formats. Publishers may prefer that libraries deal directly with them, and, therefore, offer little to vendors in the way of discounts or incentives. Law libraries tend to change vendors very infrequently.

In contrast, medical libraries include both medical school and hospital libraries. The medical school libraries tend to be larger and more academic in service type, while the hospital libraries have fewer staff, are more corporate in service type, and are seeing more consolidation and outsourcing of materials and services. The titles that are purchased by medical libraries are often highly specialized, very expensive, published by foreign publishers, and may offer higher publisher discounts, therefore being more attractive to vendors. However, this is a very volatile market with increasing electronic access.

Common to both law and medical libraries is the fact that their materials may require special handling. The customer service representative with prior experience is valued, and some vendors may even have specialized divisions to handle these materials. The patrons of both types of libraries have the same need for very current information and a growing reliance on electronic sources. A majority of the information in these specialized areas may be controlled by a minority of publishers, and the quantity and cost of the information is growing exponentially. Both types of libraries prefer common expiration dates on their subscriptions whenever possible, and the library staff readily utilize electronic listservs to stay in touch with other similar libraries and their vendors and publishers. Publishers' discounts to particular vendors and subscription agents can vary, and that may cause variations in the arrangements different agents can offer a library for the same material.

For the future, there will probably be a continuing decline in the number of subscription agencies. Transaction related benefits are of diminishing value to publishers; they want more help in reaching and retaining key markets. Discounts will continue to drop and eventually disappear altogether due to (1) increased shareholder pressures for profits, and (2) the flat market for journals. As the serials industry changes, vendors are caught in the middle. Some of them are looking to their own future, creating value through services such as table of contents and article databases.

McKee closed by suggesting the following points to consider when selecting a vendor: (1) Market–Is it segmented or specialized? Is the vendor knowledgeable in that market? (2) Location of the vendor–Does use of email and other online functions alleviate concerns about distance, time zones, etc.? (3) Service–Is there a single contact or a team approach? What is the level and type of training provided? (4) Sales representative–Is an MLS important in this position? Is previous experience in a library setting required? (5) Services offered–What are the invoicing, claiming, and renewal options? What will they cost? Can the vendor interface with a local automated system? (6) Perception of the future–Does the agent have realistic plans for the future? Each library must consider its "special" situation before selecting a vendor.

How to Build and Use a Customized Serials Information Database on Your Personal Computer

Rick Ralston

Workshop Leader

Robb M. Waltner

Recorder

SUMMARY. Librarians now have the capability, using a personal computer, to integrate bibliographic data, collection-use data, and even data from ILL requests into a customized serials database for the purpose of conducting automated use studies and qualitative collection analysis. This workshop builds upon a previous NASIG workshop and offers further ideas and enhancements for libraries creating customized databases. A general discussion of the issues and techniques related to building a customized serials database is presented, along with costs, benefits, and future considerations. *[Article copies available for a fee from The Haworth Document Delivery Service: 1-800-342-9678. E-mail address: getinfo@haworth.com]*

Rick Ralston is Head of Technical Services, Indiana University School of Medicine, Ruth Lilly Medical Library.

Robb M. Waltner is Periodicals Librarian, University of Evansville Libraries, Evansville, IN.

[Haworth co-indexing entry note]: "How to Build and Use a Customized Serials Information Database on Your Personal Computer." Waltner, Robb M. Co-published simultaneously in *The Serials Librarian* (The Haworth Press, Inc.) Vol. 31, No. 1/2, 1997, pp. 261-265; and: *Pioneering New Serials Frontiers: From Petroglyphs to Cyberserials* (ed: Christine Christiansen and Cecilia Leathem) The Haworth Press, Inc., 1997, pp. 261-265. Single or multiple copies of this article are available for a fee from The Haworth Document Delivery Service [1-800-342-9678, 9:00 a.m. - 5:00 p.m. (EST). E-mail address: getinfo@haworth.com].

This session was a follow-up to a workshop Rick Ralston co-presented at last year's North American Serials Interest Group (NASIG) conference in Durham, N.C. Reading the report of the previous workshop entitled "Automating Journal Use Studies: A Tale of Two Libraries" is recommended since many of the ideas presented during last year's workshop served as the basis of this presentation.[1] Further information may also be found in Ralston and Francq's article on gathering statistics in a serials collection.[2]

This year's workshop was attended by approximately 60 conference attendees, mostly librarians. As an introduction, Ralston discussed the management of a serials collection. For three years, the Ruth Lilly Medical Library has conducted an automated use study of the serials collection using portable barcode readers and *Paradox* database software. The result of this project is a customized serials database with use statistics for every title. Despite the fact that many libraries are automated and often have access to some automated serials control, the construction of a customized serials database maintained on a personal computer facilitates data gathering and provides valuable information in support of serials collection management. Two key reasons for creating and maintaining this database are:

1. No automated library system incorporates all the data needed to make collection decisions.
2. No automated library system offers report-generating capabilities which are flexible enough for use in serials management. This is especially true of mainframe-based automated library systems which often require difficult and lengthy consultation with personnel not associated with the library to extract useful data and reports.

PROCEDURES FOR BUILDING THE DATABASE

Below is an outline of the steps which facilitate the creation of a customized serials database:

1. *Collecting data:* When evaluating potential sources of data, the emphasis should be on making use of readily available electronic data over manually-keyed data. Sources of data that went into the creation of the original database produced at the Ruth Lilly Medical Library included bibliographic records produced by library management software and electronic files available from Ebsco, the library's vendor. The availability of electronic data will vary depending on the circumstances and systems at each library, but the primary goal should be to reduce the amount of time and labor required to enter data manually.

Interlibrary Loan (ILL) requests will soon be incorporated into the Lilly Library database. This will be accomplished by replacing all paper-based ILL requests with a Web-form. Request information will be entered by patrons through a Web page and downloaded from the Web server by the ILL Department. A Common Gateway Interface (CGI) script has been written to convert the Web-form information to an ASCII delimited text file. This file will then be imported into *Paradox,* the same database management system (DBMS) used in the serials use study. ILL staff will then complete processing of the request in this format. Since there is not as yet a link between *Paradox* and OCLC, ILL staff will be required to transfer this data to OCLC manually. Ralston is currently investigating ways of automating the delivery of this data to OCLC and other suppliers. The most significant point, however, is that once transferred into the DBMS, the ILL request information will be available for analysis along with the other elements in the database and will provide a more comprehensive analysis of serials activity.

2. *Managing data*: Two issues were discussed. First was the question of database design. Ralston cited an article which was important conceptually to his design.[3] The most important consideration was organizing the data into manageable portions and not attempting to accomplish too much with a single database table. The second issue discussed was backing up the database. No definitive preferences were outlined, for once again the circumstances of each library creating a customized database will vary. However, these two crucial issues need to be addressed during planning stages.

3. *Reporting data*: Examples of reports produced from the customized database were presented. The first example was a report which summarized the titles most frequently requested through ILL during the month of June 1996. A second example showed requests which were submitted to ILL even though the issues were already held by the library. These reports would then be used to identify collection deficiencies (e.g., new titles to order) or to indicate needed changes in processing and operational areas such as binding, shelving, etc.

COST/BENEFIT ANALYSIS

The costs associated with building a customized serials database consist of hardware, software, and human resources. In Ralston's use study, two portable barcode scanners are used to gather barcode data from shelf locations. Communication software is used to transfer this information to *Paradox*. The barcode readers and communication software were purchased from a vendor. The *Paradox* software was available via the campus network. The use of staff to scan barcodes while shelving has had no negative impact on the shelving operations at Lilly Library. Also, the librarian in charge of the database is required to plan, manage, and make use of the data. It was Ralston's opinion that this commitment of time and effort is still more efficient than working in coordination with ancillary computing services.

Two benefits were outlined as the results of having access to a customized database of serials collection data. First, Ralston reported that his collection, after three years of compiling use data, is starting to reflect better ratios between cost and use. In other words, low-use titles have been canceled. The reports now being produced indicate that the titles currently in the collection are consistently used, and the collection has little deadwood. The plan is to monitor the ILL data which will soon be added to the database for an indication of which new titles might need to be acquired.

Second, the reports produced from the database have played an important role in library administration and accreditation proceedings. Database reports are capable of showing effective utilization of the serials budget by the library and indisputable use of serial resources by patrons. Other reports have been produced which track each discipline's use of the collection as a percentage. These reports have proved worthwhile during accreditation and curricular reviews.

GETTING STARTED

There are four steps required to move forward in the development of a customized serials database:

1. Learn a database management system or spreadsheet program.
2. Investigate the sources and format of serials data at your institution.
3. Assess the need and availability for additional staff and funding to conduct the use study, purchase hardware, software, etc.
4. Plan the database based on the resources available.

TOWARD THE FUTURE

Further refinements are expected in automating data collection and manipulation. First, Ralston is working towards automated processing of online search results so that these results can be submitted electronically as document delivery requests. This would eliminate the need for patrons to enter data manually into an ILL Web-form. Second, the uploading of electronic borrowing requests to OCLC or other suppliers, such as Docline, is being investigated in order to eliminate manual data entry by ILL staff.

CONCLUSIONS

The recent era of serials cost increases and subscription cancellations has placed a high priority on effective and reliable stewardship of the serials budget and management of the serials collection. Institutions make a substantial investment in serial resources and often have little substantive justification for the expenditures. The two workshops presented on this subject have presented a highly automated and yet accessible process for implementing an automated use study, for building a customized serials database, and for enhancing it with the inclusion of ILL data. The workshops have inspired many librarians to re-think the efficacy of manual use studies or to begin an assessment of their own collection. Assessment has become a high priority for libraries because of serials inflation and decreasing collection budgets. Librarians who can plan and implement a customized serials database benefit in several ways:

1. Access to the database assists in making informed decisions about managing the collection by bringing all the relevant data together in an accessible format.
2. Relevant qualitative data is made available which demonstrates consistent use of serial resources, providing further justification for institutional support of the collection.
3. A collection analysis project, such as the construction of a customized serials database, demonstrates proactive management of serials resources through the removal of "under-utilized" resources from the collection and subsequent replacement with subscriptions which meet relevant curricular needs.

NOTES

1. Karen Cargille, "Automating Journal Use Studies: A Tale of Two Libraries," *The Serials Librarian* 28, no. 3/4 (1996): 349-353.
2. Rick Ralston and Carole Francq, "Subscription Statistics for Collection and Budget Decisions," *Indiana Libraries* 14, no. 3 (1995): 65-71.
3. Sal Ricciardi, "Database Design: Redundancy and Normalization," *PC Magazine* 13 (January 25, 1994): 285-287.

Expanded Roles:
Qualities That Serialists Can Bring
to Other Aspects of Information Work

Sandy Folsom
Marilyn Geller
Workshop Leaders

Jos Anemaet
Recorder

SUMMARY. Increasingly today, serials librarians have to accept additional responsibilities outside their primary areas of expertise. The skills serialists have gained in handling the complexities of serials cataloging make a solid foundation upon which to build proficiency in other areas of work within as well as outside the traditional library. Two professionals show how such skills are needed in the changing world of information services. *[Article copies available for a fee from The Haworth Document Delivery Service: 1-800-342-9678. E-mail address: getinfo@haworth.com]*

THE CHANGING ROLE OF THE SERIALIST
IN ACADEMIC LIBRARIES

Sandy Folsom, Serials Cataloger/Reference Librarian at Central Michigan University, began by describing the changing roles and responsibili-

---

Sandy Folsom is Serials Cataloger/Reference Librarian, Park Library, Central Michigan University.
Marilyn Geller is Internet Product Specialist, Readmore Academic Services, Inc.
Jos Anemaet is Cataloger, The Valley Library, Oregon State University.

[Haworth co-indexing entry note]: "Expanded Roles: Qualities That Serialists Can Bring to Other Aspects of Information Work." Anemaet, Jos. Co-published simultaneously in *The Serials Librarian* (The Haworth Press, Inc.) Vol. 31, No. 1/2, 1997, pp. 267-271; and: *Pioneering New Serials Frontiers: From Petroglyphs to Cyberserials* (ed: Christine Christiansen and Cecilia Leathem) The Haworth Press, Inc., 1997, pp. 267-271. Single or multiple copies of this article are available for a fee from The Haworth Document Delivery Service [1-800-342-9678, 9:00 a.m. - 5:00 p.m. (EST). E-mail address: getinfo@haworth.com].

ties of serialists and the reasons for these shifts within libraries. Performing an array of services and functions has been common for librarians in smaller libraries, but when university libraries experienced rapid growth in the 1960s, academic librarians tended to specialize in one subject or one area of service. An idealistic change from specialization to a more holistic, integrated model as envisioned by theorists like Michael Gorman[1] occurred in the late 1970s. While there were always some librarians who, from a need for personal satisfaction, chose to expand their technical services roles by accepting some public services responsibilities, by the 1990s the integration of positions was more often due to shrinking budgets, fewer staff, and a desire to provide better customer service. Many librarians were pushed into new areas by forces beyond their control. Today, the trend is toward reorganizing, down-sizing, and despecializing as libraries try to respond to greater user expectations with less money and ever-increasing prices for materials.

Folsom's presentation had two objectives. She wished to outline the qualities serialists bring to other areas of academic libraries and she also wanted to provide them with specific aids that would help their transition from technical services into a more public services role. Folsom is a prime example of a serials cataloger branching out into public services for many of the reasons mentioned. She started at Central Michigan University in 1984 as a serials cataloger in a traditional cataloging department. Her responsibilities included serials control and supervision of support staff. By 1990, Folsom had become deeply involved in the automation, upgrades, and retro conversion projects of the library. She also cataloged serials in a small departmental library and taught a 1-credit Bibliographic Instruction course each year. In 1995, after Folsom assumed the added responsibility of collection development in Women's Studies, her library decided to out-source all cataloging except serials. The elimination of the cataloging department and its staff resulted in the retirement of one of the professionals. The remaining two catalogers accepted reassignment. Folsom agreed to a 50% serials cataloging–50% Reference position and a changed job title.

QUALITIES SERIALISTS BRING TO OTHER ASPECTS OF LIBRARY WORK

Technical Knowledge and a Fresh Approach

Although the transition to unfamiliar work can be unsettling, serialists should remember that they have many skills to share with patrons and other librarians. They have a detailed knowledge and understanding of the online catalog and automated systems. Catalogers, in particular those who have been involved in recon projects or setting up automated systems, know what is and is not in the system or why it is not. They know what the preferred access terms are and the origin of and reasons for the cryptic messages in the OPACs. Serialists may also be able to save patrons' time and aggravation by recognizing and correcting errors in the online catalog. They are skilled at tracking down material because they are familiar with the workflow and procedures in technical services. Coming from technical services, serialists can bring a sense of novelty to their public services role and may inspire other librarians to expand into different areas. Because serialists often manage large, complicated projects, they are adept at working on multiple levels. Serialists are used to change and technological innovations and are good at explaining automated systems. However, their extensive and detailed understanding of the online system may need to be adjusted to the particular information needs of the patron.

TRANSITIONAL AIDS

The transitional aids Folsom offers the serialist going into unfamiliar territory may serve anyone moving into any new position equally well. She cautions that it is important to have a positive attitude. Try to assimilate new duties gradually, find a mentor, request and offer feedback. Resist the urge to use technical jargon that may not be helpful to patrons or colleagues and may cause ill will. Have a formal job description. All parties must have a clear understanding of the expectations, especially when more than one manager is involved. Make clear what you do and do not know so people understand your training needs. A systematic, ongoing training program is of utmost importance when embarking on a new venture, because the "sink or swim" approach is doomed to fail.

Folsom found that it takes time to "switch gears." It is important to know your own comfort level and habits and to avoid excessive fragmentation. For instance, she has a difficult time settling down again after working at the reference desk or teaching, so she prefers to do her cataloging work in the mornings. Have realistic expectations, for the serialist who goes from full-time to half-time cataloger cannot hope to provide the previous level of service or remain an expert. As the profession continues to face cut-backs and reorganization in the future, Folsom believes that we may all have to give up our expertise and be generalists. This trend seemed the most disturbing to the audience and Folsom did not have an answer to the question posed by a colleague: "Who will teach the entry-level library professional when all the experts have retired?"

SERIALISTS OUTSIDE THE LIBRARY

Marilyn Geller, Internet Product Specialist at Readmore Academic Services, covered the expanding roles of serialists from the perspective of a serials cataloger who branched out into a non-library setting. After Geller received her M.L.S., she first became a general cataloger and, for the next 10 years at MIT, a serials cataloger. Toward the end of her library career, she developed an interest in the Internet and its uses in the library. Her training as a serials cataloger made it easier to accept the intricacies of the Internet and the requirement for specific numbers or coding even if she did not always understand their meaning. This interest eventually led to a job offer from a serials subscription agency. Her skills as a serials cataloger continue to help her create products and services that are useful to libraries.

Serial Catalogers' Personality Traits

Geller attributes to serials catalogers certain unique personality traits that allow them to see catalogs as resources, not objects; make them tolerant of ambiguity and conscious of the impact of records on the rest of the world; cause them to be detail-oriented and flexible about change; but most of all, impel them to love crossword and/or jigsaw puzzles.

Serialists combine an understanding of the overall organization with an ability to deal with minutiae and a gift for gathering information from a variety of sources. However, just collecting materials is not enough. They must make it easier for patrons to recover the information or it may be useless. Serialists manage important details such as changes in titles, prices, numbers, and currency rates. They learn to analyze this data and put it all together. They understand the value of coding data and organizing it so it can be retrieved for they are familiar with different ways to catalog information, whether it is MARC formats, account and fund codes, or holdings records.

Commercial Environments

Libraries and commercial organizations that support libraries, such as vendors and subscription agencies, may be distinct environments, but they have similar goals that can benefit from the skills of librarians. Both types of organizations carefully select the kinds of information they need before they acquire it. They process this material and package it, providing a useful end product or service. Thus the skills and personality traits of the serialist are equally valuable in a library and a commercial organization.

For instance, commercial ventures like Integrated Library System (ILS) vendors create platforms that provide solutions for managing library collections, integrate discrete but related data sets, and automate routine library functions. A serialist's understanding of technical services and ability to handle coded data are invaluable for such work.

Geller is most familiar with the world of the subscription agents who collect information from publishers and libraries, code it for easy access, extract certain data for different reports, and offer an organized database with supporting services to clients. In this world all major vendors employ people with library degrees. These people know when publishers have not provided essential information, such as publishing history or ISSN numbers. They are also able to talk more easily to library clients.

One area where librarians are needed, but remain mostly absent, is publishing. However, those publishers who attend conferences like NASIG and provide added value through organized packaging are more likely to recognize the benefits of the serialists' expertise. Electronic publishing and the Internet in particular need the qualifications of good serials catalogers or the personality traits just described. The electronic information super-highway has become a chaotic maze. To sort, code, categorize, organize, evaluate, and create some sort of order out of the confusion on the Internet requires all the skills catalogers and information specialists have.

Catalogers are familiar with concepts like metadata that require scholarly journals and Internet files to have imbedded headings with author, title, and other important publishing information included. Serialists know the level of detail needed to make these files accessable. As files move around the Internet and change URLs, catalogers are needed to keep users informed. Geller feels confident that the future of serialists is secure as the Internet continues to expand and becomes ever more difficult to navigate, requiring increasingly more sophisticated search engines. Someone questioned whether it is enough that serialists understand that they are needed in this industry, if vendors and publishers are not convinced of the value of librarians. Geller responded that commercial organizations are being educated through conferences such as NASIG and EDUCOM, while librarians are already being hired to perfect searching tools like Yahoo and InterNIC. In this well-received presentation, Folsom and Geller offered a helpful and encouraging array of possibilities to librarians, who feel that traditional avenues are closing.

NOTE

1. Michael Gorman, "On doing away with Technical Services Departments," *American Libraries* 10 (July/August 1979): 435-437 and Michael Gorman, "The Ecumenical Library," *The Reference Librarian* 9 (fall/winter 1983): 55-64.

Claiming on the Net

Tina Feick
Tim McAdam

Workshop Leaders

Robert M. Cleary

Recorder

SUMMARY. The availability of EDI (Electronic Data Interchange) to process routine serial claims is attractive to librarians, agents and publishers. This workshop presented one such project using the electronic claiming module developed by Innovative Interfaces Inc. The preparation required by the vendor and library was demonstrated, and advantages, problems and future enhancements were discussed. *[Article copies available for a fee from The Haworth Document Delivery Service: 1-800-342-9678. E-mail address: getinfo@haworth.com]*

The presenters of this workshop demonstrated the steps required for electronic claiming using the claiming module developed by Innovative Interfaces Inc. Tina Feick, Sales Manager-North America for Blackwell's Periodicals Division and Tim McAdam, Acquisitions Librarian at the Uni-

---

Tina Feick is Sales Manager for North America, Periodicals Division, Blackwells.

Tim McAdam is Acquisitions Librarian, University of California, Irvine.

Robert M. Cleary is Serials Acquisitions Librarian, University of Missouri-Kansas City.

[Haworth co-indexing entry note]: "Claiming on the Net." Cleary, Robert M. Co-published simultaneously in *The Serials Librarian* (The Haworth Press, Inc.) Vol. 31, No. 1/2, 1997, pp. 273-278; and: *Pioneering New Serials Frontiers: From Petroglyphs to Cyberserials* (ed: Christine Christiansen and Cecilia Leathem) The Haworth Press, Inc., 1997, pp. 273-278. Single or multiple copies of this article are available for a fee from The Haworth Document Delivery Service [1-800-342-9678, 9:00 a.m. - 5:00 p.m. (EST). E-mail address: getinfo@haworth.com].

versity of California, Irvine, represented the vendor and library perspectives on this project. The audience included many librarians, subscription agents, publishers and automation systems vendors. Feick began by summarizing subscription agents' efforts in the area of EDI (Electronic Data Interchange) and claiming serial issues. Agents have been accepting electronic claiming information from libraries via the Internet. Claims sent by free-text E-mail require manual rekeying by the agent. Claims sent by File Transfer Protocol (FTP) or by E-mail using X12 guidelines, as well as free-text claims, require processing by an EDI translator before being sent to a publisher. Claims are then processed through the agent's online system. Feick stressed that using EDI for claiming is appropriate for routine claiming, not complex claiming problems. Interest in EDI among libraries is growing and Innovative Interfaces has been involved in a number of projects to facilitate electronic claiming. In 1995 the Serials Industry Systems Advisory Committee (SISAC) published EDI guidelines in X12, the U.S. EDI standard. The standards for the format of serials claims have been tested, approved and published.

VENDOR PREPARATION

Blackwell's participated in a beta test of the Innovative Interfaces electronic claiming module in cooperation with the University of California, Irvine (UCI). In order to enable machine processing of the claims produced using this system, links between the vendor and library's records had to be established. For this project, the Agent's Subscription ID (ASID) and the Serial Issue and Contribution Identifier (SICI) were chosen as X12 match points. Blackwell's provided the title, ISSN (International Serial Standard Number), along with bar codes for UCI's order record number and Blackwell's unique Subscription ID number. Files of UCI's order numbers had been sent previously via FTP. Since not all serials have an ISSN, it could not be used as a control number. These bar codes were then printed and sent for input by staff at the UCI Library. The bar codes utilized the Code 128 barcode language, which reads SISAC bar codes. The order number barcode was provided to speed up location of the proper record, and title and ISSN were provided for verification that the proper record had been found. Wanding the Subscription ID barcode inserted the number in the vendor title ID field in the order and checkin records.

LIBRARY PREPARATION

Tim McAdam then described how the UCI Library prepared to interact with Blackwell's to facilitate electronic claiming. The system requires that a special vendor record be set up with certain indicators. An "s" in the CODE2 field indicates that the vendor can receive Internet claims in the X12 format for Order status inquiry-869 (claims). In the NOTE2 or NOTE3 field, the vendor's designated E-mail address to receive claims must appear, preceded by "$EDI." This involved creating one new vendor record for Blackwell's for electronic claiming.

Inputting of the Subscription ID was accomplished on a project basis. The UCI Library decided that they needed the Subscription ID in both their order and checkin records, since there was no vendor-related information in their checkin records. Three personal computers were set up and three people were able to input the necessary information on one thousand records in approximately two hours. The first barcode brought up the correct record and then the title and ISSN provided with the bar codes were checked for a match. If there were no discrepancies, the Subscription ID barcode was used to input the number in the vendor title field in the order record. Then a macro was used to get to the current checkin record from the summary, and the inputting process was repeated for the checkin record.

McAdam stated that this project provided an opportunity to standardize vendor codes since different vendor codes in UCI's integrated system had been used to indicate the same vendor. McAdam stated that if other fixed fields need to be changed this could easily be accomplished during this process by creating a bar code to reflect fixed field information. A small percentage of ISSN provided by Blackwell's were in conflict with the existing ISSN in current records. These records were turned over to UCI's Cataloging Department for further examination.

McAdam presented overheads of the various screens used in the electronic claiming process. The example showed that while fifty-nine electronic claims were ready to send via E-mail, not all fifty-nine were actually sent. In most cases, the problem was the lack of a Subscription ID. These problematic records were either corrected or set up for print claiming only.

Feick described how after the file is retrieved from the dedicated mail box, it goes to an EDI Translator, for mapping to the Blackwell's Periodicals System. All claims are reviewed by a customer service person at Blackwell's and then they are sent to the publisher. Blackwell's has found that they can sometimes answer claims from the X-12 formatted "Ship Notice Manifest" (Despatch) data that they receive from certain publishers. This works well for claims that are made before an issue has been published. Blackwell's tries to reduce the amount of unnecessary claims they send to publishers. Responses are then sent back to the library.

ADVANTAGES FOR VENDORS

Receiving claims electronically has reduced the amount of rekeying necessary and therefore increases accuracy of claims information. Claim information using the Innovative Interfaces claiming module comes directly from the bibliographic record, which is typically downloaded from a national database, and from the checkin record and/or the order record. Specific issue information for the SICI is taken from the checkin box and is usually extrapolated by the system, although enumeration and chronology can be keyed-in by a staff person. This further ensures the accuracy of the information that is received by Blackwell's. Blackwell's staff also do not have to rekey the pertinent information and do not have to process paper claims. Response to claims is faster and allows staff to concentrate on other work.

ADVANTAGES FOR LIBRARIES

McAdam reported that the advantages of electronic claiming for the UCI Library were greater control of the process, speed of transmission, faster receipt of missing issues, less errors in claiming, decreased time spent processing paper claims, and savings on paper, envelopes and postage. In addition, this project was a team effort requiring participation from several library units. The library was able to implement industry-specific standards in terms of EDI and was able to report that they were accomplishing more with less staff. McAdam reported that approximately 75 percent of all claims for their three largest serials vendors are sent electronically and that the staff now have more time to work on claiming reports.

PROBLEMS WITH ELECTRONIC CLAIMING FROM THE VENDOR'S PERSPECTIVE

Feick reported confusion with any free-text that appeared in the PID field, which is supposed to be used as a Media Type Code Identifier. Libraries were using this field to indicate that additional issues were being claimed. Any free-text appearing in this field is bounced out by the system and has to be rekeyed. For electronic claiming to work effectively without human intervention, Feick stressed that each claim must claim one issue only. Another problem was the limitation on claim reason codes in the

Innovative Interfaces electronic claiming module. The SISAC X12 list of Mandatory Data Elements for a Serials Claim allows for five other claiming reasons; only one is available in the claiming module. Membership package titles also cause problems, since only one Subscription ID is assigned to a package that may consist of many titles. Feick stressed that these titles were more suitable for traditional print claiming or personal attention.

PROBLEMS WITH ELECTRONIC CLAIMING FROM THE LIBRARY'S PERSPECTIVE

McAdam also reported problems with claiming membership titles and attributed that to the fact that separate Subscription IDs had not been assigned to those titles. There is no claim note field to add free text which can be processed effectively by Blackwell's on the receiving end, as there is with printed claims. The UCI Library still manually inputs the Subscription ID for general changes and for new orders.

FUTURE ENHANCEMENTS DESIRED BY VENDORS

Feick stated that they would prefer to receive EDI claims via FTP. In order to be in full SISAC compliance, all claim reason codes should be made available by systems vendors. There also needs to be a better way to handle free-text notes that will not be bounced out by the system. Currently, only a handful of publishers and systems vendors participate in electronic claiming. Feick stressed that greater participation will speed up improvements.

FUTURE ENHANCEMENTS DESIRED BY LIBRARIES

McAdam mentioned that it would improve the claiming process if they could receive claim responses electronically. Some claim responses require that predictive received dates be adjusted manually. In the future, when machines are communicating back and forth, a claim will be sent out and the response would automatically insert a corresponding note and update predicted dates for a particular issue. He also cited the need to receive Subscription ID numbers electronically for changes and new orders.

DISCUSSION AND CONCLUSION

In the general discussion, the need to claim at all was raised. Because of claiming limits, and the opportunity to predict when an issue will be received based on previous receipt patterns, libraries feel that it is better to claim than not claim. Libraries have limited access to revised publishers' schedules. Agents can filter some of these claims using the dispatch data they receive from the major publishers who provide it. If publishers set a schedule and then stick to it, claims could be dramatically reduced. Since not many publishers are providing dispatch data, libraries will continue to claim issues that are late in arriving. Another opinion expressed was that libraries should be examining their claiming procedures if they consistently claim before an issue is published.

Other discussions centered around the actual procedure for entering the unique Subscription ID, since not all libraries are set up to wand in information using bar codes. Other libraries already have the Subscription ID in their records and wanted to know what would happen to that field if an additional field was added. The electronic claiming module will use the first Vendor Title ID it sees. For the UCI Library, one day-and-a-half was spent in wanding in the Subscription ID.

Other questions involved the library/agent relationship. One participant wondered if such a project committed a library to keep their subscriptions with a particular agent, since much effort is expended to set up electronic claiming. Another asked if agents would be giving discounts on service charges to set up electronic claiming. One participant replied that their agent would not raise the service charge on titles that were claimed electronically.

At this stage, electronic claiming is limited to those systems vendors, agents and publishers who are willing to make the investment in the technology. While agents and libraries are enthusiastically involved in the process and reaping the benefits, publishers and systems vendors have a lesser degree of participation. In terms of sending electronic claims, the systems vendor is the key participant in that process. If a library cannot use their claiming system to send electronic claims, they cannot participate at all. In the area of responses, still more development remains. The Innovative Interfaces electronic claiming module cannot receive responses and not many publishers are providing them. The participants in this project are enthusiastically moving forward with electronic claiming by solving current problems, determining possible improvements and asking for enhancements.

Format Integration and Serials Cataloging

Crystal Graham

Workshop Leader

Judith Johnston

Recorder

SUMMARY. Format integration has achieved some goals: Seriality of nonprint materials can be expressed. Materials in several physical formats can be described. Archival control of non-print materials can be designated. Content designation has been standardized. Validation routines have been simplified or eliminated. Documentation has been much reduced. Format integration also brings new problems and issues. Bibliographic records are more complex, partly due to the nature of the material, but also due to new fields. Format specialists must learn new cataloging rules and content designation. Optional fields can impede shared cataloging. Local systems may be unable to correctly use some of the new codes. Format integration runs counter to the proposed use of a single record for multiple versions. Catalogers have a great deal to consider in formulating policies. *[Article copies available for a fee from The Haworth Document Delivery Service: 1-800-342-9678. E-mail address: getinfo@haworth.com]*

The USMARC formats were developed and are maintained by the Library of Congress, with advice of the ALA Committee on Machine-

Crystal Graham is Serials Librarian, University of California, San Diego.
Judith Johnston is Catalog and Authorities Librarian, University of North Texas, Denton, TX.

[Haworth co-indexing entry note]: "Format Integration and Serials Cataloging." Johnston, Judith. Co-published simultaneously in *The Serials Librarian* (The Haworth Press, Inc.) Vol. 31, No. 1/2, 1997, pp. 279-287; and: *Pioneering New Serials Frontiers: From Petroglyphs to Cyberserials* (ed: Christine Christiansen and Cecilia Leathem) The Haworth Press, Inc., 1997, pp. 279-287. Single or multiple copies of this article are available for a fee from The Haworth Document Delivery Service [1-800-342-9678, 9:00 a.m. - 5:00 p.m. (EST). E-mail address: getinfo@haworth.com].

Readable Form of Bibliographic Information (MARBI). There are five types of formats: bibliographic, authority, holdings, classification data, and community information. Format integration only affects the bibliographic formats. Its purpose is to integrate the seven separate formats which exist for books, serials, maps, music, visual materials, computer files, and archives and manuscripts control (AMC). (OCLC separates the music format into scores and sound recordings, for eight formats.)

Each bibliographic format was developed with its own data elements specific to the type of material, e.g., frequency for serials and scale for maps. As technology advanced, new formats evolved, new combinations of materials appeared, and libraries expanded the scope of their collections. Having separate formats for different types of materials caused a number of problems for catalogers and online systems. For example, for some non-print materials, such as maps and music, the workforms did not have a 362 field. The serials format lacked material specific fields such as the 007 used for sound recordings. Catalogers could not properly code the catalog records for these materials. Materials composed of several formats lacked fields to describe accompanying material, e.g., a serial with a map or CD-ROM. Another problem was in archival control. The AMC format was developed for use with paper materials described by S. Hensen's *Archives, Personal Papers, and Manuscripts.* This was not really appropriate for other archival materials such as oral histories or collections of photographs.

Learning slight differences between formats also caused confusion and difficulty. For example, frequency was entered in a 310 field in the serial format, but in the 315 field for the maps format. It was particularly difficult to design and maintain computer validation tables used for these various formats. As new fields were approved, it was necessary to determine for which formats to approve them. Validation tables had to be rewritten, and the utilities' as well as libraries' systems had to be updated. The need for extensive documentation was another disadvantage. OCLC published eight separate format documents, and the USMARC bibliographic format used half-page columns showing which fields were valid in which formats.

A solution was very much needed. MARBI came up with a proposal to make all the data elements valid for all the formats, which is what we now call format integration. It is important to understand that format integration does not abolish the formats; it integrates them. The cataloger must still select a primary format in choosing a workform. Instead of asking "Is a specific field valid on this format?" the cataloger chooses the most appropriate tags for the material. The validation model has been replaced with the appropriateness model.

The idea for format integration was first presented in 1983 in a MARBI discussion paper by John Attig. Catalogers began to see changes in 1991, when fields that were judged useless were declared obsolete, such as indicators in the 260 and 550. These changes were documented in *USMARC Format for Bibliographic Data Update no. 3*.

PHASE 1 HIGHLIGHTS

The main feature of phase 1, in 1995, was the validation of all variable fields and the standardization of their usage across formats. *USMARC Format for Bibliographic Data, Format Integration edition* was issued. Phase 2, in 1996, saw changes to fixed fields and control fields (001-008). *USMARC Format for Bibliographic Data, Format Integration edition, Update # 1* documented these changes. Some aspects of phase 1 which affected serials cataloging included abolishing some serials-specific variant titles fields (211, 212, and 214) in favor of the 246; abolishing the acquisitions address and price (265 & 350) in favor of the 037; narrowing the use of the 730 to mean related/analytical titles in catalog entry form; and adding the 740 field for related/analytical titles not in catalog entry form. In the 246 field the ‡i was introduced for use when the second indicator is insufficient to describe the source of the variant title. The first indicator of the 246 was defined for card production/display. This seems ironic just when many libraries are discarding their card catalogs. However, catalogers still have the obligation to code correctly for our colleagues with card catalogs, and/or the eventuality that our local systems will be able to use the indicators. The University of California, San Diego library has written a macro for OCLC Passport for Windows that automates the inputting of various 246 fields. Libraries can go to the UCSD web site (http://tpot.ucsd.edu/Pass/passport.html) and get the details, if they wish to set up this macro in their own libraries.

PHASE 2 HIGHLIGHTS

The purpose of phase 2 of format integration was to standardize and extend all the fixed field and control field elements across all formats.

In a MARC bibliographic record the Leader indicates what type of record it is, i.e., whether it is a national level record, an AACR2 record, or a new or corrected record, etc. For format integration the most important elements are the Leader/06 (Type of record) and the Leader/07 (Bibliographic level). The 008 field has a special relationship with the Leader and the two are displayed as a single fixed field block on OCLC and RLIN. Positions 00-17 and 35-39 of the 008 are identical for all formats; elements such as Country, Language, and Dates are consistent across formats. The other bytes, in positions 18-34, are format-specific. Leader 06 (Type) and 07 (Bibliographic level) determine the meaning of bytes 18-34 in the 008. Codes for Frequency and Regularity are examples of format-specific bytes. The specific workform command in bibliographic utilities signals the systems to provide a workform with the appropriate Leader bytes and corresponding 008 fields: for example, in OCLC the workform command "wfs" yields a Leader/06 = a, Leader/07 = s, and mnemonics for printed serials. Under format integration, the default on the workforms used for nonprint serials is Leader/07 = m, so serials catalogers must remember to change it.

The biggest change with phase 2 of format integration is a policy change on the selection of primary format. The serials format is now used only for print serials. Non-print serials are now entered on the respective non-print formats, i.e., computer file serials are entered on the computer file workform, serial sound recordings are entered on the sound recording format, etc. One of the questions which catalogers face is which format specialist cataloger will catalog these materials?

How are those missing serials fixed field elements coded into these other formats now? A new field, the 006, is used. This field can be used for secondary aspects such as serial aspects of a serial computer file, or for material-specific aspects of secondary material, such as accompanying material. Just as the Leader byte for Type controls the meaning of the 008 fixed field bytes, the Type byte of the 006 controls the meaning of the remaining bytes of the 006. The meanings are the same as bytes 18-34 in the 008 of the format type specified.

Catalogers can also use the 006 to indicate seriality of loose-leafs, which are considered books with serial aspects. However, adding a 006 to a loose-leaf monograph doesn't add much information. Some elements are redundant, such as Conference, Content, and Government publication. Frequency and Regularity are probably the most important serial characteristics that can be recorded in coded form. Ironically, the OCLC system does not allow a corresponding 310 field to be added to loose-leaf records. This prohibition is counter to the spirit of format integration.

Another questionable 006 field is for a serial computer file with accompanying books. The 006 fields for the accompanying book, such as a user's manual, might be useless, containing only data elements redundant to those in the serial 006. An important point to remember is that the 006 is optional, and libraries will need to develop their policies for using it.

Other changes to the Leader were made. The Leader/17 (Encoding level) now has a code 4, meaning core level record. In Leader/06 (Type) two new codes, code p (mixed materials format) and code t (manuscript language material) have been added. These new Type codes are not used for serials. Earlier the problem of coding archival controlled nonprint materials was mentioned. It was decided that it was an error to use the bibliographic format code to equal a type of control of material. Therefore, in Leader/06 (Type) code b (AMC format) is eliminated. This separates the type of material from the type of control. The Leader/08 byte for Control, valid for use with all formats, was defined. Defining archival control may not be an important issue for most serial catalogers now, but it might become more of an issue as we become more involved in archiving electronic journals. It is not appropriate to use the archival control designation on records for preservation microform masters. ARL standards mandate a single record for all generations, with an 007 field for each generation. Archival status is coded in the ‡i of the appropriate 007.

Format integration validates the 007 field for all formats. The 007 is now defined for computer file characteristics. The 007 is also optional, and libraries will need to determine their policies on use of this field. Deciding what format to use, and when to use the 006 and 007 can be confusing. A helpful table is provided at the end of the report.

Format integration has achieved several goals: Seriality of nonprint materials can be expressed, now that variable fields are valid across all formats and the 006 field can be added. Materials in multiple formats can be described. Archival control of non-print materials can be designated with the creation of the new Leader/08 byte. Content designation has been standardized. Validation routines have been simplified or eliminated, since variable fields are valid across formats. Documentation has been much reduced; for example, OCLC has reduced its manuals from eight documents to one.

PROBLEMS AND ISSUES OF FORMAT INTEGRATION

Format integration also brings new problems and issues. Bibliographic records are more complex, partly due to the nature of the material, but also due to new fields. Format specialists must learn new cataloging rules and content designation. Optional fields can impede shared cataloging. Local systems may be unable to accept, display, or index some of the new codes.

For example, when the 246 ‡i was first introduced, NOTIS was unable to index the ‡a when it followed ‡i. Local systems may not recognize the dual nature of material indicated in an 006 field. The format code is especially important, because it may govern the OPAC display of a system. It can trigger the display of the material type designation, or the order of display of records. Some systems display current receipts for serials based on the format code. Another very important situation is where the format code engages the serials control system.

Some catalogs are divided and format-specific, such as the University of California Melvyl catalog and the RLIN database, so users must select a format before searching. The change in treatment of non-print serials results in a lack of predictability where one will find a record and also causes a division between the print and non-print versions of the same serial. The Library of Congress delayed implementing format integration due to reprogramming for CONSER to accept serials with a Leader Type other than a. Products sold by the Library of Congress are also affected, since format codes are used to generate products. Serials union lists may also be affected, since format codes are used to select records for output, and will have to be reprogrammed to accept records not on the serials format.

Duplicate detection programs which use Leader codes will be affected. Format codes are also used to generate statistics and to limit searches, so both statistics and search strategies and results will be impacted. Will materials with multiple material types be mapped into both indexes in systems?

What is the relationship between format integration and multiple versions? Format integration aids in describing one item with various aspects; multiple versions concerns several different items with identical content. AACR2 mandates separate records for multiple versions and format integration requires that those separate records for print and nonprint versions be on different formats. There is widespread sentiment that users are better served by a single bibliographic record. Many libraries use a single record, especially for preservation digitization. The ALA CC:DA's *Guidelines for Bibliographic Description of Reproductions* gives tacit approval for using a single record. Another reason for putting electronic and print versions on the same record is because in a Webcat the record can provide holding statements for both versions, and clickable hypertext links to the Internet version. (For an example, link to http:// pactech.ucsd.edu and see the record for *Classical and quantum gravity*.) Format integration, with its requirements to describe different versions on different formats, takes a step backward from the progress toward a single record for multiple versions. MARBI discussion paper no. 97 questions whether cataloging all digital material as Leader/06 m (Computer file) is useful. It suggests that identifying the primary record type by content rather than carrier better serves users, and recognizes that many catalogers are adding information about digital items to records for originals, especially for Internet documents. Several precedents for coding for content over carrier are cited: music CDs are coded as music; digitized cartographic materials are coded as maps; and microforms are coded as printed material. The paper suggests redefining Leader/06 m for use only when computer file characteristics are the primary aspect of the item. The information may be numeric data, computer software, or a mixture of various types of computer files. The paper also notes that a new definition does not mandate whether or not to use a separate record for a digitized item, but leaves it up to the cataloger. MARBI welcomes input from various constituencies, and may be contacted through the USMARC listserv at usmarc@loc.gov.

What computer file serials are then primarily textual? Would the definition include digital reproductions of print serials, simultaneous digital and print versions, selected portions of print serials online, and electronic journals? Can users be expected to know whether the material also exists in print? What about serials that can't exist in print, such as databases or interactive multimedia? It will not be easy to create guidelines. Catalogers have a great deal to consider in formulating policies.

BIBLIOGRAPHY

Attig, John C. "The Concept of a MARC Format," *Information Technology and Libraries* 2 (Mar. 1983): 7-17.

Caplan, Priscilla. "USMARC Format Integration. Part I, What, why and when?" *The Public-Access Computer Systems Review* 3:5 (1992), pp. 131-134. Available online: gopher://info.lib.uh.edu:70/00/articles/e-journals/uhlibrary/pacsreview/v3/n5/caplan.3n5

Caplan, Priscilla. "USMARC Format Integration. Part II, Implications for Local Systems," *The Public-Access Computer Systems Review* 4:1 (1993), pp.13-17. Available online: gopher://info.lib.uh.edu:70/00/articles/e-journals/uhlibrary/pacsreview/v4/n1/caplan.4n1

Crawford, Walt. *MARC for Library Use: Using Integrated USMARC.* 2nd ed. Boston: G.K. Hall, 1989.

Format Integration and Its Effect on Cataloging, Training, and Systems: Papers Presented at the ALCTS Preconference Implementing USMARC Format Integration, American Library Association Annual Conference, June 26, 1992, San Francisco, California. Edited by Karen Coyle. Chicago, ALA, 1993.

Format Integration and Its Effect on the USMARC Bibliographic Format. Washington, D.C.: Cataloging Distribution Service, Library of Congress, 1995.

Glennan, Kathryn. "Format Integration: The Final Phase," *MC Journal: The Journal of Academic Media Librarianship* 3:2 (1995). Available online: http://wings.buffalo.edu/publications/mcjrnl/v3n2/glenna.html

Graham, Crystal and Rebecca Ringler, "Serial Computer Files under Format Integration." October 24, 1995. Available online: http://tpot.ucsd.edu/Cataloging/Current/cg1.html

Hirons, Jean. "Format Integration and Its Impact on Serials: a Speech Given at the ALCTS Institute on Serials in the Age of Format Integration," San Francisco, Oct. 7, 1995. Available online: http://tpot.ucsd.edu/Cataloging/Current/jean.hirons.html

Lin, Su-jing. "QuickRef246." Available online: http://tpot.ucsd.edu/Pass/Macro/rflst246.html

MARBI. *Discussion Paper no.97. Coding Digital Items in Leader/06 (Type of Record) in the USMARC Bibliographic Record.* May 6, 1996. Available online: gopher://marvel.loc.gov:70/00/.listarch/usmarc/dp97.doc

OCLC. *Technical Bulletin 206: Format Integration Phase 1.* 1995. Available online: http://www.oclc.org/oclc/tb/tb206/tb2061.htm

OCLC. *Technical Bulletin 212: Format Integration Phase 2.* 1996. Available online: http://www.oclc.org/oclc/tb/tb212/tb2121.htm

Research Libraries Group. *RLIN Fixed Field and Other Changes for Format Integration.* May 3, 1996. Available online: http://www.rlg.org/fi.html

APPENDIX 1. Fixed Fields for Different Types of Publications

	Leader/06 Leader/07	008	006	007
Printed serial	Type: a Blvl: s	serial		
Microform serial	Type: a Blvl: s	serial		microform
Serial computer file	Type: m Blvl: s	computer file	serial	computer file
Printed music (score) serial	Type: c Blvl: s	music (score)	serial	
Printed map serial	Type: e Blvl: s	map	serial	map
Projected medium (videos etc.) serial	Type: g Blvl: s	projected medium	serial	video, motion picture, graphic
Nonmusical sound recording serial	Type: i Blvl: s	music (sound recording)	serial	sound recording
Musical sound recording serial	Type: j Blvl: s	music (sound recording)	serial	sound recording
Printed serial with accomp. CD-ROM	Type: a Blvl: s	serial	computer file (optional)	computer file (optional)
Printed loose-leaf with serial updates	Type: a Blvl: m	books	serial (optional)	

Voice of the Customer: Feedback Strategies for Libraries and Vendors

Adrian W. Alexander
Mary Lou Goodyear

Workshop Leaders

Cathy Kellum

Recorder

SUMMARY. Reliable customer feedback data is vital to all service organizations, including libraries and subscription vendors. Quality should be defined by the customer, not by the service organization's specifications. A subscription vendor and a library administrator provide an overview of various methods for capturing useful, and usable, information with discussions of quality service dimensions and issues, strategies to foster effective customer feedback, and methods to develop better communication between libraries and their vendors. *[Article copies available for a fee from The Haworth Document Delivery Service: 1-800-342-9678. E-mail address: getinfo@ haworth.com]*

Adrian W. Alexander is Sales Manager, Western Region and Academic Marketing Manager, The Faxon Company.
Mary Lou Goodyear is Associate Dean of Libraries, University of Kansas.
Cathy Kellum is Training Supervisor, OCLC Services, SOLINET, Atlanta, GA.

[Haworth co-indexing entry note]: "Voice of the Customer: Feedback Strategies for Libraries and Vendors." Kellum, Cathy. Co-published simultaneously in *The Serials Librarian* (The Haworth Press, Inc.) Vol. 31, No. 1/2, 1997, pp. 289-294; and: *Pioneering New Serials Frontiers: From Petroglyphs to Cyberserials* (ed: Christine Christiansen and Cecilia Leathem) The Haworth Press, Inc., 1997, pp. 289-294. Single or multiple copies of this article are available for a fee from The Haworth Document Delivery Service [1-800-342-9678, 9:00 a.m. - 5:00 p.m. (EST). E-mail address: getinfo@haworth.com].

This workshop, led by a serials vendor, Adrian Alexander of Faxon, and a library administrator, Mary Lou Goodyear of the University of Kansas, discussed issues critical to library personnel and the organizations that provide products and services to them. Two examples of these service organizations are serials subscription agents and bibliographic networks. In order to set the stage, the workshop leaders began with an informative discussion of why information gleaned from the workshop was vital to cultivate effective communication between those parties.

LIBRARY ENVIRONMENT

Technological Change. First of all, the current changing environment in today's libraries, along with their response to and preparation necessary for those changes, is an important consideration that must be addressed before a full understanding of the issues can be realized. Obviously, rapid technological change is a major factor, with technologists such as Bill Gates of Microsoft and major bookstore chains like Barnes & Noble in "competition" with libraries for their audiences. Libraries in today's world must position themselves as players in this competitive atmosphere–the idea of competition itself being a concept that may be alien to many librarians.

Increased Accountability. Increased accountability to higher administration and/or other funding bodies is also a major factor in library record-keeping processes, such as tracking contributions both of a monetary nature as well as gifts of books and other materials. Today's libraries are also discovering they must demonstrate their value to both their institution and their patrons as well as to their governing bodies. Many libraries have responded to these pressures focusing on quality, with Deming's philosophy of Total Quality Management (TQM) being the critical link. While the relationships between libraries and their vendors have traditionally been thought of as adversarial, Deming proposes a "partnership model" in which working together more effectively is the goal. A current example of this is the 3M Corporation, where some of their employees are located on-site with several of the company's suppliers and vendors under long-term contracts. Ideally, to strengthen the bond with vendor staff and foster better communication, 3M and the suppliers involved in the agreement have found that while their profits are the same, their costs are now 5-10% lower than before the on-site relationships were established.

New Ways of Managing. Another environmental factor is the search for new ways of managing library functions. Not unusual is the need for the serials librarian to frequently serve as a "boundary spanner" concerning serials functions between Public Services and Technical Services, and also be somewhat of a mediator of the issues between library administrators, financial office staff, subscription vendors and/or bibliographic networks, all the while keeping in mind the needs of the ultimate end user of the materials being procured, the library patron.

LIBRARY RESPONSE TO CUSTOMER FOCUS

Team Management. Often the impetus to begin a partnership utilizing TQM concepts either within the library or with outside companies is a result of an administrative mandate. In order for these relationships to get off on the right foot, administrators should allow an avenue for team members to "buy in" to the concept in some manner, possibly by allowing them to be involved in the initial decisions concerning methods or procedures. Combining staff from both the library and the service organization on the same teams fosters better communication and a good working environment. Company auditors may question this plan, but should be convinced of its merits.

A possible suggestion is to incorporate a requirement into the initial bid process that both parties (library and vendor) must be able to demonstrate a dedication toward the concepts of TQM before the relationship can be effected. Included in the agreement among those involved should be definitions of "Quality Service Dimensions" so that all parties are aware of their parameters. Definitions of those factors follow:

> *Tangibles*–the appearance of physical facilities, equipment, and personnel
> *Reliability*–the ability to perform the promised service dependably
> *Responsiveness*–the willingness to help customers and to provide prompt service
> *Competence*–possession of required skills and knowledge to perform the service
> *Courtesy*–politeness, respect, consideration
> *Credibility*–trustworthiness, believability, honesty
> *Security*–freedom from danger, risk, or doubt
> *Access*–approachability and ease of contact
> *Communication*–keeping customers informed in language they can understand
> *Understanding the Customer*–making an effort to know customers and their needs.

An exercise at this point in the workshop was for the attendees to identify the three most important quality dimensions for themselves, both as suppliers and recipients of services. Group responses were compared to a study from management literature. The audience statistics were similar to those of the study: 32% chose *reliability* as the most important factor, with *responsiveness* in second place with 22%. Receiving the lowest rating was *tangibles*.

Restructuring/Reengineering. Reengineering, downsizing, rightsizing, and self-directed work teams are current buzz words associated with what libraries formerly referred to simply as reorganization. Often a result of the implementation of TQM, or merely an effort to find a better, more efficient way of accomplishing tasks, the goal is to restructure the organization of the library staff. Effective cross-training may be either the method or the end result of this process.

Customer Feedback. Strategies for gathering information were also covered. It was suggested that several methods be used in order to get the total view of the customers' needs. A warning, however, was issued that customer expectations color the responses in most of these methods; some of those expectations may be unrealistic. Attendees were advised to include factors such as quality standards, performance gaps, delivery gaps, and customer expectations when using the information gathered from evaluating services using any of the suggested methods.

Service Quality and Performance Evaluation. "Quality Service Issues" when evaluating the performance during a contractual agreement among libraries and vendors were also discussed, with examples of questions to be included. When evaluating vendor performance, the following questions should be asked:

- Are invoices/reports well designed?
- Are we receiving the materials we ordered?
- Are orders and claims processed promptly?
- Does my vendor understand the market?
- Am I treated well when I call the vendor?
- Am I receiving accurate price projections?
- Is my prepayment secure?
- Can I reach my customer service representative via e-mail?
- Can I get regular updates on my account?
- How long has it been since my vendor stopped by to see what I need?

Questions relating to the evaluation of library performance are:

- Are work areas well-designed?
- Are check-in records well-maintained?

- Are claims sent to the vendor promptly?
- Does my staff understand how publishers operate?
- Are problems with vendors handled in a professional manner?
- Are my budget projections accepted by the administration?
- Are current periodical issues safe from theft?
- Is order status information easily obtained by the rest of the library?
- Am I keeping faculty informed regularly about price increases?
- Do I know what is most important to customers who order serial titles?

MODELS OF CUSTOMER/SUPPLIER RELATIONSHIPS

Traditional Model. Factors in the traditional model of customer service are:

1. Price is paramount (competitive bid process).
2. Quality service only dealt with in its absence (complaints).
3. Trust is low.
4. Positional bargaining.

Partnership Model. In the partnership model of customer service, the following factors are considered important:

1. Focus on improvement of process and service.
2. Reduction of errors before they occur.
3. Close cooperation/sharing of data on performance standards and fiscal health.
4. Incentive to improve on quality.
5. Price based on cost, not market.
6. Teams of employees communicate to improve services.
7. Build long-term relationships.

TECHNIQUES FOR GATHERING INFORMATION

Goodyear shared with the audience a chart she is proposing to use in a study which is still in progress, concerning the strategies for gathering customer service information. The techniques she suggests utilizing are:

Transactional Surveys. A survey done immediately after the service transaction. This type of survey measures customer perceptions while they are fresh.

Total Market Surveys. A survey done on a less frequent basis, but that includes all aspects of the service provided. This tool measures the customers' overall satisfaction with the service *relative* to the customers' perceptions of the service to be rendered.

Mystery Shopping. Posing as customers to gather information about how well employees meet performance standards.

Service Reviews. Periodic visits with customers to discuss the service relationship.

Customer Advisory Panels. A group of customers formed to review services. Feedback is normally given in meetings or through telephone interviews. Interaction between panel members that results in new ideas is the strongest facet of this type of feedback.

Declining, Former Customer Surveys. Surveys to those who are limited in their service relationship with you. These surveys assist in determining the reasons for lost customers.

Focus Group Interviews. Specific topic interviews with a group of customers or potential customers to receive feedback on ideas or to work through an issue.

Employee Field Reporting. Employees' reports concerning communications with customers.

Employee Research. Soliciting ideas and comments from employees on how to improve service.

The workshop leaders entertained questions throughout the session, fully answering each and encouraging discussion on the topics in question. Attendees at this session were skillfully guided through the myriad concepts, terms, and theories regarding customer service and feedback.

BIBLIOGRAPHY

1. Leonard L. Berry, *On Great Service: A Framework for Action* (New York, NY: The Free Press, 1995).

2. Charles C. Poirier and William F. Houser, *Business Partnering for Continuous Improvement* (San Francisco, CA: Barrett-Koehler Publishers, 1993).

3. Valarie A. Zeithaml, A. Parasuraman, and Leonard L. Berry, *Delivering Quality Service: Balancing Customer Perceptions and Expectations* (New York, NY: The Free Press, 1990).

The SISAC Barcode
and the Periodicals Analysis Database

Nancy Deyoe
Kathy Payne
Workshop Leaders

Amey L. Park
Recorder

SUMMARY. This workshop described the development of two serials management databases at Wichita State University (WSU) in Kansas. The databases facilitate periodical labeling, checkin, and use data collection. Usage information is loaded into another database which serves collection development needs. Nancy Deyoe, Principal Cataloger at WSU, described the labeling and checkin processing and workflow features. Kathy Payne, previously Science Librarian at WSU and currently Head of Reference at Weber State University, described the development and use of the collection development program. Both presenters demonstrated the use of the two databases. *[Article copies available for a fee from The Haworth Document Delivery Service: 1-800-342-9678. E-mail address: getinfo@haworth.com]*

PROJECT DEVELOPMENT

Prior to 1991, Wichita State University (WSU) used handwritten LC and SuDocs call number labels for loose periodical issues. Writing and

Nancy Deyoe is Principal Cataloger, Wichita State University Libraries.
Kathy Payne is Head of Reference, Weber State University Library.
Amey L. Park is Serials Librarian, Kent State University, Kent, Ohio.

[Haworth co-indexing entry note]: "The SISAC Barcode and the Periodicals Analysis Database." Park, Amey L. Co-published simultaneously in *The Serials Librarian* (The Haworth Press, Inc.) Vol. 31, No. 1/2, 1997, pp. 295-299; and: *Pioneering New Serials Frontiers: From Petroglyphs to Cyberserials* (ed: Christine Christiansen and Cecilia Leathem) The Haworth Press, Inc., 1997, pp. 295-299. Single or multiple copies of this article are available for a fee from The Haworth Document Delivery Service [1-800-342-9678, 9:00 a.m. - 5:00 p.m. (EST). E-mail address: getinfo@haworth.com].

attaching the label and completing NOTIS checkin took 1.25 minutes per piece. In addition, collecting intermittent use information for periodical cancellation projects was labor-intensive and represented only a snapshot view of journal usage.

In 1991, Jasper Schad, Director of the WSU library, directed John Williams, Periodicals Supervisor and the technical expert for this project, to improve journal labeling and to develop a system that would collect journal use information. The resulting test of the production of smart barcode labels for loose issues proved so successful for labeling, checkin, and collection of use data that the entire collection was eventually barcoded according to SISAC specifications.

WORKFLOW FOR LABEL CREATION AND NOTIS UPDATING

When a piece is received at WSU Libraries, a student examines it, finds the ISSN, and searches it in the barcode database, which uses Worthington Data Solution's LabelRIGHT barcode software. The ISSN is used as the link between the SISAC barcode and the receipt screen in NOTIS. If the ISSN cannot easily be found on the piece, the title is searched in NOTIS and the ISSN found there is used. Records that lack ISSN have been given pseudo-ISSN. Publisher-produced SISAC barcodes located on some journal issues are not used because the data on them is not always correct and the barcode is not found on all journals.

A template record is retrieved from the barcode database. One template exists for each of the 4,000 LC-classified and 400 SuDocs-classified serials received by the library.

The student updates the template to reflect the piece in hand, which requires possibly changing a three-digit chronology code and a four-digit enumeration code, as well as changing the template to reflect the piece's actual chronology and enumeration. Students are able to memorize most of these codes.

A barcode is then printed using dot matrix printers on acid-free paper stock with archival adhesive. Above the barcode is a human-readable location and call number (including enumeration and chronology) which facilitates shelving. The barcode is followed by a line of numbers which interprets the barcode and contains the eight-digit ISSN, a 900-series number designating a chronology descriptor, the piece's actual chronology, a four-digit code designating the enumeration, and the piece's actual enumeration. The journal title also appears on the label.

Updating the template and producing the barcode takes 10-20 seconds for an LC-type label, with a SuDocs-type label requiring slightly more time.

The barcode is affixed to the front cover of the piece. No standard location is used; the only goal is never to cover the publisher-supplied enumeration, chronology, table of contents, or other valuable information.

Switching to NOTIS, the barcode is scanned. The NOTIS LSER serial module record is retrieved and updated following ANSI level-4 standards for holdings, requiring three keystrokes and 10 seconds.

STAFF AND FINANCIAL SAVINGS

An original investment of $1,000 was required for the barcoding equipment and software. This cost has paid for itself in staff and time savings. Although building the initial template database for the 4,400 serials involved staff commitment and time, fewer staff are now needed for serials checkin and labeling. Since this project was implemented in 1991, the staff required for all serials checkin and labeling work has been reduced by 1.25 FTE, in spite of the unit's adding to their workload the responsibility for all receipt, cataloging, and processing of government documents. Serials checkin and labeling currently requires .75 student FTE for the handling of approximately 150 daily issues.

PROBLEMS AND ERROR RATE

Government Document periodicals, which are processed two times each week, have proven to be difficult to work with. Most lack ISSN and it can be difficult to find the correct title in the barcode database. In addition, documents require more time to process because they were initially loaded into a separate processing unit.

Few errors occur through the use of the barcode software. Errors resulting from barcode creation are caught by NOTIS when it is updated. Every three months, approximately one error is detected during subsequent use data collection scanning.

COLLECTION AND USE OF DATA

Use data can be analyzed to the issue level as well as collected for both in-house and external circulation. Portable scanners called Tricoders are used several times each day to collect internal and external use data.

Bound periodicals are not barcoded. Instead, a notebook containing a barcode for each title, arranged by call number, is used. The barcode in the notebook is scanned to allow for the collection of use data for bound volumes. Scanning requires 5-7 minutes for each loaded truck.

The Tricoders can store over 7,500 scans. Continuous use data collected by them is uploaded to a collection development database once each month, allowing the monitoring of data across several years.

PERIODICALS ANALYSIS DATABASE (PAD)
DEVELOPMENT AND USE

Kathy Payne described the use of PAD. It was created to store collection analysis information and was evolutionary in nature, beginning with a Quattro Pro spreadsheet which was eventually replaced by Paradox, a more flexible and sophisticated database.

PAD is used to support cancellation decisions and requests for additional funds for serial expenditures and to demonstrate that the library is making responsible serials funding decisions. The library has received additional monies because of data generated from PAD. The database also provides information to collection development librarians, facilitates the assignment of journal titles to subject bibliographers, and has been found to be particularly helpful as an orientation tool for new librarians, allowing them to become quickly familiar with the titles for which they are responsible.

DATA ELEMENTS IN PAD

Data elements in PAD include the ISSN or pseudo-ISSN, previous ISSN, title, whether the title is classified by the LC or SuDocs classification scheme, the call number itself, location, subscription number, publisher's name, frequency, ISI impact factor, whether or not the title is indexed, peer reviewed or refereed, whether the title is foreign or domestic, librarian assignment, department assignment, target audience, fund code, current issue use data, bound volume use data, summation of use, baseline (1985) cost, current cost, current issue cost/use, current issue and bound volume cost/use, a code for core/curricular/research use, and a code for primary usage by undergraduate students, graduate students, or faculty.

Most information in PAD can be automatically updated including changes to the ISI impact factor, information about other Kansas libraries that hold the title, and expenditures. Variables which require manual updating include names of librarians to whom the title is assigned, as well as code changes.

REPORTS GENERATED FROM PAD

Many statistics can be gathered by PAD and many reports can be generated and printed from it. Use and administrative reports provide information about the cost, original cost, annual use, and cost/use of a journal or group of journals (both current and bound volumes) by LC class number, subject department, or librarian assignment since 1985 (the year WSU began using NOTIS).

Collection management reports provide journal information including title, call number, cost, cost/use, ISI impact factor, and other people to contact before the journal is canceled for each title assigned to a particular librarian. They also list subjects assigned to each librarian as well as a comprehensive subject report which provides a listing of journal titles by LC call numbers and a code for each librarian to which the title is assigned.

The use of QBE (Query By Example) reports to search PAD tables for desired data elements allows for the creation of customized reports.

FUTURE DEVELOPMENTS

In the future, the library will be networked, making PAD more accessible to collection development librarians. Other future developments include creating a database for government documents and seeking a federal grant for further enhancement of PAD, such as the importation of ILL use data and use data collected from online databases.

An article describing this project tentatively entitled, "The Development and Implementation of the Periodicals Analysis Database," and written by Kathy Payne, John Williams, and Dr. Mohammed Dadashzadeh will be published in an upcoming issue of *Serials Review.*

The two workshops were attended by approximately 88 NASIG attendees. The audience was attentive and impressed with the work and time savings. Questions from the audience concerned details of working with the two databases. One participant noted that WSU appears to have developed a system that provides features which an automated vendor could have provided, an observation that was agreed upon by the presenters.

Improving In-House Communication About Serials

Jeanne Baker
Sherry Palmiter

Workshop Leaders

Christa Easton Reinke

Recorder

SUMMARY. Numerous departments are involved in the serials processing chain, with functions becoming more inter-related in the online environment. At the University of Maryland at College Park, no one person or individual acted as a central clearing house for planning, implementing, or disseminating information about serials processing. This workshop examines function and process of a continuous quality improvement (CQI) team which studied the issues surrounding processing of serials, as well as the team's recommendations and their implementation. *[Article copies available for a fee from The Haworth Document Delivery Service: 1-800-342-9678. E-mail address: getinfo@haworth.com]*

Jeanne Baker is Head of the Serials Cataloging Unit, McKeldin Library, University of Maryland at College Park.

Sherry Palmiter is Head of the Serials Acquisitions Unit, McKeldin Library, University of Maryland at College Park.

Christa Easton Reinke is Serials Librarian, University of Houston Libraries.

[Haworth co-indexing entry note]: "Improving In-House Communication About Serials." Reinke, Christa Easton. Co-published simultaneously in *The Serials Librarian* (The Haworth Press, Inc.) Vol. 31, No. 1/2, 1997, pp. 301-305; and: *Pioneering New Serials Frontiers: From Petroglyphs to Cyberserials* (ed: Christine Christiansen and Cecilia Leathem) The Haworth Press, Inc., 1997, pp. 301-305. Single or multiple copies of this article are available for a fee from The Haworth Document Delivery Service [1-800-342-9678, 9:00 a.m. - 5:00 p.m. (EST). E-mail address: getinfo@haworth.com].

This workshop related an examination of serial functions and an attempt to coordinate these functions within a large academic library. The University of Maryland at College Park, where this case took place, addressed this issue through the use of a Continuous Quality Improvement (CQI) team. The Serials Communication Team, which involved staff from public and technical services, sought input from library staff regarding areas of confusion in serials processing. Using CQI techniques, the team examined all aspects of communication regarding serials and developed recommendations, which were then submitted to library administration. This workshop examined both the team process, in general and specifically, and the team's recommendations and their implementation.

The decision to use a CQI team to address communication problems related to serials was driven largely by a university-level mandate to use CQI to solve problems. The University's Office of Continuous Quality Improvement provided a CQI trainer who gave a basic overview of the CQI process to all library staff. After training, library administration solicited ideas for topics to be examined by CQI teams.

Several factors created the need for clarifying communication about serials within the Libraries. Serials functions were spread throughout technical services rather than being integrated into a single unit, and public service and other units also perform serial functions and rely on serial records. The Libraries had recently moved to an integrated online system, Victor, which meant that units which had previously maintained their own, often manual, records were now reliant on the same record. Projects such as shifting materials to compact storage, retrospective conversion, and inventory lacked overall coordination and led to units "tripping over" each other. Finally, inaccurate coding of the serials management screen in the online system made extracting accurate statistics from the system difficult, and served as a harbinger of potential future problems with database integrity if serials functions were not better coordinated.

With the problem identified, team formation was the next step. Teams were divided between full and quasi teams. Full teams included members of the Libraries' divisions. The team which examined serials communication issues was a quasi team, made up largely of members of the Technical Services division. The Associate Director of Technical Services served as the team's sponsor, with the Head of Serials Cataloging acting as Team Leader. They developed a team charter and selected team members. Staff from acquisitions, catalog management, cataloging, the main library's periodicals services unit, and a branch library were named to the team, and a facilitator selected. The team included professional and paraprofessional staff, some of whom had never served on a committee before.

One of the team's initial assumptions was that reorganization of serials units within technical services was not an option, since reorganization had been discussed at length and rejected as part of a decision to fill a department head position. The team began by brainstorming to identify basic needs. They then categorized these needs into basic groups: documentation, training, and communication about serials in general. Throughout this process, the facilitator worked to keep discussion focused on the team's charter and to avoid dwelling on overly specific problems. Having identified some concerns of those who worked directly with serials, the team then sought information about how the rest of the library staff felt about the same issues. The team developed a questionnaire which they sent out to all library staff. The team enjoyed a 46% return rate on questionnaires, with many including comments, some substantial.

All team members participated in compiling the team's final report, whether by writing recommendations or compiling statistics and creating graphs. The team then gave two reports–one to the Associate Director for Technical Services and Technical Services department heads and one to all library staff. The team encountered delays due to conferences, summer vacations, and staffing shortages. In all, the team's work took nine months rather than the four months originally projected.

The team's recommendations fell into three categories: documentation, training, and coordination. For documentation, the team suggested that documentation should be written pertinent to one's position and geared towards entering data into Victor, the online system. Each department should write its own documentation as needed and review it continuously to ensure that it reflects current policy and procedure. In addition, a general procedures manual should be written in a form that is readily updated, to include the basics that every staff member needs to know, including jargon. Finally, documentation should be mounted on the technical services division's home page, including cataloging terms, a contact list, and answers to frequently asked questions. In the area of training, new employees should be trained as soon as possible after their arrival, with emphasis on workflow and who-does-what with serials. The implementation of new cross-departmental procedures should immediately trigger coordinated training for all serials staff. Regular serials training should be available to non-serial technical services staff, and serials training should also be available to non-technical services staff as needed.

One suggestion which the team doubted could be implemented was the establishment of a new position of Serials Coordinator. They envisioned that the person in this role would review documentation, develop training, coordinate policies and procedures, and serve as a contact person for questions from non-serials staff. The team also suggested the creation of a Serials Round Robin Group, consisting of the department/unit heads of technical services serials units, who would discuss serials issues and new assignments in their units which would affect other units. Finally, they suggested that all serials units use the technical services division's mail reflector to discuss issues internally, as well as using the library-staff reflector and library newsletter to make announcements regarding serials issues.

Library Administration's response and the implementation of selected recommendations came soon before this presentation in June, 1996. Responsibility for documentation, including reviewing, clarification, and placing documentation on the technical services home page was assigned to the Head of Catalog Management. A serials cataloger is now responsible for general training in serials control on Victor and OCLC, while in-depth training is the responsibility of the individual serial unit. The duties of coordinating serials communication fell to the head of Serials Acquisitions, who chairs the Technical Services Serials Group and the University of Maryland at College Park Serials Group. In addition to calling meetings and setting agendas, this person is responsible for monitoring the technical service and Library Staff mail reflectors and responding appropriately to serials issues raised in the forums.

Because implementation of recommendations came only slightly before this presentation, it is difficult to assess the effects these changes will have on communication related to serials. Sherry Palmiter, Head of Serials Acquisitions and the coordinator of serials communication, reported that she began to receive questions regarding serials as soon as her new role became known. The presenters indicated some frustration at trying to schedule meetings of the Serials Round Robin Group, though scheduling meetings has been a problem throughout the team process. Finally, they indicated concern that documentation may bottleneck, since one person will have responsibility for reviewing it all.

Much of the discussion centered on the situations in which teams can be effective for dealing with issues of serials communication. While the function of teams must be at the grassroots, there must be administrative support for the work of the team, especially since it can be nearly impossible to make changes from the bottom up. Also, participants noted that teams are not an effective way of dealing with resistance, although administrators may try to apply them in that situation.

Other discussion centered on areas which are still unknown because these changes have been implemented so recently. These included whether or not there would be formal standards for documentation and what type of training would be offered. As part of discussion, the workshop leaders clarified that the team did not identify any need to overhaul procedures for serials, but simply to make information about serials processing more freely available throughout technical services and the library.

The Culture of Technical Services

Debbie Kalvee

Workshop Leader

Julie Tao Su

Recorder

SUMMARY. Libraries are reevaluating technical services processes and making technological, organizational, and workflow changes in order to optimize productivity with ever shrinking resources and provide effective user services in the rapidly changing information environment. However, regardless of how much tinkering we do with streamlining processes, little will change until the culture of technical services changes. This workshop discusses the culture of the library profession and presents a case study of one library's attempt to transform that culture. *[Article copies available for a fee from The Haworth Document Delivery Service: 1-800-342-9678. E-mail address: getinfo@haworth.com]*

What is the corporate culture in our workplace and in our library profession? What has our value system done for the profession and our patrons? Can these values we hold sustain librarianship in the ever evolv-

Debbie Kalvee is Head of the Bibliographic Management Access Department, Elmer E. Rasmuson Library, University of Alaska, Fairbanks.

Julie Tao Su is Serials Cataloging Librarian, Indiana University-Purdue University at Indianapolis.

[Haworth co-indexing entry note]: "The Culture of Technical Services." Su, Julie Tao. Co-published simultaneously in *The Serials Librarian* (The Haworth Press, Inc.) Vol. 31, No. 1/2, 1997, pp. 307-313; and: *Pioneering New Serials Frontiers: From Petroglyphs to Cyberserials* (ed: Christine Christiansen and Cecilia Leathem) The Haworth Press, Inc., 1997, pp. 307-313. Single or multiple copies of this article are available for a fee from The Haworth Document Delivery Service [1-800-342-9678, 9:00 a.m. - 5:00 p.m. (EST). E-mail address: getinfo@haworth.com].

ing information landscape? Debbie Kalvee, Head of the Bibliographic Access Management Department, Elmer E. Rasmuson Library at the University of Alaska, presented a case study on professional culture and one library's attempt to transform that culture.

The Elmer E. Rasmuson Library at the University of Alaska Fairbanks is the largest library in Alaska with circa 2 million holdings. It is also the largest and oldest federal depository in the state. The library plays a significant role in statewide planning and development of information services. Since 1995, when the Division of Computing and Communications merged with the library, Rasmuson has also been responsible for all academic, administrative computing and networking on campus.

The Division of Libraries has 17 library faculty and 51 staff members. Librarians are tri-partite faculty, having responsibilities in teaching, research, and library, university and public service. The Division consists of five departments: Instructional Media Production and Communications Technology; Collection Development; Alaska and Polar Regions; Reference and Instructional Services; and Bibliographic Access Management (BAM). There are five units in the Bibliographic Access Management Department: Acquisitions; Monographs; Serials; Government Documents and Maps; and the Biosciences Library. Similar to the Division of Libraries, BAM's organizational structure is matrix in design and very flat. Almost everyone reports to two or three people, and works in overlapping units.

In early 1994, when Kalvee assumed the position as the department's head, she inherited a highly competent and experienced staff. However, she observed low morale, little communication, workload inequity, and an extreme hierarchical reporting structure in the department. Although the workflow previously had been streamlined so that Acquisitions staff who received materials also performed copy cataloging and processing, a sizable cataloging backlog accumulated over the years, which would cost several hundred thousand dollars to outsource, at the rate of $22-25 per title.

Since then many changes have been implemented in BAM which include the following.

MANAGEMENT CHANGES

- Responsibility and authority have been delegated to librarians. Professionals are now managers for work groups such as Acquisitions, Monographs and Serials. Professionals have shifted from being primarily the creators of bibliographic records to serving as managers of the cataloging process.

- To enhance communication, all personnel have participated in fun activities such as personality preference tests, which are shared with everyone, to learn individual strengths and levels of flexibility, etc.
- The Department is continually examining processes and evaluating workflow to eliminate invalid tasks and discard procedures not of benefit to the patrons. The departmental principle when examining any process is: "what does this do for the patron?"

TECHNOLOGICAL CHANGES

- The UAF campus network was upgraded. The department has received many new workstations, resulting in all employees having their own workstations and Internet access.
- The current VTLS-based online system has the capability to download records from OCLC and upload these into the online system. These records in turn are exported via tapeload to WLN, thus eliminating the rekeying of OCLC records into WLN.

CATALOGING CHANGES

- The goal to get current receipts, including gifts, to the public stacks within one month has been established.
- Cataloging records are directly input into WLN without using worksheets or being reviewed by a "cataloging guru."
- Rush, original cataloging has shifted to support staff under the direction of the professionals.
- Only key access points are corrected such as author, title, imprint information, call number, and subject headings.
- The cataloging backlog has been closed; therefore, nothing is being added.

OUTSOURCING

- A portion of the Library's budget, circa $70,000 per year, has been redirected to outsourcing the cataloging backlog.
- Approval books are received with bibliographic records, supplied by BNA.

- Firm orders purchased with BNA will be received shelf-ready with accompanying bibliographic records.
- Newly received federal documents are automatically processed for the collection using MARCIVE's cataloging services.

PERSONNEL CHANGES

Due to the economic and political conditions on campus, the Department has lost support staff positions, and some professional staff, and time due to job reassignments. The department has been forced to do more with fewer staff. Moreover, a number of key personnel have recently retired. Up to 11 more are potential candidates for early retirement, should an early retirement incentive program be approved.

There is no guarantee that vacant positions will be filled, due to budget constraints. All professional positions are being reviewed by the campus administration for recruiting approval. Based on previous cases, it is highly unlikely cataloging librarians will ever be hired.

Many changes have been implemented with varying degrees of success. There certainly have been significant accomplishments and incremental progress, and some changes have produced very positive results. For instance, communication within the department has greatly improved. The department has become more efficient and people are working even harder, but they also have experienced some setbacks or resistance to change. Many personnel, for example, are reluctant to adopt the new policy of editing only key access points. They still clean up the entire bibliographic record. The 15% return rate of the BNA approval plan presents a problem, and records received from the approval profile are also disappointing. In-house programs need to be written to allow proper importation of records from different vendors, and it can take up to a year for such transactions to be successfully implemented.

Despite the technological and organizational changes, Kalvee noted that production did not significantly improve. It can still take several months for books or serials to reach the shelves. The technical services units in Rasmuson are still not able to stay current in cataloging and processing material. Items continue to go to the backlog.

The technology change continuum has three phases: replication (or mechanization), acceleration, and transformation. Rasmuson is mired in the second stage where they still add new applications to what they currently do. What is keeping the organization from moving forward to the final phase of transformation where REAL CHANGES occur? Kalvee contends it is the culture of technical services, or by extension, of the library profession. Regardless of how much tinkering is done to streamline processes, little will change until the culture changes. Is this possible? In these mercurial times, we are asking staff who are naturally inclined to build an ordered environment and to be in control, to become risk takers and to invent solutions. Can we expect them to sublimate into another kind of personality?

The following are values identified among personnel in the BAM Department which are applicable to the library profession in general:

1. Structure, order, control and detail are highly regarded. These values are particularly strong in the technical services areas. On the downside, these values foster specialization, extreme complexity, inflexibility, and by extension, they result in needless segmentation of the profession.
2. Library workers tend to defer to authority. This inclination can lead to strict adherence to established rules and procedures. Unfortunately, the rules used to catalog materials focus on describing the physical pieces rather than the contents. Such information is of less value to patrons than indexing and abstracting and table of contents services provided by commercial vendors. Although many articles have been written exhorting us to simplify and rethink our blind devotion to the rules, little changes.
3. Personnel are very competent, and are therefore pre-disposed to not tolerate mistakes or inaccuracies. This can discourage risk taking.
4. Librarians are perfectionists. This characteristic has fostered uniformity among libraries, which can make it easy for patrons to find material. However, librarians tend to spend too much time on striving for the ideal. As a result, very little is accomplished and progress is slow.
5. Librarians at Rasmuson have a very strong service commitment. All personnel, regardless of their primary responsibilities, are expected to work at the public service desks.
6. Most decisions are reached by consensus. Conformity is encouraged and valued. However, circumstances may not allow colleagues the time they need to get to the place we need them to be, or they may never want to get there.
7. Personnel have a strong belief in democratic values, free speech, and preservation of world knowledge.

Many of the above values have contributed significantly to the profession, but some of these become speed bumps on the changing library highway. For instance, the library culture lacks aggressiveness, entrepreneurialism, and decisiveness, which are imperative in the process of organizational change.

In order to successfully manage organizational change, the corporate culture–in this case, the library culture–must be transformed. Although it is still too early to tell if the attitudes in the BAM Department have really changed, people are coming around and many new ideas have been implemented which would not have been acceptable a year ago.

Kalvee believes we can make dramatic changes, but someone must set the direction and lead the way. It is imperative we coax out "stars" in the organization who will propose seemingly outlandish, and sometimes innovative, new ideas. Furthermore, there must be optimistic, yet skeptical risk takers, or "early adopters" who are willing to take up the challenge to implement the good suggestions. Obviously, strong administrative support is also essential. Supervisors should be prepared to help personnel set priorities and allow them to let go of less important tasks. Some practices must end before others begin. Introducing projects that can be completed in the near future is an excellent morale booster. Finally, attitudes towards control and security must be relaxed to allow for innovative thinking.

Library personnel as well as patrons are expected to change their attitude and mythical vision of a "library." It is difficult, and can be very upsetting for some conservatives who do not want the "library," as they see it, to be destroyed. For the benefit of the organization, it may be necessary to marginalize/neutralize personnel who do not come along, and are being particularly nasty about it. Getting naturally passive people to participate actively in the change process also remains a challenge; however, public acknowledgment and reward of such initiative and creativity can facilitate increased involvement.

In conclusion, Kalvee noted that the experience can be fun, tiring, and rewarding. Although the process is generally frustrating and initially unpleasant, one can mature as an individual and as a manager in such intense times. In order to make *real* changes happen, we need to re-evaluate our professional values, transform or discard those that hinder our progress, and keep those that have served us well. To become true information (rather than library) professionals, we need to look beyond our "edifice," i.e., the library building (which we use to define ourselves), and look to other professions for some answers.

Kalvee closed the workshop by presenting questions for discussion:

- What has the value system done for us and for our patrons?
- Can we and the values we hold keep librarianship a viable profession in the current information environment?

- Should we handle everything the same way? Will we ever be satisfied with a permanent abbreviated record?
- Should we look towards getting out of traditional services and move into something else, such as mediated instruction, teaching, and building better tools for information retrieval?
- Can we outsource the cataloging, processing, and organizing functions?
- Should we go back and recon monographic titles with table of contents summary notes?
- Do we have any aggressive risk takers?
- Are we information professionals?

In response to a question from the audience, Kalvee noted that Rasmuson outsources a specialized collection, mostly Alaskan materials, to WLN for cataloging. When books are returned from WLN, a trained student uploads the records via diskette to the online system, barcodes and links the item, and cursorily reviews the records for accuracy.

One member of the audience expressed concern that technical services staff may lose their cataloging skills if cataloging is outsourced. A second participant commented it is almost impossible to outsource serial materials because of their complexity and changing nature. Another participant suggested that outsourcing should not only be applied to technical service, but also to public service functions. Enhanced access points provided by technical services may help patrons become such sophisticated searchers that they no longer need assistance from the reference desk. Kalvee responded that, in her experience, many patrons will still require reference services and that perhaps we need to make library systems more convenient and intuitive for our patrons. Reference services are analogous to bank services: many patrons want to use the ATM, while others prefer to speak to tellers.

There were also comments and discussion about technical service personnel staffing the public service desk, and at the repeat session, there was discussion on how to have one's ideas heard and how to become a risk taker in library organizations.

Web Worlds and Hyperspace: Exploring More Advanced Topics in Web Authoring

Birdie MacLennan
Steve Oberg

Workshop Leaders

Mary Ann Sheble

Recorder

SUMMARY. The workshop provided an opportunity for participants to expand their knowledge of the World Wide Web and become better Web authors through exploring advanced Web authoring topics in a hands-on environment. The workshop began with a discussion of ideas for creative linking within and between documents, special character formatting, creating graphics, and coding tables. The second part of the workshop provided information on how to use external media, Common Gateway Interface (CGI) scripts, and Hypertext Markup Language (HTML) editors and converters. *[Article copies available for a fee from The Haworth Document Delivery Service: 1-800-342-9678. E-mail address: getinfo@haworth.com]*

Birdie MacLennan is Serials Coordinator, University of Vermont.
Steve Oberg is Head of Bibliographic Control, University of Chicago.
Mary Ann Sheble is Associate Director for Technical Services and Systems, University of Detroit Mercy Libraries, Detroit.

[Haworth co-indexing entry note]: "Web Worlds and Hyperspace: Exploring More Advanced Topics in Web Authoring." Sheble, Mary Ann. Co-published simultaneously in *The Serials Librarian* (The Haworth Press, Inc.) Vol. 31, No. 1/2, 1997, pp. 315-325; and: *Pioneering New Serials Frontiers: From Petroglyphs to Cyberserials* (ed: Christine Christiansen and Cecilia Leathem) The Haworth Press, Inc., 1997, pp. 315-325. Single or multiple copies of this article are available for a fee from The Haworth Document Delivery Service [1-800-342-9678, 9:00 a.m. - 5:00 p.m. (EST). E-mail address: getinfo@haworth.com].

315

Steve Oberg (Head, Bibliographic Control, University of Chicago) and Birdie MacLennan (Serials Coordinator, University of Vermont) emphasized that the workshop was designed for World Wide Web (Web) authors who consider themselves at the intermediate level; it was specifically intended for those who are currently creating Web pages but would like to expand their skills. The workshop was held in the University of New Mexico Zimmerman Library computer lab. Since this was a hands-on workshop, attendance was limited to two participants per computer, a total of twenty participants at each of the two sessions. Rick Ralston (Automated Processing Manager, Indiana University School of Medicine) and Robert Persing (Assistant Head of Serials, University of Pennsylvania) acted as workshop "free-floaters" and assisted workshop participants with some of the hands-on computer tasks. Workshop participants were provided with handouts (derived from a complete set of Web pages) that guided them through the hands-on exercises and gave them Uniform Resource Locator (URL) links for further information on topics covered in the workshop.

TOPICS ON WEB PAGE DESIGN

Part one of the workshop was provided by MacLennan. It was entitled, "Topics in Web Page Design (or: the Tapestry of HTML)." The presentation began with an overview of basic elements of Web page design and advanced to an in-depth discussion and demonstration on how to create document links, graphics, and tables.

ELEMENTS OF WEB DESIGN

MacLennan began the workshop with a discussion of techniques for creative Web page design. Prior to building a Web page, authors must define the scope and purpose of the site, and think about the design of the page in terms of the intended audience. Good designs begin with a search of the network to gather resources. Building a Web page is a two-step process: gathering information from the network, and weaving the information into a Web page.

MacLennan recommended that authors try to construct Web page designs that strike a balance between text and graphics. Because large graphics files slow retrieval of documents, they should not be used extensively. To accommodate both graphical browsers and text-only browsers, alternate text codes can be used to display text in non-graphical browsers. For example, the following would display the NASIG logo to those with graphical browsers and would provide as an alternative, the message "NASIG Logo" to those with text-only browsers:

<img scr=images/logomed.gif" alt=NASIG Logo">

During the process of constructing a Web page, MacLennan suggested that authors toggle between the Web browser and editor to view "work in progress" so that the author will continuously have an idea of what the user will see. Web pages should always be signed and the latest revision date should be placed on each document. Because information at Web sites changes frequently, links in Web documents should be checked regularly and information should be updated as necessary. After becoming familiar with basic Hypertext Markup Language (HTML) coding, authors may want to try one or more of several HTML editors. To keep up-to-date on HTML innovations, Web authors may want to peruse various style guides and coding sources that are offered on the Internet.[1]

CREATIVE USE OF LINKING

Three types of Web page links were demonstrated:

- Links within a document
- Links between documents
- Links between graphic images.

LINKS WITHIN A SINGLE DOCUMENT

Occasionally, authors may want to link one section of their Web document to another section. This may be useful to provide links between a table of contents and relevant sections of a document. To provide links between sections of a single document, Web authors must first name the section of the text they wish to link to:

<a name="link">Creative Use of Linking</a>

To link to that portion of the text, a hypertext reference anchor (a href=) must be used, followed by the hash sign (#) and the "name" of the section. The anchor must be closed with an </a> code:

<a href=#link>Creative Use of Linking</a>

The link will appear in the document as: *Creative Use of Linking.* When users click on this link, they will be routed to the section of the document that has been named, "Creative Use of Linking."

LINKS BETWEEN DOCUMENTS

Establishing a link between a Web page document and a remote document is relatively easy. A hypertext reference anchor (a href=) must be provided, followed by the URL of the document to which the author wishes to link, and the display term or phrase (for example, "NASIG-Web")

a href= "http://nasig.ils.unc.edu>NASIGWeb</a>

This will display as *NASIGWeb.* When users click on this term, they will be routed to the connecting "NASIGWeb" document.

LINKING IMAGES

It is possible to provide links between images within a single document and between documents. To illustrate the use of linking images within a document, MacLennan provided an example from her workshop Web page, "Topics in Web Page Design." The table of contents in this Web page contains an image of a quilt. At the conclusion of the various sections of the Web page, smaller quilt images are used. To provide the link between small quilt images and the larger table of contents image, MacLennan embedded the "img scr" file that she wished to link within a hypertext reference anchor (a href=). She then closed the anchor with an </a> code. In HTML code, the link between one of the smaller quilt images to the larger table of contents image appears as:

href=#contents> <img src= "quilt.gif></a>

To provide a link between an image and a remote document, authors must use a hypertext reference anchor to a URL. For example, to link an image with the name "nasig2.gif" to the NASIG New Mexico Conference page, the HTML code would appear as:

<a href= "http://http:www.unm.edu /-nasig. >

<img scr= "nasig2.gif"> NASIGWeb</a>

SPECIAL CHARACTER FORMATTING

Special formatting is necessary to display characters that are used in HTML code, such as ampersands and angle brackets. To display these characters in a document as "legitimate" characters, the following codes should be used:

< = *the code for* < *(left-angled bracket)*

> = *the code for* > *(right-angled bracket)*

& = *the code for* & *(ampersand)*

Additional codes support a number of non-ASCII characters and diacritical marks. A full list of these characters can be viewed through retrieving the document, "HTML Coded Character Set."[2]

GRAPHICS: WEB ARCHIVES AND CREATING YOUR OWN

It is possible to use a wide variety of colors for Web page graphics. You can either retrieve graphics files from other documents and incorporate them into your Web page or create your own. MacLennan provided information on several sites for downloading graphics: "Yahoo Graphics" and "Yahoo Icons."[3] A third resource, the "University of Vermont (UVM) Buttons, Balls, and Icons" encourages Web authors to link to UVM resources, rather than download files.[4] The first step in constructing a color graphics file is defining the background color. The use of the attribute BACKGROUND="URL.gif" is a part of the proposed HTML 3.0 code and is supported by browsers such as Mosaic and Netscape. Background colors and text colors are Netscape rather than HTML 3.0 extensions. To view these features, a Netscape Navigator browser version 1.1N or higher should be used. The use of Netscape extensions should not break the ability of a non-compatible browser to view the document.

To create color graphics, Web authors should familiarize themselves with a few basic codes for defining colors:

BACKGROUND = to define a graphical file as a background . . . or;
BCOLOR = to define a BackGround color
LINK = color of links
TEXT = color of unlinked text
VLINK = color of visited links

Hexadecimal color codes for links or background attributes should be defined in the *BODY* of Web documents. Web authors can become familiar with hexadecimal values for color attributes through viewing charts on the Internet. MacLennan suggested the following resources: "IFLA HTML: Backgrounds and Colour Notes," and Doug Jacobson's "RGB Hex Triplet Color Chart."[5]

A simple way to experiment with a number of color and background options is to visit Sam Choukri's "ColorMaker" page. This is an interactive color design program tutorial. The tutorial makes it easy to choose colors and backgrounds, and tailor them to Web pages.[6]

There are several software packages that make it easy to create, edit, and convert graphics files. Two examples mentioned by MacLennan are LView, a shareware package and Paintbrush, a Windows application.

TABLES

Creating tables in Web documents can be a good way to present detailed information in a form that is easy for users to understand. MacLennan mentioned several resources to help Web authors become familiar with coding tables: "TableMaker," "NCSA Mosaic Tables Tutorial," and "Tables as Implemented in Netscape 1.1."[7] All contain a number of examples. "TableMaker" is an interactive program and tutorial by Sam Choukri, and may be especially useful for Web authors who are just learning the art of table coding.

COMPONENTS FOR THE NEXT STEP IN WEB AUTHORING

The second part of the workshop was presented by Oberg. It was entitled, "Components for the Next Step in Web Authoring: External Media, CGI Scripts, and HTML Editors/Converters." This part of the workshop involved a combination of show-and-tell and hands-on work. Due to time and technology constraints, the purpose of the presentation was to provide highlights for further exploration, rather than in-depth instruction.

USING EXTERNAL MEDIA

Oberg began by explaining that one way to become familiar with using or viewing audio and video on the Web is to have a basic knowledge of the various file formats used to create these files. The easiest way to recognize the format of a file is by interpreting the file extension. For example, one popular video format, Quicktime, has files with the extensions "qt." and ".mov." A common file format for audio files is AIFF (Audio Interchange File Format). AIFF files have the extension ".aiff." Oberg cautioned that the process of incorporating external media into Web pages is more complex than integrating text and images. For example, to retrieve and use external media files, Web authors must have a properly configured Web browser that will "point" to what are commonly termed "helper apps." Helper apps are basically application programs that play audio and video files after Web browsers have downloaded files from remote Web pages. Examples of helper apps are LView and Media Player. Other requirements for integrating external media files into Web presentations may include a sound card and speakers, especially for IBM-compatible machines. Oberg noted that audio and video files are very large in comparison to other file types and cannot be retrieved quickly, especially for those who access Web pages via dial-up connections.

Two recent, frequently talked about Web developments are Java from Sun Microsystems and Adobe Acrobat. Java is a programming language based on C++. A Java-capable browser (such as HotJava or Netscape 2.x for X-Windows) is able to download and run *applets* (small applications written in Java) to local workstations. These applets are essentially miniature application programs that can perform an astonishing array of functions, such as automatically adding new features to Web browsers and running real-time animation. Oberg reminded the audience that Web pages enhanced with Java applets are generally viewable only by browsers that run on Windows 95, Windows NT, and UNIX.

Adobe Acrobat files can be recognized by their *.pdf* extension. They are created by a proprietary program that stores files in a format called Portable Document Format (PDF). With an Adobe Acrobat Reader, files created in PDF format can be displayed and printed across a number of platforms (such as Macintosh and Windows) with all layout schemes and fonts intact. While the program to write files in PDF is relatively expensive, the Adobe Acrobat Reader software is free.

COMMON GATEWAY INTERFACE SCRIPTS (CGI)

Common Gateway Interface (CGI) is the scripting language used to write gateway scripts for server software. Most commonly, CGI is written in object-based programming languages such as Perl and C. CGI scripts reside on Web server machines and are used to process information from Web browsers. A CGI script operates as a behind-the-scene interpreter of information from a Web browser, instructing the Web server software on how to respond.

Oberg discussed two ways in which CGI scripts are commonly used: for image maps and for forms. Image maps (sometimes referred to as clickable image maps) are graphic images with discrete areas mapped from portions of the image to provide hypertext links to other files or resources when clicked-on by a mouse. Image maps are created by mapping coordinates from areas of the image to a coordinate file, and then creating a CGI script that will take the mouse click coordinates from the browser, compare them to coordinates in the coordinate file, and open the correct link. After Web authors have determined what graphic image they will use to create an image map, they can determine coordinates using a graphics software package, such as Paintbrush or PaintShop Pro.

To enable workshop participants to better understand image maps, Oberg retrieved the main Yahoo screen. At the bottom of the screen, there are coordinates for an image map. When the user clicks on the image map, the server is directed to the correct location to retrieve the requested information.

Another use of CGI scripts is for forms that users can complete on the Web through entering information into text boxes, check boxes, radio buttons, or selection lists. To create forms, Web authors will need the following:

- UNIX operating system (or another operating system with CGI capability)
- CERN HTTPD or NCSA HTTPD Web server
- Programming knowledge of Perl, C, or similar language
- Access to cgi-bin directory on a server machine, or work with sysadmin.

To illustrate features of these forms, Oberg had workshop participants enter responses on an online form ("NASIG Workshop Guest Book") that he created for the workshop. Other applications of these forms were discussed and examples were provided:

- CGI enables users to enter validation information to provide access to restricted databases. CGI will take user identification and password information, and compare it to a file of authorized users. The *Wall Street Journal Interactive Edition* uses CGI scripts for user validation.
- Through clicking on appropriate points on a form, users are provided with an interactive search engine to a database of information. AltaVista was provided as an example.

- CGI scripts enable users to conduct electronic business transactions. Users can make selections through clicking on appropriate boxes on a form. Amazon.com Books was provided as an example.

HTML EDITORS AND CONVERTERS

Oberg discussed three types of HTML editors and converters:

- UNIX editors, such as emacs and vi
- "Standalone" editors, such as HTML Writer for Windows and HTML Edit for Macintosh
- "Integrated" editors/converters, such as Microsoft's Internet Assistant and ClarisWorks.

Different editors may be best for different situations. To compare editors, Oberg suggested that workshop participants refer to an article from *Internet World,* "Web Authoring Tools."[8] The workshop concluded with a hands-on practice session. Workshop participants viewed the HTML coded document for Oberg's workshop handout and practiced setting up a Web page, using HTML Writer.

NOTES

1. See for example, *A Beginner's Guide to HTML* (Urbana, IL: National Center for Supercomputing Applications)
http://www.mcsa,uiuc.edu/General/Internet/WWW/HTMLPrimer/html and
    Grobe, Michael. *HTML Quick Reference Guide* (Lawrence, KS: University of Kansas, Academic Computing Services)
http://www.cc.ukans.edu/info/HTML_quick.html
2. HTML Coded Character Set
http://www.w3.org/pub/WWW/MarkUp/html-spec/html-spec_13.html
3. Yahoo Graphics
http://www.yahoo.com/Computers_and_Internet/Graphics/Yahoo Icons
http://www.yahoo.com/Computers_and_Internet/World_Wide_Web/Programming/Icons/
4. University of Vermont (UVM) Buttons, Balls, and Icons
http://www.uvm.edu/icon/
5. IFLA HTML: Backgrounds and Colour Notes
http://www.nlc-bnc.ca/ifla/I/training/colour/ colour.htm/
    RGB Hex Triplet Color Chart
http://www.phoenix.net/-jacobson/rgb.html

6. ColorMaker
http://www.missouri.edu/-c588349/colormaker.html
7. TableMaker
http://www.missouri.edu/-c588349/tablemaker.html
NCSA Mosaic Tables Tutorial
http://www.mcsa.uiuc.edu/SDG/Software/Mosaic/Tables/tutorial.html
Tables as Implemented in Netscape 1.1
http://www.netscape.com/assist/net_sites/tables/html
8. "Web Authoring Tools," *Internet World* 7/4 (April, 1996)
http://www.internetworld.com/Apr96/toc.html

RECOMMENDED RESOURCES
External Media

Audio Formats FAQ
http://www.cis.ohio-state.edu/hypertext/faq/usenet/audio-fmts/top.html
Sound Information (Yahoo)
http://www.yahoo.com/Computers/Multimedia/Sound/
Alison Zhang's Multimedia File Formats on the Internet: Movies
http://ac.del.ca/-dong/movies.htm/
JavaSoft
http://www.javasoft.com/
Adobe Acrobat
http://www.adobe.com/

CGI Scripts

Original CGI Documentation
http://hoohoo.ncsa.uiuc.edu/cgi/
Original NCSA Forms Documentation
http://hoohoo.ncsa.uiuc.edu/egi.forms.html
http://www.ncsa.uiuc.edu/SDG/Software/Mosaic/Docs/fill-out-forms/overview.
html
Information about Perl (Yahoo)
http://www.yahoo.com/Computers/Languages/Perl/

HTML Editors and Converters

Microsoft's Internet Assistant
http://www.microsoft.com/msword/Internet/IA/default.htm
HTML Writer (Windows)
http://lal.cs.byu.edu/people/nosack/

HTML Edit (Macintosh)
http://www.stonehand.com/murray/htmledit.html

General Web Publishing Resources

Lemay, Laura. *Teach Yourself More Web Publishing with HTML in a Week.* (Indianapolis, IN: SamsNet, 1995).
Lynch, Patrick. *Web Style Manual.* (New Haven: Yale Center for Advanced Instructional Media).
http://info.med.yale.edu/caim/StyleManual_Top.HTML/
Web4Lib Electronic Discussion List and Archives
http://sunsite.berkeley.edu/Web4Lib/

GILS,
Government Information Locator Service:
Blending Old and New
to Access U.S. Governmental Information

Judy Andrews

Workshop Leader

Lucy Duhon

Recorder

SUMMARY. U.S. government information resources, because of their vast quantity and lack of organization, and because of redundancies among agencies, have never been simple to locate. A budding electronic system, the Government Information Locator Service (GILS), is beginning to put structure into government information as well as to provide online pointers to government resources. This workshop explained the legislation behind the making of GILS, described its mission, and demonstrated actual searches for government information using the locator service. *[Article copies available for a fee from The Haworth Document Delivery Service: 1-800-342-9678. E-mail address: getinfo@haworth.com]*

Judy Andrews is Documents Librarian, James Madison University, Harrisonburg, VA.

Lucy Duhon is Assistant Serials Librarian, University of Toledo, Toledo, OH.

[Haworth co-indexing entry note]: "GILS, Government Information Locator Service: Blending Old and New to Access U.S. Governmental Information." Duhon, Lucy. Co-published simultaneously in *The Serials Librarian* (The Haworth Press, Inc.) Vol. 31, No. 1/2, 1997, pp. 327-333; and: *Pioneering New Serials Frontiers: From Petroglyphs to Cyberserials* (ed: Christine Christiansen and Cecilia Leathem) The Haworth Press, Inc., 1997, pp. 327-333. Single or multiple copies of this article are available for a fee from The Haworth Document Delivery Service [1-800-342-9678, 9:00 a.m. - 5:00 p.m. (EST). E-mail address: getinfo@haworth.com].

FOUNDING FATHERS

Judy Andrews, Documents Librarian of James Madison University, in Harrisonburg, Virginia, opened the workshop to a group of 45 mostly documents librarians by highlighting the history of government documents in the United States. A show of hands confirmed the truth that in most libraries documents have traditionally been relegated to the basement (or even the attic). Now, although documents command more respect, they are still as complicated as ever.

"In the late eighteenth century, when the 13 rebellious British colonies decided to strike out on their own, the first thing they did was publish a government document!" Andrews declared, drawing laughter from the group. She continued with a recitation from the Declaration of Independence, in which the founding fathers "solemnly publish and declare . . . that these united colonies are . . . free and independent states . . . "

In 1822, James Madison wrote to W. T. Barry, "A popular Government, without popular information, or the means of acquiring it, is but a Prologue to a Farce or a Tragedy . . . a people who mean to be their own Governors, must arm themselves with the power which knowledge gives."[1] At least one of our early leaders clearly recognized that the public must have access to government information. This was the foundation for the depository library system.

EXPANDING FAMILY

There are 1400 depository libraries in the United States today. Their function is to provide storage and access to government documents. All depository libraries must keep their documents for at least five years, except for regional depositories, which must keep the material permanently. Andrews noted that this will probably change, because of the Internet and electronic publishing. The United States is reputedly the largest publisher in the world. Its publications range from small one to two page pamphlets to volumes hundreds of pages long. In 1994, the Government Printing Office (GPO) distributed 101.8 million publications. Keeping up with this information is difficult, especially when the only constant is change.

BIRTH OF A SYSTEM

The Government Information Locator Service (GILS) is a recent attempt to organize government information on the Internet. Since the

1980s, Charles McClure, of Syracuse University, has conducted studies on the way users find and use government information. In 1992, McClure and William Moen completed a report to the Office of Management and Budget (OMB), the National Archives and Records Administration (NARA), and the General Services Administration, which showed who was using government documents.[2] This report set the general design for a network-based locator of government information, and set the stage for the legislation that would make this possible.

In February 1993, the Clinton-Gore administration published a strategic plan for using technology. Promoting the dissemination of federal information was an "action item."

> Every year the federal government spends billions of dollars collecting and processing information . . . while much of this information is very valuable, many potential users either do not know that it exists, or do not know how to access it. We are committed to using new computer and networking technology to make this information more accessible to the taxpayers who paid for it. . . . federal information is [to be] made available at a fair price to as many users as possible while encouraging growth of the information.[3]

On June 8, 1993, P.L. 103-40 established the GPO as "a means of enhancing electronic public access to a wide range of federal electronic information."[4] This was the first time that a public law recognized that electronic information was government information, and that it should be part of the GPO depository library program. This battle had been fought since the Reagan administration, and so this was a big victory. P.L. 103-40 mandated that federal publications be stored in electronic format. The law also contained a provision that access to directories and documents be made available to depository libraries without charge.

Concurrently to this legislation, the OMB was publishing Circular A-130, "Management of Federal Information Resources."[5] This encouraged agencies to ensure public access to government information regardless of form or medium. It also established the use of aids, such as catalogs and directories, and required that any fee exacted would equal no more than the cost of dissemination.

In September 1993, the National Information Infrastructure Task Force published their Agenda for Action. One of the objectives of this agenda was to provide access to government information. Interestingly, this task force suggested something that librarians have used all along–the "virtual card catalog." It "will indicate the availability of government information in whatever form it takes."[6]

In summary, these are the steps that laid the groundwork for the establishment of GILS:

- a report that identified a need and set the design
- a strategic plan for technology that prominently included government information
- a law that established a directory of federal information in electronic format
- a regulation that required electronic format for federal publications
- the inclusion of public information in NII Agenda for Action

OMB Bulletin 95-01, which was issued in furtherance of the Circular, describes the function of GILS as follows:

> GILS will identify published information resources throughout the federal government, describe the information available in those resources, and provide assistance in obtaining the information. It will also serve as a tool to improve agencies' electronic records management practices. GILS will consist of decentralized agency-based locator records, and associated information services. It will use off-the-shelf communications and information technology products and services, so that government information can be stored and retrieved in a variety of ways and in a variety of locations.[7]

With 108 major agencies in the United States, not to mention the subsets of those agencies, it is easy to see why decentralization might be necessary. Agencies, better than anyone else, have the expertise to organize and disseminate their information, and for political reasons prefer local responsibility for cost and control.

The idea for GILS came about because of Eliot Christian's model for the United States Geological Survey (USGS).[8] His vision was to provide "one stop shopping." Selling the idea meant choosing the least expensive method possible–electronic access. OMB Bulletin 95-01 requires that each agency develop and make available to the public a locator service for those information products that are publicly available. To do this, agencies may use one of four methods: either using their own information resources, through an information processing service organization in another agency (such as GPO), through an interagency cooperative effort, or through a contractor. Internet access should be free of charge, particularly to depository libraries. Agency GILS are to be established in accordance with the Federal Information Processing Standard (FIPS Pub.) 192. If GILS cannot make a direct link to the desired information, it will provide the necessary contact to request or receive that information, possibly in another format.

LEARNING TO WALK

The plan was that by December 31, 1995, each federal agency would have compiled an inventory of its automated information system records and locators. By June 30, 1996, a review is scheduled to check for completeness in establishing a record disposition schedule. By December 31, 1996, each agency should give this schedule to the Archivist of the United States. Although Eliot Christian's model was meant to be simple and cost-effective, agency decentralization inevitably makes it necessary to enforce some standard. There is some controversy concerning the use of off-the-shelf software, and about whether it should be tied to the Z39.50 standard. This relates to the issue of quick obsolescence of software and hardware. Who will keep the equipment and documentation to transmit and display older information? It is because of these unresolved issues that NARA accepts only three to five percent of material in electronic format.

Access and preservation were the two big issues at the recent Federal Depository Library Conference in April of this year. In 1995, Congress proposed that all government information be put into electronic format within two years. The more realistic counter-offer proposed by the GPO, in May 1996, was that *half* of all government information be transferred within *seven* years. How useful GILS is, and will become, depends largely on politics. There is still no consensus between the White House and Congress over who will control GILS. Andrews expressed some doubt as to the savings GILS will provide–the GPO has already hired two new employees, just for GILS, and resources keep being shifted to cover the new regulation.

GRADING GILS

The second half of the workshop consisted of group work. First Andrews demonstrated GILS on the World Wide Web. By entering the main site (http://www.usgs.gov/gils), she was able to go into *GPO Access* and conduct a search. Menu choices included, *All Records on GPO Access GILS sites; Pathway GILS records created by GPO* [those records on GPO's server]; and *Pointer Records to Other GILS sites* [those records on other servers]. *Individual Agency GILS databases on GPO Access* was yet another menu option.

As an example, Andrews submitted a search–the phrase "population and housing," which yielded 14 hits (the default is 40). Hits scoring highest appear at the top of the list. *Word weight* rates a word highest if it appears in a headline or title and less if it appears only in the text. *Term weight* refers to the frequency of occurrence of words over all documents in the database. Here weight is dependent upon uniqueness. Therefore, words that appear frequently are not rated as highly; some are so common that they become stop words. One audience member asked for clarification on whether selecting a number from the returned list will retrieve the text for the user. Andrews explained that the user will only get the GILS core record, which is a locator for the actual information.

After this brief demonstration, Andrews put the workshop attendees to work. The classroom split off into nine groups of four or five, and each group was given a sample printout of an agency located through GILS. They were instructed to examine their particular printout and note the agency, its mission, the type of resource, the good points of the locator record, and what could be improved. In general, each group was to decide whether their sample record carried out the GILS mission effectively. The groups discussed their agencies' records among themselves for ten minutes, then each one reported its findings before the class. Among the complaints were: that subject terms were too broad, that they were not searchable, and that there were not enough actual "hot links." Some positive observations included the extensive points of contact, availability information, links, subject terms, and cross references the records held.

ROOM TO GROW

At the end of the workshop, the group had questions concerning the relationship between GPO Access and GILS, about the role librarians will play in contributing to and updating GILS records, and whether there would be available an online government organization manual and other lists of resources.

There is still much work to be done with this locator service. Librarians, as users, need to campaign to those creating GILS, explaining what the records need to make them more useful. For example, there is a need for online access to journals. It is a beginning, however, that these GILS records are based on the MARC format.

Providing this locator service in a decentralized manner will assure the most complete and accurate information possible, but it also means that different agencies will define the GILS mandate in different ways, and this risks redundancy. One of the reasons GILS was created in the first place was to avoid redundancy in disseminating government information. To sum up GILS: It's a baby. The baby will grow.

NOTES

1. Saul K. Padover, Ed., *The Complete Madison: His Basic Writings* (New York: Harper & Brothers Publishers, 1953), 337.
2. Charles R. McClure, Joe Ryan, and William E. Moen, *Identifying and Describing Federal Information Inventory/Locator Systems: Design for Net-worked-based Locators*, 2 vols. (Bethesda, MD: National Audio Visual Center, 1992).
3. William J. Clinton and Albert Gore, Jr., *Technology for America's Strength, A New Direction to Build Economic Strength* (Washington, DC: Government Printing Office, February 1993).
4. U.S. Statutes at Large 107 (1993): 112-114. *Government Printing Office Electronic Information Access Enhancement Act of 1993.*
5. Office of Management and Budget. *Federal Information Resources Management, Revision: Notice* (OMB Circular No. A-130), Federal Register 58, no. 126 (July 2, 1993), 36068-86.
6. Department of Commerce. NTIA NII Office. Information Infrastructure Task Force. *The National Information Infrastructure: Agenda for Action* (Washington, DC, September 15, 1993).
7. Office of Management and Budget. *Establishment of Government Information Locator Service* (OMB Bulletin 95-01).
8. Eliot J. Christian, *Government Information Locator Service (GILS)* (May 2, 1994). Available by anonymous FTP (File Transfer Protocol) via the Internet at 130.11.48.107 as /pub/gils.text (ASCII) text format.

Using Focus Groups
to Match User Expectations
with Library Constraints

Sheryl Williams

Workshop Leader

Elizabeth Parang

Recorder

SUMMARY. Focus groups can furnish needed user input in a short time frame. The issues to be discussed must be clearly identified and questions formulated. Appropriate participants can then be selected. Care should be exercised in selecting a facilitator, a meeting location, and recording equipment. Sessions transcripts can be readily analyzed using a matrix which can then be utilized to compile a written report summarizing both the overwhelming feeling of group and other points brought out. *[Article copies available for a fee from The Haworth Document Delivery Service: 1-800-342-9678. E-mail address: getinfo@haworth.com]*

This workshop was based on the use of focus groups to elicit user input desired for inclusion in a decision-making process concerning space plan-

Sheryl Williams is Head of the Serials Department, University of Nebraska Medical Center Library.

Elizabeth Parang is Coordinator of Periodicals, Pepperdine University, Malibu, CA.

[Haworth co-indexing entry note]: "Using Focus Groups to Match User Expectations with Library Constraints." Parang, Elizabeth. Co-published simultaneously in *The Serials Librarian* (The Haworth Press, Inc.) Vol. 31, No. 1/2, 1997, pp. 335-339; and: *Pioneering New Serials Frontiers: From Petroglyphs to Cyberserials* (ed: Christine Christiansen and Cecilia Leathem) The Haworth Press, Inc., 1997, pp. 335-339. Single or multiple copies of this article are available for a fee from The Haworth Document Delivery Service [1-800-342-9678, 9:00 a.m. - 5:00 p.m. (EST). E-mail address: getinfo@haworth.com].

ning at the University of Nebraska Medical Center Library. After describing the present situation, Sheryl Williams, Head of the Serials Department, went on to talk about structuring the focus groups, including developing the questions, selecting the participants, scheduling the meetings, evaluating the materials, and wrapping up.

Williams began the workshop by describing the Leon S. McGoogan Library of Medicine at the University of Nebraska Medical Center. The library moved into its 60,000 square foot location in 1970 and currently has six linear miles of journal shelving, housing 158,00 volumes. The library is at approximately 92% capacity with an estimated five years of growth for journal shelving. The library serves as the primary medical and research library for the University of Nebraska Medical Center, Nebraska health professionals, and the citizens of Nebraska. Materials support five basic functions: clinical practice and health care services; research by faculty, staff, and students; education and training of health professionals; administration of health care services and educational programs; and preservation of institutional publications or related materials. McGoogan Library pays careful attention to weeding unwanted materials and to maintaining and preserving retrospective materials. Discussion within the library centered on three possible solutions to the space problem: converting older holdings to microform, withdrawing holdings from the collection completely, or placing materials in an off-site storage facility.

The Library believes in open communications with its users, both for publicizing services and for determining service needs. The two most appropriate methods for gathering information from users concerning space requirements were determined to be surveying users or conducting focus groups comprised of selected users. At this point, Williams involved the workshop participants in identifying the differing attributes of focus groups and surveys and determining which one is best used in a specific situation. Since McGoogan Library had surveyed the users on several topics in the past few years, focus groups were selected as the preferred method. Another advantage to focus groups is the ability to administer them in a short period of time while surveys may dribble in over an extended period of time.

As a first step in developing questions for the focus groups, the library department heads brainstormed to identify topics which could affect the users of the journal collection. Sheryl conducted such a brainstorming session with the workshop participants identifying aspects of the space problem, noting the basic areas apparent in these topics, and outlining objectives of the focus groups. These objectives were to identify user information needs and sources, to find out how customers feel about different formats, and to answer the question, "Are interlibrary loan, off-site storage and compact storage acceptable to the users?" Similarly, the McGoogan librarians grouped their topics into three basic areas: use of the collection, access to information, and availability of materials. The goals of the focus groups were developed from these areas. Questions were developed by a committee composed of those directly affected by this project: Head of Reference, Head of Serials, Head of Circulation, and Head of Collection Development. The order of questions flowed from general to specific. The McGoogan focus group questions were included in the packet of materials Sheryl furnished to workshop participants.

Next, workshop participants discussed the pros and cons of choosing a professional facilitator, a trained interviewer who can get participants to stay on track while drawing them out. Advantages included having no vested interest and thus being less likely to react to perceived criticism, resulting in the group members being more open, being less likely to guide the group, having no history of interaction, being an expert in group dynamics, and possessing the equipment and facilities to effectively conduct focus groups. Disadvantages included not following up on questions because of a lack of knowledge, expense, having his/her own agenda, lack of a vested interest, and not developing in-house expertise. The facilitators purpose and objectives must match those of the library. The McGoogan Library chose to use a consulting firm that had been used for a previous study conducted by the Midcontinental Region office of the National Library of Medicine. The firm's transcription services were used but the library chose to analyze the findings in-house at considerable savings. The Library Director and Head of Serials met with the facilitator to discuss the issues and ensure he had the background needed to understand what information the library was seeking as well as to acquaint him with such topics as UnCover and the limitations of electronic journals. As part of the process, a formal proposal was drawn up including the scope of the project (conducting six focus groups composed of medical students, medical faculty and medical staff), the purpose, the objectives, and the approach. A focus group cost estimate was obtained; both the proposal and the cost estimate were included in the packet of information given NASIG workshop participants.

Participants should be selected keeping in mind that focus groups are not quantitative surveys and, therefore, are not statistically representative of all users. Groups are generated based on pre-determined characteristics and rationale. There must be enough commonality within the group for members to be comfortable in the discussion, although a variety of participants is needed if a variety of questions is asked. Workshop participants discussed who should be selected and why. For its focus groups, the McGoogan Library identified groups including each of the Colleges, the faculty senate, researchers, clinical faculty, student senate, and other users (including special privilege users and the non-UN users who dial-in to the on-line system). Information about area librarians could be obtained through Interlibrary Loan statistics. Participants in these groups were known users of the library, members of the Library Advisory Committee and individuals from the Medical Center administrative offices. Students were not included as they would not have the experience to discuss the current journal collection. The groups were gender balanced and diverse. The participants wore name tags so the facilitator could address them by name.

Suggested honorariums for workshop participants included food and on-line searches. Because of funding constraints McGoogan Library could not afford breakfast or lunch and settled on providing coffee and rolls to morning groups and coffee, soda, and cookies to afternoon groups. In order to achieve the optimum size of 8-10 participants per group, McGoogan librarians had composed lists of 15-25 names in order to allow for "no shows" or declines. A preliminary letter was sent from the Vice-chancellor for Academic Affairs, a strong supporter of the library, to the selected participants, describing the importance of these focus groups and encouraging participation. One week later telephone invitations were made following a prepared script. Sheryl's handout included both this script and a confirmation letter sent to the participants. All persons contacted were eager to participate.

A specific calendar period should be selected for scheduling the groups. McGoogan wanted the groups to meet within a two-week period for one hour each and could hold no more than two per day. The master campus schedule was consulted to determine what time periods were most desirable. Clinical faculty had to be scheduled early in the morning; nursing students had to be scheduled around classes; national meetings, Grand Rounds and accreditation visits had to be considered, as did spring break and final exams. Although the Library has a conference room which would have been adequate for the focus group meetings, it was felt that holding the discussions away from the library would contribute to the neutrality of the discussions. The sessions were tape-recorded and the room selected was not acoustically ideal for recording, resulting in some unintelligible comments. Perhaps using more than one tape recorder or an omni-direction microphone rather than the built-in microphone on the recorder would have helped.

As mentioned previously, the Library had chosen to analyze the sessions in-house. Both the audio-cassettes and the transcriptions, both on paper and on disk, were received from the facilitator. A hidden advantage to analyzing the material in-house was the greater understanding gained of the feelings behind the comments included in the reports. Originally, each member of the committee was to analyze one group in order to avoid inundating any one individual. However, Sheryl found she enjoyed the analysis and took on the responsibility for the entire work, spending approximately three hours on each group's transcript. A matrix was developed which briefly described each topic and each group. Analysis must be verifiable and appropriate to the study. Comments included in this matrix were representative of the group. At this point in the workshop, participants attempted to fill out a sample matrix using sample transcript excerpts. The McGoogan Library matrix was 4 pages. The written analysis is based on this matrix so each question must be adequately identified.

As part of wrapping up the project, focus group participants should be acknowledged. A small thank-you card with a brief message from the library director was sent to each. A written report was distributed to selected individuals. The written analysis included what was known, then confirmed or challenged, such as the fact that most materials used were published within the last 5-10 years; what was suspected, that the foreign language materials were not needed; and what was new, such as comments about moving out study tables. Sheryl included a page from the focus groups summary which illustrated the use of a paragraph summarizing the response of all groups followed by comments that typify what each group felt. An executive summary was prepared which also specified the criteria for withdrawing or keeping materials.

In reviewing the focus groups experience, Williams identified areas which could have been improved including the use of better recording equipment and limiting the size of the groups. Because few persons on their lists declined, the McGoogan focus groups were often 12-15 persons resulting in some being difficult to manage; the next time they would prioritize the list. This workshop was organized so that participants contributed throughout, recounting both good and bad experiences with focus groups.

Educating/Retraining Serialists for Change

Barbara Hall

Workshop Leader

Markel Tumlin

Recorder

SUMMARY. Changes in libraries and the need to improve staff skills make it necessary for librarians to develop and maintain practical skills training programs. An overview of the planning of training programs is provided. Included are the five primary steps of successful training programs: assessment, planning, selecting methods, using principles of adult learning, and evaluation. A real-life example from the University of Southern California is described. *[Article copies available for a fee from The Haworth Document Delivery Service: 1-800-342-9678. E-mail address: getinfo@haworth.com]*

This workshop was designed to present the basic components of practical skills training programs for serials staff members. It was conducted by Barbara Hall, the Head of the Acquisitions Department at the University of Southern California, who was introduced to workshop attendees by Cynthia Coulter, Head of Acquisitions at the University of Northern Iowa.

Barbara Hall is Head of the Acquisitions Department, University of Southern California.

Markel Tumlin is Head of the Periodicals Department, University of San Diego.

[Haworth co-indexing entry note]: "Educating/Retraining Serialists for Change." Tumlin, Markel. Co-published simultaneously in *The Serials Librarian* (The Haworth Press, Inc.) Vol. 31, No. 1/2, 1997, pp. 341-345; and: *Pioneering New Serials Frontiers: From Petroglyphs to Cyberserials* (ed: Christine Christiansen and Cecilia Leathem) The Haworth Press, Inc., 1997, pp. 341-345. Single or multiple copies of this article are available for a fee from The Haworth Document Delivery Service [1-800-342-9678, 9:00 a.m. - 5:00 p.m. (EST). E-mail address: getinfo@haworth.com].

In her introduction of Hall, Coulter commented that NASIG Conference participants had heard about many new developments affecting serials work, but would be dependent upon their staffs to implement necessary changes. She further indicated that Hall would provide strategies to help those in attendance assist their workers in learning needed skills.

Hall began her presentation by stating her purpose: to provide tips and general guidelines for practical skills training. Most hands went up in the audience of approximately 35 (mostly librarians) when Hall asked if any of the participants had done training in the previous year or would be doing training in the coming year; this response highlighted the relevance of the workshop to those attending. Hall provided an outline of her presentation and then asked for audience volunteers to provide a definition of training (as distinguished from teaching). Training, it was determined, is often concerned with changing a behavior or attitude with regard to specific procedures and/or tasks; often, there is a "hands-on" component.

Before launching into a discussion of strategies for developing training programs, Hall listed some of the reasons that libraries devise and institute them. Calling training a "key ingredient in organizational success," Hall identified several factors that create a need for the training of library employees. Technological change in libraries topped the list; Hall emphasized that such change leaves librarians no choice in whether or not to provide training; training is necessary to address these conditions. Organizational change was given as another reason that training is needed; people changing jobs must often learn new skills. Training is also sometimes needed to address the performance problems of individual employees (such as high error rates); such training may enhance worker productivity and quality. Bringing staff members up to newly desired skill levels within their established positions is also a legitimate reason to implement training programs. The object of training is to close the skills gap between where the person is and where he or she needs to be.

A discussion of the five basic steps to success in developing training programs followed, constituting the lengthiest part of the presentation. The five distinctive steps identified by Hall included assessing the need for training, planning the sessions, selecting methods of training, utilizing principles of adult learning, and evaluating results. Hall explored each step as a necessary component in an overall training program.

In assessing whether or not training is needed, one must be able to decide if a situation, a problem, or change within the library requires training or if another type of action is more appropriate. For example, there may be personnel issues that are problematic but can't be solved by training. One must first identify exactly what the problem or needed change is and then decide if the situation can be improved by reducing or eliminating a skills gap between current practice and some desired outcome or targeted goal. An example of this might be to improve communication within the library by training people in the use of electronic mail. This assessment can only be made by gathering information, both through effective communication (talking to both staff members and other supervisors) and from records (e.g., checking them for error rates).

Once one has determined that the problem can be addressed by showing staff how to improve their practical skills, one must plan the actual sessions. Several questions must be answered at this stage for the sessions to be effective. The first thing that must be decided is what exactly is the desired outcome. Once this has been established, one can and must gear the course content to address the specific skills targeted. The aims and objectives of the training session must be established. The aims tend to be fairly general (e.g., to teach people electronic mail), while the objectives tend to be more specific and measurable (e.g., "here are the things you need to know to send and receive electronic mail").

Personnel questions must also be considered at this point; who will be trained and who will do the training. The people to be trained are those requiring the skills identified for addressing the problem. The trainer is often their supervisor (in this case, the Serials Librarian), but may be somebody else from within the library or parent organization. Hall stressed that it is often beneficial to explore other resources available within the institution. For example, it is not uncommon for university computing centers to have instructors available to teach certain computer skills.

Other questions to be answered during the planning stage are "how, where, and when?" One must determine which instructional methods and training aids are best suited to address identified aims and objectives. Predicting the number of needed sessions is also necessary. Selecting a venue that will maximize learning is important, as is a determination of how soon the skills are needed. One must exercise time management and set priorities.

The third part of Hall's "five steps to success" approach was a discussion of many of the training methods available to the trainer. Job instruction, the first method mentioned, is often done in a one-on-one setting with a new employee. Methods of training for larger groups include lectures and modified lectures (in which the trainees have the opportunity to ask questions). These methods are somewhat abstract and perhaps best suited for general knowledge training. Demonstrations, on the other hand, are essential for quality training in the use of motor skills. Other methods include group discussion (not very effective for practical skills training), student practice (good for increasing competence once skills have been "learned"), student reading, role-playing (better for teaching behaviors than for teaching skills), and programmed instruction (e.g., help screens, tutorials). In addition, the trainer must select training aids that enhance and do not interfere with understanding. Materials from which to choose include such things as videos, overhead transparencies, slides, whiteboard, flipcharts, and handouts.

The actual planning of the lesson(s) includes preparing notes, considering timing within the lesson, and taking care of equipment needs. All should address aims and objectives. Hall recommended providing three unique demonstrations for each skill to be transmitted; the first demonstration should be done at normal speed, the second at a slower and more explanatory rate, and the third performed after asking for instructions from the student(s). Trainees must also be given the opportunity to assist so that they can practice these skills.

As the fourth of her basic steps, Hall stressed the importance of utilizing the principles of adult education during each practice session. While it is unlikely that a trainer would be able to incorporate all of them every time, Hall suggested that it would be beneficial if at least two or three of the principles could be utilized in each lesson. Adult learning can be implemented in a variety of ways. The first is to engage the participant in active learning, to allow him or her to learn by doing. This is particularly meaningful for skills training. It is also important to make the learning appropriate by showing the trainee how a need is being met and by using familiar examples. Trainees should know what the desired outcome is. In addition, they should also be motivated; this can often be accomplished by an enthusiastic trainer who successfully explains how the training will improve the trainee's job.

A component of adult learning that was heavily stressed by Hall was that of multiple-sense learning. It is valuable to let the trainee see and experience as well as just to hear. Greater retention of information is accomplished by appealing to as many of the senses as possible. The trainer must also be sensitive to encouraging two-way communication, thus allowing the trainee to more actively participate in the training. In addition, the trainer must provide feedback, using positive reinforcement whenever possible. The concept of "repeat, recap, and review" can also play a vital role in allowing the trainee to absorb the skills through practice, although Hall warned that extremely long sessions often detract from retention. Finally, Hall stressed that first impressions ("primacy") and last impressions ("recency") are often those most easily retained by trainees.

The last of the five steps described by Hall concerns evaluation. Hall stressed that evaluation is necessary to ensure that the required skills have been sufficiently absorbed by the trainee. Methods of evaluation include interviewing trainees, taking a written survey, testing trainees on acquired skills, observing the trainees using their new skills, and monitoring job performances. The failure of the trainees to exhibit competence in their new skill areas may require the trainer to design new and different training sessions or to work one-on-one with trainees who are having problems.

Hall then provided a real-life example to illustrate the concepts she had presented. When her library at the University of Southern California brought in new computer systems, a lot of retraining of longtime employees was necessary. She noted the phenomenon of established employees being required to learn new technologies with which they were uncomfortable. In describing the results of the training sessions, she noted that they were very popular with the staff and had unexpected results, such as certain staff members, initially nervous about the training, who adapted well and learned much.

After summarizing her major points (and, in effect, reemphasizing the "recency" component of adult learning), Hall suggested to the attendees that they start working on training programs immediately and also provide a program of ongoing training. She further stated that as supervisors, the participants of the workshop knew best what their staffs needed.

Hall's presentation was followed by a series of questions and comments. One participant mentioned the issue of training student workers rather than regular staff members; the possibility of using students already knowledgeable on computers to train other students in a "buddy" system was mentioned. One participant asked Hall if USC had implemented an ongoing training system; Hall responded that while that had not yet happened, it had been suggested and was likely. One participant commented on her staff's enthusiasm for training. Another mentioned that she had come to librarianship after a career in teaching and reemphasized the importance of ongoing training. Finally, one participant stressed that different people have different learning styles and rates; it is important for trainers to recognize this; in addition, it is important to note that some staff members perform well but aren't skilled teachers.

Participants of this workshop left with some excellent handouts that outlined Hall's major points. A lesson plan and session plan form were also provided. It was impossible to leave this session without a good understanding of the basic structure for planning and implementing a training program.

Pioneering Document Delivery

Terry Sayler
Clare MacKeigan

Workshop Leaders

Becky Schwartzkopf

Recorder

SUMMARY. The provision of materials through document delivery has become a critical issue for all libraries as the costs for materials skyrocket. This workshop described examples of pioneering document delivery from Maryland and Canada. The presenters provided examples of a public and a commercial document delivery system. *[Article copies available for a fee from The Haworth Document Delivery Service: 1-800-342-9678. E-mail address: getinfo@haworth.com]*

Terry Sayler and Clare MacKeigan each provided their unique perspectives of document delivery services to an audience of 60 which was comprised mostly of interlibrary loan or document delivery providers. As Head of Interlibrary Loan at the University of Maryland at College Park, Sayler presented the perspective of a practitioner and user of SAILOR,

---

Terry Sayler is Head of Interlibrary Loan, University of Maryland, College Park.

Clare MacKeigan is Marketing Director of Network Support, Inc.

Becky Schwartzkopf is Serials Librarian, Mankato State University, Mankato, MN.

[Haworth co-indexing entry note]: "Pioneering Document Delivery." Schwartzkopf, Becky. Co-published simultaneously in *The Serials Librarian* (The Haworth Press, Inc.) Vol. 31, No. 1/2, 1997, pp. 347-351; and: *Pioneering New Serials Frontiers: From Petroglyphs to Cyberserials* (ed: Christine Christiansen and Cecilia Leathem) The Haworth Press, Inc., 1997, pp. 347-351. Single or multiple copies of this article are available for a fee from The Haworth Document Delivery Service [1-800-342-9678, 9:00 a.m. - 5:00 p.m. (EST). E-mail address: getinfo@haworth.com].

Maryland's Online Public Information Network. MacKeigan, Marketing Director of Network Support, Inc., concentrated on the process of developing the IntelliDoc system into a marketable document delivery system, RELAIS.

Sayler began her presentation by reviewing the rapid changes which are occurring in the document delivery field within libraries. Libraries of a few years ago provided quick and accurate access to material which they had purchased. This changed rapidly with the advent of online/electronic technology and the onset of expedited delivery methods which shifted the focus to providing access in addition to purchasing materials. A population of patrons who are never seen is being created.

SAILOR, the Online Information Network for Maryland was the focus of Sayler's presentation. The impetus for SAILOR developed from a white paper issued in 1989 by the Maryland State Department of Education, Division of Library Development and Services entitled "Toward the Year 2000." The mission as stated in the paper was to "provide the residents of Maryland with rapid, easy access to information, materials, and services from any available information source." Sayler distributed a handout entitled: "SAILOR INTERNET Reference Manual," which is being used to train individuals on the SAILOR system.

Sayler used the University of Maryland at College Park home page on the World Wide Web to access and demonstrate SAILOR. The Web address is:

http://www:ITD.umd.edu/UMS/UMCP/PUB/umcp_home.html

An important link from this home page is to SAILOR. (A more direct link to SAILOR is available at: http://sailor.lib.md.us/). Interesting features on the home page include a link to SAILOR's collection development policies for the Web. All linked sites are collected and reviewed in a similar fashion to print materials. A goal is to provide Maryland citizens with "good" sites from the Web. Also available is a continuously updated union list of periodicals from all Maryland libraries–research, university, public and special.

To exemplify the availability of document delivery on SAILOR in a public library setting, Sayler used the Anne Arundel county link. Among other services, this link provides all citizens with access to full text databases anytime of the day or night. Sayler contends that this is expedited document delivery–pioneering document delivery for the end of the twentieth century.

Sayler showed the thirteen campus University of Maryland system link to provide an example of what is available to users in a university setting. All student, faculty and staff have access to services either in the library or remotely. A hold/recall feature allows patrons to request material from the shelf of another library and choose one of twenty-four sites for delivery of the materials. The material is usually in hand within three to four days. For articles identified through such services as UNCOVER or ArticleFirst, patrons may expedite delivery through FAX by registering and having charges billed directly to them.

A number of issues for the future of SAILOR were raised by Sayler. SAILOR is currently free but the local telephone company is now considering charges for telecommunications use. Access to reference databases and online catalogs has caused business within the University of Maryland at College Park's Interlibrary Loan offices to grow astronomically for both borrowing and lending. Remote access requires citizens to have equipment and telephone access to utilize the system and services. Supporting this requirement has become a burden for some public school districts. In addition, funding from the federal government will dry up at the end of the year and state or local constituents will need to provide additional support. Sayler encouraged the audience to visit the sites of two other states which are pioneering state document delivery systems, the Alaska State Library Home Page (http://sled.alaska.edu/) and the Utah State Library Home Page (http://www.state.lib.ut.us/www.htm).

A lively discussion of issues related to provision of online access to databases and sources took place throughout Sayler's presentation. Questions centered around funding issues, password access, delivery methods and educating patrons. Sayler stated that for interlibrary loan the advent of online resource availability has become an issue of educating the public: "the information revolution has also become an education revolution in terms of making information available and making people understand it."

The next presentation given by Clare MacKeigan included the background of IntelliDoc and how the commercial document delivery system RELAIS emerged from it. MacKeigan cautioned that she would be using the terms interlibrary loan and document delivery interchangeably. Handouts detailing the RELAIS system and describing CISTI (Canada Institute for Scientific and Technical Information) were distributed.

MacKeigan provided background information about IntelliDoc which is an acronym for Intelligent Document Delivery. IntelliDoc was developed as a document delivery system for CISTI. Participants were encouraged to visit CISTI's Web site (http://www.cisti.nrc.ca/cisti/). A major objective of IntelliDoc is to transform lending requests for materials into an electronic format as early as possible and remain in that format throughout the document delivery process. IntelliDoc provides the following advantages:

- accepts requests from multiple sources
- identifies client preferences for delivery
- routes requests to the closest stack location
- manages problem requests
- converts document to the format requested
- calculates invoice amounts
- tracks request from entry to delivery
- keeps statistics.

MacKeigan explained that CISTI is the premier collection of scientific, technical and medical journals, and is North America's largest document delivery system handling up to 2,000 requests per day. CISTI's catalog may be accessed free at the Web site noted above. IntelliDoc was developed to provide for CISTI's continuous growth in volume, the need for faster turn around time, more flexible delivery methods, and reliable delivery of documents.

According to MacKeigan, one of the keys to the IntelliDoc system is the electronic scanning workstation. The workstation, which includes a modified Fijitsu scanner, is ergonomically efficient and easy to use. The twenty-inch monitor allows an 8 1/2" × 11" page to be scanned while touch controls increase the operator efficiency. The ability to scan in the landscape rather than the portrait mode allows for quicker processing of documents. The station also includes a barcode reader which is used to scan the barcode of the item and request, and electronically update the request status in the IntelliDoc system.

RELAIS is the commercial product which was developed from IntelliDoc and is now being marketed by Network Support, Inc. The University of Alberta is the first site to use RELAIS. MacKeigan described RELAIS as a complete interlibrary loan system which provides both borrowing and lending components. RELAIS provides access to the catalog through the Web, has a system for small or large institutions, and will support an electronic reserves module.

MacKeigan noted that one of the key features of RELAIS is automatic searching with fifty percent of requests to the printer without staff intervention. The system utilizes the scanner workstations described above, and provides for several electronic delivery options–FAX, Ariel, FTP, or local or remote printing. The following benefits of using RELAIS were noted: multiple delivery options, reduced cycle times, reductions in human resource requirements, reduced delivery costs, and improved staff work conditions. MacKeigan closed her session by describing some future goals for RELAIS: multi-catalog searching, interlibrary loan protocol standards processing, and modified auction model utilization.

During MacKeigan's presentation many questions and comments from the audience centered on the scanning workstation concept which she had described. Network Support Inc. is looking at other brands of workstations to fill future needs and requirements. MacKeigan praised the Fijitsu model for its ability to provide both clear text and illustration images. MacKeigan noted that the storing of text to provide for future requests is both a copyright and economic issue and is not currently being done by RELAIS. The session ended with a plug for RELAIS by a librarian from the University of Alberta where 94 percent of their requests are filled within twenty-four hours.

Document Delivery is an area of interest to a variety of constituents—librarians, publishers, vendors, and suppliers. The high interest level from the audience was reflected by the many comments and questions throughout this workshop session. Sayler and MacKeigan successfully illustrated the significance of document delivery in the serials information chain. Issues of concern raised at this session that will continue to be discussed in the future include: system password controls, licensing agreements, online system compatibility, copyright law, delivery methods, telecommunication connections, and fee schedules.

Virtual Trailblazing:
Incorporating Electronic Journals
into an Academic Library

Karen Howell
Rayette Wilder
Lorraine Perrotta
Workshop Leaders

Joan Lamborn
Recorder

SUMMARY. The World Wide Web makes it possible for patrons to link easily to electronic journals but does not resolve problems of selection, acquisition, serials control, and cataloging. A pilot project undertaken at the University of Southern California Libraries involved creating a subject and title index to e-journals of interest to the USC faculty on the Web with links to the journals. Upon completion of the pilot, maintenance of the collection was assigned to the Serials Department in the University Library. It then became necessary to mainstream e-journal collection maintenance into the technical services operations of the library. *[Article copies available for a fee from The Haworth Document Delivery Service: 1-800-342-9678. E-mail address: getinfo@haworth.com]*

Karen Howell is Head of Networked Information Development, Center for Scholarly Technology.
Rayette Wilder is Project Librarian, Center for Scholarly Technology.
Lorraine Perrotta is Serials Librarian, University of Southern California.
Joan Lamborn is Acquisitions/Serials Librarian, University of Northern Colorado.

[Haworth co-indexing entry note]: "Virtual Trailblazing: Incorporating Electronic Journals into an Academic Library." Lamborn, Joan. Co-published simultaneously in *The Serials Librarian* (The Haworth Press, Inc.) Vol. 31, No. 1/2, 1997, pp. 353-359; and: *Pioneering New Serials Frontiers: From Petroglyphs to Cyberserials* (ed: Christine Christiansen and Cecilia Leathem) The Haworth Press, Inc., 1997, pp. 353-359. Single or multiple copies of this article are available for a fee from The Haworth Document Delivery Service [1-800-342-9678, 9:00 a.m. - 5:00 p.m. (EST). E-mail address: getinfo@haworth.com].

This workshop described the planning and implementation of the Electronic Journal Pilot Project at the Center for Scholarly Technology of the University of Southern California Libraries and the initial integration of project maintenance into technical service operations of the University Library. Karen Howell, the head of networked information development at the Center for Scholarly Technology, began with a description of the goals of the project, the environment in which the project was developed, and the issues that were raised during project development. Rayette Wilder, project librarian at the Center for Scholarly Technology, described the actual development and implementation of the project. Lorraine Perrotta, the serials librarian at the University of Southern California, concluded the presentation with a discussion of mainstreaming the project into the technical services operations of the University Library. About one hundred people attended the workshop, primarily librarians.

PROJECT CONCEPTION AND GOALS

In her introduction, Karen Howell, of the Center for Scholarly Technology, described the beginnings of the project. The emergence of electronic journals presents special challenges to libraries. Electronic journals can be elusive and difficult to track. There are different protocols for retrieving electronic journals, and their electronic addresses may change quite unexpectedly. Providing access to backfiles and archiving are also problematic. Libraries may store electronic publications on a local computer or provide access to a remote site. Given rapidly changing technology, the choice of format for archiving electronic publications is also unclear. Cataloging electronic resources presents other problems. By 1993/94 the Dean of the University Southern California Libraries felt it had become necessary to develop coordinated, organized access to electronic journals for members of the USC community and directed the Center for Scholarly Technology to deal with the issue.

Given the goal of providing organized access to electronic journals, it was also necessary to establish some guidelines for the project:

1. Selection of electronic journals to be included in the project would be based upon the research interests of the faculty.
2. The scope of the project would be electronic journals accessed via gopher, listserv and the World Wide Web.
3. Electronic journals would be accessed bibliographically by subject and title.
4. Physical access would be available from numerous locations on the campus–computer laboratories, the main and branch libraries–as

well as from remote locations, such as faculty offices and student dormitory rooms, via the campus network.

5. Backfiles and archives would be made available.

ENVIRONMENT FOR THE PROJECT

In 1993/94, the University Library was not in a position to undertake a pilot project for managing electronic journals. Both the serials and acquisitions librarian positions were unfilled. A kardex-based serial check-in system was still in place, and a new integrated library system was under consideration. However, a research and development unit did exist in the library, the Center for Scholarly Technology (CST). While CST offered staff with expertise to explore opportunities to apply technology to meet the academic needs of the university community, its role was limited to starting a pilot project. If CST were to take on the pilot project, a sponsor to continue the project had to be identified. It was acknowledged that a department in technical services would become the sponsor, but the specific department and position were not determined until after the pilot project was underway.

Personnel in the University Library and in the Information Services Department provided the expertise necessary for project development. Librarians brought experience delivering services to patrons. Information Services staff could provide technical support. CST sponsored a library intern, Rayette Wilder, to develop the project. Once the internship was completed, she was hired in a temporary position as project librarian to continue development of Web pages for the project and to determine who should assume responsibility for mainstreaming the project. At that point it was decided that the Acquisitions Department would assume responsibility for acquiring electronic journals and that the serials librarian would be responsible for mainstreaming all electronic journal procedures, with assistance from CST as needed.

DEVELOPMENT ISSUES

The project database was designed with the intention of developing a model that could be adopted by other libraries. Documentation was considered very important for internal consistency and for transferability to other library situations. The documentation included research conducted by the intern during the planning phase of the project, selection guidelines, and cataloging practices.

The importance of publicity was recognized. Members of the university community needed to be aware of the project to use the collection as a resource and to contribute to its development by recommending journal titles to the selectors. Publicity had to reach library personnel as well so that they could inform patrons of the project. It was also considered necessary for publicity to be continuous to counteract turnover within the university community.

Another important part of project development is evaluation. An evaluation will be needed to determine how often the database is used, which titles in the collection are being used, and whether infrequently used titles should be removed from the collection.

DEVELOPMENT OF THE PROJECT

Rayette Wilder, the project librarian, described the development of the project. After reviewing the literature and listservs, she selected four academic electronic journal collections to use as case studies. The collections were selected based on the size of the collection, titles included, and the stated goals of each collection. The four selected were: the Mr. Serials Project at North Carolina State University; the CICNet E-Serials Archive developed by the Committee on Inter-institutional Cooperation; the State University of New York at Morrisville electronic journal collection; the Scholarly Communications Project at Virginia Polytechnic Institute and State University.

Based upon an analysis of those collections, it was decided that a hypertext model would be best for the University of Southern California collection. It was also decided to apply the existing collection development criteria to the selection of electronic journals for the project. Marginal titles were included in case of doubt. Preference was given to journals on the Web for technical reasons, but gopher-protocol journals are also included. The collection began with free journals. Later fee-based journals were added with access restricted by IP address.

After providing a description of the development of the project, Rayette Wilder accessed the USC Electronic Journals Collection on the Web (http://www.lib.usc.edu/Info/Acqui/Ejournals/index.html) so that attendees could view the collection firsthand. There are currently seventy-eight journals in the collection, including foreign titles. Since USC is part of the Association for Research Libraries Latin American project with an active selector in this area, the collection includes a large number of Latin American materials. The collection can be searched by title or by broad subject area representing the schools within the university: arts and humanities, social sciences, science and technology. A subject search retrieves a list of journals. For foreign journals, the country of origin and language is noted in parentheses after the title. Clicking on an entry leads to a web page for the individual electronic journal which in turn provides a link to the journal itself.

To provide access to the collection for USC sites that do not have Web access, such as the branch libraries, a gateway interface was created from USCInfo, USC's campus information service. The service allows for text only viewing of the collection. Further project developments will include:

1. Improved functionality of the title index: As the collection gets larger, the title index will become more difficult to manage. To address that problem, the list could be subdivided into alphabetic sections so that smaller files would be manipulated in title searches. Different software could also help to alleviate the problem of file size.
2. Improved bibliographic access: Bibliographic records with subject headings will be entered in the online catalog to increase access to the electronic journal collection once the integrated library system is in place.
3. Maintenance of the URL's: URL's will be maintained so that patrons can continue to access journals that have changed location.

Archiving is not currently being done as part of the pilot project. Archiving at the consortial level through the Southern California Electronic Library Consortium is being considered.

A VIEW FROM THE TRENCHES IN TECHNICAL SERVICES

Lorraine Perrotta, serials librarian at USC, described the context for current serial operations at USC and the process underway for incorporating collection development and maintenance of the USC Electronic Journals Collection into the technical services operations in the University Library.

The University of Southern California Libraries is a multi-library system consisting of seventeen libraries. The libraries maintain over 16,000 current subscriptions and standing orders. The standing orders are received on the GEAC 8000 system. Subscriptions are handled manually using a kardex. The Serials Department consists of four full-time members and 1.5 student FTE. The department is preparing to consolidate serial operations onto the SIRSI system.

Implementing an integrated library system is a high priority and demands much staff time and attention. Nevertheless, first steps have been taken to make the transition from pilot project to a regularly maintained electronic journal collection. To ensure the ongoing development of the Web interface for the project, the project librarian trained the serials librarian in the maintenance and development of electronic journal Web pages. The staff have received intense training to develop windows-based computer skills. PC's with Web access have been installed. Access to the electronic journal Web pages has been streamlined so that serials staff can maintain the e-journal collection.

Policies to support the collection are not yet in place. The collection development policy on electronic formats that has been in place since 1994 needs to be updated to respond to the growing number of electronic journals. A cataloging policy for electronic formats will need to be developed before records for electronic materials are created in the new online catalog. Acquisition procedures may need to be changed to accommodate the acquisition of electronic journals that do not always follow the print model.

Electronic resources present issues for all aspects of collection development and maintenance: selection, acquisitions, serials control, and cataloging. While presenting challenges, electronic resources can also encourage teamwork as library personnel consult with one another and reach solutions for handling the new format.

SELECTION

The overall issues related to selection are common to all types of resources, not just electronic. A current collection development policy is critical if the collection is to match the needs of the library community. Consistent involvement of the selectors is also important. Frequently, the level and awareness of interest in electronic resources varies among selectors. Uneven activity among selectors leads to uneven representation of subject areas in the collection. Selectors also need to deal with the question of whether to keep the electronic or print version or both.

ACQUISITIONS

With limited staff and funding, it can be difficult to justify allocating staff to create and maintain extensive records for electronic journals, particularly since many electronic journals are currently free. However, that situation may change. Archiving decisions also need to be made. Electronic journals may be archived on a local file server, or patrons may be directed to a remote site.

SERIALS CONTROL

Holdings records for electronic journals raise several questions. Should holdings information for electronic journals be provided on the Web pages as in the online catalog? Should the holdings information be presented as an open summary holdings statement or as a list of issues received? If holdings are made available on the Web, who should maintain them?

CATALOGING

What resources are cataloged depends upon the definition of the library collection. If the collection includes remote electronic resources and records are created in the catalog, certain technical issues need to be addressed. The holding library for the electronic resource needs to be designated in the library system. Policies need to be developed for titles held in both print and electronic formats. A URL hotlink in the online catalog record to the electronic resource that provides easy access for the patron needs to be maintained.

In summary, for electronic resources to be incorporated into an academic library collection, there must be consensus and commitment throughout the organization. The library administration must understand the cost implications and resource requirements. Necessary policies must be formulated and put in place.

A brief question/answer period followed the final presentation. Access to fee-based electronic journals was discussed. There was general agreement that password access does not work and that limiting by IP address is preferable. Concern was expressed that use may be lower with password access. In answer to a question about IP address limiting for remote users, modem access to a PPP connection to USC was suggested. A lower cost option would be to telnet to USCInfo. The problems of site licenses and responsibility for web page maintenance were also raised.

Technical Services
Within a Team-Based
Information Services Environment

Jos Anemaet
Janet Lee-Smeltzer

Workshop Leaders

Kathryn Loafman

Recorder

SUMMARY. In 1994, the Oregon State University merged the libraries
into a new Information Services unit. The process of reorganizing
the new IS unit into teams is described, with an evaluation of how
the reorganization has affected Technical Services. *[Article copies
available for a fee from The Haworth Document Delivery Service:
1-800-342-9678. E-mail address: getinfo@haworth.com]*

About five years ago, Oregon State University[1] faced having to cut up
to 30% from the budget due to a voters' initiative to cut taxes. The univer-

---

Jos Anemaet is Cataloger, Oregon State University.
Janet Lee-Smeltzer is Catalog Librarian, Oregon State University.
Kathryn Loafman is Head of the Cataloging Unit, University of North Texas
Libraries, Denton, TX.

[Haworth co-indexing entry note]: "Technical Services Within a Team-Based Information Services
Environment." Loafman, Kathryn. Co-published simultaneously in *The Serials Librarian* (The Haworth
Press, Inc.) Vol. 31, No. 1/2, 1997, pp. 361-366; and: *Pioneering New Serials Frontiers: From Petro-
glyphs to Cyberserials* (ed: Christine Christiansen and Cecilia Leathem) The Haworth Press, Inc., 1997,
pp. 361-366. Single or multiple copies of this article are available for a fee from The Haworth Document
Delivery Service [1-800-342-9678, 9:00 a.m. - 5:00 p.m. (EST). E-mail address: getinfo@haworth.com].

sity administration hired an outside management firm, KPMG-Peat Marwick. After reviewing the entire organizational structure of the university, the recommendations were to downsize the existing sixty upper management positions to under twenty-six. They also recommended combining areas performing similar functions in order to realize savings by consolidating administrative activities.

KPMG-Peat Marwick recommended areas involved with information gathering, storage, and retrieval be merged into a new unit, Information Services. Four departments were combined: the OSU libraries (consisting of the main library, OSU Valley Library, and the branch library, Hatfield Marine Science Center/Guin Library), the Computer Center, Telecommunications, and the Communications Media Center.

In January 1994, a new Associate Provost for Information Services was hired and tasked with the merger. Eight short-term teams were created, each team including one member from each of the four departments. These teams were charged with identifying the areas critical to fulfill the university's mission, and they came up with The List of Nine Hot Issues:

1. Instructional Labs
2. Multi-media production
3. Local area network support
4. Front-line user support
5. Equipment repair and maintenance
6. Instruction and training
7. Large systems
8. Administration
9. Services to extension faculty.

They also recommended the creation of transitional teams to address these Hot Issues. Both of the transitional teams (and some of the eight short-term teams) recommended that Information Services be reorganized into a team-based structure.

This recommendation was accepted. A survey was sent out to the staff asking them to describe their current position and special skills. The surveys were used by the administration to assign staff to teams. At the reorganization kick-off meeting, each staff member received a packet which included a list of the teams to which they had been assigned. More than thirty teams were introduced. Some teams had only one or two members, while others had more than twenty. Everyone in the Cataloging Division had been assigned to one big Cataloging Team. Many of the staff were (and are) on several teams.

Each team is composed of a sponsor, facilitator, coordinator, notetaker, and team participants.

The sponsor is a manager who meets with the team but is not a member of the team. Sponsors are responsible for setting parameters, framing issues, and serving as liaisons with the IS Senior Managers and with other team sponsors. The sponsor's role changes as the team develops.

Facilitators are not usually members of the team. The facilitator keeps the discussion focused on the agenda and notifies the team when the time allotted for an agenda item has expired. The team members then decide either to drop items from the current agenda and continue the discussion or move the discussion to another agenda. The facilitator also assists the team to do a meeting review (in which the team evaluates the progress made during the meeting) and helps the team develop a realistic agenda for the next meeting.

The coordinator convenes the team meetings and is responsible for scheduling the meeting, distributing the agenda, meeting notes, and reports. They serve as the contact person for the participants.

Each team must display competency before moving on to the next level of responsibility.

Stage 2 competency is participatory management. In S2 teams, the sponsor works with the team and is held accountable for the team's achieving its goals. Stage 3 competency is team-based management. In S3, the sponsor transmits the IS Goals to the team, reviews the team's proposals, and coaches the team; but it is no longer clear who is really accountable for the team's success. The sponsor is accountable since she has veto power over the team's activities, but the team is accountable because it is the team's plan. This is the beginning of shared accountability. The sponsor evaluates the team members in the S2 and S3 stages; but the sponsor may or may not evaluate team members in S4. Stage 4 competency is self-managed teams. In S4, the sponsor serves as team consultant at the team's request and helps evaluate the performance standards the team is setting, but the team is held responsible for meeting the team goals.

Of the thirty teams, only five were designated as Formal Teams. Formal Teams would deal with one or more of the Hot Issues, and would receive immediate team training. The remaining teams were called Informal Teams, and would receive team training at a later, unspecified, date.[2]

Before reorganization, the libraries' Technical and Automation Services consisted of three divisions: Acquisitions, Cataloging, and Automation; and one unit, Materials Preparation. After the reorganization (fall 1995), there were six teams in Technical Services.

Two members of the Automation Division staff formed the Oasis[3]

Team, dealing with systems problems of the library's on-line catalog. The rest of the Automation Division staff were moved out of the libraries, joining the LAN Support Team and the Electronic Support Services Team. The University Webworks Team was moved into Technical Services, but the team is still in the process of formation.

In the Acquisitions Division, the Monographs Acquisitions Unit and the Serials Acquisitions Unit each became a team: Monographs Acquisitions Team (6 members) and Serials Acquisitions Team (8 members). The head of the Acquisitions Division is the sponsor of both teams. There are no outside facilitators and the entire team acts as facilitators. Two members of each team volunteered to be coordinator and notetaker.

The Cataloging Division had two brainstorming sessions, and reorganized as a Monographs Cataloging Team (9 members), a Serials Cataloging Team (5 members), and an Oasis Database Maintenance Team (2 members). The head of the Cataloging Division is the sponsor of both the Serials Cataloging Team and the Oasis Database Maintenance Team, and the Assistant Head is sponsoring the Monographs Cataloging Team. The functions previously carried out by the Materials Preparation Unit have been integrated into the Acquisitions and Cataloging teams.

At the moment, the Monographs Cataloging Team and the Serials Cataloging Teams are the only active teams in the Cataloging Division. The teams meet weekly. The coordinator's job is rotated every four weeks and the notetaker's job every other week, because taking meeting minutes is a time-consuming task. At the beginning, both teams had facilitators who were members of the team, but it was difficult for the facilitators to remain outside of a discussion that would affect their own work assignments. Currently, both teams have outside facilitators.

Technical Service started the team process without any prior team training. An IS training coordinator was hired last year to provide training in the areas of team-based management, effective team meetings, and project planning. In addition, there will be intensive training focused on communications, interpersonal relationships, group process, team decision making and problem solving. Each team is encouraged to attend these sessions together as a group; however, the sponsors will not normally attend the training with their teams.

The Acquisitions and Cataloging staff have mixed feelings about the reorganization. Cataloging staff in general have a more positive attitude. They feel the team-based organizational structure will increase efficiency and help provide better services. They are more involved in the decision making process, and they believe that decisions are being made in a more timely fashion. Cataloging Divisional meetings are much shorter now since so much is being discussed at the team meetings, but staff who are on only one team feel they are not getting as much information. The team structure also breaks up the cohesiveness of the Cataloging Division as a whole. The Acquisitions staff feel that team process has been given higher priority than service. However, they do feel that meetings are more structured, and decisions are being documented because the teams are required to keep minutes. Technical Services staff do not see the team decision process as being efficient. Instead of asking one person for a decision, problems must be discussed in teams. This is a serious drawback when dealing with time-sensitive issues.

Both Cataloging and Acquisitions staff agree that moving the Automation Division out of the libraries has had an adverse effect. In addition, the Library LAN was migrated into the IS LAN. Not only are there fewer automation support staff in the library building, but the libraries are given a lower priority. There has not been the same level of software training for the library staff since the merger; in particular, they lack the software training targeted for library applications. In response to these problems, a Departmental Computer Assistant system was established. There is still not the same level of service as before, but things have improved within the libraries.

Technical Services has yet to benefit from team reorganization. Things seem more confused, there are problems with communications, and staff morale is low. However, OSU-IS is only in the beginning of the team process and still in transition. It will take time for the organizational culture to change.

WORKSHOP QUESTIONS AND ANSWERS

Q. We went through a team-based reorganization at my institution two years ago. We found there was a problem in having members on the team who supervised other members of the same team. Some staff were very reluctant to be in this environment. Was that your situation as well?

A. None of the team members were supervisors of other members of the same team, and none of the classified staff were required to supervise other members of the same team.

Q. Could the Team Sponsors veto the team decisions? I would think that the ability of teams to make decisions would be undermined if the upper level administrators could change team decisions.

A. The teams are at different stages of competency. In the Team Charge, there are parameters on what kind of decisions the team can make based on the team's competency. As the team becomes more competent, some of the management's roles can shift over to the teams. Right now the sponsors are still managers and they still have the authority. They are definitely trying to move us to the S4 level where all the decisions are ours and the sponsors no longer have veto powers. There will always be situations when the decision is contextual and still depends on the other teams or the circumstances.

Q.   You have varying levels of staff participating in the teams. Are all the staff qualified to participate in the decision making processes?

A.   We are hoping that extensive training will address this problem.

Q.   On my campus they tried the team approach in small groups throughout the campus. One of the places they started a team was in part of the library. Now I am at a different campus, where the team approach is being imposed from the top. My feeling is that the upheaval is greater where I am now, but they are working through it together. Whereas, at the place I was before, there was a lot of resentment and I'm not sure they are ever going to get over it.

A.   It is important that upper management communicates that they are committed to the team-based approach.

NOTES

1. For information about Oregon State University, the libraries, and the reorganization, see http://www.ORST.EDU.

2. There was one title the staff found useful as a self-training aid: Harrington-Mackin, Deborah. *The team building tool kit: tips, tactics, and rules for effective workplace teams* (New York: AMACOM, 1994).

3. Oasis is the name of the OSU online catalog, a Geac Advanced System.

Seven Myths
About the ISSN

Regina Reynolds

Workshop Leader

Ann Ercelawn

Recorder

SUMMARY. An understanding of how International Standard Serial Numbers (ISSN) are assigned and used is fundamental to the work of all participants in the serials information chain. This workshop sought to dispel many of the common misconceptions about the ISSN by exploring the "myths" and presenting the facts. *[Article copies available for a fee from The Haworth Document Delivery Service: 1-800-342-9678. E-mail address: getinfo@haworth.com]*

Regina Reynolds, Head of the National Serials Data Program since 1992, conducted a workshop exploring the many myths surrounding the ISSN for an audience composed of serials librarians, publishers, and subscription agents. Reynolds presented a fictitious case study of a "hook to holdings" project undertaken by a brash and ill-informed cartoon charac-

Regina Reynolds is Head of the National Serials Data Program, Library of Congress.

Ann Ercelawn is an Original Cataloger at the Vanderbilt University Library, Nashville, TN.

[Haworth co-indexing entry note]: "Seven Myths About the ISSN." Ercelawn, Ann. Co-published simultaneously in *The Serials Librarian* (The Haworth Press, Inc.) Vol. 31, No. 1/2, 1997, pp. 367-372; and: *Pioneering New Serials Frontiers: From Petroglyphs to Cyberserials* (ed: Christine Christiansen and Cecilia Leathem) The Haworth Press, Inc., 1997, pp. 367-372. Single or multiple copies of this article are available for a fee from The Haworth Document Delivery Service [1-800-342-9678, 9:00 a.m. - 5:00 p.m. (EST). E-mail address: getinfo@haworth.com].

ter called Serial Sam, who is instructed by his boss, Mona Monograph, to acquire ISSN information for all the records in his library's catalog in order to link them to records provided by abstracting and indexing services. As Reynolds related the tale of Serial Sam's misadventures, she challenged workshop attendees to note where Serial Sam fell victim to many of the common misconceptions about the ISSN, as they would be asked to identify Serial Sam's errors at the conclusion of the fable. In the story, Serial Sam immediately runs into trouble trying to match titles between the catalog and A&I databases, consulting a serials directory and periodical issues in the stacks to locate ISSN, attempting to determine what to do with title changes, foreign titles, the same title in different formats, etc. Desperate to acquire missing ISSN data for his records, he tries to bribe the agency responsible for assigning the ISSN into giving him numbers immediately, and ultimately resorts to making them up himself! When Serial Sam's completed "hook to holdings" project is unveiled at a formal ceremony and proves a total disaster, Serial Sam wails, "Where did I go wrong?"

Perceptive workshop attendees responded enthusiastically to Serial Sam's plea for help by correctly identifying many of his mistakes. A lively interchange ensued between Reynolds and the audience in discussing the major myths surrounding the ISSN. Fourteen (rather than seven!) myths and the accompanying facts were summarized by Reynolds in a handout distributed to participants:

Myth: The ISSN has embedded meaning like the ISBN.

Fact: Unlike the ISBN, which contains country and publisher prefixes, the ISSN has no embedded meaning.

Discussion: Blocks of ISSN are assigned to ISSN national centers by the ISSN International Centre. Blocks are generally assigned sequentially, with lower numbers indicating earlier publications, but there are some exceptions. The last digit of the ISSN is a check-digit which allows for machine validation of the numbers in systems which have algorithms designed to check ISSN.

Myth: If an ISSN printed on an issue conflicts with one on a MARC record, the one printed on the issue is the correct one.

Fact: More often than we wish, publishers often change titles without getting a new ISSN. They also misprint ISSN. ISSN in NSDP-authenticated records or in ISSN International Centre products are the best source of accurate and current ISSN.

Myth: Serials can have either ISSN or ISBN, but not both.

Fact: ISSN and ISBN are both used on serials such as directories and monographic series. The ISBN identifies the particular year or volume, the ISSN identifies the serial or series.

Myth: The plural of ISSN is ISSNs.

Fact: According to ISSN standards, "ISSN" is used for both singular and plural.

Myth: Publishers who have an ISSN are entitled to lower postal rates.

Fact: Although the U.S. Postal Service uses the ISSN as a control mechanism for publications which are granted second class mailing rates, and requires printing of ISSN confirmed by NSDP, publishers with ISSN pay the same rate as publishers without ISSN.

Discussion: Reynolds explained that as part of NSDP workflow, the agency reviews all applications for second class mailing rates. However, not all publications that qualify for these rates are assigned ISSN. Publications that are of a very local nature and unlikely to be cited or indexed, such as Boy Scout newsletters, are not routinely assigned ISSN. However, if a publisher specifically requests ISSN assignment, NSDP will comply and provide an ISSN.

Myth: ISSN are assigned by national libraries worldwide.

Fact: Most ISSN centers are located in national libraries but several are housed in national scientific and technical centers.

Myth: NSDP can assign an ISSN to any serial.

Fact: NSDP can only assign ISSN to serials published in the U.S., with some exceptions. ISSN for publications of international bodies (e.g., the United Nations) are assigned by the ISSN International Centre, located in Paris. Responsibility for certain multinational publishers is divided among ISSN centers in the countries in which they publish.

Myth: ISSN are only assigned at the request of the publisher.

Fact: ISSN are also assigned at the request of abstracting and indexing services, the U.S. Postal Service, and as part of the Library of Congress serial cataloging workflow.

Discussion: Workshop attendees inquired as to how they could assist the ISSN assignment process. Reynolds noted that although NSDP generally cannot respond to requests from individuals due to staffing shortages, there are ways that serialists can help. Vendors can assist by advising publishers that they should acquire ISSN for new titles and for title changes. Librarians can notify NSDP when they discover misprinted ISSN on current serial publications; NSDP will follow-up by contacting publishers to correct the situation or forward requests for correction to non-U.S. centers for foreign publications. Librarians can also contact publishers to request that they acquire ISSN (the process is completely free, but generally requires several weeks to complete). A wealth of information about ISSN, including downloadable and interactive application forms, is available on NSDP's new web site (http://lcweb.loc.gov/issn/). Applications for print serials must be accompanied by a piece or surrogate, but Reynolds noted that publishers of electronic publications may submit ISSN applications by using the interactive form and including a URL or other access information. NSDP uses the form completed by the publisher as a cost-effective basis for a cataloging record by manipulating publisher-supplied data.

Myth: One ISSN is assigned to the basic serial regardless of how many formats it is published in.

Fact: Separate ISSN are required for each physical format in which a serial is published, except for reproduction microforms which carry the ISSN of the original serial.

Myth: Publishers self-assign ISSN.

Fact: While ISBN are self assigned by publishers, ISSN are assigned by ISSN centers worldwide.

Myth: A serial published in 1950 could not have an ISSN.

Fact: Even though the ISSN system didn't get started until the early 70s, older and ceased serials are eligible for ISSN and many such serials have had ISSN assigned to them.

Myth: Having an ISSN means no one else can use that title.

Fact: The ISSN confers no rights to a title. If the title is not unique, the ISSN center adds a qualifier to make it unique. Protecting a title requires a trademark.

Discussion: One workshop participant inquired what happens when 2 publishers issue the same title and each publisher claims that it publishes the true version. Reynolds responded that the ISSN center with jurisdiction for that title decides who is entitled to the ISSN. Alternatively, the ISSN center might decide that the old publication had ceased and assign two new ISSN.

Myth: The ISSN stays the same for the life of the serial, regardless of title changes.

Fact: Most title changes require new ISSN. However, some minor changes such as changes in prepositions, conjunctions, or spelling do not. ISSN centers make these decisions.

Discussion: A question about situations in which revised cataloging rules for determining title changes would result in a record merger elicited the response from Reynolds that such cases are reviewed on a case-by-case basis. ISSN in such situations are not routinely canceled. Canceled ISSN sometimes result from double assignment by 2 catalogers in the same or different agencies. A canceled ISSN is entered in the subfield z of the 022 field of a serial record. The subfield y in the 022 field reflects ISSN found on issues of serials, either misprinted by the publisher or no longer valid due to a title change.

Myth: Serials directories are the best sources of ISSN.

Fact: Serials directories usually get at least some of their ISSN from the publisher who may not have gotten a new ISSN for a title change, or may have confused ISSN among various publications. The best sources for ISSN are OCLC, the CONSER database, the U.S. MARC tapes for U.S. serials, and for non-U.S. serials, ISSN Compact or other products of the ISSN International Centre.

In conclusion, Reynolds outlined some of the challenges currently facing the National Serials Data Program. The Program is coping with inadequate funding and staffing. She expressed some concern that a proposal to reorganize NSDP into a Library of Congress cataloging section might dilute the primary mission of the program, which is to assign and promote ISSN. Further, she noted that serials publications themselves are providing significant challenges due to proliferating formats, and that web sites with constantly changing material are challenging conventional definitions of what constitutes a serial publication. On a lighter note, Reynolds ended her fable of Serial Sam by having him attend remedial serials school, join NASIG to further his serials education, contribute to AmIs (American ISSN friends), marry Mona Monograph, and begin raising either a future technical processing department, or (as was suggested during the second session), a family of loose-leaf services. Workshop participants were delighted by the happy conclusion to the story (and both entertained and informed by Reynolds' presentation).

Serials Exchanges:
Streamlining and Elimination

Carol Pitts Diedrichs
Trisha L. Davis

Workshop

Martin Gordon

Recorder

SUMMARY. A full reexamination of serials exchange programs at the project level may reveal fertile ground for academic libraries striving to achieve both efficiency and economy of scale in collection management. Both institutional factors such as reduced staffing levels as well as global political shifts clearly justify such a review. The results of one such study are detailed with emphasis upon statistical correlation and procedural requirements. Methods by which inter-departmental cooperation can be achieved are also outlined. *[Article copies available for a fee from The Haworth Document Delivery Service: 1-800-342-9678. E-mail address: getinfo@haworth.com]*

This workshop described in detail the steps taken at the Ohio State University Libraries to streamline and thereby enhance the value of the serial exchange program. Carol Pitts Diedrichs, Head, Acquisitions

---

Carol Pitts Diedrichs is Head of the Acquisitions Department, Ohio State University Libraries.

Trisha L. Davis is Head of the Continuation Acquisition Division, Ohio State University Libraries.

Martin Gordon is Acquisitions Librarian, Franklin and Marshall College.

[Haworth co-indexing entry note]: "Serials Exchanges: Streamlining and Elimination." Gordon, Martin. Co-published simultaneously in *The Serials Librarian* (The Haworth Press, Inc.) Vol. 31, No. 1/2, 1997, pp. 373-378; and: *Pioneering New Serials Frontiers: From Petroglyphs to Cyberserials* (ed: Christine Christiansen and Cecilia Leathem) The Haworth Press, Inc., 1997, pp. 373-378. Single or multiple copies of this article are available for a fee from The Haworth Document Delivery Service [1-800-342-9678, 9:00 a.m. - 5:00 p.m. (EST). E-mail address: getinfo@ haworth.com].

Department, Ohio State University Libraries, spoke on behalf of herself and co-author Trisha L. Davis, Head, Continuation Acquisition Division, Ohio State University Libraries. She described the historical background inspiring the project, the project's proposal and design, its effect on the collection management program, it impact upon campus publishing, statistical analysis, and the project's results.

BACKGROUND

Serials exchange has traditionally been a component of large, modern academic libraries' collection development and materials acquisitions programs, especially those whose parent institutions have a strong international studies curriculum. Kovacic provides the most oft-expressed rationale for these programs stressing that they should make available material that is otherwise not obtainable or is not economical to purchase.[1] In the early 1970s, 95% of all ARL libraries surveyed had gift and exchange programs. However, even at that time, librarians were ambivalent regarding their value and some expressed a growing concern as to the relative impact upon the overall library budget. By 1989, a study confirmed the de-emphasis of exchange programs at ARL libraries, especially when measured in terms of staff devoted to those programs. In addition, the study revealed that discounts on local university press publications influenced heavily the dynamics of serial exchange. Those libraries not having access to discounted publications to offer on exchange accounted for only 30% of all the programs.[2]

At Ohio State University, eight staff positions were funded by the Office of the Provost for International Affairs for exchange programs. Primarily bibliographic and language specialists, one position, however, was assigned to the Libraries' Acquisition Department for exchange management. However by 1990, the University no longer was expressing the same degree of interest in the types of academic endeavors that the exchange program primarily supported, and the need for the reevaluation of the program within the Libraries became more and more evident. A visit to Indiana University and the University of Michigan confirmed the authors' suspicions that their home institution had to either significantly enhance the support of the exchange program (in terms of staffing) or minimize the program and acquire needed serials through other channels.

PROJECT PROPOSAL

In May, 1991, a proposal was submitted to the Ohio State University Libraries' Materials Budget Committee to investigate the exchange program with an eye toward streamlining the entire process. Justification for the proposal included the labor intensive nature of the work, the expense in terms of staffing, the lack of any recent title review, the change in the global political scene, and the sense that paid acquisitions might better fulfill these subscriptions in a timely manner than as the case in the early 1970s. Finally, and perhaps most significantly, the authors felt that the expenses involved in purchasing subscriptions might be balanced by the curbing of subscriptions placed for exchange. The materials budget could also more easily absorb some increase in costs than could the personnel line budget accommodate the need for additional staff.

Approval was received for the project with the stipulation that collection managers would be central to the process allowing them to weigh the relative merits of titles that the library was exchanging for what was being received. This would be done on a title-by-title basis. However, the Acquisitions Department would retain the right to decide *how* to obtain material that was felt to be needed. Collection managers' budgets would not benefit by a decision either to cancel a title received on exchange title or to retain it.

A three year time period was determined to be appropriate for the project so as not to disturb other higher priorities of either the Acquisition Department or collection managers.

PROJECT IMPLEMENTATION AND EXECUTION

From the outset, collection managers were kept well-informed as to the rationale behind the review and the procedures to be used to carry it out. This was accomplished to a great extent by use of the already established quarterly meetings with the group at large. Positive anticipated benefits for collection managers were highlighted including the increased ability that the Acquisitions Department would have to meet their overall needs through the redirection of staff energies.

Collection managers were also appraised of the various procedures that would be employed. Master records for each exchange review would be transferred from manual to automated files as had already occurred with the actual receipt records themselves. Collection managers would indicate on the appropriate forms whether or not to retain a title. Wherever possible, serial and non-serials subscriptions would be transferred to a paid basis.

Finally, collection managers were assured that in no instance would an exchange be terminated for titles that were to be retained until the first receipt for the retained title was received under paid subscription.

Collection managers, working with forms designed to provide them with as much information as possible concerning each title and the corresponding title(s) given on exchange, recorded their decisions as to whether or not each title warranted a place in the ongoing, active collection. They then submitted their decisions to the Acquisitions Department, keeping a copy of the form for their files.

Three actions were possible, based upon those decisions:

- If a title was to be canceled, Ohio State University suppliers were notified to cease shipment of the exchange serial as of a certain date. Exchange partners were also notified.
- If a title was to be retained, and it was to be fulfilled through paid subscription, that new subscription was placed. When the first issue was received then, and only then, was the exchange partner notified and the exchange title(s) canceled with the supplier. In some cases a partial exchange could be maintained.
- If a title was to be retained and the exchange was to be maintained, a confirmation letter was sent to the exchange partner verifying the partner's address and the name of the contact person for the exchange.

In all instances, the Acquisitions Department's records were updated and the collection manager was notified.

IMPACT ON CAMPUS PUBLICATIONS

As the review process progressed, every effort was made to keep campus publishers of exchanged material aware of the ongoing results so that they could have optimum time in which to assess the impact of cancellations upon their subscription base. All titles from each publisher were reviewed whenever possible as a group. It was soon apparent from conversations with these publishers that spring was the best time for them to be advised as to the extent of the following renewal year change in subscriptions placed for exchange. As a further assistance to publishers, the Acquisitions Department provided each exchange partner with the clear information as to how to renew the canceled subscription on a paid basis, should they choose to do so.

One by-product of the dialog with publishers was the avoidance in many instances of increased subscription rates for remaining subscriptions because there was time to negotiate with the supplier. For example, in one case 200, hitherto free exchange subscriptions were thereafter to have been provided only at the full subscription rate. The Acquisitions Department was able to negotiate a 40% discount for the duration of the review period with the understanding that, at its closure, remaining subscriptions would be paid at the full institutional rate.

PROJECT RESULTS

At the onset of the project in 1991, 1,721 titles were listed as being received on exchange, 516 of which were published in the United States. The total cost of the 1,143 titles sent in exchange for these titles was $14,554, including $10,000 for 271 copies of the *Ohio Journal of Science.*

It was possible to fulfill almost all of the domestic titles and the vast majority of foreign ones via paid subscriptions. Foreign exchanges, however, did have a decidedly higher retention rate, especially in areas of the world where currency exchanges are volatile. And, it should be noted, exchange retention was also at a higher rate for materials received from areas of the world such as the former Soviet Union where publication schedules are less reliable.

It was found that, overall, costs for purchasing titles received on exchange were not significantly higher than the costs of titles that were purchased previously to be sent in their fulfillment.

By project's end, 67 exchanges were retained, of which all but two were foreign. While the project was being undertaken, communication was received from many exchange partners indicating that they, too, were reviewing their own programs. Many of these letters indicated that, for reasons similar to those motivating the Ohio State University Libraries' review, they would no longer be continuing the exchange.

The majority of titles retained via exchange were published by special societies, and by university presses located in the Far East–Pacific Rim nations–as well as those countries formerly a part of the Soviet Union. Ohio State University Libraries still receive far more titles than are sent.

CONCLUSION

Streamlining Ohio State University Libraries' exchange program has proved to be beneficial both in terms of cost as well as from a management perspective. However, the availability of funds to enable the Acquisitions Department to switch to paid based subscriptions was a necessary underpinning of the project's success. Content based analysis of the titles received on exchange, an acknowledged objective of transfer of retained titles to a paid subscription basis and the movement of all support records for titles received on exchange from manual to automated files were the three primary goals set forth for the project.

All of these goals were achieved.

As evidenced by the project's meticulous planning and execution, as well as the positive responses from the first session's forty-odd participants, most of whom were academic librarians bringing with them an avid interest in the subject at hand, the authors Diedrichs and Davis have given the profession a well-emblazoned trail to tread. Despite the obvious difficulties inherent in this massive undertaking, such as the volume of detail involved, lack of consistency in earlier record keeping and the need for inter-library, campus and off-campus communication throughout, the success of this project will stand as a paradigm for others who need to address this important aspect of academic collection management.

NOTES

1. Kovacic, Mark, "Gifts and exchanges in U.S. Academic Libraries," *Library Resources and Technical Services* 24 (Spring 1980): 160.

2. Deal, Carl, "The Administration of International Exchanges in Academic Libraries: A Survey," *Library Acquisitions: Practice and Theory* 13 (1989): 201-202.

11th Annual NASIG Conference Registrants, University of New Mexico, June 1996

Conference Registrants	*Institutions*
Anderson, Elma	Marywood College
Aaron, Amira	Readmore, Inc.
Adams, Agnes	University of Nebraska
Adrian, Philip	Rush University
Aiello, Helen M.	Wesleyan University
Akie, Ron	Faxon
Alessi, Dana	Baker & Taylor
Alexander, Adrian	Swets & Zeitlinger, Inc.
Alexander, Whitney	Texas A & M University
Algier, Aimee	Santa Clara University
Anderson, Amy	Southwestern University
Anderson, Bill	Library of Congress
Andrews, Judy	Carrier Library, James Madison University
Anemaet, Jos	Oregon State University
Anspach, Karen	Data Trek, Inc.
Archer, Cynthia	University of Windsor
Ashby, John	Faxon Canada
Ashton, Jonathan	
Astle, Deana	Clemson University
Atkins, Julie	Oxford University Press
Ayers, Leighann	University of Michigan
Badics, Joe	Eastern Michigan University
Baia, Wendy	University of Colorado
Bailey, Clare	The Bureau of National Affairs
Baker, Jeanne	University of Maryland
Baker, Maryellen	Cal Poly University Library
Baker, Theresa	University of Kansas Medical Center

Ball, Katharine — University of Windsor
Banach, Pat — University of Massachusetts/ Amherst
Bannerman, Ian — Blackwell Science Ltd.
Baron, Joel H. — Dawson Publishing
Basch, Buzzy — Basch Subscriptions Inc.
Beach, Regina — Mississippi State University
Beckett, Chris — B.H. Blackwell Ltd.
Beier, Mike — Brigham Young University
Belcher, Dana Marie — University of Oklahoma SLIS
Bell, Carole R. — Northwestern University Library
Bender, Mary L. — University of Wyoming
Benham, Ann — Blackwell North America
Bennett, Marsha — Boston Public Library
Benson, Polly — George Mason University
Beran, Mary Lou — Idaho State University
Bergin, Edward — Rice University
Bernards, Dennis — Brigham Young University
Bernstein, Vivian — American Institute of Physics
Binegar, Patricia — Faxon
Bircher, Elizabeth — EBSCO Federal Government Division

Blair, Margaret K. — Health Sciences Library
Blatchley, Jeremy — Bryn Mawr College
Blixrud, Julia C. — CAPCON Library Network
Bloss, Alex — University of Illinois at Chicago
Bloss, Marjorie — Center for Research Libraries
Blosser, John P. — Northwestern University Library
Boissy, Robert W. — The Faxon Company
Bolman, Pieter S.H. — Academic Press
Bonk, Sharon C. — Queens College, CUNY
Born, Kathleen — EBSCO Information Services
Bracken, Lee — Harvard Business School
Bradley, Melissa — Denver Public Library
Branham, Janie — Southeastern Louisiana University
Brash, Brian — International Publishing Distributor
Brass, Evelyn — University of Houston
Breed, Luellen L. — UW–Parkside
Breedlove, Rebecca — University of Massachusetts
Breithaupt, John — Allen Press Inc.
Brennan, Molly — Radford University

Briscoe, Georgia	University of Colorado Law Library
Broadwater, Deborah	Vanderbilt University
Broadway, Rita	University of Memphis
Bross, Valerie	CSU Stanislaus
Brown, David	Carl Corporation
Brown, Ladd	Georgia State University
Brown, Lynne Branche	Yankee Book Peddler, Inc.
Brown, Michael	UNM General Library
Brumley, Richard	Oregon State University
Bruno, Gloria	Oxford University Press
Buchanan, Nancy L.	University of Houston
Bueter, Rita	Blackwell North America
Bull, Greg	University of St. Thomas
Burk, Martha	Babson College
Burk, Mary	San Francisco State University
Burks, Suzan K.	Ball State University
Bussell, Jody	UC Berkeley
Butler, Joan	University of Michigan
Buttner, Mary	Stanford University Medical Library
Button, Leslie Horner	University of Massachusetts/ Amherst
Cabanero, Jennifer	New Mexico Highlands University
Caelleigh, Addeane	Academic Medicine
Callaghan, Jean	Wheaton College
Cap, Maria	L.A. County Law Library
Cargille, Karen	UC San Diego
Carlson, Bobbie	Medical University of South Carolina
Carlson, Melvin	University of Massachusetts/ Amherst
Casados, Tebols	LANL
Casetta, Prima	Getty Center Library
Celeste, Eric	MIT Libraries
Chaffin, Nancy	Arizona State University West
Champagne, Thomas	University of Michigan
Chang, Hui-yee	University of California, Santa Cruz
Chang, Ling-li	Loyola University Chicago
Chen, Cecilia	CSU Dominguez Hills
Chou, H. Charlene	Columbia University Libraries
Chressanthis, June	Mississippi State University

Christensen, John O.   Brigham Young University
Christiansen, Christine   University of Miami
Chrzastowski, Tina   University of Illinois
Cianfarini, Margaret   Harvard Law School Library
Clack, Mary Beth   Harvard College Library
Clark, Terri   Creighton University
Clay, Genevieve   Eastern Kentucky University
Clayton, Cheryl T.   Brigham Young University
Cleary, Robert M.   University of Missouri-Kansas City
Cochenour, Donnice   Colorado State University
Cohen, Donna   Rollins College
Cohen, Eileen   University of New Mexico Law
                              Library

Collins, Dorothy
Collins, Kelly   Readmore Academic
Collins, Michelle   College of William & Mary
Conant, Roy   The Book House, Inc.
Conger, Mary Jane   Jackson Library - UNCG
Congleton, Robert   Temple University
Conway, Cheryl L.   University of Arkansas, Fayetteville
Cook, Eleanor   Appalachian State University
Copeland, Nora S.   Colorado State University Libraries
Corrsin, Stephen   Columbia University
Coulter, Cynthia M.   University of Northern Iowa
Courtney, Keith   Taylor & Francis
Cox, Brian   Elsevier Science
Cox, Jennifer   University of Arizona
Cox, John   Carfax Publishing Company
Crooker, Cynthia   Yale University
Crowell, Loretta   Waye State University
Crowley, Christy   University of New Mexico
Crump, Michele   University of Florida
Cuesta, Emerita M.   Hofstra University
Curtis, Jerry   Springer Verlag
Czech, Isabel   Institute for Scientific Information

Dalton, Bobbie Lou   Davidson College Library
Dane, Stephen   Kluwer Academic Publishers
Darling, Karen   University of Orgon
Davis, Carroll N.   Columbia University
Davis, Renette   University of Chicago Library

Davis, Susan	University of Buffalo
Dawson, Julie Eng	Princeton Theological Seminary
Day, Nancy	Linda Hall Library
De Maurivez, Halina	University of Ottawa
Dean, Otis A.	Blackwell Publishers
Deeken, Joanne	Clemson University
Degener, Christie T.	UNC-CH Health Science Library
Deyoe, Nancy	Wichita State University
Di Biase, Linda	University of Washington Libraries
Diaz, Stephanie	Los Alamos Research Library
Dickerson, Eugene	Villanova University
Diedrichs, Carol Pitts	Ohio State University
Dobson, Vinita	Texas Christian University
Douglass, Janet	Texas Christian University
Drabek, Hilda	University of Connecticut
Drake, Paul	Kansas City Public Library
Druesedow, Elaine	Duke University
Drum, Carol	University of Florida
Drummond, Rebecca C.	Georgia State University Library
Duffy, Suzanne	Texas Tech University Library
Duhon, Lucy	University of Toledo Libraries
Dunlop, William	University of Vermont
Dyer, Sandra	University of North Carolina Law Library
Dykas, F. Ann	University of Missouri–Kansas City
Edwards, Jennifer	M.I.T.
Eldredge, Jon	UNM Health Sciences Center Library
Ellis, Kathryn D. (K.D.)	University of Tennessee
Emery, Jill	Texas Southern University
Ercelawn, Ann	Vanderbilt University
Estella, Kathy	EBSCO Information Services
Evans, Dexter R.	The Faxon Co., Inc.
Fairfield, John R.	ICI
Fairley, Craig	Information Dynamics
Farber, Anita	University of Texas at Austin
Farley, Lorraine M.	Center for Research Libraries
Farwell, Anne	CANEBSCO Information Services

Gimmi, Robert D.	Shippensburg University
Ginsparg, Paul	Los Alamos National Laboratory
Gisonny, Karen	New York Public Library
Gitchoff, Miriam	SDSU Library
Glatzer, Ken	The Faxon Company
Gobin, Kip R.	UVA Law Library
Goldich, Terri J.	Homer Babbidge Library, University of Connecticut
Gonzales-Small, Grace	New Mexico State University
Goodyear, Marilu	University of Kansas
Gordon, Martin	Franklin & Marshall College
Gormley, Alice	Marquette University Library
Gottardi, Angela	University of New Hampshire
Graf, George	Trinity College
Graham, Crystal	University of California, San Diego
Grande, Dolores	John Jay College
Grant, Georgia	University of Alberta
Graves, Shirley	Loma Linda University
Green, Brian	EDItEUR
Green, Mary Beth	Troy State University
Greene, Audrey	EBSCO
Greene III., Philip E. N.	EBSCO
Gregory, Chris	Baker & Taylor
Griffith, Joan	Harrassowitz
Groth, Mike	Kluwer Academic Publishers
Grover, Diane	University of Washington
Gurshman, Sandra J.	Readmore, Inc.
Haas, Ruth S.	Harvard College Library
Hall, Barbara	University of Southern California
Halpin, Libby	Indiana University School of Dentistry Library
Halpin, Lola	Emory University
Hamilton, Fred	Louisiana Tech. University
Hanson, Mary Ellen	UNM General Library
Harnad, Stevan	Southampton University
Harris, Sandra R.	Linda Hall Library
Harrison, John C.	Northern Arizona University
Hart, Patricia	University of Washington
Harwell, Rolly	East Tennessee State University
Hashert, Cynthia	Auraria Library

Hattink, John   Kluwer Academic Publications
Hauselt, Gretchen   Cambridge University Press
Hawthorn, Margaret   Erindale College University of
                               Toronto
Haynes, John   IOP Publishing
Heckman, Stephen P.   Heckman Bindery, Inc.
Hedberg, Hilding   Richards Memorial Library
Hedberg, Jane   Wellesley College
Hedin, Lise   Library of Michigan
Heinze, Linda   Weber State University
Helinsky, Suzana   BTJ Library Service
Henderson, Charlotte   Southern University
Henderson, Kittie   EBSCO
Hendren, Carol   CCLA
Henebry, Carolyn   University of Texas at Dallas
Hepfer, Cindy   Serials Review/Suny Buffalo
Heras, Elaine   Lewis & Clark College
Heterick, Bruce   The Faxon Company
Hillery, Leanne   Ball State University
Hinders, Tom   Oberlin College Library
Hing, Trevor   B.H. Blackwell LTD
Hinger, Joseph   Detroit College of Law Library
Hirons, Jean   Library of Congress
Hodge, Stan   Ball State University
Hofsas, Elizabeth   Yale University Library
Holland, Jeff   University of Nevada
Holley, Beth   University of Alabama
Holley, Sandra H.   University of Texas Health Center
Holt, Thomas   Stanford University
Hopkins, Randall   University of Maryland
Hor, Annie   CSU Stanislaus
Horiuchi, Linda   Idaho State University
Horn, Marguerite E.   Northern Arizona University
Howell, Gail M.   Faxon
Howell, Karen   University of Southern California
Huesmann, James   Linda Hall Library
Hughes, Katherine   Loyola University
Hurd, Sandra H.   EBSCO Information Services
Hutchins, Carol   New York University

Ireland, Lee — Data Research Associates, Inc.
Irvin, Judy — Louisiana Tech. University
Israel, Jodi L. — The Faxon Company
Ivins, October — University of Texas - GSLIS

Jacox, Corinne — University of Nebraska–Lincoln Libraries
Jaeger, Don — Alfred Jaeger, Inc.
Jakubowski, Kathi — University of Wisconsin–Milwaukee
Janes, Judith — Cleveland Clinic Foundation
Jayes, Linda D. — University of Chicago
Jewell, Timothy D. — University of Washington
Jo, Julitta — Suny Stony Brook
Johnson, David L. — Princeton University Library
Johnson, Judy L. — University of Nebraska
Johnson, Kay G. — University of Tennessee
Johnston, Judith Ann — University of North Texas
Jones, Daniel H. — Briscoe Library-UTHSCSA
Jones, Douglas — University of Arizona
Jones, Stephanie N. — Ameritech Library Services
Jordan, K. Paul — Brigham Young University
Julian, Gail — University of South Carolina
Jurries, Elaine F. — Auraria Library

Kalvee, Debbie — Ramuson Library, University of Alaska
Kannel, Ene — National Library of Canada
Kara, William J. — Cornell University
Kascus, Marie A. — Central Connecticut State University
Kaser, Richard T. — NFAIS
Katz, Stephen J. — Colorado School of Mines
Kay, Mary H. — Humboldt State University
Keates, Gwenda — Wiley Europe
Kellogg, Martha — University of Rhode Island Library
Kellum, Cathy — SOLINET
Kelly, Robert A. — The American Physical Society
Kennedy, Kit — Readmore Academic
Khosh-khui, Sam A. — SWTSU
Kim, Peg — Washington University Libraries

Lucas, John	University of Mississippi Medical Center
Luetkemeyer, Mark	St. Louis University
Luther, Judy	ISI
Lutz, Linda	University of Western Ontario
Lynch, Paula M.	Thomas Jefferson University
Macadam, Carol	Swets
Macarthur, Susan	Bates College
Macdonald, Patricia A.	National Library of Canada
Macewan, Bonnie	Penn State
Mackeigan, Clare	Network Support Inc.
Macklin, Lisa A.	Georgia Tech
Maclennan, Birdie	University of Vermont
Macwithey, Mary	HAM-TMC Library
Maddox, Jane	Harrassowitz
Magenau, Carol	Dartmouth College Library
Malawski, Susan	John Wiley & Sons, Inc.
Malinowski, Teresa	California State University
Mann, Marjorie F.	National Library of Medicine
Mapes, Frank	EBSCO Information Services
Marill, Jennifer	Washington Research Library Consortium
Markley, Susan	Villanova University
Markwith, Michael	Swet + Zeitlinger, Inc.
Martin, Sylvia	Vanderbilt University Library
Martinez, Joanne	University of Arizona
Matthes, Meg	Nova Southeastern University
Matthews, Pamela A.	Missouri Western State College
Maxwell, Kimberly A.	Catholic University of America
May, Bill	The Faxon Co., Inc.
McAdam, Tim	University of California
McCafferty, Patrick	Case Western Reserve University
McCallon, Mark	Abilene Christian University
McCarthy, Patrick	Saint Louis University
McClary, Maryon	University of Alberta
McClure, Wanda L.	University of Kentucky
McCutcheon, Dianne	National Library of Medicine
McDougald, Barbara T.	U.S. Patent & Trademark Office
McGrath, Kat	University of British Columbia
McHugo, Ann	Dartmouth College Library

McIlhinney, Joanne	CISTI
McKay, Bea	Trinity University
McKay, Sharon Cline	Blackwell's Periodicals
McKee, Anne	Blackwell's Periodicals
McLeod, Rebecca	MIT Press Journals
McNair, Alison	Dalhousie University
McNair, Richard	Canadian Armed Forces
McShane, Kevin	National Library of Medicine
Medaglia, Victoria J.	Babson College
Meiseles, Linda	Hofstra University
Meneely, Kathleen	Cleveland Health Sciences Library
Mercurio, Marianna	Washington University
Mering, Margaret	University of Nebraska
Merrill-Oldham, Pete	Acme Bookbinding
Merriman, Faith A.	Central Connecticut State University
Mestecky, Phil	Elsevier Science Ltd.
Metz, Allan	Drury College
Middeldorp-Crispijn, Ineke	Martinus Nijhoff International
Milam, Barbara	Kennesaw State College
Miller, Judith K.	Valparaiso University
Mills, Vicki	University of Arizona Library
Milner, Lesley A.	Ball State University
Moff, Maria	University of Akron
Moles, Jean Ann	Univ. Ark. for Medical Sciences
Moore, Wendy	Furman University
Moran, Sheila E.	Massachusetts General Hospital
Morris, Ruth	NM Health Sciences Center Library
Mouw, James	University of Chicago
Mulcahey, Kathy	Rapid Science Publishers
Mullins, Teresa	The UnCover Company
Murden, Steve	Virginia Commonwealth University
Murray, Dana	Faxon Canada
Nanna, Laura	University of California
Neal, James G.	Johns Hopkins University
Nelson, Catherine	UC Santa Barbara
Nelson, Janice	University of Colorado
Newman, Bryan	UCHSC
Newsome, Nancy	Western Carolina University
Nez, Ann	University of Washington Law Library

Nguyen, Hien — National Library of Medicine
Nissley, Meta — California State University Chico
Nosakhere, Akilah — Georgia State University
Novak, Denise D. — Carnegie Mellon University

O'Brien, Leslie — Virginia Tech
O'Leary, Susan — EBSCO
O'Neill, Ann — College of Library & Information Science, USC
Oberg, Steve — The University of Chicago Library
Olivieri, Rene — Blackwell Publishers
Ouderkirk, Jane — Harvard University

Page, Mary — Rutgers University
Palmiter, Sharron Snyder — University of Maryland
Pangrac, Kelly Dugan — Kansas City Public Library
Paradis, Olga — Baylor University
Parang, Elizabeth — Pepperdine University
Park, Amey L. — Kent State University Libraries
Parker, Laura — Elsevier Science
Patrick, Carol — Cleveland State University
Payne, Kathryn — Weber State University
Perez-Vargas, Magda — Interamerican University of Puerto Rico
Perrotta, Lorraine — University of Southern California
Perry, Sara — CISTI
Persing, Robert — University of Pennsylvania
Persons, Jerry — Stanford University
Peterson, Jan — Academic Press
Philipp, Fred — Readmore, Inc.
Phillips, Patricia A. — University of Texas at El Paso
Pintozzi, Chestalene — University of Arizona
Pitts, Linda M. — University of Washington
Pizarro-Escobar, Luz D. — Interamerican University of Puerto Rico
Popilskis, Edvika — R.R. Bowker/Reed Reference
Prabha, Chandra — OCLC
Pratt, Kathleen — Los Alamos National Laboratory
Presley, Roger L. — Georgia State University

Qualls, Martha Jane	The University of Memphis
Radbourne, Margaret	Wiley Europe
Ragone, Nina	The Faxon Company
Ralston, M. Joan	Villanova University
Ralston, Rick	Indiana University
Randall, Kevin M.	Northwestern University
Randall, Mike	UCLA
Rankin, Juliann	California State University Chico
Rast, Elaine	Northern Illinois University
Rawling, Phyllis C.	University of Delaware
Reijnen, Marian	Martinus Nijhoff International
Reinalda, Roy J.	Faxon
Reinig, Twyla S.	University of New Mexico
Reinke, Christa	University of Houston
Reynolds, Regina	Library of Congress
Riley, Cheryl	Central Missouri State University
Rioux, Margaret A.	MBL/WHOI Library
Risher, Carol A.	Assoc. of American Publishers
River, Sandra	Texas Tech University Library
Roach, Dani	Macalester College-DeWitt Wallace Library
Roberts, Constance F.	University of Connecticut
Robinson, Trina R.	Loyola Law Library
Robischon, Rose	U.S. Military Academy
Robnett, Bill	Vanderbilt University
Rogers, Marilyn	University of Arkansas
Rohe, Terry	Millar Library Portland State University
Rosenberg, Frieda B.	UNC Chapel Hill
Rossignol, Lucien R.	Smithsonian Institution Libraries
Roth, Alison C.	Blackwell's Periodicals
Rothaug, Caroline	John Wiley & Sons, Inc.
Ruelle, Barbara	Emory University
Rumph, Virginia A.	Irwin Library, Butler University
Ruthenberg, Donnell	Data Research Associates, Inc.
Salk, Judy	R.R. Bowker/Reed Reference Publishing
Salomon, Patricia H.	Bowling Green State University

Sanders, Susan	NIST
Saudargas, Thom	CCLA
Savage, Steve	Library of Michigan
Saxe, Minna C.	City University of New York Grad School
Saxton, Elna L.	University of Cincinnati
Sayler, Terry Ann	University of Maryland
Schader, Barbara	UCLA
Scheffler, Eckart A.	Walter De Gruyter, Inc.
Schein, Anna	West Virginia University Libraries
Schimizzi, Anthony J.	Sterne Library–UAB
Schmitt, Brian	American Institute of Physics
Schmitt, Stephanie	University of Mississippi
Scholl, Miki	Hamline University School of Law Library
Schwartz, Marla	American University Law Library
Schwartzkopf, Becky	Mankato State University
Scott, Sharon	University of Nevada, Reno
Seal, Robert	Texas Christian University
Selness, Sushila	USD Legal Research Center
Shadle, Steve	University of Washington
Shaffer, Barbara	University of Toledo
Shaffer, Carolyn	Johnson County Library
Shea, Marsha	San Diego State University
Sheble, Mary Ann	University of Detroit Mercy
Sheffield, Becky	Ball State University
Sibley, Debbie	University of Massachusetts Medical Center
Sievers, Arlene Moore	Case Western Reserve University
Simon, Rebecca	University of California Press
Simpson, Pamela	Penn State
Singleton, Alan	Institute of Physics
Sleeman, Allison M.	University of Virginia
Sleep, Esther L.	Brock University Library
Smets, Kristine	Joint Bank/Fund Library
Smith, Alan	Blackwell's Periodicals
Smith, James L.	EBSCO Information Services
Smith, Patricia	Colorado State University
Smith, Sharon	Los Alamos National Lab
Smith, Sue	Blackwell's Periodicals
Smith, Susan P.	University of Connecticut

Somers, Michael S.	LSU Libraries
Sonberg, Paul A.	Readmore
Soper, Mary Ellen	GSLIS, University of Washington
Sorensen, Sally	Texas Christian University
Southern, Diana	John Wiley & Sons Ltd.
Spence, Duncan	Carfax Publishing Comapny
Sprague, Nancy	LANL
Springer, Fran	American Grad. School of International Management
Stamison, Christine	Blackwell's Periodicals
Steele, Heather	Blackwell's Periodicals
Steinsiek, Sabra	UNM-School of Law Library
Stephens, Catherine	University of Nevada, Las Vegas
Stephens, Joan	Georgia State University
Stevens, Hannah M.	Boston Library Consortium
Stickman, Jim	University of Washington
Su, Julie	IUPUI
Sugnet, Chris	University of Arizona
Sullivan, Eugene V.	University of South Alabama
Sullivan, Kathryn	Winona State University
Sullivan, Sharon	UCLA
Summers, Lorna	Turpin Distribution
Sutherland, Laurie	University of Washington
Swanek, Lavina	Creighton University
Sweet, Kathleen A.	Phoenix College Library
Swets, Ariane V.	Swets Subscription Services
Taffurelli, Virginia	Pratt Institute
Tagler, John	Elsevier Science
Talley, Kaye	University of Central Arkansas
Tallman, Karen Dalziel	University of Arizona
Taylor, Kay E.	University of Minnesota
Teague, Elaine	SAS Institute Inc.
Teaster, Gale	Winthrop University Library
Teel, Kay	New York University
Tenney, Joyce	University of Maryland Baltimore County
Terry, M. Nancy	Grand Valley State University
Thomas, Suzanne L.	University of Pittsburgh
Thornton, Christopher P.	CWRU Library
Tijerino, Cathy	University of New Orleans

Timberlake, Phoebe	University of New Orleans
Tong, Dieu Van	University of Alabama, Birmingham
Tonkery, Dan	TDT Ventures
Tonn, Anke	Nicholls State University
Trolley, Jacqueline H.	Institute for Scientific Information
Truitt, Marc	Princeton University Libraries
Tumlin, Markel	University of San Diego
Turitz, Mitch	San Francisco State University
Tusa, Sarah	Lamar University
Tuttle, Marcia	University of North Carolina
Urka, Mary Ann	George Washington University
Valino, Nenita M.	Anne Arundel Community College Library
Van Auken, Gayle	Linda Hall Library
Van Goethem, Jeri	Duke University
Van Reenen, Johann	University of New Mexico
Van Schaik, Joann	Texas Tech HSC Library
Van Snellenberg, Richelle	Student Grant Recipient
Varjabedian, Kathy	Los Alamos National Lab Research Library
Vent, Marilyn	University of Nevada, Las Vegas
Vogt, Norman	Northern Illinois University
Wakeford, Paul	University of California
Wakeling, Will	UKSG/University of Birmingham
Wallace, Patricia M.	University of Colorado
Wallas, Philip	EBSCO Publishing
Walsh, Harry	National Library of Canada
Walther, James H.	LEXIS-NEXIS
Waltner, Robb	University of Evansville
Wang, Margaret K.	University of Delaware
Ward, Colleen	Oklahoma City University
Warren, Karen T.	USC School of Medicine Library
Watkinson, Anthony	Chapman and Hall
Weber, Joe	Christopher Newport University
Weigel, Friedemann	Harrassowitz

Weiss, Amy K.	Ball State University
Weiss, Paul J.	University of New Mexico
Weng, Cathy	Temple University Library
Westall, Sandy	Innovative Interfaces
Weston, Beth	George Washington University
Whipple, Marcia	NCCUSC RDTE DIV Tech. Lib.
Whiting, Peter C.	Prairie View A & M University
Whitney, Marla	CARL Corporation
Whittaker, Martha	Carl
Wild, Judith W.	Brooklyn College
Wilder, Rayette	University of Southern California
Wilhelme, Judy	University of Michigan
Wilhite, Marjorie	University of Iowa
Wilke, Mary I.	Center for Research Libraries
Wilkes, Helen H.	University of Georgia Libraries
Wilkinson, Frances C.	University of New Mexico
Williams, Allen	Grand Valley State University
Williams, Geraldine	Northern Kentucky University
Williams, Jill	Cleveland-Marshall Law Library
Williams, Linda F.	Arizona Health Sciences University of Arizona
Williams, Sheryl	University of Nebraska Medical Center
Williams, Sue	University of Colorado at Boulder
Willis, Barbara H.	University of Colorado at Boulder
Wilson, Betty Jean	Morehead State University
Wilson, Jenni	Readmore Academic
Wilson, Margaret	University of Kansas
Wilson-Higgins, Suzanne	B.H. Blackwell Ltd.
Winchester, David	Washburn University
Wineburgh-Freed, Maggie	USC Norris Medical Library
Winjum, Roberta	University of Hawaii at Manoa
Wisniewski, Ken	Academic Book Center
Withington, Charles	Kluwer Academic Publishers
Witkovski, Ruth	Creighton University Health Sciences
Witsenhausen, Helen	John Wiley & Sons
Wolfe, Garry R.	RoweCom
Woodford, Barbara	EBSCO Information Services
Woodley, Mary S.	Getter Center

Xu, Amanda   MIT Libraries

Yanney, Donna Sue   Prairie View A & M University

Zendzian, Lynda K.   Bowdoin College Library
Zhang, Wei   Northwestern University Library
Zuidema, Karen   University of Illinois at Chicago
Zuriff, Susan Rom   University of Minnesota

Index

AACR2, 110-111,114,142,281,284
abstracting and indexing, 57,59,84,
    93,143
  hook to holdings, 368
  medical, 257
acquisitions, 258-259,358-359,374
Adobe Acrobat, 153,157,321
Agent's Subscription ID (ASID), 274
Alta Vista, 132,138,322
American Association of Law
    Libraries, 256
American Libraries, 132
American Mathematical
    Society(AMS), 201
American Physical Society (APS),
    100,163,165-168
AmIS (American ISSN friends), 372
archives, 87,93-94,144,165,195,
    354-355
  APS, 167-168
  authoritative, 91,158
  consortial, 145-146,195,197,
    356-357
  digital, 163,225
  electronic journals, 79,358
  e-print, 78,85-86,152,165-166
  integrity, 84
  preprint, 75,83,86,165
ARIEL, 11
ArticleFirst, 349
Association for Computing
    Machinery (ACM), 46,201
Association of American
    Universities (AAU), 99,104
Association of Research Libraries
    (ARL), 99-100,104
Audio Interchange File Format
    (AIFF), 321

Author State Inquiry System (ASIS),
    167
automated use studies, 261-264,
    295-297

BISAC (Book Industry Systems
    Advisory Committee), 10,
    16
Blackwell, 274-276
Book Industry Study Group (BISG),
    7
books, 32-35,37,39,98
Brandywine Project, 222
*Bulletin of the American
    Mathematical Society,* 201

Cambridge Scientific Abstracts, 133
catalog-as-gateway, 139-140
cataloging. *see* electronic serials
    cataloging; Internet,
    cataloging
CatchWord, 45
CBISAC/CSISAC-Canada, 7
CD-ROM, 43,45,84,133,139
  licensing, 173-174,177
checkin, 144,295
CIC Center for Library Initiatives
    (CLI), 194-195,199
CIC Electronic Journals Collection
    (CIC EJC), 138,141,145,
    191-192,195-197,199-202
CICNet, 191-192,194-196,198,202
CICNet E-Serials Archive,
    191,195-196,356
CISTI (Canada Institute for
    Scientific and Technical
    Information), 349-350

Haworth
DOCUMENT DELIVERY
SERVICE

This valuable service provides a single-article order form for any article from a Haworth journal.

- *Time Saving:* No running around from library to library to find a specific article.
- *Cost Effective:* All costs are kept down to a minimum.
- *Fast Delivery:* Choose from several options, including same-day FAX.
- *No Copyright Hassles:* You will be supplied by the original publisher.
- *Easy Payment:* Choose from several easy payment methods.

Open Accounts Welcome for ...
- Library Interlibrary Loan Departments
- Library Network/Consortia Wishing to Provide Single-Article Services
- Indexing/Abstracting Services with Single Article Provision Services
- Document Provision Brokers and Freelance Information Service Providers

---

MAIL or *FAX* THIS ENTIRE ORDER FORM TO:

Haworth Document Delivery Service
The Haworth Press, Inc.
10 Alice Street
Binghamton, NY 13904-1580

or FAX: 1-800-895-0582
or CALL: 1-800-342-9678
9am-5pm EST

PLEASE SEND ME PHOTOCOPIES OF THE FOLLOWING SINGLE ARTICLES:

1) Journal Title: _____

    Vol/Issue/Year:_____Starting & Ending Pages:_____

Article Title:_____

_____

2) Journal Title: _____

    Vol/Issue/Year:_____Starting & Ending Pages:_____

Article Title:_____

_____

3) Journal Title: _____

    Vol/Issue/Year:_____Starting & Ending Pages:_____

Article Title:_____

_____

4) Journal Title: _____

    Vol/Issue/Year:_____Starting & Ending Pages:_____

Article Title:_____

_____

(See other side for Costs and Payment Information)

COSTS: Please figure your cost to order quality copies of an article.

1. Set-up charge per article: $8.00
     ($8.00 × number of separate articles)   _____

2. Photocopying charge for each article:
               1-10 pages: $1.00   _____

               11-19 pages: $3.00   _____

               20-29 pages: $5.00   _____

               30+ pages: $2.00/10 pages   _____

3. Flexicover (optional): $2.00/article   _____

4. Postage & Handling: US: $1.00 for the first article/
               $.50 each additional article   _____

               Federal Express: $25.00   _____

               Outside US: $2.00 for first article/
               $.50 each additional article_____

5. Same-day FAX service: $.35 per page   _____

                    GRAND TOTAL: _____

METHOD OF PAYMENT: (please check one)
❑ Check enclosed   ❑ Please ship and bill. PO # _____
               (sorry we can ship and bill to bookstores only! All others must pre-pay)
❑ Charge to my credit card: ❑ Visa; ❑ MasterCard; ❑ Discover;
                    ❑ American Express;

Account Number:_____ Expiration date:_____

Signature: *X*_____

Name: _____ Institution: _____

Address: _____

          _____

City: _____ State:_____ Zip:_____

Phone Number: _____ FAX Number: _____

MAIL or *FAX* THIS ENTIRE ORDER FORM TO:

Haworth Document Delivery Service	**or FAX:** 1-800-895-0582
The Haworth Press, Inc.	**or CALL:** 1-800-342-9678
10 Alice Street	9am-5pm EST)
Binghamton, NY 13904-1580	